ARGONAUT LIBRARY
OF ANTIQUITIES

ANCIENT COINS ILLUSTRATING
LOST MASTERPIECES OF GREEK ART

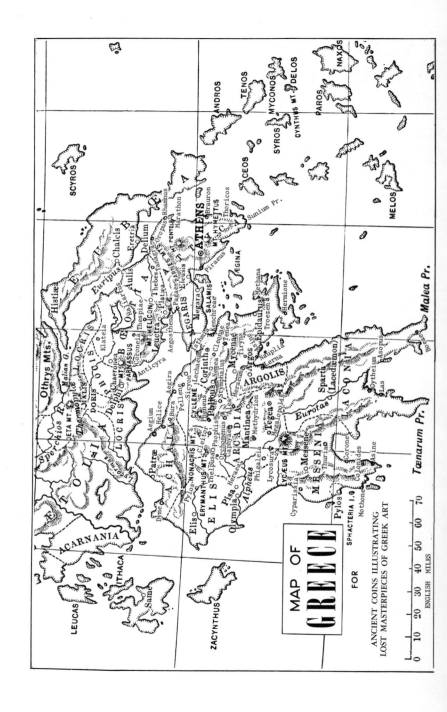

MAP OF GREECE

FOR

ANCIENT COINS ILLUSTRATING
LOST MASTERPIECES OF GREEK ART

0 10 20 30 40 50 60 70
ENGLISH MILES

ANCIENT COINS ILLUSTRATING LOST MASTERPIECES OF GREEK ART

A Numismatic Commentary on Pausanias

by

F. W. Imhoof-Blumer

Late Professor of Archaeology and Numismatics at the University of Basel and Late Director of the Swiss National Museum.

Percy Gardner

Late Professor of Archaeology and Numismatics at the Universities of Cambridge and Oxford. Coins and Medals at the British Museum

NEW ENLARGED EDITION WITH INTRODUCTION, COMMENTARY AND NOTES BY

Al. N. Oikonomides

ARGONAUT, INC., PUBLISHERS
CHICAGO
MCMLXIV

Library of Congress Catalog Card Number: *LC 64-23435*

PREFACE

The immortal work of Imhoof-Blumer and Gardner belongs to a period of productive and creative scholarship to which we owe most of our reference books and manuals on the sciences of antiquity. The enthusiastic scholars of this period did not write for the satisfaction of university boards and museum trustees, but for the self-satisfaction of creating works giving a more complete and effective knowledge of antiquity. Their works were needed, and they knew in what directions their research had to take them to lead to the creation of sound background materials for study by future generations.

The study of the books by Pausanias, "The Description of Greece," thoroughly edited, commented upon and emended by a team of inspired scholars beginning about 1700 A.D., provided the foundation for the scientific study of archaeological topography from which methodic excavation was born. But even the most brilliant and extensive study of these books could not proceed alone, without valuable contributions from other branches of the antiquarian sciences. The history of Greek art, architecture, epigraphy, numismatics, etc. profited greatly from the study of Pausanias, and in return, gave back enormous amounts of knowledge in the form of verifications of the author's original information which had previously been considered by some scholars to be an unreliable combination of mythology, history and monumentology.

An historian of Greek art, working at the start of the nineteenth century, must have felt lost, depressed and insecure in studying the text of Pausanias, because, surrounded by an ocean of copies of famous sculptures created from the late Hellenistic to the end of the Roman periods, as well as a wealth of minor miniature copies of famous pieces used for decorative purposes on industrial products, but relatively few surviving originals, he could not know, nor could he identify, which were copies or imitations of what and by whom. The development of the study of stylistic improvements provided some guidelines later, dividing archaic, classic, Hellenistic and Post-Hellenistic (called 'Roman') art. But then, by what means could he subdivide these enormous categories into local schools and attribute works to specific artists as mentioned by the surviving literary and epigraphical sources?

It was here that the study of numismatics came, in the mid-nineteenth century, to provide the bridge between literary evidence and actual surviving works of art, unifying the two into one secure knowledge. Luckily, beginning during the late-Hellenistic period, it became the custom for city-states of the Greek world to use their coinage as an advertising medium for their prestige-bringing art treasures and local marvels. This custom became increasingly common during the Roman era, and at that time it was not uncommon for authors to write special treatises on famous works of art and the treasures of famous cities.

Pausanias toured Greece the same way that a modern American travel writer might wish to do. However, it would seem that Pausanias was much more systematic than one could possibly be today, for he possessed an amazing and complete knowledge of ancient Greek history, mythology and topography based on sources, most of which are now lost. He also had a remarkable background in the lives and works of the most famous artists of the past when he toured Greece between 166 and 174 AD. He travelled over the whole of the Peloponnese, Attica, Boeotia, Locris and Phocis. It is inexplicable why the islands of the Aegean and Ionian Seas, Crete, Thessaly, Macedonia and Epirus did not attract his attention, unless the books of his work covering some or all of these areas have not survived. But, as far as we know, his travel chronicles are accurate and as detailed as a military log; so detailed, in fact, as to make one wonder if he was not bored to death in writing them thus. He recorded everything in his path worth noting, as well as many things en route which were less than interesting. Mountains, cities, towns, statues, sanctuaries, festivals, legends, genealogy, folk lore, mythology, temples and local cults are all logged in his diary. It is not difficult to see how these descriptive records can be helpful in identifying art as shown on coins, and how the identifications of their shapes in turn can be used to identify other echoes of the said works of art, even of those, in many cases, which have been lost, destroyed, or are as yet undiscovered. They also enable one to search for possible surviving statuary or miniature copies amongst what we now possess of ancient works of art.

It was not before the mid-nineteenth century that the importance of statuary representations on coins was realized. And from that time to this, this work has remained the most organized effort in comparing the written evidence of Pausanias with the pictorial evidence of coins. It is unique in its careful cataloguing, and is as complete as the authors at that time could make it. Sir J. G. Frazer depended completely upon the interpretations of Imhoof-Blumer and Gardner in numismatic matters for his monumental commentary to Pausanias, and this book, to date, has not been replaced, or, in fact, even approached by any more modern work. In this "Greekless age" a reissue of the present work could not be attempted without translating the passages from Pausanias which were originally given by the authors only in Greek. Therefore, the translations have been provided on the following pages, together with the references to the plates on which are represented the coins discussed, as well as the pages of the authors' commentaries. In some cases, in order to make a passage more readable for those not well acquainted with Pausanias, I have extended the quotation given in the original. These parts are found enclosed in double parentheses. In simple parentheses are added names or explanatory words, such as the English equivalents of the names of gods' epithets, etc. Where a reference is designated *(Ref.)*, no picture of the coin exists in the plates, but the original text contains information as to where it can be found. Those passages which required special attention I translated directly from the original, while those which presented no particular problems were based on the translations of Shilleto and Jones.

As for the coins of Athens, where new discoveries, excavations and research have given us more knowledge for the satisfactory interpretations of literary and numismatic evidence in the last seventy five years, I have found it necessary to add a new chapter reconsidering the coins collected by Imhoof-Blumer and Gardner. It would have been easy to add new material, especially from tetradrachms of Athens of the reformed style, but I believe that this was unnecessary because any questions about the representations of art treasures on this particular type of coinage can be answered easily by referring to the excellent and extensive work of Margaret Thompson: *The New Style Silver Coinage of Athens* (New York, 1962).

Notes have been added in cases of coins where a new and more valid interpretation has been recently proposed, and where I felt that I could bring more evidence to the attention of fellow archaeologists and numismatists. It is a fact that we have a fine handbook in French by L. Lacroix, *Les reproductions de statues sur les monnaies grecques* (Liege, 1949). This book can be used as a reference wherever questions of identification arise, in parallel with the work of P. W. Lehman, *Statues on Coins of Southern Italy* (New York, 1946). For more detailed bibliographical information up to 1956, the reader may consult the compilation by Cornelius Vermeule, *A Bibliography of Applied Numismatics* (London, 1956).

The title, *Ancient Coins Illustrating Lost Masterpieces of Greek Art* has been selected in preference to the original for the benefit of coin collectors and young scholars who, not being active in the field of archaeology, may not be familiar with Pausanias, therefore requiring a title more indicative of the book's contents. Actually I believe that the new title is the one which belongs to the book. But to avoid any voices of discontent, the original title has been preserved as an explanatory subtitle for those who wish it.

The edition in book form, if my information is correct, was not issued in more than 500 copies, and I have personally never had an opportunity to see or to use such a copy in a library more than once. In somewhat greater supply is the three-part original edition published in article form in, "Journal of Hellenic Studies," Vol. VI, 1885, pp. 50-101, Vol. VII, 1886, pp. 57-113, and Vol. VIII, 1887, pp. 6-63. But even these journals are not readily available outside of major reference libraries, so this new enlarged edition, incorporating new translations and notes, has been issued in light of the ever increasing interest in the study of Greek art and numismatics.

This enlarged edition of the *Numismatic Commentary to Pausanias* under its new title, is the editor's second step toward the much needed improved reissues of classical reference books for the study of Greek and Roman antiquities. The first step was the enlarged edition of the invaluable *Masterpieces of Greek Sculpture* by Adolf Furtwaengler (Argonaut, Chicago, 1964), the cordial acceptance of which convinced the publishers to dedicate more effort in this direction. Now this edition of *Ancient Coins Illustrating Lost Masterpieces of Greek Art*, dealing mainly with sculptures known from literary descriptions and numismatic representations which for the most part have not survived or been recognized in copies, closes more completely the circle which I hope to close entirely with an extended and revised edition of the famous reference work by H. S. Jones, *Passages from Ancient Writers Illustrative of the History of Greek Sculpture*, to be published in the near future.

AL. N. OIKONOMIDES

Chicago, September, 1964

TABLE OF CONTENTS

TRANSLATIONS OF PAUSANIAS' TEXTS

MEGARA (Plates A, i-xv. FF, i-iii; Pages 4-8, 154)

1. *Paus. I. 40,2*—cf. Pl.A, i
   And not far from this conduit is an ancient sanctuary . . . and there is a bronze statue of Artemis called by the name of Saviour . . . and this statue of Artemis was made by Strongylion.

2. *I. 41,3*—cf. Pl.A, ii
   And not far from the monument of Hyllos . . . is a temple of Apollo and Artemis . . . and Alkathus, son of Pelops . . . who, as they say, built this sanctuary ((when he killed the lion of Kithairon)), dedicating it to Artemis Agrotera (Huntress) and Apollo Agraios (Hunter).

3. *I. 40,4*—cf. Pl.A, iii
   And next, as you enter the sacred precinct of Zeus, called the Olympieion, there is a temple well worth seeing . . . The head of this statue of Zeus is of ivory and gold, but the other parts are of clay and gypsum; and they say it was made by Theokosmos, a native, with the assistance of Pheidias.

4. *I. 43,6*—cf. Pl.A, iv
   And in the neighboring temple, Lyssipus has made the Muses and a bronze Zeus, *cf. I. 40,6.* A roofless temple of Zeus Konios (dusty).

5. *I. 40,6*—cf. Pl.A, v
   Having ascended the Acropolis . . . is a temple of Dionysus called Nyktelios (Nocturnal). *I. 43,5.* And Polyidos also built the Shrine of Dionysus and dedicated a statue of the god which is now all veiled except for the face . . . this they call Dionysus Patroos (Ancestral), and another they call Dionysus Dasyllios (the Vineripener), etc.

6. *I. 40,6*—cf. Pl.A, vi-vii
   And statues of Asklepios and Hygeia, both made by Bryaxis.

7. *I. 44,2*—cf. Pl.A, viii
   And there is, in the ancient gymnasium, near the gates called the Nymphades, a stone shaped like a small pyramid; this they call Apollo Karinos.

8. *I. 42,5*—cf. Pl.A, ix-x. FF, i-ii
   The old temple of Apollo was built of brick; but later the Emperor Hadrian built it of white stone. From the statues in it, the one called Apollo Pythios and the other called Apollo Dekatophoros are very like the Egyptian statues, but the other, the one they call Archegetes, is similar to the sculptures of the Aeginetan school. *cf. I. 44,2.* To the

right is a temple of Apollo Prostaterios . . . in it is a statue
of Apollo well worth seeing; also Artemis, and Leto, and
other statues, [and Leto and her sons] by Praxiteles. *cf. I.
42,2.* And then, when he was building the wall, (Alkathos)
as the Megarians say, Apollo assisted him, and laid his lyre
down on the stone; and if one chances to hit it with a pebble,
it sounds like a lyre playing.

9. *I. 42,4*—cf. Pl.A, xi. FF, iii

And on the hill where the citadel stands, is a temple of
Athena, and in it is a gilded bronze statue of the goddess,
except the hands and feet which are, like the face, of ivory.
And there is another temple here of Athena called Nike
(Victory) and another of Athena Aiantis.

10. *I. 40,6*—cf. Pl.A, xii-xiii

Here too is the Megaron (sacred chamber) of Demeter.
cf. I. 42,6. There is also a temple of Demeter Thesmophoros
(Lawgiver).

11. *I. 43,6*—cf. Pl.A, xiv

Near the shrine of Aphrodite is a temple of Tyche (Fortune). The statue in it is by Praxiteles.

12. *Other types:* Pl.A, xv

PAGAE (Plates A, i-vii. FF, iv; Pages 8-9, 154)

1. *Paus. I. 44,4*—cf. Pl.A, i-ii

At Pagae still is preserved a bronze statue of Artemis called
Saviour, in size and shape exactly like the statue of the goddess at Megara.

2. *Other types:* Pl.A, iii-vii. FF, iv

AEGOSTHENA (Plate A, i; Pages 9-10)

1. *Paus. I. 44,5*—cf. Pl.A, i

At Aegosthena is a sanctuary of Melampous, the son of
Amythaon, and a man of no great size is carved on a stele.
((And they sacrifice to Melampous and have a festival to
him every year. But they say he has no prophetic powers,
either in dreams or any other way)).

CORINTH (Plates B, i—G, cxliv; Pages 10-28, 154-158)

Paus. II. 2,6

The notable things in the city are partly the remains of
antiquity which can still be seen, but the greater part of
them are those which were produced during the more recent flourishing of the city.

1. *Paus. II. 1,3*—cf. Pl.B, i-viii

As you go forward the famous pine was to be seen, even
in my time, near the seashore; and there was an altar to

Melicertes. For they say that this was the place to which
the boy was conveyed by the dolphin . . . and it is at the
head of the Isthmus.

II. 1,7—cf. Pl.B, ix-x

And on the temple (of Poseidon at Isthmia), which is not
very large, there stand bronze Tritons. And there are statues in its Pronaos (fore-temple); two of Poseidon, one of
Amphitrite and Thalassa (the Sea), also of bronze. And
inside the temple, Herodes the Athenian, dedicated in our
time, four horses, gilded but for the hoofs which are of
ivory, and two Tritons are near the horses, gold above, and
ivory below the waist. On the chariot (drawn by the four
horses) Amphitrite and Poseidon are standing, (and in
this group belongs also) Palaimon represented as a child
standing on a dolphin, also made of gold and ivory.

II. 2,1—cf. Pl.B, xi-xiii

Inside the precinct of the sanctuary there is, on the left
hand, a temple of Palaimon, and there are in it statues of
Poseidon, Leukothea and Palaimon himself.

II. 3,4—cf. Pl.B, xiv-xvii

Next to the statue of Hermes are Poseidon and Leukothea
and Palaimon on the dolphin.

2. *II. 1,9*—cf. Pl.B, xviii-xxiv

And there are also dedicated statues of Galene (Calm) and
of Thalassa (the Sea), and a horse with the body and fish-
tail of a sea monster beyond its chest. (There are also
dedicated statues of Ino, Bellerophontes and the horse,
Pegasus).

3. *cf. II. 2,4*—cf. Pl.C, xxv-xxx

((In front of the city of Corinth is a grove of cypresses
called)) Craneion. Here is a sanctuary of Bellerophontes
((and a sanctuary of Aphrodite Melainis)).

4. *II. 3,5*—cf. Pl.C, xxxi-xxxii

And there are several fountains . . . the most handsome
is the fountain-building by the statue of Artemis and on
it is a figure of Bellerophontes (riding Pegasus) and the
water flows from the hoof of Pegasus.

5. *II. 1,6*—Ref.

The Corinthians say that Poseidon had a controversy with
Helios (the Sun) about their land, ((and that the Briareos
was the arbitrator, awarding the Isthmus and all in that
direction to Poseidon, and giving the height above the city
to Helios. From this time on they say that the area of

Isthmus belongs to Poseidon)).

6. *II. 1,5&6*—cf. Pl.C, xxxiii-xxxix. FF, v
   The Isthmus of Corinth extends in one direction to the sea at Kenchreae, and in the other, to the sea at Lechaion.

7. *The two harbors, Lechaion and Kenchreae*—cf. Pl.C, xl

8. *II. 2,2*—cf. Pl.C, xli-xlviii
   The Isthmian games did not fall into disuse when Corinth was destroyed by Mummius, but as long as the city lay desolate, the surveillance of the games was given to the city of Sicyon, and when Corinth was rebuilt, the old honor came back to it.

9. *II. 1,7*—cf. Pl.D, xlix-l
   And as you approach the temple (of Poseidon at Isthmia), there are portrait statues of the athletes who have been victors in the Isthmian games on one side, and on the other, pine trees planted in a row, in a nearly straight line. And on the temple, which is not very large, can be seen (as akroteria?) bronze Tritons.

10. *II. 1,7*—cf. Pl.D, li-lix
    cf. Corinth 1. *(Paus. II. 1,7)* cf. *II. 2,3*
    There is, at Lechaion, a sanctuary of Poseidon, and in it, a bronze statue of the god. cf. *II. 2,8*. A fountain building and a bronze Poseidon on it. Under the feet of the god is a dolphin spouting water.

11. *II. 2,3*—cf. Pl.D, lx-lxv. FF, vi
    And at Kenchreae there is a temple of Aphrodite and in it a stone statue of the goddess. And next to it, on the breakwater running into the sea, a bronze statue of Poseidon. And on the other side of the harbor are sanctuaries of Asklepios and Isis.

12. *II. 2,3*—cf. Pl.D, lxvi-lxix
    And on the road to Kenchreae, which begins at the Isthmus, is a temple of Artemis and an ancient statue (xoanon) of the goddess. *cf. II. 3,5*. Next to his (Poseidon's) statue stands a statue of a hunting Artemis.

13. *II. 2,4*—cf. Pl.D, lxx-lxxii, FF, vii-viii
    cf. Corinth 3. *(Paus. II. 2,8)* A statue of Aphrodite made by Hermogenes of Kythera.

14. *II. 2,4*—cf. P.E, lxxiii-lxxvi
    And the tomb of Lais with a lioness set (in relief?) on it, holding a ram in her fore-paws.

15. *II. 2,6*—Ref.
    In the marketplace is . . . a sanctuary of Artemis the

Ephesian, etc.

16. *II. 2,6*—cf. Pl.E, lxxvii-lxxxii

And there are two ancient statues of Dionysus, wholly gilded, except the faces which are painted with red ointment. One they call Dionysus Lysios, and the other, Baccheios. The tradition about these statues I will also record.

17. *II. 2,8*—cf. Pl.E, lxxxiii-lxxxv

There is also a temple of Tyche (Fortune). The statue of the goddess is standing, and made of Parian marble.

18. *II. 2,8*—cf. Pl.E, lxxxvi-lxxxviii

And there are also two bronze statues of Hermes, both in standing posture, and one of them has a temple built for it.

19. *II. 2,8*—cf. Pl.E, lxxxix-xc. FF, ix

And there are three statues of Zeus also in the open air. One has no special epithet; the second is call Zeus Chthonios (Earthly) and the third, Zeus Hypsistos (Highmost, Supreme, Heavenly).

20. *II. 3,1*—cf. Pl.E, xci-xciii. FF, x-xi

In the middle of the market place is a bronze statue of Athena ((and on its pedestal are sculpted figures of the Muses)).

21. *II. 3,1*—cf. Pl.E, xciv-xcvi

And above the marketplace is a temple of Octavia, the sister of Augustus ((who was emperor of the Romans after Caesar, the founder of modern Corinth)).

22. *II. 3,2*—cf. Pl.F, xcvii-cii

And as you go out from the marketplace, getting the road towards Lechaion, there are propylaea (gateways) on which are set two gilded chariots, one with Phaethon, the son of Helios, and the other with Helios (the Sun) himself, in it.

23. *II. 3,2*—cf. Pl.F, ciii. FF, xii-xiii

((And a little distance from the Propylea (gateways) to the right)) is a bronze statue of Herakles. *cf. II. 4,5.* An ancient statue (xoanon) of Herakles, naked, which they say is the work of Daedalos.

24. *II. 3,2*—cf. Pl.F, cv-cviii

And next to it (the statue of Herakles) is the entrance (to the fountain building) leading to the springwaters of Peirene.

25. *II. 3,2*—cf. Pl.F, cix. FF, xiv

There is also near Peirene, a statue and a sacred enclosure of Apollo. *cf. II. 2,8.* And there is also a bronze statue of

Apollo called Klarios.

26. *II. 3,4*—cf. Pl.F, cx-cxi

And as you go on the straight road leading to Lechaion, there is a bronze statue representing Hermes, seated, and by him, a ram, ((but the story about Hermes and the ram in the ceremony of the cult of the Mother of the gods, though I know it, I purposely do not relate)).

27. *II. 3,5*—Ref.

And there are several fountains placed throughout the city . . . and the most noteworthy is the one by the statue of Artemis, and on it is a figure of Bellerophontes (and the water flows through the hoof of the horse, Pegasus).

28. *Fountains*—cf. Pl.F, cxii-cxv. FF, xv

29. *II.4,1*—cf. Pl.F, cxvi

And not far from the tomb (of Mermeros and Pheres) is the sanctuary of Athens Chalinitis (the Bridler) . . . her statue is an ancient one (xoanon). The head and hands and feet are of white stone.

30. *II. 4,5*—cf. Pl.F, cxvii-cxviii

Close to this gymnasium (the ancient one, not far from the theatre and the spring called Lerna) there are temples of the gods; one of Zeus, one of Asklepios, and the statues of Asklepios and Hygeia (Health) are of white stone ((and the one of Zeus is bronze)).

31. *II. 4,6*—cf. Pl.F, cxix

As you go up to Acro-Corinthos, there are two sacred precincts of Isis ((surnamed Pelagia (Marine) and Egyptian, and two of Serapis)).

32. *II. 4,7*—cf. Pl.F, cxx

And above is a temple of the Mother of the Gods.

33. *II. 5,1*—cf. Pl.F, cxxi-cxxxiv. FF, xvi

On the ascent to Acro-Corinthos is a temple of Aphrodite and statues of her in full armor, and Helios (the Sun) and Eros holding a bow.

34. *Other types*—cf. Pl.G, cxxxv-cxliii. FF, xvii

TENEA (Page 158)

1. *Paus. II.* 5,4—Ref.

Tenea is about 60 stadia distant from Corinth . . . Apollo is the god they hold in highest honor.

SICYON (Plates H, i-xx, FF, xviii; Pages 28-31, 158)

1. *Paus. II. 7,2*—cf. Pl.H, i-ii

The Sicyonians bury their dead in a uniform manner: they deposit the body in the ground and they build over it a stone platform with columns, and on these they build something like the pediments of a temple.

2. *II. 7,5*—cf. Pl.H, iii

In the citadel now used is a sanctuary of Tyche Akraia, and next to it, one to the Dioscuri. Their statues are ancient ones (xoana) as well as the one to Tyche Akraia.

3. *II. 7,5*—cf. Pl.H, iv-vii

And next to the theatre is a temple of Dionysus. The statue of the god is made of gold and ivory and by it are statues of Bacchantes of white stone.

4. *II. 7,8*—cf. Pl.H, viii-ix

((And as you enter the marketplace there is a temple of Peitho (Persuasion), also without a statue. Peitho's worship was established among them on the following grounds: Apollo and Artemis, after slaying Pytho (Python), went to Aegialeia (the ancient name of Sicyon) to purify themselves. But, being seized with some panic in the place which they now call Phobos (Fear) they turned aside to Crete . . . and a pestilence came upon the people of Aegialeia and they were ordered by the seers to propogate Apollo and Artemis)). And they sent seven lads and seven maidens to the river Sythas as suppliants.

5. *II. 7,9*—Ref.

The temple of Apollo is in the present marketplace and they say it was originally built by Proetos because his daughter was cured of madness here. The temple and statue that I saw were dedicated by Pythokles.

6. *II. 9,6*—cf. Pl.H, x

There is also (a statue of) Zeus Meilichios . . . made with an obvious lack of art; Meilichios' image is something like a pyramid. And in the open area of the marketplace is a bronze statue of Zeus, a work of Lysippos.

7. *II. 10,1*—cf. Pl.H, xi

And in the gymnasium, which is not far from the marketplace, is dedicated a statue of Herakles made of stone, the work of Skopas. There is also elsewhere a shrine to Herakles.

8. *II. 10,2*—cf. Pl.H, xii

And as you enter the temple of Asklepios, on one side of the entrance is a statue of Pan seated. *cf. II. 11,1.* An altar of Pan.

9. *II. 10,2*—cf. Pl.H, xiii-xiv

The temple of Asklepios . . . and, being in it, (you can see) the gold and ivory statue of the god, represented beardless, a work of Kalamis. He has a scepter in one hand, and in the other, a pine cone.

10. *II. 10,4*—cf. Pl.H, xv-xvi

Next is the sanctuary of Aphrodite . . . the seated statue of the goddess is the work of Kanachos, the Sicyonian . . . and it is made of gold and ivory. The goddess is represented having the modius (corn measure) on her head, and in one hand holds a poppy, and an apple in the other.

11. *II. 10,7*—cf. Pl.H, xvii-xix

((And as you ascend from here to the gymnasium)) on the right is a temple of the Pheraean Artemis; the Sicyonians say that the ancient statue of the goddess (xoanon) was brought from Pherae.

12. *II. 11,2*—cf. Pl.H, xx

And as you descend to the plain, there is a shrine of Demeter. And they say it was built by Plemnaeos ((in gratitude to the goddess for rearing his son)).

13. *II. 11,1*—Ref.

There is a temple of Athena . . .

14. *Other types:* Pl.FF, xviii

PHLIUS (Plates H, i, FF, xix-xx; Pages 31-32, 158-159)

1. *Paus. II. 12,4*—cf. Pl.H, i

Asopos ((said to be the son of Celusa and Poseidon)) discovered the water of the river ((which they call Asopos)).

2. *II. 13,3*—cf. Pl.H, i

((On the citadel of Phlius . . . a sanctuary, which from ancient times has been held to be the holy of holies)). The goddess to whom the shrine belongs is called by the earliest people of Phlius, Ganymede, but the later call it Hebe.

3. *II. 13,5*—cf. Pl.FF, xix, Ref.

There is also a bronze statue of Artemis, which looks to me like an ancient one.

4. *II. 13,5*—Ref.

And as you descend from the citadel, there is, on the right, a temple of Asklepios, and the statue is a beardless one. ((Below this temple is the theatre)).

4a. *II. 13,7*—Ref.

And not far away is what is called Omphalos (navel) ((the center of all the Peloponnese, if indeed their account is correct)).

5. *II. 13,7*—Ref.

There is an ancient sanctuary of Dionysus.

5a. *II. 13,7*—cf. Pl.FF, xx

And there is also one sanctuary of Apollo, and another of Isis. The statue of Dionysus can be seen by anyone, as well as that of Apollo, ((but that of Isis may only be seen by the priests)).

CLEONAE (Plates H, i-ii, FF, xxi; Pages 32, 159)

 1. *Paus. II. 15,1*—cf. Pl.H, i

((On the road from Corinth to Argos, you come to the small town of Cleonae)) . . . there is a shrine of Athena, in which is a statue made by Skyllis and Dipoenos ((pupils of Daedelos)).

 2. *Other types:* Pl.H, ii, FF, xxi

NEMEA, Coins of Argos (Plate I, i-x; Pages 33-34, 159)

 1. *Paus. II. 15,2*—cf. Pl.I, i

And on these mountains is still shown the cave lair of the Nemean lion.

 2. *II. 15,2*—cf. Pl.I, ii-ix

((At Nemea is a temple well worth seeing of Nemean Zeus, only the roof has fallen in, and there is no longer any statue there; but there is a grove of cypress around the temple)), here it is, they say, that Opheltes, placed on the grass by his nurse, was devoured by a big snake . . . here too is the grave of Opheltes . . .

 3. *II. 15,3*—Ref.

(The Argives) offer a contest here in a race for armored men in the winter meeting of the Nemean games.

 4. *II. 15,3*—Ref.

And above Nemea is the mountain Apesas, where they say Perseus sacrificed first to the Apesantian Zeus.

4a. *Other types:* Pl.I, x

THE ARGIVE HERAEUM, Coins of Argos (Plate I, xi-xvi; Pages 34-35)

 5. *Paus. II. 17,3*—cf. Pl.I, xi

In the Pronaos (fore-temple of the Heraeum) are, on the one side, some old statues of the Charites (the Graces) ((and on the right, the couch of Hera)).

 6. *II. 17,4*—cf. Pl.I, xii-xiv

The huge statue of Hera sitting on the throne is made of gold and ivory, and is a work of Polykleitos. There is a crown on the head of the statue on which are worked the Charites (Graces) and the Horae (the Seasons). In one hand she holds a pomegranate, and a scepter in the other . . . and a cuckoo sits on the scepter.

II. 17,5—Pl.I, xv
They say that the statue standing beside Hera represents
Hebe. It is a work of Naukydes, made too of ivory and gold.

7. *II. 17,6*—cf. Pl.I, xvi
And a peacock made of gold and bright precious stones, a
dedication of the Emperor Hadrian.

ARGOS (Plates I, xvii. L, lvi. FF, xxii. GG, vi; Pages 35-42,
159-161)

8. *Paus. II. 18,1*—cf. Pl.I, xvii-xxi, FF, xxii
And as you go from Mycenae to Argos, there is on the left
of the road a hero-shrine to Perseus.

9. *II. 19,3*—cf. Pl.FF, xxiii, Ref.
Of the sanctuaries and temples of the city of the Argives,
the most notable is the one of Apollo Lykios. The statue
which I saw was a work of Attalos the Athenian. ((The
original temple and the ancient statue (xoanon) were the
offerings of Danaos)).

II. 19,8—cf. Pl.I, xxii-xxiv
Next is a statue of Apollo Agyieus (guardian of the
streets).   *cf. II. 24,1.*
A temple of Apollo . . . the bronze statue of the god is in
a standing posture and it is called Apollo Deiradiotes.

10. *II. 19,4-7*—Ref.
Outside the temple there is a well mouth on which is
represented in relief, the fight between the bull and the
wolf, and a young girl throwing a stone at the bull. ((They
think that this maiden represents Artemis)).

11. *II. 20,1*—cf. Pl.K, xxv-xxvii
And there is a seated statue of Zeus Meilicheios made of
white marble, a work of Polykleitos. *cf. 19,7.* An ancient
statue of Zeus (xoanon). *cf. 19,8.* An altar of Zeus Hyetios
(the rain-bearer). *cf. 20,6.* A shrine to Zeus Soter (the
Saviour). *cf. 21,2.* An altar of Zeus Phyxios (God of
Flight). *cf. 22,2.* An old statue of Zeus. *cf. 24,3.* and on
the summit of Larisa is a temple of Larisaean Zeus. The
statue, which is made of wood, ((stands no longer on its
pedestal)). There are several votive offerings there and an
ancient statue of Zeus (xoanon) with the usual two eyes
and a third in the forehead.

II. 20,3—cf. Pl.K, xxviii
And opposite this (the relief of Kleobis and Biton) is a
temple of Nemean Zeus with a bronze standing statue of
the god, a work of Lysippus.

12. *II. 20,3*—cf. Pl.K, xxix-xxxi

And further from the temple of Nemean Zeus is a most ancient temple of Tyche (Fortune) ((since Palamedes, the inventor of dice, made a votive offering of his invention to this temple)).

13. *II. 19,6*—cf. Pl.K, xxxii-xxxiii

Here are also ancient statues (xoana) of Aphrodite and Hermes; the latter is the work of Epeios, and the former, the offering of Hypernnestra. *cf. 19,7.* And a statue of Hermes depicted making a lyre from a tortoiseshell.

14. *II. 20,3*—cf. Pl.K, xxxiv

And near are carved in relief on stone, Kleobis and Biton, who themselves drew the cart with their mother in it to the temple of Hera.

15. *II. 21,1*—cf. Pl.K, xxxv

((And as you descend thence and turn to the marketplace ... and the)) temple of Asklepios.

16. *II. 21,9*—cf. Pl.K, xxxvi-xxxviii, FF, xxiv

And not far from the trophy (victory memorial) is the sanctuary of Leto. The statue is a work of Praxiteles (and the Argives call) the maiden figure standing beside the statue of the goddess, Chloris (Pale) ((saying that she was a daughter of Niobe, called Meliboea at the first)).

17. *II. 22,1*—cf. Pl.K, xxxix. GG, i

Just opposite the tomb of the women is a sanctuary of Demeter surnamed Pelasgia ((because Pelasgos, the son of Triopas, built it, and not far from the temple is Pelasgos' tomb)). *cf. 18,3.* A temple of Demeter surnamed Mysian. *cf. 21,4.* Pyrrhus' bones lie in the temple of Demeter.

18. *II. 22,5*—Ref.

And next is the temple of Dioscuri. ((The statues represent the Dioscuri themselves, their sons Anaxis and Myasinous, and their mothers Hilaeira and Phoebe. They are made of ebony wood by Dipoenos and Skyllis ...)).

19. *II. 22,6*—cf. Pl.K, xl

And near this temple of Dioscuri is a sanctuary of Eileithuia, a votive offering of Helen. *cf. 18,3.* .... is a shrine of Eileithuia.

20. *II. 22,6*—cf. Pl.K, xli

And beyond (the temple of Eileithuia) is a sanctuary of Hecate. (The cult) statue is a work of Skopas, and made of stone. The two bronze statues of the goddess opposite it are made, the one by Polykleitos, and the other by his brother Naukydes, the son of Mothon.

21. *II. 22,9*—cf. Pl.GG, ii, Ref.

In the gymnasium of Kylarabos is a statue of Athena Kapaneia (corr. to Pania) *cf. 21,3.* And there is a temple of Athena under the name Salpinx (Trumpet) which, as they say, was built by Hegeleos.

22. *II. 24,3*—cf. Pl.K, xlii-xlv

And on the summit of Larisa ... there is also a temple of Athena well worth seeing. *cf. 24,2.* And next to the temple of Apollo Deiradiotes is a temple of Athena Oxyderkes (Sharp-eyed), the votive offerings of Diomedes. *cf. 23,5.* (The Argives) say ... that they have the statue of Athena which was carried away from Ilion (Troy) (by Diomedes).

23. *II. 23,1*—cf. Pl.K, xlvi

As you go thence on the road called the hollow way ((there is, on the right hand, a temple of Dionysus. The statue of the god, as they say, came from Euboea)). *cf. 23,7.* Temple of Dionysus Kresios (of Crete). *cf. 24,7.* The feast of Dionysus.

24. *II. 23,4*—cf. Pl.K, xlvii-xlviii, GG, iii.

The most notable Asklepieion at Argos, when I visited it, contained a seated statue of Asklepios made of white stone, and Hygeia standing by him. There are also, seated near, statues of those who made the statues, Xenophilos and Straton.

25. *II. 23,7*—cf. Pl.L, xlix

An underground building on which was the chamber of bronze built by Akrisios for the safe custody of his daughter (Danae).

26. *II. 24,1*—Ref.

And as you go up to the citadel (Larisa), there is also a temple of Hera Akraia (of the heights).

27. *II, 24,2*—Ref.

The Stadion (Race-course) where they hold the games in honor of Nemean Zeus and of Hera (Nemea and Heraia).

28. *II. 24,2*—Ref.

((On the left of the road to the citadel)) is a monument to the sons of Aigyptos. ((Their heads are here, apart from their bodies, for the bodies are at Lerna where the murder of the young men was perpetrated, and when they were dead, their wives cut off their heads to show their father their desperate deed)).

29. *II. 25,1*—cf. Pl.L, l-li

((On this road (from Argos to Mantinea) is a temple with
a double entrance; one facing west, another east)). At the
east end is an ancient statue of Aphrodite (xoanon), and
on the west end, of Ares. These statues are, they say, votive
offerings of Polyneikes ((and the Argives who were associated with him on his expedition (Seven against Thebes))).

30. *Other types:* Pl.L, lii-lvi, GG, iv-vi

EPIDAURUS (Plates L, i-viii, GG, vii-viii; Pages 42-44, 161)

1. *Paus. II. 26,3-6*—cf. Pl.L, i-ii

And the district was especially held sacred to Asklepios for
the following reason: ... (Coronis) ... exposed the new-
born child ... and as he was exposed there, one of the she-
goats feeding on the mountain gave him milk, and the
watchdog of the flock guarded him ... and Aresthanas (the
herdsman), when he found the child, desired to take him
away, etc.

2. *II. 27,2*—cf. Pl.L, iii-v, GG, vii

The statue of Asklepios is made of ivory and gold and is
in size half that of Zeus Olympios at Athens. The inscription shows that it was made by Thrasymedes, the son of
Arignotos from the island Paros. The god sits on a throne
holding a staff in one hand and he holds his other hand
above the head of the serpent, and a dog is lying at his feet.

3. *II. 27,6*—cf. Pl.L, vi-vii. GG, viii

Antoninus (the Roman senator) ... built a temple to Hygeia, and another to Asklepios and Apollo, surnamed the
Egyptians. *cf. 27,5.* And within the sacred grove ... there is
... a statue of Epione. *cf. 29,1.* There is a sanctuary of
Asklepios (in the city of Epidaurus) and in it statues of
the god himself and Epione, who they say was his wife,
and those statues are made of Parian marble and are in
the open air.

4. *II. 27,7*—Ref.

((And there are two mountains above the grove, one called
Titthion (Nipple) and the other)) Kynortion. And on the
latter, a sanctuary of Apollo Maleatas. This sanctuary is
one of the later ones.

5. *II. 28,1*—Ref.

All kinds of snakes, and especially those which incline to be
tawny in color, are considered sacred to Asklepios.

6. *Other types:* Pl.L, viii

AEGINA (Plates L, i-viii, GG, ix; Pages 44-46, 161)
1. *Paus. II. 29,6*—cf. Pl.L, i
   Near the chief harbor ... is a temple of Aphrodite.
2. *II. 29,6*—Ref.
   And in the most notable place of the city is the Aiakeion
   (the hero-shrine of Aiakos). ((A square court of white
   stone at the entrance of which are statues of the envoys
   who were sent by the Greeks to Aiakos)).
3. *II. 30,1*—cf. Pl.L, ii, GG, ix
   The ancient naked statue of Apollo (xoanon) is of native
   art (Aeginetan school).
4. *II. 30,2*—cf. Pl.L, iii
   And of all the gods the Aeginetans honor most Hecate ...
   ((and within the enclosure is a temple containing)) an
   ancient statue of the goddess, a work of Myron. It has one
   face and one body. ((Alkamenes, as I believe, was the one
   who first made a tri-bodied and tri-faced statue of
   Hecate)).
5. *II. 30,3*—Ref.
   As you go towards the mountain of Panhellenian Zeus, you
   reach the sanctuary of Aphaea.
6. *II. 30,4*—cf. Pl.L, iv
   The mountain Panhellenian has nothing of note but the sanctuary of Zeus, which, as they say, was established by Aiakos.
7. *Other types:* Pl.L, v-viii

TROEZEN (Plates M, i-xii, GG, x-xvi; Pages 46-49, 161-162)
1. *Paus. II. 30,6*—cf. Pl.M, i-ii
   They worship Athena under the names Polias (Urban) and
   Sthenias (Strength-giver) and Poseidon surnamed Ba-
   sileus (the King). And so their ancient coins have on them
   a trident and a head of Athena.
2. *II. 32,5*—cf. Pl.M, iii-v
   And in the citadel there is a temple of Athena Sthenias
   and the ancient statue of the goddess (xoanon) is the work
   of Kallon of Aegina ((who was the pupil of Tektaios and
   Angelion, who made the statue of Apollo at Delos, and they
   are recorded as pupils of Dipoinos and Skyllis)).
3. *II. 31,1*—cf. Pl.M, vi
   In the marketplace of Troezen is a temple and statues of
   Artemis Soteira (Saviour). *cf. 30,7.* He (Saron, king of
   Troezen) built the sanctuary dedicated to Saronian Artemis. *cf. 31,4.* Near the theatre is a temple of Artemis
   Lykia which Hippolytus built.

4. *II. 31,6*—cf. Pl.GG, x, Ref.
   They say that the shrine of Apollo Thearios was built by
   Pittheus. *cf. 32,2.* And within the sacred precinct (of Hippolytus' shrine) is a temple of Apollo Epibaterios, a votive
   offering of Diomedes ((when he escaped the storm which
   fell on the Greeks as they were returning from Troy)).

5. *II. 31,6*—cf. Pl.M, vii
   And the cult statue (of Apollo Thearios) is a work of Her-
   mon of Troezen who also made the ancient statues of the
   Dioscuri (xoana).

5a. *II. 31,10*—cf. Pl.GG, xi-xii
   And there is a statue of Hermes, called Polygios.

6. *II. 31,10*—Ref.
   There is also a shrine of Zeus Soter (Saviour).

7. *II. 32,1*—cf. Pl.M, viii, GG, xiii
   And to Hippolytus, the son of Theseus, a most notable
   sanctuary is dedicated and a temple in it with an old statue.

8. *II. 32,3*—cf. Pl.M, ix
   And above it is a temple of Aphrodite Kataskopia (Peep-
   ing). *cf. 32,6.* Temple ... of Aphrodite Akraia (of the
   Heights). *cf. 32,7.* And a shrine of Aphrodite Nymphia
   (Bride) ((which was built by Theseus when he married
   Helen)).

9. *II. 32,4*—cf. Pl.GG, xiv, Ref.
   And the statue of Asklepios is a work of Timotheos, but
   the people of Troezen say that it does not represent Asklepios, but Hippolytus.

10. *II. 32,4*—cf. Pl.M, x, GG, xv
    I saw also the house of Hippolytus, and in front of it the
    fountain building, built on the spring, which, as the people
    of Troezen say, was discovered by Herakles.

11. *II. 32,7*—cf. Pl.M, xi
    And a rock called Theseus' rock ((which, in former times,
    used to be called the altar of Zeus Sthenios)) but had its
    name changed because Theseus found the shoes and sword
    of Aegaeus under it. *cf. 31,1.* Theseus ... when he returned
    to Troezen from having killed Astereion, the son of
    Minos, ...

12. *Other types:* Pl.M, xii, GG, xvi

METHANA (Plate M, i-iv; Pages 49-50)

1. *II. 34,1*—Ref.
   At a distance of about 30 stadia from the small town (of
   Methana) are some baths at a (warm) mineral spring.

And they say that the spring of water first appeared there when Antigonos, the son of Demetrios, was king of Macedon.

2. *Other types:* Pl.M, i-iv

HERMIONE (Plates M, i-iii, GG, xvii; Pages 50-51, 162)

1. *Paus. II. 34,10*—cf. Pl. GG, xvii, Ref.

   And even now there are several sanctuaries, one of Poseidon at the beginning of the headland, and as you go from the sea to the heights is a temple of Athena ((and by it the foundations of a Stadion (Race-course))).

2. *II. 34,11*—Ref.

   ((But what I select as most worthy of record are)) the temple of Aphrodite Pontia (Marine) and Aphrodite Limenia (of the Harbor), and in it is a large statue (of the goddess) of white stone, a work of art truly worth seeing. And there is another temple of Aphrodite ((which has other honors from the people of Hermione and this special one: that maidens or widows intending to marry must all sacrifice here before their weddings)).

3. *II. 35,1*—cf. Pl.M, i

   And next is a temple of Dionysus Melanaegis (Black-shielded).

4. *II. 35,3*—cf. Pl.M, ii

   And the sanctuary of Tyche (Fortune), as the people of Hermione say, is the newest one that they have, and in it is a colossal statue of Parian marble.

5. *II. 35,4*—Ref.

   The temple most worthy of notice is that of Demeter on the Pron ... *cf. 35,5.* ((And Demeter is called Chthonia there, and the annual festival held in her honor during the summer is called Chthonia too)).

6. *II. 35,6*—cf. Pl.M, iii

   And the procession is followed by some people who lead a full-grown heifer from the herd, tightly bound with ropes and bucking wildly, etc. (Description of the Chthonia festival)

ASINE (Plate M, i-ii, Pages 51, 163)

1. *Paus. II. 36,5*—cf. Pl.M, i

   ((The Argives razed (the city) to the ground and added it to their territory)) but they left the sanctuary of Apollo Pythaeus standing and it can still be seen.

2. *Other types:* Pl.M, ii, GG, xxiii

LERNA & NAUPLIA, Coins of Argos (Plates L, li-M, ii. GG, xviii-xx; Pages 51-52, 162)
1. *Paus. II. 37,2*—cf. Pl.L, li
   And a statue of Aphrodite of stone near the sea. *cf. II. 19,6; 19,7; 20,8; 23,8; 25,1; 38,1.*
2. *II. 37,4*—cf. Pl.M, i
   And at the spring of Amymone grows a planetree under which, they say, the Hydra was reared.
3. *II. 38,2*—cf. Pl.M, ii, GG, xviii-xx
   The hero-settler of Nauplia was Nauplios, son of Poseidon and Amymone ... and a sanctuary of Poseidon and harbors at Nauplia ((and a spring called Kanathos)).

LACEDAEMON (Plates N, i-xix, GG, xxi; Pages 54-60, 163)
1. *Paus. III. 10.7*—cf. Pl.N, i-ii
   And a third branch from the high road on the right leads to Karyae and the shrine of Artemis, for the area of Karyae is sacred to Artemis and the Nymphs. And there, in the open field, stands a statue of Artemis Karyatis (Caryatide).   *cf. III. 14,2.*
   And there are shrines of Poseidon Hippokurios (Horse-raiser) and the Aeginaetan Artemis. And as you retrace your steps to the Lesche (Club) there is a shrine of Artemis Issoria which they also call Limnaea, though she is not actually Artemis but the Cretan goddess Britomartis. But about her I spoke in the chapter on Aegina. *cf. III. 18,4.*
   Those are the stories they tell about Artemis Knagia. Knageus, they say, was a native (of Sparta) ((who joined the expedition of the Dioscuri against Aphidna (in Attica))).   *cf. III. 20,7.*
   Not far from it (the place called Lapitheion on Mount Taygetos) is Dereion where, in the open air, is a statue of Artemis Dereatis.
   III, 25,3—cf. Pl.N, iii-iv, GG, xxi
   And the sanctuaries at Pyrrhichos are two: one for Artemis surnamed Astrateia (Anti-militarist) and the reason for this surname is that here the Amazons were stopped from any further advance, and one of Apollo Amazonios. Both have ancient statues (xoana) and they say that they were votive offerings of the women from Thermodon (Amazons).
2. *III. 11,11*—cf. Pl.N, v-vii
   There is also ((in the city of Sparta)) a statue of Hermes Agoraios (of the Marketplace) carrying the child Dionysus.

3. *III. 12,8*—cf. Pl.N, viii-ix

And the Lacedaemonians have an altar of Apollo Akritas, and a sanctuary of the earth called Gasepton (Venerable Earth), and above it is ((shrine? temple?)) of Apollo Meleatas. *cf. 13,3.* And Karneios, whom they surname Oiketas (House-guarder) was honored in Sparta even before the return of the Herakleidae; his statue was erected in the house of Krios, the son of Theokles the prophet. *cf. 13,4.*

4. *III. 14,6*—Ref.

And as you go further away from Dromos (the Course) you come to the sanctuaries of the Dioscuri and the Charites (Graces).

5. *III. 15,3*—cf. Pl.N, x

And there are shrines of Helen and Herakles; hers near the tomb of Alkman, and his very near the city wall, and in it is a statue of Herakles armed. ((Herakles was so represented in this statue they say because of his fight against Hippokoon and his sons)).

6. *III. 16,6*—Ref.

And the Lacedaemonians have a sanctuary for Lycurgos their lawgiver, as if he were a god.

7. *III. 16,7*—cf. Pl.N, xi-xii

At the site called Limnaion is a sanctuary of Artemis Orthia (Standing). The ancient statue (xoanon), as they say, is the very one which Orestes and Iphigeneia formerly stole from the Tauric (peninsula). And the Lacedaemonians say that it was brought to their country when Orestes extended his kingdom thence. And their account seems to me more probable than the one of the Athenians ... but it seems that it was forgotten by the Athenians ((during the preparations to abandon the land)) and became a prey to the Medes, and it was carried from Brauron to Susa and afterwards the Syrians of Laodikeia received it as a gift from king Seleukos and they still have it.

8. *III. 17,2*—cf. Pl.N, xiii-xiv

The Lacedaemonians, many years afterward, completed the temple and made a bronze statue of Athena, a work of Gitiadas, a native, who also composed Doric poems and a hymn to the goddess Athena. Many of the labors of Herakles and many of his other adventures, and several actions of the Dioscuri, and the rape of the daughters of Leukippos, and Hephaistos freeing his mother from her bonds are wrought in relief on the bronze (in this temple).

9. *III. 19,2*—cf. Pl.N, xvi-xvii

And here the statue stands, the height of which I could not find anyone who knew, but in conjecture it appears to be about 30 cubits tall ((about 50 feet)). And this is not a work of Bathykles, but ancient and not artistically made, for except for the face, feet and hands, it resembles a bronze column. There is a helmet on the head and a lance and bow in his hands. And the base of the statue is like an altar and they say that Hyacinthos is buried in it.

10. *Other types:* Pl.N, xviii-xix

GYTHEIUM (Plates N, xxl-O, ix; Pages 60-63, 163)

1. *Paus. III. 21,8*—cf. Pl.N, xx-xxii

The people of Gytheium assign no mortal as founder of their city, but say that Herakles and Apollo, when they quarreled about the tripod and reconciled afterward, jointly settled the town; and in their marketplace they have statues of Apollo and Herakles.

2. *III. 21,8*—cf. Pl.N, xxiii-xxiv

And on another site (in the city) is a statue of Apollo Karneios.

3. *III. 21,7*—Ref.

Near them (the statues of Herakles and Apollo in the marketplace) is a statue of Dionysus. *cf. 22,2.* There is a mountain sacred to Dionysus which they call Larysion ((and here at the beginning of spring they have a feast to Dionysus.

4. *III. 21,7*—cf. Pl.O, i-ii

((And on another site of the town)) ... is a bronze statue of Asklepios in a roofless temple, and a fountain sacred to the god.

5. *III. 21,7*—Ref.

And a holy sanctuary of Demeter.

6. *III. 21,7*—cf. Pl.O, iii

... and a statue of Poseidon Gaieochos (Earth-holder).

7. *III. 21,9*—cf. Pl.O, iv

And the gates (((of the city wall))) here are called Kastorides (Sacred to Kastor).

8. *III. 21,9*—Ref.

And on the citadel there is a temple and a statue of Athena.

9. *III. 22,1*—cf. Pl.O, v

Facing the island (((Cranae, opposite Gytheium))) on the mainland is the sanctuary of Aphrodite Migonitis (Uniting) and the entire place is called Migonion, and this sanctuary, according to what they say, was established by Alexander (((Paris, the Son of Priam))).

10. *Other types:* Pl.O, vi-ix

ASOPUS (Plate O, x-xiii; Page 63)

  1. *Paus. III. 22,9*—cf. Pl.O, x

    ((And the town of Asopus on the sea is about 60 stadia distant from Akriae))...and there is a sanctuary of Athena called Kyparissia (Cypress goddess) on the citadel.

  2. *Other types:* Pl.O, xi-xiii

BOEAE (Plate O, xiv-xvi; Pages 63-64)

  1. *Paus. III. 22,12*—Ref.

    The oracle told them that Artemis would show them where to dwell...and they call Artemis Soteira (Saviour).

  2. *III. 22,13*—cf. Pl.O, xiv-xv

    And elsewhere in the city are shrines of Asklepios and Serapis and Isis.

  3. *III. 23,2*—cf. Pl.O, xvi

    And as you sail from Boeae to the promontory of Malea, there is a harbor called Nymphaion, with a statue of Poseidon standing.

LAS (Plate O, xvii-xxi; Pages 64-65)

  1. *Paus. III. 24,6*—cf. Pl.O, xvii

    ((To the right of Gytheium is Las, 10 stadia from the sea, and 40 from Gytheium))...and there are still visible ruins of the old town, and standing before the city wall is a statue of Herakles.

  2. *III. 24,7*—cf. Pl.O, xviii

    And there is among the ruins a temple of Athena surnamed Asia, erected, as they say, by Castor and Pollux on their safe return from Colchis.

  3. *III. 24,8*—cf. Pl.O, xix-xx

    And on Mount Ilion there is a temple of Dionysus, and at the very summit a temple of Asklepios. ((On Mount Knakadion is an Apollo called Karneios)).

  4. *III. 24,9*—cf. Pl.O, xxi

    And on a promontory by the sea is a temple of Artemis Diktynna, whose feast they hold annually.

THURIA (Plate O, xxii-xxiv; Pages 65-66)

  1. *Paus. IV. 31,2*—cf. Pl.O, xxii-xxiv

    And Augustus gave Thuria to the Spartans. For, when he (the future emperor of Rome) was at war with (Mark) Anthony, himself a Roman, several Greeks, especially Messenians, fought (for Anthony) because the Lacedaemonians espoused the side of Augustus. Accordingly, Augustus punished the Messenians and others who had opposed him, some more, some less. And the people of Thuria left their ancient city built on a height and went to dwell in the plain. Not that they abandoned the upper city altogether, for there are still standing ruins of walls and a sanctuary there for the cult of the Syrian goddess.

MESSENE (Plate P, i-vii; Pages 66-68)

1. *Paus. IV. 31,9*—Ref.

There is a holy shrine of Demeter at Messene.

2. *IV. 31,10*—cf. Pl.P, i

There are many, and worthwhile, statues to see at the sanctuary of Asklepios. For beside the statues of the god and his sons, ((and beside those of Apollo, the Muses and Herakles, there are statues of a personification of the city of Thebes, Epameinondas, the son of Kleommis, and of Tyche (Fortune) and of Artemis Phosphoros (Light-bringer). Those in stone are the work of Damophon, the only Messenian sculptor I know of who has produced any remarkable statues)).

IV. 31,11—cf. Pl.P, ii

There is also a temple of ((the Heroine)) Messene, the daughter of Triopas, and her statue is made of gold and Parian marble ((instead of ivory)). *cf. 31,6.* ((And the most notable (in the marketplace of Messene) is a statue)) of the Mother of the Gods of Parian marble, by Damophon.

3. *IV. 31,10*—Ref.

And a statue of Herakles ... *cf. 32,1.*

4. *IV. 31,7*—cf. Pl.P, iii

And by the said Damophon is the statue of ((Artemis)) which the Messenians call Laphria.

5. *IV. 33,2*—cf. Pl.P, iv-v

The sanctuary of Zeus Ithomatas (of Ithome). And the statue of Zeus is the work of Ageladas, and it was originally made for the Messenians who settled at Naupaktos.

IV. 31,6—Pl.P, vi

In the marketplace is a statue of Zeus Soter (Saviour).

6. *Other types:* Pl.P, vii

CORONE (Page 68)

1. *Paus. IV. 34,6*—Ref.

There is also in the citadel in the open air a bronze statue of Athena with a red-legged crow in her hand. *cf. 34,6.* And a temple of Dionysus.

COLONIDES (Plates P, x, GG, xxii; Pages 68, 163)

1. *Paus. IV. 34,8*—cf. Pl.P, x, GG, xxii
   ((And adjoining the town of Corone is the town of Colonides. Its inhabitants say that they are not Messenians, but were brought by Kolaenos from Attica, who according to an oracle, followed a crested lark there. And in the process of time, they picked up the Dorian dialect and customs. And the town of Colonides is on a height not far from the sea)).

MOTHONE (Plate P, viii-ix, xi-xiv; Pages 68-69)

1. *Paus. IV. 35,1*—cf. Pl.P, viii
   ((and Mothone, which before the expedition against Troy, and even subsequently to that war, was called Pedasos, afterwards changed its name to Mothone from the daughter of Oeneus, as the inhabitants say)) ... but in my opinion it was the rock called Mothon which gave its name to Mothone because this rock is the one which forms a natural harbor, for it is primarily submerged under the water and narrows the entrance for ships, and at the same time is a sort of breakwater against the wildness of the waves.

2. *IV. 35,8*—cf. Pl.P, xi-xii
   At Mothone is a temple of Athena Anemotis (Mistress of the Winds). Diomedes they say dedicated the statue of the goddess and gave her that surname ((for violent unseasonable winds used to blow over the place and do much harm, but after Diomedes prayed to Athena, no disaster from fierce winds came to them)).

3. *IV. 35,8*—cf. Pl.P, xiii
   There is also a sanctuary of Artemis here.

4. *Other types:* Pl.P, ix, xiv

PYLOS (Plates P, xv-xvi, GG, xxiv; Pages 69-70, 164)

1. *Paus. IV. 36,2*—cf. Pl.P, xv, GG, xxiv
   There is a temple here of Athena Koryphasia (Dweller of the Peaks).

2. *Other types:* Pl.P, xvi

CYPARISSIA (Plate P, xvii-xix; Page 70)

1. *Paus. IV. 36,7*—cf. Pl.P, xvii
   And as you go toward Cyparissia from Pylos, there is a spring under the city close to the sea; they say the water welled up when Dionysus struck the ground with his thyrsos, and so they call the spring Dionysias.

2. *IV. 36,7*—cf. Pl.P, xviii-xix

There is also in Cyparissia, a shrine of Apollo and a shrine of Athena Cyparissian.

3. *IV. 36,5*—Ref.

And at the site called Aulon there is a temple of Asklepios Aulonios and a statue of the god. ((Here flows the river Neda, forming a natural boundary between Messenia and Elis)).

ELIS (Plate P, xx-xxiv; Pages 70-74)

1. *Paus. V. 10,7*—Ref.

And at the edge of the pediment lies the river god Kladeos.

V. 14,6—Ref.

And next to those altars we have mentioned there is one on which they sacrifice to Alpheios and Artemis together ... and at a short distance from this is another altar to Alpheios.

2. *V. 11,1*—cf. Pl.P, xx-xxiii

The statue of the god (Zeus) is made of gold and ivory and is seated on a throne and a crown is on his head imitating the branches of an olive tree. In his right hand he holds Nike (Victory), ((a crowned statuette)) also made of ivory and gold, and holding a garland. In the left hand of Zeus is a scepter decorated with every kind of precious stone. And the bird seated on the scepter is an eagle. *cf. V. 24,1.* As you go toward the great temple, starting from the Bouleuterion (Council Chamber), there is on the left a statue of Zeus crowned, as it were, with flowers, and having in his right hand a thunderbolt.

3. *V. 13,1*—Ref.

And within Altys there is a separated sacred enclosure for Pelops. Among all of the heroes in Olympia, Pelops is the mostly highly preferred of the heroes by the inhabitants of Elis, even as is Zeus from among all of the gods.

4. *V. 17,1*—Ref.

((And at the temple of Hera)) ... the statue of the goddess is seated on a throne ((and standing by is (Zeus?) bearded and wearing a leather cap (of the Phrygian type) on his head, and the workmanship is very primitive)).

5. *VI. 25,1*—cf. Pl.P, xxiv. Page 73

And within the sacred enclosure (of Aphrodite, at the city of Elis is a stone platform and on it is a bronze statue of Aphrodite seated on a bronze he-goat. This is a work of Skopas and is known as Aphrodite Pandemos (Common).

6. *VI. 26,1*—Ref. Page 74

And there is an old theatre between the marketplace and the sanctuary of the goddess Mene (Crescent Moon), [as well as a new theatre] and a shrine of Dionysus. The statue (of Dionysus) is a work of Praxiteles. And of all the gods, one of the most respected by the people of Elis is Dionysus and they say that he frequents their festival in his honor called the Thyia ((in a place about 8 stadia from the city)).

V. 19,6—Ref.

And there too is a statue of a bearded Dionysus lying down in a cave, clad in a long chiton and holding a bowl in his hands. And there are clusters of vines around him and apple and pomegranate trees.

DYME (Page 74)

1. *Paus. VII. 17,5*—Ref.

((The boundaries between Achaia and Elis are)) the river Larisos, on the banks of which is a temple of Athena Larisaea, and Dyme, a town of the Achaeans, about 30 stadia from the river.   *cf. VII. 17,9.*

There is also at Dyme, a temple of Athena and a very old statue of the goddess; ((they have as well a sanctuary for the worship of Mother Dindymene and Attis)).

PATRAE (Plates Q, i-R, v; Pages 74-82, 164)

1. *Paus. VII. 18,2*—Ref.

Not far from Patrae the river Glaukos flows into the sea.

VII. 19,5—Ref.

It was on account of this sacrifice that the river which flowed by the sanctuary of Triklaria was called Ameilichos (relentless). It had long had no name. *cf. 19,9.* And the river was given its present name Meilichos (mild).

2. *VII. 19,6*—cf. Pl.Q, i-iv

And after the sack of Ilion (Troy), when the Greeks divided the spoils, Eurypylos, the son of Euaemon, received a chest in which there was a statue of Dionysus, the work, as some people say, of Hephaistos himself, which was given to Dardanos (the founder of Troy) as a gift from Zeus.

VII. 21,1—cf. Pl.Q, v

And in this part of the city is also a sanctuary of Dionysus, surnamed Kalydonios because the statue came from Kalydon.

VII. 21,6—Ref.

And there are here statues of Dionysus, the same number, and named after the ancient towns of the Achaeans, Mesateus and Antheus and Aroeus.

3. *VII. 18,9*—cf. Pl.Q, vi-x

Augustus gave to the people of Patrae valued spoils from
Kalydon, and one of them was the statue of the Artemis
Laphria which, up to my day, is honored on the citadel of
Patrae. *VII. 18,10.* The statue's figure is that of a huntress,
and is of ivory and gold. It is the work of Menarchomos
and Soidas, both of the city of Naupaktos. It is conjectured
that they are not much later than the period of Kanachos
the Sicyonian, or Kallon of Aegina ((the sculptors)).

4. *VII. 19,1*—cf. Pl.Q, xi-xii

Those of the Ionians who dwelt at Aroe and Antheia and
Mesatis, having a sanctuary in common, and a temple of
Artemis Triklaria, used to celebrate her annual festival all
night long. *VII. 20,7.* Just opposite the marketplace by this
exit is the sacred precinct and temple of Artemis Limnatis
(Mistress of the Lake).

5. *VII. 18,12*—cf. Pl.Q, xiii

They have a most splendid procession to Artemis in which
the virgin priestess rides last in a chariot drawn by stags.

6. *VII. 20,2*—cf. Pl.Q, xiv-xv

And within the sacred precinct of Artemis Laphria is a
temple of Athena called Pan-Achaeis, and the statue of the
goddess is ivory and gold.

7. *VII. 20,3*—cf. Pl.Q, xvi

And as you go downtown you come to the temple of Mother
Dindymene, where Attis is also honored. His statue is not
shown. The one of the Mother is made of stone.

8. *VII. 20,3*—cf. Pl.Q, xvii

And in the marketplace there is a temple of Zeus Olympios.
The god is represented seated on a throne, and a statue of
Athena is standing by him.

9. *VII. 20,3*—cf. Pl.Q, xviii

Next to the temple of Zeus Olympios is a statue of Hera
((and a sanctuary of Apollo)).

10. *VII. 20,3*—Ref.

A sanctuary of Apollo, and the statue represents him nude,
without any dress, ((and sandals are on his feet, and one
foot rests upon the skull of an ox)). *VII. 20,6.* Next to the
marketplace is the Odeion. And there is a statue well worth
seeing of Apollo which was made from the spoils received
by the people of Patrae, when they alone of the Achaeans
helped the Aetolians against the army of the Gauls. *VII.*

21,11. In this sanctuary there are temples of Apollo and Aphrodite. Their statues are made of stone.

11. *VII. 21,7*—cf. Pl.Q, xix-xxiii

And at the harbor is a temple of Poseidon with a statue of stone, erect.

12. *VII. 20,9*—cf. Pl.Q, xxiv

The statue of Asklepios, save for the dress, is entirely of stone. *VII. 21,14.* There is also a sanctuary of Asklepios at Patrae, beyond the citadel and near the gates (of the city wall) which lead to Mesatis.

13. *VII. 21,10*—Ref.

Also at Patrae, not very far from the sanctuary of Poseidon, are sanctuaries of Aphrodite.

14. *VII. 21,10*—Ref.

There are also some bronze statues very near to the harbor; one of Ares and one of Apollo.

15. *VII. 21,13*—Ref.

And near the grove at Patras are two sanctuaries of Serapis, and in one of them is the grave monument of Aigyptos, son of Belos.

16. *Other types:* Pl.R, i-v

AEGIUM (Plate R, vi-xxiv; Pages 82-88)

1. *Paus. VII. 23,5*—cf. Pl.R, vi-viii

And at Aegion they have an old temple of Eileithyia; her statue is veiled from head to foot with a finely woven veil, and is made of wood except for the face, hands and feet which are of Pentelic marble. One of the hands is outstretched and in the other she holds a torch ... the statue is a work of Damaphon the Messenian.

2. *VII. 23,7*—cf. Pl.R, ix-xi

And at a short distance from the temple of Eileithyia is the sacred precinct of Asklepios and statues in it of Hygeia and Asklepios. The iambic epigram inscribed on the pedestal says that the sculptor who made them was Damophon of Messene.

3. *VII. 23,9*—cf. Pl.R, xii-xiv

There is also, in the marketplace, a sacred precinct of Zeus Soter (Saviour) and two bronze statues at the left as you enter; the beardless one seems to me to be the older. *VII. 24,4.* There are several other bronze statues at Aegion: Zeus as a boy, and Herakles, also beardless, works of Argeladas of Argos.

4. *VII. 24,2*—cf. Pl.R, xv-xvi

   And a sanctuary of Homagyrios (the Gatherer). Here are statues of Zeus, Aphrodite and Athena. And Zeus was surnamed Homagyrios because Agamemnon gathered together ((at this place, the most famous men in Greece to deliberate together in common how to attack the realm of Priam)).

   VII. 24,3—cf. Pl.R, xvii-xix

   And next to Zeus Homagyrios is the temple of Pan-Achaean Demeter.

5. *VII. 23,9*—cf. Pl.R, xx

   At Aegion there is also a temple to Athena and a grove sacred to Hera. And there are two statues of Athena of white stone ((but the statue of Hera may be seen by no one else except the woman who holds the office of Hera's priestess)). *VII. 23,10.* ((And in a building)) ... are bronze statues of Poseidon, Herakles, Zeus and Athena, and they call them the Argive gods.

6. *VII. 24,1*—cf. Pl.R, xxi-xxii

   At Aegion there is also near the marketplace a common temple for Apollo and Artemis; and in the marketplace, a sanctuary of Artemis represented as an archer.

7. *VII. 24,2*—cf. Pl.R, xxiii

   And near the sea at Aegion is a sanctuary of Aphrodite, and next to it, one of Poseidon.

8. *Other types:* Pl.R, xxiv

HELICE (Page 88)

1. *Paus. VII. 24,5*—Ref.

   ((Forty stadia away from Aegion is a place by the sea called Helice)). Here was once the city of Helice, and the Ionians had here their most holy sanctuary, the one of Poseidon Helikonios.

BURA (Plate S, i-iii; Pages 88-89)

1. *Paus. VII. 25,9*—cf. Pl.S, i

   There are temples here; one of Demeter, one of Aphrodite and Dionysus, and a third of Eileithyia. Their statues are made of Pentelic marble and were done by Eukleides the Athenian, and the statue of Demeter is robed. ((There is also a sanctuary of Isis)).

2. *VII. 25,10*—cf. Pl.S, ii-iii

   And as you descend from Bura to the sea, there is a river called Buraikos and a statue of Herakles, which is not too big, in a cave. And the surname of Herakles is Buraikos.

AEGIRA & PHELLOE (Plate S, iv-ix; Pages 89-91)
1. *Paus. VII. 26,3*—cf. Pl.S, iv-v

   ... And they built a sanctuary of Artemis Agrotera (the Huntress) thinking that this trick against the Sicyonians would not have occurred to them were it not for Artemis. *cf. VII. 26,5.* ... And a temple of Artemis with a contemporary statue. *VII. 26,11.* And there are sanctuaries of Dionysus and of Artemis. The statue of the goddess is a bronze one showing her removing an arrow from her quiver. ((Dionysus' statue has touches of vermilion paint)).

2. *VII. 26,4*—cf. Pl.S, vi

   And Aegira presented, as a worthy sight for the visitor, a sanctuary of Zeus with a statue of the god seated, made of Pentelic marble, a work of Eukleides the Athenian.

3. *VII. 26,4*—cf. Pl.S, vii

   In this shrine (of Zeus) stands also a statue of Athena. The face, hands and feet are of ivory; the rest of the statue is wooden, gilded, and richly variegated.

4. *VII. 26,7*—Ref.

   ((There is also a very ancient temple of Apollo)) ... and there are erect statues of Asklepios standing in the temple, and in another place statues of Serapis and one of Isis, these too being of Pentelic marble.

5. *VII. 26,8*—cf. Pl.S, viii-ix

   I have also seen and visited another building in Aegira. In this building was a statue of Tyche (Fortune) carrying a horn of Amaltheia (cornucopia), and by her, a winged Eros ((to symbolize to men that success in love is due to chance rather than beauty)).

PELLENE (Plate S, x-xiv; Pages 91-93)
1. *Paus. VII. 27,2*—cf. Pl.S, x

   On the way to the city there is also a temple of Athena built of local stone. The statue of the goddess is of gold and ivory. And they say that Pheidias made it much earlier than he did the statues of Athena on the Acropolis at Athens and in Platea.

2. *VII. 27,3*—cf. Pl.S, xi

   And opposite the grove of Artemis Soteira (Saviour) enclosed by a wall is the shrine of Dionysus Lampter (the Lighter). For him they celebrate a festival called Lampteria and during it they carry torches in the shrine by night and they place wine bowls all over the city.

3. *VII. 27,4*—cf. Pl.S, xii

There is also a sanctuary of Apollo Theoxeonios (the Stranger's God) at Pellene, and the statue (of the god) is made of bronze ... Near the sanctuary of Apollo is a temple of Artemis, and the statue represents the goddess as an archer.

4. *VII. 27,11*—cf. Pl.S, xiii

Not far from Mysaion is a temple of Asklepios called Kyros where people are cured by the god.

ARCADIA (Page 93)

1. *Paus. VIII. 1,6*—Ref.

Pelasgos ... discovered that the acorns of some, but not all, oak trees were good.

2. *VIII. 3,6*—Ref.

((Lykaon had many sons, but only one daughter, Kallisto. According to the tradition of the Greeks, Zeus fell in love and mated with her. And when Hera discovered it)) she turned Kallisto into a she-bear whom Artemis killed with her arrows to please Hera. And Zeus sent Hermes with orders to save the child which Kallisto was carrying ((and he turned her into the constellation known as the Great Bear)) ... (The baby was Arcas, and became the hero of the Arcadians).

MANTINEIA (Plate S, xv-xx; Pages 93-95)

1. *Paus. VIII. 9,1*—cf. Pl.S, xv

And in Mantineia is a double temple divided near the middle with a wall. On one side is a temple on Asklepios with a statue of the god made by Alkamenes.

2. *VIII. 9,1*—cf. Pl.S, xvi-xvii

The second shrine is a shrine of Leto and her children. Praxiteles made those statues, the third generation after Alkamenes, ((On the pedestal of these are depicted the Muses and Marsyas playing the flute)). *cf. VIII. 15,5.* After turning to the left for about a stadion, you come to a temple of Apollo Pythios, quite fallen to decay, and in ruins.

3. *VIII. 9,2*—Ref.

The people of Mantineia also have several other shrines, such as the one to Zeus Soter (Saviour) and another to Zeus called Epidotes (Bountiful).

4. *VIII. 9,2*—cf. Pl.S, xviii-xix

There is also a shrine of the Dioscuri.

5. *VIII. 9,3*—cf. Pl.S, xx

And near the altar of Hera is the tomb of Arcas, the son

of Kallisto. ((His remains were brought from Maenalos in accordance with the oracle at Delphi)). *cf. p. xxxvii.*

6. *VIII. 9,7*—Ref.

And they worship also Athena Alea and have a shrine and a statue of her.

7. *VIII. 9,7*—Ref.

They also regard Antinous as a god, and of the temples in Mantineia his is the newest ... And he was honored in Mantineia for this reason: Antinous originated from the town of Bithynion in Bithynia (Asia Minor), beyond the river Sangarios, and the Bithynians were originally Arcadians from Mantineia.

8. *VIII. 10,2*—Ref .

And by the foot of the mountain (Alesion) is a shrine of Poseidon Hippios (Horsebreeder). Not far from the stadium of Mantineia ... the sanctuary which I have seen was recently built by Emperor Hadrian.

ORCHOMENUS (Plates S, xxi-T, iii; Pages 95-97)

1. *Paus. VIII. 13,1*—cf. Pl.S, xxi-xxiv

On the left of the road from Anchisia, on the slope of the mountain, is a sanctuary of Artemis Hymnia. *VIII. 13,2.* And near the town is an ancient statue (xoanon) of Artemis, set in a large cedar tree, whence the goddess is surnamed Kedreatis (of the Cedar Tree).

2. *VIII. 13,2*—cf. Pl.T, i

((And among the notable sights ·in the city are)) ... sanctuaries of Poseidon and Aphrodite. Their statues are stone.

3. *Other types:* Pl.T, ii-iii

PHENEOS (Plate T, iv-viii; Pages 97-98)

1. *Paus. VIII. 14,5*—Ref.

... The people of Pheneos say that Odysseus ... erected a temple there to Artemis and named the goddess Heurippe (Horsefinder) on the spot in Pheneos' land where he found the horses.

2. *VIII. 14,10*—cf. Pl.T, iv-vi

And of all the gods, the people of Pheneos honor most Hermes and they hold a festival called Hermaia. And they have a temple of Hermes with a stone statue, which is made by Eucheir, the son of Eubulides the Athenian.

3. *VIII. 15,1*—cf. Pl.T, vii-viii

At Pheneos they also have a sanctuary of Demeter called Eleusinian, and they celebrate the rites of the goddess just the same as at Eleusis, according to their statement.

CLEITOR (Plate T, ix; Page 98)
1. *Paus. VIII. 21,3*—cf. Pl.T, ix
   The most notable sanctuaries of Cleitor are those dedicated to Demeter, Asklepios ((and Eileithyia)).
2. *VIII*. 21,4—Ref.
   The people of Cleitor have also a sanctuary of the Dioscuri at a distance of about 4 stadia from the city, and they call them the Great Gods and their statues are of bronze.
3. *VIII. 21,4*—Ref.
   And on the summit of a mountain, a distance of about 30 stadia from the city, is a temple and a statue of Athena Koria.

STYMPHALUS (Plate T, x-xii; Page 99)
1. *Paus. VIII. 22,7*—cf. Pl.T, x-xii
   At Stymphalus there is also an ancient sanctuary of Artemis Stymphalis; the statue is an ancient one (xoanon), most of it gilded. And on the roof of the temple are represented the Stymphalian birds. It is difficult to see clearly whether these are made of wood or gypsum, but I conjecture that they are of wood. *VIII. 22,5.* Those birds are as large as a crane and they look like the ibis, but their beaks are stronger and not curved like the ibis.

ALEA (Page 99)
1. *Paus. VIII. 23,1*—Ref.
   ((And next to Stymphalus comes Alea, a town of the Argolic league founded, they say, by Aleus, the son of Aphidas)). Their sanctuaries here are those of Artemis Ephesia (of Ephesus) and Athena Alea. ((And there is a temple of Dionysus with a statue of the god)).

CAPHYAE (Plate T, xiii-xvii; Page 100)
1. *Paus. VIII. 23,3*—cf. Pl.T, xiii
   ((The town clearly gets its name from Kepheus, the son of Aleus ... and the inhabitants trace their origins to Attica. They say they were expelled from Athens by Aegeus and fled to Arcadia and supplicated Kepheus to allow them to dwell there ...)). In Cephyae there are shrines of Poseidon and the Knakalesian Artemis. And in their city belongs Mount Knakalos where they celebrate an annual feast to Artemis.
2. *VIII. 23,6*—cf. Pl.T, xiv
   And about a stadion from Caphyae is a place called Kondylea where there is a sacred grove of Artemis and a temple of the goddess who is here called Kondyleatis, as of old.

3. *Other types:* Pl.T, xv-xvii

PSOPHIS (Plate T, xviii-xxi; Pages 100-101)

1. *Paus. VIII. 24,1*—Ref.

The founder of Psophis was, as some (authors) say, Psophis, the son of Arrhon (the son of Erymanthos, the son of Aristas, the son of Parthaon, the son of Periphetes, the son of Nyktimos), but others say Psophis was the daughter of Xanthos, the son of Erymanthos, the son of Arcas.

2. *VIII. 24,5*—Ref.

And it is said that Herakles, at the command of Eurystheus, hunted the boar (which exceeded all others in size and strength) near Erymanthos (the mountain).

3. *VIII. 24,12*—cf. Pl.T, xviii

The people of Psophis also have a temple and a statue of Erymanthos (the River God) on the banks of the Erymanthos river.

4. *VIII. 21,2*—Ref.

There are various kinds of fish in the river Aroanios, especially some variegated ones which have, as the people say, voices like the thrush. ((I have seen them caught, but I have never heard their voices, although I have waited by the river side till sunset when they are said to be the most vocal)).

5. *VIII. 23,8*—cf. Pl.T, xix-xx

You will come to the oak-copse Soron on the road which passes through Argeathae, Lycuntes and Scotane. Soron is on the road to Psophis and it, as well as all the other Arcadian oak-copses, shelters various wild animals such as boars, bears and immense tortoises.

6. *VIII. 24,4*—Ref.

The sources of the river Erymanthos are on the mountain Lampeia, and this mountain they say is sacred to Pan.

7. *Other types:* Pl.T, xxi

THELPUSA (Plate T, xxii-xxiv; Page 102)

1. *Paus. VIII. 25,4*—cf. Pl.T, xxii

And near Thelpusa, at the site of the shrine of Demeter, the river Ladon flows downward to Onkeion, and the people of Thelpusa call the goddess Erinys (Fury), etc.

VIII. 25,7—cf. Pl.T, xxiii

And they say that Demeter bore a daughter by Poseidon, whose name they will not reveal to the uninitiated, and a son, the foal Arion.

2. *Other types:* Pl.T, xxiv

HERAEA (Plate T, xxv-xxvi; Pages 102-103)

1. *Paus. VIII. 26,1*—Ref.

The founder of Heraea was Heraeus, the son of Lykaon, and the town lies on the right of the river Alpheios.

2. *VIII. 26,1*—cf. Pl.T, xxv-xxvi

There are also two temples of Dionysus. The one is called Polites (citizen) and the other, Auxites (Increaser), and there is also a special building where they celebrate the orgies (Mysteries) of Dionysus.

3. *VIII. 26,2*—Ref.

There is also at Heraea a temple of Pan who is a native god for the Arcadians. As for the temple of Hera, only some ruins and the columns were remaining at the time of my visit.

MEGALOPOLIS (Plate V, i-viii; Pages 103-105)

1. *Paus. VIII. 30,2*—cf. Pl.V, i

((The marketplace is built in the north section to the right of the river's course)). There is in it a precinct made of stone, and a sanctuary of Zeus Lykaios, but there is not entrance to it.

VIII. 30,10—cf. Pl.V, ii

Very near this stoa, towards the east, is a shrine of Zeus Soter (Saviour) adorned with columns all around. Zeus is represented seated on a throne, and by him stands a personification of the city goddess Megalopolis, and on the left is a statue of Artemis Soteira (Saviour). All these statues are of Pentelic marble and were sculpted by Kephisodotos and Xenophon, the Athenians. *VIII. 32,4*. And in this district there is a hill towards the east and on it is a temple of Artemis Agrotera (Huntress), this too dedicated by Aristodemos.

2. *VIII. 38,5*—cf. Pl.V, iii-iv

There is also, on Mount Lykaion, a sanctuary of Pan, and around it, a grove of trees and a hippodrome (race-course). And in front of it, the Stadion (race-track). *cf. VIII. 30,3.* And there is a statue of Pan (in the temple of Zeus Lykaios at the Agora of Megalopolis) made of stone and they call it Oenois ((from the nymph Oenoe who used to be with the other nymphs and was privately Pan's nurse)). (The manuscripts of Pausanias give the version "Sinoeis" for the epithet and "Sinoe" for the nymph's name).

3. *VIII. 30,3*—cf. Pl.V, v

And in front of this sacred enclosure ((of Zeus Lykaios))
is a bronze statue of Apollo worth seeing, about twelve feet
high. It was brought here from Phygalia as a contribution
for the embellishment of Megalopolis.

4. *VIII. 30,7*—Ref.

And behind these public administration buildings is a
temple of Tyche (Fortune) with a statue in stone of the
goddess, five feet high, more or less.

5. *VIII. 31,3*—cf. Pl.V, vi-vii

There is also a statue of Herakles close to the one of
Demeter about a cubit high. This Herakles was one of the
Idean Dactyli, as Onomacritos says in his epics. There is a
table in front of him ...

6. *VIII. 31,5*—cf. Pl.V, viii

And inside the precinct ((of the Great Goddesses)) ... is a
sanctuary of Aphrodite. *cf. VIII. 32,2.* The sanctuary of
Aphrodite too was in ruins and nothing remains of it except the pronaos (fore-temple) and three statues of the
goddess; one was called Urania (Heavenly), the second
Pandemos (Common) and the third had no appellation.

METHYDRION (Page 105)

1. *Paus. VIII. 35,8*—Ref.

At a distance of about 30 stadia downward from Krounoi is
the grave of Kallisto, a high mound of earth with many
trees, wild and tended, growing on it. And on top of this
earth mound is a shrine of Artemis surnamed Kalliste
(Most Beautiful).

LYCOSURA (Pages 105-106)

1. *Paus. VIII. 38,5*—Ref.

There is also on Mount Lykaion ... a Stadion, where in
olden times they celebrated the Lykaian games. *See
appendix.*

PHIGALEIA (Plate V, ix-xix; Pages 106-107)

1. *Paus. VIII. 39,5*—cf. Pl.V, ix-x

And there is a temple of Artemis Soteira (Saviour) and
her statue of stone in an erect position. And from this
shrine it is their custom to start the processions.

2. *VIII. 39,6*—cf. Pl.V, xi-xii

And in the gymnasium there is a statue of Hermes represented wearing a cloak and the statue does not end in legs,
but as a square pillar.

3. *VIII. 39,6*—Ref.

There is also a temple of Dionysus whom the natives call Akratophoros (Bearer of Pure Wine). ((The lower parts of the statue are not visible, being covered with leaves of laurel and ivy. And all of the statue which can be seen is painted with shiny vermilion so as to look very gay)).

4. *VIII. 41,2*—cf. Pl.V, xiii

And the river called Lymax flows into the lake called Neda passing beside Phigaleia. And they say that Lymax got its name because of the purifications (cleansing) of Rhea.

5. *VIII. 41,10*—cf. Pl.V, xiv

A temple of Aphrodite is in the place called Kotilon and it has a statue of the goddess, but its roof is now gone.

6. *VIII. 42,1*—cf. Pl.V, xv-xviii

The other mountain, Elaion, is about thirty stadia away from Phiagaleia. There is a cave of Demeter Melaina (Black).

7. *Other types:* Pl.V, xix

TEGEA (Plate V, xx-xxiv; Pages 108-109)

1. *Paus. VIII. 45,6*—cf. Pl.V, xx

On the pediment in front of the temple is represented with sculptures the hunting of the boar of Kalydon and the boar appears right in the center. And at its one side is Atalanta ((and Meleager and Theseus and Telamon and Peleus and Pollydeukes and Iolaos (the companion of Herakles in most of his labors) and also the sons of Thestios, Prothous and Kometes, the brothers of Althaea; and on the other side of the boar, Ancaeos, already wounded, and Epochos, supporting him as he drops his weapon, and near him, Castor and Amphiaraos, the son of Oekles, and beside them, Hippothoos (the son of Kerkyon, the son of Agemedes, the son of Stymphalos) and lastly, Peirithous. On the gable at the back is a representation of the single combat between Telephos and Achilles on the plain of Caicus)). *VIII. 47,2.* And among the most notable votive offerings in the temple is the hide of the Kalydonian boar.

2. *VIII. 45,4*—cf. Pl.V, xxi

The ancient sanctuary of Athena Alea at Tegea was built by Aleos. *VIII. 46,4.* The statue of Athena Alea, ((you may see it now as you enter the Forum of Augustus in Rome)) ... is made throughout of ivory and is a work of Endoios. *VIII. 47,1.* The statue of Athena now at Tegea was brought recently from the suburb of Manthourii, and it was called by the people there, Athena Hippia (Horse-breeder).

3. *VIII. 47,5*—cf. Pl.V, xxii-xxiii

They say that it was a boon of Athena to Kepheus, the son of Aleos, that Tegea should never be sacked, and they also say that the goddess cut off some of the hairs from Medusa's head and gave them to him for the protection of the city.

4. *VIII. 48,7*—Ref.

And they say that Telephos was exposed on Mount Parthenion and a deer suckled the abandoned baby.

5. *VIII. 48,7*—Ref.

And the people of Tegea worship Eileithyia and they have in their market a temple of the goddess with a statue in it known as "Auge on her knees."

6. *Other types:* Pl.V, xxiv. *cf. VIII. 48,6.* A square statue; the Arcadians seem to delight in this type of statue.

PLATEA (Pages 110-111)

1. *Paus. IX. 2,7*—Ref.

There is also at Platea a temple of Hera well worth seeing ((for its size and the beauty of the statues in it. Entering, you see a statue of Rhea carrying the stone to Cronus)). They call Hera "Teleia" (Full-grown). Her statue is in a standing position and of huge size. Both these statues are of Pentelic marble and are works of Praxiteles. There is also another statue of Hera in a sitting position, a work of Kallimachos, and they call it "Bride" for the following reason . . .

THEBES (Plate X, i-ii; Pages 111-113)

1. *Paus. IX. 11,7*—Ref.

Above the rock called "Chastizer" is an altar of Apollo surnamed Spodios (Ash keeper) and it is made of the ashes of sacrificed animals.

2. *IX. 11,4*—Ref.

Here is a (sanctuary of Herakles) Herakleion and its statue is of white stone, a work of Xenokritos and Eubios, the Thebans, and they call it Promachos (Champion). The ancient statue (xoanon) is thought by the Thebans to be one of the works of Daedalos and it also looks so to me. *cf. IX. 11,6.* And on the pediments Praxiteles is the one who sculpted most of the twelve labors of Herakles.

3. *IX. 12,4*—cf. Pl.X, i

Very near is a statue of Dionysus, and this is also one of the works of Onasimedes, and it is bronze, filled ((most bronze statues were hollow)), and the altar is the work of the sons of Praxiteles. *IX. 16,6.* And very close to the theatre is a temple of Dionysus surnamed Lysios (Deliverer).

4. *IX. 16,1*—cf. Pl.X, ii

((A sanctuary of Tyche (Fortune), and in it is a statue representing the goddess carrying the child Plutos (Wealth))). According to the Thebans, the hands and face of the statue were made by Xenophon the Athenian; the rest of it by Kallistonikos, a native of Thebes. It was clever of them to place Plutos in the arms of Tyche (Fortune) like a baby carried by its mother or nurse. But no less clever was the idea of Kephisodotos who made the statue in Athens of Eirene (Peace) to carry Plutos (Wealth) in her arms. *IX. 25,3.* A sanctuary of the Dindymene Mother, the votive offering of Pindar. The statue is the work of Aristomedes and Socrates, the Thebans.

5. *IX. 16,5*—Ref.

((The shrine of Demeter Thesmophoros (Law giver) was of old, as they say, the house of Kadmos and his descendants. And the statue of Demeter is only visible down to the chest)). *IX. 25,5.* ((And about twenty-five stadia (from the city of Thebes?) is the sacred grove of Demeter (Cabeiria) and Kore (Persephone) and the entrance to it is permitted only to the initiated ones)). ((The sanctuary of the Cabeiroi is at a distance of seven stadia, more or less, from this grove)).

TANAGRA (Plate X, iii-xvii; Pages 113-116)

1. *Paus. IX. 19,6*—cf. Pl.X, iii-v

At this place the Euripos parts Euboea from Boeotia. ((On the right is the sanctuary of Demeter the Mycalessian, and a little farther on is Aulis)) ... there is here a temple of Artemis and two stone statues of her, one holding torches, and the other as an archer ... and palm trees grow in front of the sanctuary.

2. *IX. 20,1*—cf. Pl.X, vi

The people of Tanagra say that the founder of their city was Poemander ... and Poemander married Tanagra, the daughter of Aeolos; though the poetess Corinna says in her poems that Tanagra was the daughter of Asopos.

3. *IX. 20,4*—cf. Pl.X, vii-ix

And in the temple of Dionysus, the statue of the god is well worth seeing. It is made of Parian marble and is a work of Kalamis. But more spectacular is the statue of Triton.

4. *IX. 22,1*—cf. Pl.X, x

At Tanagra, besides the sanctuary of Dionysus, is a temple of Themis, one of Aphrodite, and a third of Apollo, and with Apollo Artemis and Leto are adored. *X. 28,6.* Datis the Mede also showed ((his piety)) in word and deed; in word, in his address to the people of Delos, and in deed, when he found a statue of Apollo on a Phoenician ship and returned it to the people of Tanagra to re-erect it in the sanctuary of Delion.

5. *IX. 22,1*—cf. Pl.X, xi-xvi

With respect to the two shrines of Hermes called Kriophoros (Ram carrier) and Promachos (Champion) respectively, they say that Hermes got the first surname because he averted a pestilence from the city by carrying a ram on his shoulders around the city wall, and on this tradition Kalamis based his creation of Hermes carrying a ram on his shoulders . . . *IX. 22,2.* and they call Hermes Promachos (Champion) because when the Eretrians came on their warships, invading the land of Tanagra, the god himself led the Ephebes (Youths) out to battle and, appearing as an Ephebe and using a scraper as a weapon, he caused the rout of the Euboean invaders. There is also what remains of a strawberry tree preserved in the sanctuary of Hermes Promachos, for they say that the god was reared under it.

6. *Other types:* Pl.X, xvii

HALIARTOS (Page 116)

1. *Paus. IX. 26,5*—Ref.

About fifteen stadia from this mountain (((where Sphinx had her lair))), are the ruins of the city of Onchestos. They say that Onchestos, the son of Poseidon, settled here. When I was there, there remained the temple and the statue of Posidon Onchestios and the sacred grove which Homer praised. *(Iliad ii. 506—Hymns ii, 186).*

THESPIAE (Plate X, xviii-xxi; Pages 116-117)

1. *Paus. IX. 26,8*—cf. Pl.X, xviii

The statue of Dionysus and the one of Tyche (Fortune) . . .

2. *IX. 27,5*—cf. Pl.X, xix. [See appendix.]

And in another part of the town is a shrine of Aphrodite Melainis and a theatre and market place well worth seeing. There is also a bronze statue of Hesiod.

3. *Other types:* Pl.X, xx

IX. 30,3—cf. Pl.X, xxi

There too is a sacred statue of Hesiod with a harp on his

knees, which is not the appropriate instrument for Hesiod to carry ((for in his own epics *(Theogony 30)* is recorded that the poet sang holding a laurel wand)).

CORONEIA (Pages 117-118)

1. *Paus. IX. 34,1*—Ref.

Before you get to Coroneia from Alalkomenae, you will come to shrine of Athena Itonia ... and in the temple are bronze statues of Athena Itonia and Zeus, works of Akorakritos, pupil and lover of Pheidias. They also dedicated, in my time, statues of the Charites (Graces). The people also say that Iodama, the priestess of Athena, crossed the sanctuary by night and saw Athena herself, and she also saw the head of Medusa attached to her chiton.

PHOCIS (Page 118)

1. *Paus. X. 2,5-7*—Ref.

[Epigraphical verification of the names Onomarchos and Phalaekos from coin inscriptions.]

DELPHI (Plates X, xxii-Y, xiv; Pages 118-123)

1. *Paus. X. 5,1*—Ref.

There is also an ascent by Daulis to the heights of Parnassus, rather longer than the ascent from Delphi, but not as steep.

2. *X. 5,13*—Pl.X, xxii-Y, ii

The temple (of Apollo at Delphi) which exists in my time was built by the Amphictyones out of the sacred money, and its architect was Spintharos the Corinthian. *X. 19,4.* On the pediments are Artemis, and Leto, and Apollo, and the Muses ... the originals of those sculptures were designed by Praxias the Athenian, the pupil of Kalamis. *X. 24,1.* In the pronaos (fore-temple) of the temple at Delphi, several useful sayings concerning human life are written up. They are recorded as having been said by those whom the Greeks call "the wise men." *X. 24,4.* And there are also statues of only two Fates, for in the place of the third stands a statue of Zeus Moiragetes (Fate leader) and by him, Apollo Moiragetes. *X. 24,5.* In the innermost part of the temple, to which only a few have access, is another statue of Apollo, made entirely of gold.

X. 16,3—cf. Pl.Y, iii-ix

And what the Delphians call Omphalos (the navel) is made of white marble and they say that this place is the center of the whole world ...

3. *X. 8,6*—cf. Pl.Y, x-xi

And as you enter the city (of Delphi), there is a row of temples ... The fourth one is the temple of Athena Pronoia (Forethought or Fore-templar) and from the statues of the goddess in it, the one in the pronaos (fore-temple) is a votive offering of the Massaliotes, and it is bigger than the one inside. ((And this statue (in the fore-temple) is of bronze)).

4. *X. 32,7*—cf. Pl.Y, xii-xiii

But the Corycian cavern excels those I have mentioned above and you can walk through most of it even without torchlight, and the roof is at a good height from the ground and water bubbles up from springs and oozes from the roof, so there are marks of drippings from above all over the floor of the cave. Those who live around Mount Parnassus consider this cavern sacred to the Corycian Nymphs and to Pan, especially.

5. *Other types:* Pl.Y, xiv

ELATEIA (Plate Y, xv-xvi; Pages 123-124)

1. *Paus. X. 34,6*—cf. Pl.Y, xvi

At the end of the city on the right is a theatre and an old bronze statue of Athena. The goddess, they say, fought for them against the barbarian bands of Taxiles. And about twenty stadia from Elateia is a shrine of Athena Kranaia. *X. 34,8*—cf. Pl.Y, xv

And this statue of the goddess was also made by the sons of Polykles, depicting the goddess armed as for battle, and on its shield are imitated the scenes which are carved on the shield of the Parthenos statue in Athens.

ANTICYRA (Plate Y, xvii; Pages 124-125)

1. *Paus. X. 36,8*—Ref.

They also have, near the harbor, a small sanctuary of Poseidon made of unhewn stones and stuccoed and plastered inside. The bronze statue of the god is in an erect position.

2. *X. 37,1*—cf. Pl.Y, xvii

On the right of the town, at a distance of about two stadia beyond the city, is a lofty rock which forms part of a mountain, and on it is a shrine of Artemis. (The statue in it) is a work of Praxiteles; the goddess holds a torch in her right hand and has a quiver on her shoulders. She is taller than the tallest woman and at her left is a dog.

ELEUSIS (Plate EE, xix-xx; Page 152)
1. *Paus. I. 37,2, I. 37,6, I. 38,6-7*—cf. Pl.EE, xix-xx
OROPUS (Plate EE, xviii; Page 153)
1. *Paus. I. 34,2*—cf. Pl.EE, xviii
   And the people of Oropus have a temple of Amphiaraos
   and his statue is of white stone.
SALAMIS (Plate EE, xxi-xxii; Page 153)
1. *Paus. I. 36,1*—cf. Pl.EE, xxi-xxii
   At Salamis . . . ((there is a temple of Artemis)) and a
   trophy erected for the victory which Themistocles, the son
   of Neokles, engineered for the Greeks . . . and when the
   Athenians were fighting the sea battle against the Medes,
   it is said that a dragon appeared amidst the ships.
2. *Other types:* Ref.
ATHENS (Plates Y, 18-EE, 17; Pages 125-152)
   p. 126. *Paus. I. 24,5:* Transl. on p. lxxiii.

   p. 132. *Paus. I. 27,2:* About this olive tree they say nothing except that it was the testimony produced by the goddess
   (Athena) during the judgment (between her and Poseidon)
   for the land.

   p. 138. 4(b). *Paus. I. 19,6:* Transl. on p. lxv; 4(c). *Paus. I.
   23,7:* Transl. on p. lxx; 4(d). *Paus. I. 26,4:* Near the portrait
   statue of Olympiodorus stands a bronze Artemis surnamed
   Leucophryene, dedicated by the sons of Themistokles; 4(f).
   Paus. I. 29,2: A sacred precinct of Artemis with ancient
   statues (xoana) of (Artemis called) Ariste (The Best) and
   Calliste (The Most Beautiful).

   p. 140. 5(b). *Paus. I. 2,4:* Transl. on p. lx; 5(c). *Paus. I. 41,1:*
   Transl. on p. lx.

   p. 142. 6(d). *Paus. I. 20,3:* Transl. on p. lxvi.

   p. 147. 9(—). *Paus. I. 8,2:* Transl. on p. lvi.

   p. 148. 11(—). *Paus. I. 8,5:* Transl. on p. lv; 12(—). *Paus. I.
   15,1:* As we go toward the stoa (portico) which is named
   'Poikile' (painted) because of its paintings, there is a bronze
   Hermes called 'Agoraios' (of the market-place) and nearby
   is a gate; 12(+). *Paus. I. 27,1:* And in the temple of Athena
   Polias is a wooden herm (or *Hermes*) said to have been a
   dedication by Cecrops. When I was there it could not be
   seen, being covered with myrtle boughs.

p. 149. 13(−). *Paus. I. 18,1:* Transl. on p. lx; 14(−). *Paus. I. 20,3:* There was Aristion of Athens whom Mithradates used for diplomatic missions to the Greek city-states. He was the one who induced the Athenians to consider (an alliance with) Mithradates more outstanding than (the one they already had with) the Romans.

p. 150. 15(−). *Paus. I. 21,4:* Transl. on p. lxvii; 15(+). *Paus. I. 23,4:* Transl. on p. lxx.

p. 151. 18(−). *Paus. I. 21,3:* On the so-called 'south wall' of the Acropolis, and on the side which turns facing the theatre, there is a gilded head of the gorgon Medusa, and around it is wrought an aegis; 21(−). *Paus. I. 33,2:* About sixty stadia from Marathon is Rhamnus ... At a short distance inland from the seacoast is the sanctuary of Nemesis ... This marble block Pheidias sculpted and made a statue of Nemesis; on the head of the goddess is a crown adorned with deer and small statuettes of Nikae (Victories). (Nemesis) holds an apple tree branch in her left hand and in her right a bowl (phiale, patera).

1   2

1. Coin of Paphos, Cyprus, silver, reverse (B.M.C. Paphos 45). Female figure wearing long chiton, and peplos fastened on shoulder with griffin's head fibula; in left hand branch, in right phiale; probably copy of Nemesis of Rhamnus (I. xxxiii. § 3).

2. Coin of Cyzicus, electrum, obverse (B.M.C. Cyzicus 75). Harmodius and Aristogeiton, charging to right; Aristogeiton with sword in right hand, chlamys on left arm; Harmodius with right hand upraised, holding sword; copy of group (I. viii. § 5). Beneath, tunny.

A NEW COMMENTARY ON THE STATUES REPRESENTED
ON ATHENIAN COINS

by AL. N. OIKONOMIDES

In our new commentary on the coins of Athens collected by Imhoof-Blumer and Gardner (Plates Y, xviii-EE, xvii), we are considering first the connection of the numismatic representations with the text of Pausanias. The reader must remember always that some of the obvious identifications proposed in these pages are due to discoveries made several decades after the first publication of the *Numismatic Commentary to Pausanias,* and that the plates of this work are still the main collection illustrating representations of statues on coins, which the archaeologist has to use before proposing the identification of a statuary type.

It is a sad truth that since the first publication of the *Numismatic Commentary to Pausanias* the field has been thought to be completely closed to further search for a good many years. Thus, in the excellent third edition (1901) of the *Arx Athenarum a Pausanias Descripta* by O. Jahn and A. Michaelis, only one plate (xxxv) is dedicated to "Nummi, Gemmae, Tesserae Plumbeae ad monumenta arcis spectantes" and all of the references rely completely on *NCP.* Much better and more original is the use of coins in *Mythology and Monuments of Ancient Athens* by Jane Harrison and M. Verral (1890), where some identifications are proposed and an effort is made to collect new parallels between existing sculpture and vase paintings and the statuary types illustrated on the coins of *NCP.* Eight years later the monumental commentary to Pausanias by Sir J. Frazer relied completely on the *NCP* and the few "addenda" of Jane Harrison.

In books published later, the numismatic evidence is rather neglected and in *Ancient City of Athens* by Ida Thallon Hill (1953) no reference is given and no interpretation is proposed with the support of coin representations. Finally, in the companion volume (V) of the edition of Pausanias in the Loeb Classical Library (ed. by R. E. Wycherley, 1st ed., 1935, Rev. ed., 1955), the whole coverage of numismatic representations related to Pausanias' text is gloriously accomplished by illustrations of just thirty (30!) coins, not even particularly well selected; and a reference to Imhoof-Blumer and Gardner, *Numismatic Commentary on Pausanias* does not appear in the bibliography nor anywhere else.

PIRAEUS

ZEUS SAVIOUR (*Paus. I. 1,3*—cf. Pl.AA, iv) *((The sight in Piraeus most worthy of note is the sacred precinct dedicated to Athena and Zeus; both statues are of bronze; the one of Zeus holds a scepter and (a statuette of) Nike, and Athena holds a spear))*.

The "sacred precinct" (temenos) in Pausanias is mentioned as a "sanctuary" (hieron) of Zeus Soter (Saviour) in *Strabo IX, 395*. Strabo adds that at this site were also "small porticoes" (stoidia) in which were exhibited "paintings on boards" by the most famous artists, and that there were statues in the open air. From *Pliny, NH 34, 8, 74* we learn that the "excellent statue of Athena" in the temple of Zeus Soter of the port of Athens was a famous work of Kephisodotos *"cui pauca comparantur."*

The parallel subject of the above passages was pointed out by A. Milchhöfer (*Schriftquellen zur Topogr. von Athen,* p. cxi, 78-95) who connected the literary references, but in 1960, when workers digging a ditch not far from the place where the topographer had placed the sanctuary of Zeus Soter and Athena Soteira discovered an excellent bronze statue of Athena, an archaic bronze statue of a nude man (Kouros) and several other bronze and marble statues, no one thought that they could be connected with these literary sources. The archaelogist Andrew Papagiannopoulos-Palaios was the one who indicated that such a connection could be made, and also maintained that the statue of Athena definitely belonged stylistically to the work of Kephisodotos (as we know it from the copies of Eirene and Ploutos) and that the bronze statue of the nude man was the statue of Zeus Soter itself, shown beardless and still holding a part of a scepter. (See p. lxxix, 1 and Plate 4, 1.)

Completely independent of the identification of the bronze statue of Athena from Piraeus with the Athena Soteira of the literary and epigraphical sources, and unrelated as well, is the fact that the workmanship and the style of the statue support the characterization as a masterpiece of the fourth century B.C., which was once established as a cult statue in one of the sanctuaries or temples of Attica. As such, we may consider the possibility of its representation on one of the Athenian coins and I think that the coin *AA, iv* fits the statue's posture. The loss of the owl and the snake of the original statue does not invalidate the statue's identification because even though the spear was lost, traces of its existence can be seen on the inside

of the left hand which also held up the shield, the rim of which
was based on the ground (pieces discovered with the statue).
That the extended right hand was holding something is indicated by the remains of the connecting lead which can still be
seen on it.

THE CITY OF ATHENS. THE AGORA

HEPHAISTEION *(Paus. I. 14,6)* *((Above Kerameikos and the stoa
called Basileios (Regal) is the temple of Hephaistos (Vulcan).
The view of the statue of Athena standing by the one of the
god was no surprise to me, since I know the story about
Erichthonios))*.

The cult statues of Hephaistos and Athena Hephaistia by
Alkamenes have not been identified with representations on
Athenian coins. The posture of the statue of Hephaistos is
known from major and minor statuary copies (Furtwaengler,
Masterpieces of Greek Sculpture, 2nd ed., 1964, pp. 87-88) and
from the relief of an Attic lamp of the Roman period *(Ath.
Mitt.* 69/70, 1954-55, pp. 67 sqq.). The statue of Athena is still
open to question; it might well be one of the Athena statuary
types illustrated on coins, but we have no means for its identification. "There can be no doubt that Alkamenes produced several statues of Athena, with and without the helmet." (Walston,
Alcamenes, 1926, p. 180). The Athena type shown as Hephaistia
on the restored cult statue (G. Ph. Stevens, *Classical Buildings*)
and the attempt at a restoration of reliefs of its pedestal *(Ath.
Mitt.,* supra and *The Athenian Agora Guide*, 1962, p. 40) are
imaginary and not attested to by any type of reliable evidence.

TEMPLE OF ARES *(Paus. I. 8,4*—cf. Pl.DD, xxii-xxiii) *((By the
statue of Demosthenes is the sanctuary of Ares ... the statue of
Ares is a work of Alkamenes and the statue of Athena (is) by
a Parian sculptor called Lokros))*.

The cult statues of Ares and Athena Areia in the Temple of
Ares possibly were on one pedestal as were the statues of
Hephaistos and Athena Hephaistia. For the statue of Ares, a
work of Alkamenes, the identification with the Ares Borghese
proposed by Furtwaengler (See Appendix pp. 169 ff and Plate
4 for figure) can be verified as a statuary type represented on
Athenian coins. The striking resemblance of the statuary copy
with the numismatic representations, *DD, xxii-xxiii,* and the
fact that it is a proposal by the same scholar who identified
the surviving copies of the cult statue of Hephaistos, create a

strong feeling guiding us to a final acceptance of the theory. As for the Athena, definitely ascribed by Pausanias to the Parian sculptor Lokros, unknown from other sources, nothing can be said. However, if we will accept him to have been a student of Alkamenes, such a statue could have been a creation made to accompany the Ares of his master, and might be one of the Athenas of what is called the Alcamenian style (Walston, *Alcamenes*, p. 182).

Both statues must have been bronze if we may logically suppose that the Athenians would not have voted a smaller budget for a statue of the god of war than had been allowed for a statue of the god of the bronze workers in a period such as the second half of the fifth century B.C. As for the torso of Athena in Pentelic marble (Agora Museum, S. 654), considered by the excavators to be the statue of the goddess seen by Pausanias, I would like to comment that the only connection of the statue with the subject at hand is that it was found in "a Byzantine wall a few meters to the south of the Temple of Ares." (*The Athenian Agora Guide*, 1962, pp. 68, 131). The actual bronze Athena by Lokros in the temple might well be one of the unidentified statues of the goddess illustrated on Athenian coins for which as yet we have no means of identification.

METROON (*Paus. I. 3,5*—cf. Pl.CC, i) (*(There is also a sanctuary of the Mother of the Gods, whose statue is the work of Pheidias)*).

Pausanias does not question that the statue was a work of Pheidias, possibly because the inscription on the pedestal convinced him. From *Arrian (Peripl. Pont. Eux. 9)* we get the same information about the sculptor, plus the fact that the statue was seated and had a cymbal (or tympanon) and that lions were lying under its throne. (For its size cf. *Paus. viii. 37,3.*)

Now scholars became very confused amidst literary references, dedicatory reliefs and the topography of Athens due to a reference in *Pliny (N.H., xxxvi, 17)* saying that "*there is also in the same city in a shrine of the Great Mother, a work of Agorakritos.*" Having the references of the ancient writers in a state of confusion already because the manuscript copyists replaced (with one exception) the *dikasterion* (law court) in the Metroon of the Museum hill with the *bouleuterion* (council chamber) near the Metroon of the Agora, a sacred place for a second statue of the Mother of the Gods by Agorakritos "at the same city" has never been proposed.

A numismatic representation of the Pheidian Mother of the Gods can be recognized in coin *CC, i,* definitely not to be confused any longer with the Dionysus by Alkamenes. The small size of the representation accounts for the omission of the lions lying under the throne. The Mother holds a small cymbal in her left hand and a bowl (phiale) in her right.

DEMOS *(Paus. I. 3,3-I. 3,5*—cf. Pl.EE, xv; HH, v)

Pausanias has recorded two representations of Demos (the People) in the Agora. The first was one of the paintings in the Basileios Stoa where Demos was depicted with Theseus and Demokratia (Democracy) and the second was a statue in the Metroon by a sculptor named Lyson. On the relief of the amendment to the law against tyranny proposed by Eukrates in 336 B.C. appears the first known sculptural representation of Demos. Demos appears as a healthy old man seated on a throne, and behind him a standing maiden (Democracy?) is crowning him (See Page 52,4). The same scene can be recognized on coin *EE, xv* which is the second artistic record of this group.

HARMODIOS & ARISTOGEITON *(Paus. I. 8,5*—cf. Pl.DD, xiv-xv, p. 148) *((Not far away stand the statues of Harmodios and Aristogeiton, those who killed Hipparchos ... and of those statues, the new group is by Kritios, but the older ones by Antenor, and although Xerxes, when he captured Athens, carried them (the older ones) away as booty, King Antiochos long afterward returned them to the Athenians)).*

It is somehow important that we can recognize only the newer group of the Tyrannicides by Kritios and Nesiotes on the available coin representations. But neither Harmodios nor Aristogeiton can be identified with the representations on coins *DD, xvi-xviii* as proposed by Imhoof-Blumer and Gardner.

APOLLO PATROOS *(Paus. I. 3,4*—cf. Pl.CC, xx-xxi) *((... Nearby he (Euphranor) also made the statue in the temple of Apollo surnamed Patroos; as for the statues in front of it, the one called Alexilakos is a work of Kalamis and the other a work of Leochares)).*

It is believed that the headless statue of an Ionian Apollo Kitharoidos found in the excavation period of 1907 is the original statue of Euphranor *(The Athenian Agora Guide,* 1962, p. 120). A copy of this statue is considered to be the "Apollo Barberini" now in Munich (Furtwaengler, *Masterpieces,* 2nd ed., 1964, p. 87) as is a miniature found in the excavations of the Agora (*Guide*, 1962, p. 181—S. 877). The statue is represented on coins and is easily recognizable on *CC*, *xx* and *xxi*. From the coin representations we are taught that Apollo Patroos was holding a bowl (phiale-patera) in his right hand and a lyre in his left.

HERAKLES (*Paus. I. 8,4*—cf. Pl.DD, i, xi, xiii) (*(About the temple (of Ares) stand statues of Herakles, Theseus . . .)*).

The statue of Herakles in the Agora area was possibly the one echoed on the worn smooth coin *DD, xiii*. Stylistically it belongs to the type of naked standing Herakles, with the weight on the left foot, (bearded?), resting his left hand on his club and holding something in his right. Due to the worn smooth coin surface, this object (patera?) is not recognizable. But it is certain that the original did not carry a lion skin folded over his right arm.

Another statue of the youthful Herakles appears on coin *DD, i*. The hero stands with his weight on the right foot, cradling his club in his left arm and extending his right hand forward. Recently this type of Herakles has become known, from a series of dedicatory reliefs, as Herakles Pankrates. (See HERAKLES in KYNOSARGES.)

A third Herakles, the well known Lyssipean Herakles of the "Farnese" type, appears distinguishably on coin *DD, xi*. Imhoof-Blumer and Gardner immediately connected it with the statuary copy by Glykon (cf. p. 148). Strangely enough, as it becomes obvious from Johnson's references (*Lysippos*, 1926, pp. 204-205), although the city in which the original stood has not been determined, Athens has never been considered as a possible one. Such a candidacy, as far as I know, must not be excluded if we will take into consideration the fact that the one complete statuette of Herakles which was discovered in the excavation of the Athenian Agora was of the "Farnese" type (Guide, 1962, p. 181—S. 1241). *See appendix, pp. 169 ff.*

EIRENE & PLOUTOS (*Paus. I. 8,2*—cf. Pl.DD, ix-x) (*(After the statues of the Eponymous (Heroes) are statues of gods, Amphiaraos and Eirene (Peace) carrying the child Ploutos (Wealth). cf. IX. 16,2. ((Kephisodotos . . . made for the Athenians a statue of Eirene carrying Ploutos))*). See p. 147.

AMPHIARAOS (*Paus. I. 8,2 v.* supra—cf. Pl.EE, iii-iv; p. lxxviii, 5-6; Page 150). Although the type of standing Asklepios is very familiar in Attic art from dedicatory reliefs and statuettes, the cult-statue of the Asklepieion *"in the city"* was definitely a seated one. (cf. S. Papaspyridi, *Guide de Musée National d'Athenes*, Nos. 1330, 1333, 1335, 1338, 1352). Now, on the coins *EE, iii* and *iv,* the figure is a standing "healing god" as identified by the serpent rod, but it is not a representation of the cult statue of the Asklepieion "in the city." In this case we may well consider two facts: 1) If it is a statue of Asklepios in Athens, and evidently a famous one to be represented on coins, Pausanias has not recorded it, or 2) If it is a statue of another local healing god in Athens, we do not know who, or on what original statue the coin representation is based, nor if this is mentioned by Pausanias.

The statue of Amphiaraos in the Athenian Agora (if we will consider the standing image of the god in the relief of inscription *IG, II², 171* as an echo of it) is the only one to be proposed. From the inscribed dedication in *IG, II², 4441b* "To Asklepios Amphiaraos" on a small altar found near the Agora (dated 2nd c. A.D.) we may assume that the cults of the two healing gods were beginning to merge in the city of Athens in the second century A.D. I must also add that a torso of Amphiaraos' statue found at the excavations of his sanctuary at Oropus exactly fits the type indicated by the representation on these coins. The cult statue of Amphiaraos in the said sanctuary (See Pl.EE, xviii and page lxxviii, 5-6) was a seated acrolithic one made partly of white marble and partly of wood (cf. p. 153).

THESEUS (*Paus. I. 17,2*—cf. Pl.DD, v, xvi) (*(By the gymnasium (of Ptolemy) in a sanctuary of Theseus; here are paintings depicting Athenians fighting the Amazons))*. cf. *Paus. I. 8,4* (see above under HERAKLES and Pl.KK, 1-8).

A confusing situation has arisen with statue representations on two coins *DD, v* and *xvi,* of which the first is called Theseus (sans Minotaur) by the authors and the other, Harmodios from the Tyrannicides group. But it would seem that the latter identification is incorrect, inasmuch as it is obvious that *DD, xvi* is a worn example of the same minting as *DD, v.* The statue represented on both coins is obviously similar to the Harmodios of the Tyrannicides group, but it is not likely that the Tyrannicides would have been divided on a coin, especially since they are shown together on other earlier coins (*DD, xiv* and *xv*). So, if we accept the first identification, based on the similarity with the Theseus on coin *DD, iv,* thereby admitting the existence of a statue of Theseus executed in the same posture and style as the Harmodios of the Tyrannicides, we have the corroboration of both literary and monumental evidence. Kimon brought the alleged bones of Theseus to Athens from Skyros ca. 475 B.C. (*Scholiast to Aeschines* III, 13), and then built the Theseion and a sacred precinct of Theseus "in the old city," in which places such a statue would be very likely to have been placed. If a sculptor (or, why not Kritios and Nesiotes themselves?) then made a statue of Theseus, he would very possibly have been influenced by the "new style" of the Tyrannicides group of Kritios and Nesiotes erected in the Agora circa 477-476 B.C.

The existence of a statue of Theseus in ancient Athens in the same posture as the statue of Harmodios is supported by many indications on vase paintings, eclectic sculptures and mosaics. I do not believe this to be the place for a complete development of the search, but I will mention some of the most important echoes. First, in the red-figured kylix by the Kodros painter in the British Museum (E. 84), decorated inside and out with the exploits of Theseus, the strong influence of the statue appears twice (slightly modified in details only) as Theseus killing Prokroustes and as Theseus killing Skiron. From the representation on the coin, it is concluded that the figure of Theseus with Skiron is closest to the original. In general, in five out of seven illustrations of the Theseus figure by the painter, the figure is the same as the original statue from the waist downward, and the action of the feet is unchangeable. (Exterior: *Journal Hellenic Studies* 2, 1881, Pl. 10—*AJA* 55, 1951, Pl. 22; Interior: Harrison-Verral, *Myths and Monuments of Ancient Athens*, p. cxv, fig. 25). Now we can explain why this happened. The painter took a statuary representation well-known to the Athenians and modified it to fit a painted narrative of the hero's exploits. In one case the painter had an opportunity to indicate that the similarity of the Theseus statue to the Tyrannicides group was not unknown to him, and depicted the young hero attacking a sow as the Aristogeiton of the group.

The similarity of the Theseus statue to the Harmodios, as depicted on the Athenian coin and attested to by the echoes in the vase painting of Kodros and others who recorded the hero's deeds, has given ground to a group of scholars who have studied "the influence of the Tyrannicides on Attic vase-painting." The sculptor of the west frieze of Hephaistion may have used as model the statue of Theseus rather than Harmodios (Pl.KK, 3). But the most important echo of the Theseus statue was not discovered until 1957 when, in the excavations at Pella, a mosaic depicting "the Lion hunt" was uncovered. Here the figure of Theseus was used by the artist of the mosaic as the central hero figure in the scene which illustrates possibly an unknown literary exploit of Theseus or a myth connected with a local hero. The mosaics discovered in 1961, also at Pella, convince us that their creators knew well the motifs used up to that time to depict the figure of Theseus. An excellent mosaic with inscriptions showed the rape of Helen by Theseus with the help of Phorbas in the presence of Dieaneira. Another mosaic, inscribed "Gnosis made it," illustrates a deer hunt in which the central figure is again copied from the Athenian Theseus, as is his assistant. The two figures show the same modification in detail as used by the Kodros painter for the figure of Theseus with Prokroustes and Theseus with Skiron. The only difference is that the heroes are wearing cloaks blown up by the wind in the Pella mosaics. (See Plate KK, 1-8.)

The cloak does not appear either on the coin representation or on the Theseus of the Kodros painter, but it is definitely shown on an Attic sarcophagus, which has two figures based on the Theseus statue hunting the Calydonian boar (Papaspyridi, *Guide*, p. 223, No. 1186; *Cambridge Ancient History*, Plates: Vol. V, Pl. 144c) and once again in the same theme for a sarcophagus in the Eleusis museum. [For the mosaics from Pella see *Archaeology* 11, 1958, pp. 250 ff; *Balkan Studies* 1, 1960, pp. 113 ff; 4, 1963, pp. 154 ff.; *Athene* 22, 1961, No. 1; 23, 1963 Nos. 3 & 4; 24, 1964, No. 1].

Important in the interpretation of the theme of the Pella mosaics is the observation that already, in the 4th century B. C., the striking hero (first used for Harmodios and later for Theseus in Athens) was also used for the youthful Herakles as we can see on coin *T, xii* from Pheneos. In this case we cannot exclude the possibility that Herakles and Iolaos in the hunt for the Nemean lion and the Cerynitian hind are represented on two of the known mosaics from Pella.

DIONYSUS (*Paus. I. 14,1*—cf. Pl.BB, xx; CC, vii) (*(As we enter at the Odeion of Athens you see among other (statues?) worth seeing, a statue of Dionysus))*.

The statue in the Odeion is possibly the third type of Dionysus represented on Athenian coins (cf. THEATRE & TEMPLES OF DIONYSUS) and especially the one illustrated in *BB, xx* and *CC, viii*. The scepter-thyrsos does not leave any doubt as to the identification of Dionysus, but the connection with the statue seen by Pausanias is only an assumed hypothesis.

SITES AROUND AGORA AND ACROPOLIS

DIOSCURI (*Paus. I. 18,1*—cf. Pl.EE, i, p. 149) *The shrine of the Dioscuri is an old one. (In it there are images) of them standing, and of their sons on horseback.*

The archaic character of the sculpture (if it can be said that "archaic," "Classic," and "Hellenistic" styles may be recognized on the miniature representations on coins) indicates a possible connection with the Athenian sanctuary located somewhere between the Agora and the entrance to the Acropolis. ("Agora of Theseus"). In other sources this sanctuary is called *Anakeion.*

ELEUSINION (*Paus. I. 14,1*—cf. Pl.BB, xxi, xxiii-xxiv: EE, xiv) *And (in the Agora) above the fountain building called Enneakrounos (Nine-spouted) are two temples; one of Demeter and Kore, and one of Triptolemos, having a statue in it. cf. I. 2,4. And near (the "Pompeion" building after the "Dipylon" gates) is a temple of Demeter with statues in it of the goddess herself, of Kore and Iakchos holding a torch. And it is written on the wall in Attic letters that they are works of Praxiteles.*

We know from recent excavations in the Athenian Agora that the Eleusinion was located on the east side of the Panathenaic Way, exactly in the location where it was supposed to be for the topographic verification of Pausanias' account. Another temple, called "S. E. Temple" is possibly the one of Triptolemos.

The representations on the Athenian coins are not helpful for conjectures concerning the cult statues of the three main shrines of the Eleusinian deities. The seated Demeter seen only on coin *BB, xxi*, seems the more probable statue for the Eleusinion. If, on coin *BB, xxiv*, the standing torchbearer is Iakchos (instead of Triptolemos) on the chariot of snakes, the two other female standing figures are Demeter and Kore and the whole group would appear to be parallel to Pausanias' description of the statue in the temple of Demeter near the Pompeion and the Dipylon gates. (See above *I. 2,4*).

The running Kore with the torches, connected with Artemis on coin *BB, xvi* belongs to another cult, the one of the "Phosphoroi" (See PHOSPHOROI).

PHOSPHOROI (*IG, II², 1755; Agora I, 4745*—cf. Pl.BB, ix-xi, xiii-xvii; CC, viii).

The Phosphoroi are not mentioned in Pausanias, but I believe that we have important evidence of this cult on the coins of Athens collected by Imhoof-Blumer and Gardner. According to a number of epigraphic references one of the goddesses is Artemis, but the other goddess, or goddesses, unified with her in this cult is not known by name. Coin *BB, xvi* might be the key to this question, for on it we recognize the statue of a running Artemis carrying two torches (Phosphoros) and another torchbearer goddess. Thus we know that the Phosphoroi were two; now the problem is the identity of the second goddess.

Again from coin *BB, xvi* we can observe a helpful distinction. Artemis Phosphoros wears a short chiton and is in the likeness of a torchbearer "Agrotera" (Huntress) of the statuary type known as "the Artemis of Versailles" (Louvre), which is also known to have been represented on Athenian coins (cf. *BB, xii*). The second goddess wears a long chiton and looks more like Demeter or Kore (cf. p. 140).

On coins *BB, viii-xi* and *xviii* we may observe that the running torchbearing goddess wears a long chiton, definitely distinguishable from the short chiton of Artemis Phosphoros as seen on coin *BB, xvi* and also *xiv* and *xv*. The only available answer from comparison of the long chitoned torchbearing goddess type on the coins with other works of ancient art, especially vase paintings, is that she must be identified with Kore, not Demeter. This Kore is *Pherephatte (IG, II², 5074)* known as "adored" in a shrine called *Pherephattion* in the Agora. This *Pherephattion*, if the evidence of the coins is considered adequate, must also be considered as the place of the cult of Artemis Phosphoros.

NYMPHS (*Paus. I. 17,2*—cf. Pl.EE, vi) *((Above the sanctuary of the Dioscuri is a sacred enclosure of Aglauros. It was to Aglauros and her sisters, Herse and Pandrosos, that they say Athena gave Erichthonios . . . Climbing from this site the Persians entered the Acropolis (in 480 B. C.) . . .))*.

Imhoof-Blumer and Gardner consider coin *EE, vi* as illustrating *Paus. I. 22,8* (Charites by Socrates at the entry to the Acropolis). Later research has shown that the group of the three nymphs is connected with the cult of the three daughters of Cecrops, and especially with Aglauros. Another cult of three nymphs connected with the daughters of Erechtheus and the tomb of Geraistos the Cyclops is known as being located on the

hill of the Nymphs, but this second group is more or less a
secondary fertility folk-cult and is not mentioned by Pausanias.
(For further reference: M. Ervin, "The Sanctuary of Aglauros
on the South Slope of the Acropolis and its Destruction in the
First Mithradatic War" in *Archeion Pontou* 22, 1958. pp. 23-42.
See also the article of the same, "Geraistai Nymphai Genethliai
and the Hill of the Nymphs" in *Platon* 11, 1959, pp. 146-159.)

SERAPIS-ISIS (*Paus. I. 18,4*—cf. Pl.EE, ix-xi) (*(As you descend
from here (Prytaneion) toward downtown, there is a sanctuary
of Serapis)*).

The coin *EE, ix* included by Imhoof-Blumer and Gardner
among the other types of Athens, and described (p. 151) as
"Isis standing to left, lotus on head, holds flower," does not
exactly fit the known type of Attic Isis, nor the description
given. The statue illustrated is simply a standing Serapis wearing the modius (corn measure) on his head and holding a scepter
in his right hand, his left hand pendant. Pausanias reports a
temple of Serapis below the Acropolis, but this sanctuary has
not yet been found in excavation, although its existence has
been verified by several lucky archaeological finds of inscriptions and sculpture. Serapis is known to have been worshipped
together with Anoubis and Isis. Shrines of Serapis and Isis in
Athens are known to have existed, but the only evidence for one
of the several cult statues which must have been erected in the
Serapieia of Athens is the relief of a Roman lamp depicting
Serapis seated in his temple. To identify the standing figure of
this coin as the cult statue of Serapis in the Serapieion on the
north side of the Acropolis will depend on further evidence.

According to the evidence of literary sources and Attic inscriptions, Isis was adored with Serapis in the city of Athens.
The representation of her statue holding a scepter and a cornucopia is known as a common type from coin *EE, xi.* Possibly
another statue of Isis(?) is depicted on coin *EE, x.* (For further
reference see: S. Dow, "The Egyptian Cults in Athens," in
Harv. Theol. Rev. 30, pp. 182-232, A. Oikonomides, "Serapis,"
Chicago Nat. Hist. Mus. Bulletin 33, 1962, No. 12, pp. 2-3, 8.)

ZEUS OLYMPIOS (*Paus. I. 18,6*—cf. Pl.BB, iv) ... *The Sanctuary
of Zeus Olympios — Hadrian the emperor of the Romans dedicated the temple — and the statue of the god well worth seeing
... is made of ivory and gold with a remarkable artistic skill
if we may judge according to its enormous size. cf. Paus. II.*

xvii, 2. The gold and ivory statue of Asklepios (at the Epidauros sanctuary) is about half the size of the one of Olympios Zeus in Athens.

The statue at the Olympieion in Athens is considered by Imhoof-Blumer and Gardner to be a copy of the Pheidian original at Olympia (p. 138), as represented on coin *BB, iv.* J. Harrison repeats the same theory (*Mythology and Monuments,* p. 193) and the acceptance continues down to Wycherley (*Pausanias Comp. Vol. V,* p. 182, No. 3). I have already expressed my doubts about this theory earlier this year (A. Furtwaengler *Masterpieces,* 2nd ed., Chicago, 1964, pp. 417-418) based on the fact that on a dedicatory relief of the fourth century B.C. found recently in Brauron we can see a copy of a fully developed type of Zeus Olympios unrelated to the Pheidian original, but related to the statue shown on coin *BB, iv.*

APOLLO PYTHIOS-DELPHINIOS *(Paus. I. 19,1) ((Beyond the temple of Zeus Olympios, nearby is a statue of Apollo Pythios and further, a sanctuary of Apollo surnamed Delphinios)).*

The archaic statues of Apollo represented on Athenian coins *(CC, xi-xiv & xvi-xvii)* are somehow identified in a peculiar way via sculptures and literary references (cf. p. 145). I wonder if we shouldn't study further the identifications as listed by Imhoof-Blumer and Gardner.

The possibility of a representation of the cult statue in the Python or the Delphinion in Athens in the series *CC, xi-xiv* lacks supporting evidence from other sources. The recognition of an Apollo on *CC, xv* is also problematical. But the statue on coins *CC, xvi-xvii* indicates statuary work by a master of the late sixth or early fifth century B.C. (Kalamis?)

APHRODITE "IN THE GARDENS" *(Paus. I. 19,2) The statue of Aphrodite in the Gardens, a work of Alkamenes, is one of the most noteworthy things in Athens.* (See Appendix, Pl. 4, pp. 169 ff.)

Pausanias, writing in the second century A.D., expressed his admiration for the statue of Aphrodite in the Gardens. Logically we must assume that this masterpiece, also greatly admired by Lucian (*Imag.* 4 & 6), must not have escaped the attention of the "directors of the mint" who had to find, each year, several local art masterpieces to be illustrated on the reverse sides of the new coins. Logically only two things are possible: 1) The statue of Aphrodite in the Gardens was illustrated on coins not yet discovered or published, or 2) The statue is represented on coins discovered and published, but not yet identified. On the Athenian coins published by Imhoof-Blumer and Gardner no representation of Aphrodite is identified. The one possible candidate is the admirable seated statue of a goddess on coin *BB, xxii*, which reminds one of the pose and style of the seated goddesses of the Parthenon frieze. The identification and description as "Demeter seated to left on throne; holds in right hand two ears of corn, left rests on sceptre," (p. 141) simply does not fit. In any case, the "two ears of corn" used to identify Demeter are not visible in the illustration.

HERAKLES IN KYNOSARGES (*Paus. I. 18,3*—cf. Pl.DD, i & xii)
There is also a sanctuary of Herakles called Kynosarges.

The authors recognized coin *DD, i* as a possible echo of the cult statue of Theseus, but the stance is actually that of Herakles as may be seen on several Attic statues, statuettes and reliefs known to be representations of the youthful Herakles. A bearded Herakles wearing the long Ionian chiton and holding a club in his right hand, a cornucopia in the left, which can now be identified as Herakles Palaimon appears in coin *DD, xii* and the youthful Herakles of *DD, i* can be identified as Herakles Pankrates. These two new identifications are possible due to the find in 1954 on the banks of the Ilisos of a deposit of several inscriptions and many dedicatory reliefs showing these two forms of Herakles as being worshipped together, possibly even in the same shrine. Prior to this discovery the epithets "Pankrates" for the nude youthful Herakles and "Palaimon" for the bearded long-chitoned Herakles holding a cornucopia were unknown from literary and epigraphical sources.

With this discovery, also found was the head from a marble portrait statue of Alexander the Great deified as Herakles and wearing the lion helmet (see *Archeion Pontou* 22, 1958, pp. 234-243; *Athene* 22, 1961, No. 1 pp. 25-31; M. Bieber, *Alexander the Great in Greek and Roman Art*, Chicago, 1964). Through the evidence of the inscriptions and reliefs the find was connected with one of the gymnasia in Athens in the area of the Ilissos, and such a gymnasium could hardly be any other than Kynosarges, as it was first identified by A. Papagiannopoulos (*Platon* 8, 1956, pp. 126-127) and verified by a reference of Clemens of Alexandria (*Protrept*.IV, 54) mentioning that the Athenians had deified and adored as a god in Kynosarges, the father of Alexander the Great, Philip of Macedon.

APOLLO LYKIOS (*Paus. I. 19,3*—cf. Pl.CC, xviii-xix) *The site called Lykeion has its name from Lykos, the son of Pandion, and it was considered sacred to Apollo from the beginning up to the present time, and it is said that here the god was first named Lykios.*

The copies of a Praxitelean statue of an Apollo leaning slightly to the left, holding a lyre on the left and resting his right arm on the crown of his head can be identified through the mention by Lucian (*Anacharsis* 7) of the almost unique posture in Greek statuary as the statue of Apollo Lykios. The two statues represented on coins *CC, xviii-xix* appear as fitting to Lucian's description, but only the first can be accepted as an echo of the Praxitelean statue as we know it from numerous copies of the late Hellenistic period (cf. M. Bieber, *The Sculpture of the Hellenistic Age*, rev. ed. 1961, p. 18; fig. 17, 19-23; A. Furtwaengler, *Masterpieces . . .*, 2nd ed., 1964, p. 338, fig. xlviii-xlix, Pl.U; see ivory stte. from the Ath. Agora, Pl.HH, 2).

The statue of Apollo Lykios on coin *CC, xix* seems definitely archaic as a piece of sculpture and close to the style of the master who created the Apollo illustrated on coins *CC, xvi-xvii* (see p. lxiii, APOLLO PYTHIOS-DELPHINIOS). Lack of historical information does not permit us to assume that there was some need to create a replacement of the original archaic statue in the fourth century B.C., but the repairs carried on by the orator Lykourgos during the period of his administration (336-326 B.C.) may indicate two things: 1) that the gymnasium and sanctuary of Apollo at Lykeion were decaying due to old age, and 2) that the Lykeion, being outside the city's walls, was destroyed in an earlier period due to some unknown cause. The period of Lykourgos' office coincides with the style of the Praxitelean Apollo Lykios, which, as most experts of art criticism agree, is one of the master's works, and could be dated at the third quarter of the fourth century B.C.

ARTEMIS AGROTERA (*Paus. I. 19,6*—cf. Pl.BB, xii) *After crossing the Ilissus is an area called Agrae and a temple of Artemis Agrotera (Huntress). They say that when Artemis came from Delos she first hunted here, and for this reason the statue is made having a bow.*

The statue of Artemis Agrotera is shown on coin *BB, xii* (cf. p. 140). From the coin representation we recognize without difficulty the "Artemis of Versailles" as the best surviving copy of the original statue at Agrae which has been attributed to the sculptor Leochares. On the coin representation, the stag (a modern restoration on the statue) does not appear, but a hunting dog instead. The goddess was holding the bow with her left hand (M. Bieber, *Sculpture of Hell. Age*, Rev. ed. 1961, p. 63, fig. 201; Furtwaengler, *Masterpieces* . . . , 2nd ed. 1964, p. 328, 409, fig. W 4). A less known copy of Artemis Agrotera from Spain (torso only) is in the collection of the Hispanic Society of America in New York (Pl.HH, i).

SOUTH SLOPE OF THE ACROPOLIS

THEATRE OF DIONYSUS *(Paus. I. 20,3*—cf. Pl.CC, ix-x) *The oldest sanctuary of Dionysus is near the theatre.*

See the commentary of Imhoof-Blumer & Gardner on p. 143. (For recent bibliography cf. M. Bieber, *The History of Greek and Roman Theatre*, 2nd ed. 1961, and Ida T. Hill. *The Ancient City of Athens*, 1953. Restoration of the Theatre with the Sanctuary of Dionysus appears in Al. N. Oikonomides' *Acropolis*, Athens, 1958 (restor. map)).

SANCTUARY OF DIONYSUS *(Paus. I. 20,3*—cf. Pl.CC, ii-iv) *Within the precincts are two temples and statues of Dionysus, the one is called Eleuthereus and the other is the work of Alkamenes made in ivory and gold.*

For the representations of the statue of Dionysus by Alkamenes on coins *CC, ii-v*, I agree with Imhoof-Blumer and Gardner (cf. pp. 142-143). [For coin *CC, i* and *CC, vii* see above (METROON, DIONYSUS). For *CC, viii* see below (DEMETER CHLOE and KORE)]. The archaic statue of the bearded Dionysus standing and holding the Kantharos cup and thyrsos on coin *CC, vi* might be the old statue called "Eleuthereus" by Pausanias (cf. p. 143).

ODEION OF PERICLES *(Paus. I. 20,4*—cf. p. lxxviii, 3) *Near the sanctuary of Dionysus and the theatre is a structure said to be an imitation of Xerxes' tent. It has been rebuilt, for the old building was burnt by Sulla, the Roman general, when he captured Athens.*

The building, according to W. B. Dinsmoor and others, is illustrated on the leaden theatre-ticket *(tessera)* shown on p. lxxviii, 3. (For further reference see W. Bell Dinsmoor, *The Architecture of Ancient Greece*, 1950, p. 211; Ida T. Hill, *The Ancient City of Athens*, 1953, pp. 110-111 and note 16 on p. 235, and A. N. Oikonomides, *Acropolis*, Athens, 1958).

ASKLEPIOS (*Paus. I. 21,4*—cf. Pl.EE, ii-iv) *The sanctuary of Asklepios is worth seeing, both for the statues of the god and his children and for the paintings in it.*

For a discussion of the standing statue of Amphiaraos or Asklepios on coins *EE, iii-iv* see AMPHIARAOS above. The beardless statue on coin *EE, ii* would seem to represent one of the sons of Asklepios. The posture is reminiscent of the statues and statuettes of *Telesphoros* found in the sanctuary of Epidaurus.

DEMETER CHLOE AND KORE (*Paus. I. 22,3*—cf. Pl.CC, viii) *There is also a sanctuary of Ge Kourotrophos (Earth Nurse of Youth) and of Demeter Chloe (Green). You can learn all about their names by conversing with the priests.*

The cult statue of the sanctuary which represents two goddesses appears on coin *CC, viii*. A seated Demeter, clad in a long dress with two torches over her shoulders, and a standing Kore holding two torches as tall as herself are shown. Nothing of this *Kore* is mentioned by Pausanias, but happily enough we can get confirmation of the interpretation for the second statue represented on coin *CC, viii* from a group of Attic inscriptions from dedications in the sanctuary *(IG, II², 4663. 4778. 5006. 4748)*. The dedicators inscribed their offerings "to Demeter Chloe and Kore" and in one case a statue of the "Kourotrophos" is dedicated to the two goddesses. The cult statue is also represented with other deities on a vase in the Hermitage (illustrated in J. Harrison, *Myth. and Mon. Anc. Athens*, p. 99, fig. 22).

Imhoof-Blumer and Gardner interpreted the coin in connection with the cult of Dionysus (see p. 143), but they do not have supporting evidence.

BOUZYGION (*Schol. Aeschines II, 78*—cf. Pl.DD, vii-viii)

Coins *DD, vii-viii* are identified by Imhoof-Blumer and Gardner as depicting Theseus driving a bull, tentatively the Marathon bull. However, careful scrutiny will reveal that the coins show two bulls each, making the identification that of Bouzyges, who was the first man in Athens to yoke two bulls for the purpose of plowing and was thus considered a local hero. According to the Scholiast of Aeschines *(II, 78)* his family rose in importance and the priestess of Athena was chosen from among his descendants. According to the same text his plow was dedicated as a memorial on the Acropolis of Athens.

The authors have expressed wonder at the tameness of the bull(s) (p. 146) and doubt its worth as a subject for a sculptured group depicting the capture of the Marathonian bull, but with this more fitting interpretation, the tameness is indeed of prime importance.

For Bouzyges and the different interpretation of the myth see J. Harrison, *Myth. and Mon. of Anc. Athens*, pp. 96, 166-168, 426. For a representation of the myth of Bouzyges on a vase painting in Athens (Loverdos Collection) see Th. Arvanitopoulou in *Polemon* Vol. III (in Greek). The "testimonia" are collected in Jahn-Michaelis, *Arx Athenarum*, 3rd ed. 1901, p. 41.

THE ACROPOLIS

THE ENTRY (*Paus. I. 22,4*—cf. Pl.Z, iii-vii) *There is but one entry to the ascent to the Acropolis; no other is available because the hill is precipitous throughout and surrounded by a fortification wall.*

For a fine discussion of the coins representing the Acropolis — fort, temples and shrines, including the Propylaea and the staircase leading to them, see pp. 128-129. The "Testimonia" parallel to Pausanias' description as well as most of the inscriptions found during excavations up to the end of the nineteenth century are collected by A. Jahn and A. Michaelis in *Arx Athenarum a Pausania descripta* (3rd ed. 1901). A new restoration in color of buildings and monuments of the Acropolis, including those on the south slope is in my *Acropolis*, (Athens, 1958).

ATHENA NIKE (WINGLESS VICTORY) (*Paus. I. 22,5*—cf. Pl.AA, xxiv; HH, iii) *To the right of the Propylaea is a temple of Nike (Victory) wingless.*

On the coin a Victory (Nike) holding a trophy is represented. It appears more like a memorial issue for a military victory, the original of which we may assume to be one of the golden Victories in the Parthenon or the statuette of Nike carried by the ivory and gold Pheidian Athena, than a simple representation of Nike. The addition of the trophy is definitely a modification of the mint artist. I fail to see any traces of an assumed helmet (see p. 136). A parallel to the type of Nike on the coin is the bronze Nike in the collection of the Hispanic Society of America in New York (*HH, 3*), previously unpublished to my knowledge.

HEKATE "ON THE TOWER" (*Paus. II. 30,2*—cf. Pl.BB, vii) *Alkamenes, as I believe, was the first who made a statue of the tribodied and tri-faced Hekate which the Athenians call Epipyr-*

gidia (on the Tower) and it stands beside the temple of the Wingless Victory.

The statue appears on coin *BB, vii,* but Imhoof-Blumer and Gardner preferred to connect the representation with the torch-bearing Artemis (see p. lxi, PHOSPHOROI). Pausanias' passage on Alkamenes' Hekate does not appear on the list (pp. 138-139) of possible statues to be identified with coin representations, but the similarity of the figure with the "Hekateion" as it appears in copies and other works of art is obvious. The die cutter of the mint represents one view of the tri-bodied statue in a very elementary way so that the classic statue appears "archaic" as happened also in the case of Artemis Brauronia. For further reference see J. Harrison, *Myth. and Mon. of Anc. Athens,* pp. 377-379.

The similarity of the "Hekateion" with the representation of "Kore" on coin *BB, vii* is also an interesting one (see DEMETER CHLOE AND KORE). Hekate is also connected in art representations and inscriptions with the group of the three "Nymphs" or "Charites," which in turn are connected with Demeter Chloe and "Kore." The conglomeration of cults on the "Nike Tower" and below it in the area of the "Agora of Theseus" apparently go far back into prehistory, possibly even before the erection of the tower.

HERMES PROPYLAIOS *(Paus. I. 22,8*—cf. Pl.DD, xix) *At the entrance at the top of the Acropolis is a Hermes whom they call 'Propylaios' (of the Propylaea = Gateway).*

When Imhoof-Blumer and Gardner wrote their commentary the Hermes Propylaios had not been identified. This identification became possible only after 1903 when the excavations at Pergamon produced an inscribed copy of an archaic herm of Hermes. The inscription identified the original as the *"Hermes Propylaios"* adding the information that it was *"the beautiful statue by Alkamenes."* (See A. Furtwaengler, *Masterpieces* ..., 2nd ed. 1964, fig. on p. 87, App. p. 418). For the old commentary replaced by the above see p. 149. Note that the word "Hermes" in the text of Pausanias can be interpreted in two ways: 1) a terminal bust, i.e., "herm," and 2) a statue of Hermes. (See also Appendix pp. 169 ff.)

DIITREPHES *(Paus. I. 23,3*—cf. Pl.DD, xvii) *...A bronze statue of Diitrephes shot through with arrows.*

A possible echo of the statue of Diitrephes on the Acropolis of Athens is to be seen on coin *DD, xvii.* The recent article by Theophano Arvanitopoulou (*Polemon* 7, 1962) indicates a new possible copy of the famous statue by Kresilas. The figure on the above coin in the old commentary (see p. 148) is called an adaptation of Aristogeiton advancing to right, which does not appear to be the best identification, so perhaps this new attempt will lead to further investigation of the problem.

ATHENA HYGIEIA (*Paus. I. 23,4*—cf. Pl.AA, x-xi) ... *a statue of Athena surnamed Hygieia (Health).*

The inscribed statuette of Athena Hygieia found at the excavations in the sanctuary of Asklepios at Epidauros helps to identify the same pose of Athena on coins *AA, x-xi* (see J. Harrison, *Myth. and Mon. Anc. Athens,* pp. 392-393, fig. 23).

ARTEMIS BRAURONIA (*Paus. I. 23,7*—cf. Pl.BB, v-vi) *((There is also a sanctuary of Artemis Brauronia. The statue of the goddess is a work of Praxiteles and her surname is derived from a sanctuary on the site of Brauron)).* [cf. p. lxxix, Fig. 1-3.]

The statue of Artemis depicted on coins *BB, v & vi* was correctly identified by the authors as an illustration of Artemis Brauronia. Although it looks like an archaic work on the coin, today we can understand that this apparent archaism is due only to the small size in which the statue was represented on the coin. The goddess, as described, holds a patera and bow and is clad in a chiton with diplois, but her hair is not in formal curls, as we can see, but is piled high on her head. From the characteristics seen in these coins, Artemis Brauronia can be readily identified as the same statue as the one depicted in a dedicatory relief from Brauron, the Praxitelean statue in the New York Metropolitan Museum of Art, and the recently discovered bronze statue in Piraeus (cf. Furtwaengler, *Masterpieces,* 2nd ed. 1964, pp. 420, 423). As indicated by the relief of Brauron these are all copies of the Praxitelean Brauronia seen by Pausanias in the Brauroneion of the Athenian Acropolis. (See Page lxxix, 1, 2 and 3.)

The marble copy in the Metropolitan Museum in New York, definitely dated in the later fourth century B.C. was found "somewhere in Attica." In its first publication in *The Metropolitan Museum of Art Bulletin* 3, 1944, pp. 48-53, a fine premonition of Gisela M. A. Richter guided her to write about it thus (p. 53), *"In the charming head of our woman, in particular, with its delicate, oval face and serene expression, we can feel the spirit of a master's creation. Something of the radiance with which Praxiteles imbued his works is reflected in the quiet loveliness of our group."* My belief is that the copy of the Brauronia and the accompanying priestess was produced in the workshop of Praxiteles as part of the pediment sculptures for the small temple of Artemis at Brauron, also built in the later fourth century B.C. As for the priestess figure, we may note that it has a striking stylistic resemblance to the figures of the Muses on the Chaironeia base, considered also as an original of the master. (A. Furtwaengler, *Masterpieces*, 2nd ed. 1964, Pl.U, figs. U3 and U4).

ATHENA AND MARSYAS (*Paus. I. 24,1*—cf. Pl.Z, xx-xxi) ... *At this site is a work representing Athena striking Marsyas the Silenus (satyr) for he picked up the flutes which the goddess wished to be cast away forever....*

For the group recorded by Pliny as a work of Myron see the comments on pp. 132-133. For further reference see J. Harrison *Myth. and Mon. Anc. Athens*, pp. 408-410, where all of the known sculptural copies of Marsyas are listed together with the echoes of the group in artistic representations. The Athena has also been identified in sculptural copies of which the best is now in Frankfurt. For a recombination of the group from the copies see Whibley's *Companion to Greek Studies*, 4th ed., p. 292, fig. 41. The group is thoroughly studied by A. Andreu in his article "Der Lateranische Silen und die Gruppe von Athena und Marsyas" in *Opuscula Archaeologica* 3, 1944, pp. 1-36, Pls.I-VII.

THESEUS AND MINOTAUR (*Paus. I. 24,1*—cf. Pl.DD, iii & vi) ... *a representation of Theseus' fight with the Bull of Minos....*

The group on coin *DD, iii* has been more generally accepted as a representation of the work seen by Pausanias. The myth being very popular among artists of all periods, it is illustrated in many works of art, sometimes with striking originality in pose and construction. The second group illustrated on coin *DD, vi* creates a problem of preference between the two representations on coins for the selection of the group on the Acropolis. Note that the one on *DD, vi* is a work contemporary with the BOUZYGES group (see above) and possibly earlier than Myron's Athena and Marsyas.

ATHENA AND POSEIDON *(Paus. I. 24,3*—cf. Pl.Z, xi, xii, xiv, xvi)
*. . . is represented also the olive tree and Athena and Poseidon
causing the spring to gush forth.*

Note the distinction of the two groups by Imhoof-Blumer
and Gardner on pp. 130-131. The second group represents the
cult statue in the temple of Poseidon at Sounion.

ZEUS POLIEUS *(Paus. I. 24,4*—cf. Pl.BB, i-iii; DD, xviii) *And
there are two statues of Zeus, the one is a work of Leochares
and the other is called "Polieus."*

To the three sculptural types of Zeus shown on coins *BB, i-iii,*
possibly we should add coin *DD, xviii* which has been thought
to illustrate Aristogeiton (?) "advancing to right, holds sword
and chlamys." Thus far no evidence exists for the distinction
among the three types of Zeus except for Zeus Olympios (see
above and pp. 136-138). Coin *DD, xviii* may be an improved copy
of the type of Zeus hurling a thunderbolt as depicted on *BB, i.*

THESEUS "RAISING THE ROCK" *(Paus. I. 27,8*—cf. Pl.DD, ii)

This coin is well described on p. 146. Of importance is the
information given by Pausanias that "The legend is represented in bronze on the Acropolis; only the rock is actually
of stone."

THESEUS KILLING (PROKROUSTES?) (cf. Pl.DD, iv)

The coin is described on p. 146 as a variation of Theseus and
the Minotaur but if this group is represented on *DD, iii* or *vi,*
it certainly bears no resemblance to the one depicted on *DD, iv.*
Why do we not consider it to be another of the hero's exploits
e.g. Theseus and Prokroustes?

PARTHENON, ERECHTHEION & THE REST OF
THE ACROPOLIS

PARTHENON, PEDIMENT SCULPTURES *(Paus. I. 24,5) At the side
where you enter into the building (East) the sculptures you
see on what is called the pediment are all parts of a representation of the birth of Athena; the sculptures on the rear (West)
pediment represent the quarrel between Poseidon and Athena
about the domination of this land.*

For the discussion by Imhoof-Blumer and Gardner and the
coins related by them to the pediment sculptures see pp. 129-
131. Concerning coins *Z, xv* and *xvii* on which "Athena and
Poseidon are not in conflict but at rest," I suggest that they
represent the cult statue in the temple of Poseidon at Sounion.

PARTHENON, ATHENA PARTHENOS *(Paus. 1. 24,5-8*—cf. Pl.Y, xviii-xxv; HH, 4; p. lxxviii, 1-2) . . . *the statue is made of ivory and gold. On the middle of its helmet is placed a sculpted sphinx . . . and on both sides (the cheek-plates) of the helmet are sculpted griffins in relief . . . The statue of Athena, represented wearing an ankle length chiton (dress) is in a standing posture. And on the breast-plate an ivory head of Medusa is inlaid. (With the right hand she) holds a Nike (Victory statuette) about four cubits high, and with her left hand she holds a spear and a shield stands by her, and by the spear is a snake. This snake would be Erichthonios. And on the pedestal of the statue is sculpted in relief the birth of Pandora.*

The commentary on pp. 126-128 is very interesting for two reasons. First, it is an excellent collation of evidence from coin representations with information from literary sources gathered to derive a more solid idea about the lost original sculpture. Secondly, it is a valid collection of different views and aspects of a famous *dated* sculpture, a work of Pheidias, on coins.

From the coin representations the information given by Pausanias about the griffins sculpted in relief *on both sides of the helmet* was misinterpreted to mean the two sculpted Pegasi (one on each side of the sphinx) *in the middle of the helmet,* which were the supports of the two side crests. (cf. p. 127) The small copy of the Parthenos statue discovered in Athens in 1880 (the Varvakeion statuette) did little to help solve the problem. The two Pegasi and the sphinx were represented as the supports of the three crests on the helmet, but no sign of griffins was observed. See Pl.HH, 4.

Actually the problem had already been solved, but no one realized it. On the excellent copy of the Athena Parthenos bust on a gem signed by Aspasios the griffins are represented on the inner sides of the raised up cheek-plates of the helmet.

The representation of the statue on coins *Y, xviii-xxi* gives to the scrutinizing student a good example of the unreliability of coin representations for defining "style" or sculptural periods from miniatures. Judging only from the evidence of these coins we cannot even say that the statue belongs to the classic period. Instead it might easily be taken for a statue of the pre-Myronian period of sculpture.

For a comparative study of the copies from the Athena Parthenos by Pheidias see A. Furtwaengler, *Masterpieces,* 2nd

ed. 1964, Pl.E ; for the Strangford shield, *ibidem,* Pl.D ; and for
a comparative drawing of the Stangford, Lenormant and fragments of the Vatican shields, *ibidem,* p. x. The leaden tessera
at Berlin mentioned on p. 127 can be seen together with a drawing of the gem by Aspasios on page lxxviii, 1-2.

UNIDENTIFIED REPRESENTATIONS OPEN FOR RESEARCH

I can add nothing more to the identification of the numerous
statues of Athena represented on Athenian coins. The knowledge that at least one shrine or statue of the patron goddess
existed in each of the Attic demes makes any final solutions
impossible, especially when we realize that even the locations of
most of the Attic demes are still unknown and that our records
of the Attic cults of Athena are very fragmentary and
incomplete.

For instance, I would like to add that the plinth form on the
base of the cult statue in the archaic temple of Athena at
Sounion indicates a statue like the one on coin *AA, xiv.* But, even
with this small bit of evidence, any proceeding toward further
identification would be unreasonable.

For the more unique representations the chances are better.
Honorary statues are possibly represented on coins *DD, xx;
EE, v* and *xii.* Someone in the future may be luckier in identifying these with existent sculpture or with literary references.
The same can be said for the statue of a beardless hero sitting
on a rock altar resting his right hand on a club like the Lysip-
pian "Herakles Epitrapezios," except for the hair arrangement
which appears "archaic" *(EE, xvi, xvii).* Similar cases are the
naked bearded hero or god holding a priest's curled knife and
a patera *(DD, xx)* or the seated goddess *(EE, xiv)* or the trophy
on coins *EE, vii* and *viii.* Imhoof-Blumer and Gardner proposed
their ideas on the coin representations listed above convincingly.
Many later writers accepted these identifications, even as they
accepted those which we believe to be corrected on the basis
of the new evidence presented above in the commentary. But
who can say with assurance what is right and what is wrong?
Who knows if an identification appearing probable today with
the evidence at hand will stand the test of time as more new
evidence is uncovered?

CONCORDANCE BETWEEN GREEK TEXTS OF
PAUSANIAS AND THEIR TRANSLATIONS

Note: Numbers in parentheses indicate the passages commented upon. Arabic numbers in the second line of each section are the pages of the Numismatic Commentary on Pausanias on which the passages, in Greek, may be found. These numbers, following a comma, indicate pages in the supplement or appendix. Roman numerals indicate the page numbers of the translations of the Greek texts. References to the pertinent coins of the Plates may be found both in the pages of text and translation.

CORRIGENDA

Page 56. Lacedaemon. *For* III. 16,2 *read* III. 15,3.

Page 59. 9. *For* III. 19,1 *read* III. 19,2.

Page 60. 1 and 2. *For* III. 21,7 *read* III. 21,8.

Page 68. Korone 1. *For* IV. 34,6 *read* IV. 34,7; Korone 2. *For* IV. 35 *read* IV.35,2.

Page 71. Elis 2. *For* V. 11 *read* V. 11,1.

Page 72. Elis 3. *For* V. 13 *read* V. 13,1; Elis 5. *For* VI. 25,2 *read* VI. 25,1.

Page 80. *For* VII. 20,9 *read* VII. 21,11.

Page 89. Bura 2. *For* VIII. 25,10 *read* VII. 25,10; Aegina. *For* ... *read* cf. VII. 26,5.

Page 93. Arcadia 1. *For* VIII. 2,6 *read* VIII. 1,6; Mantinea 2. *For* cf. 54,5 *read* VIII. 15,5.

Page 98. Pheneos 3. *For* VIII. 15 *read* VIII. 15,1.

Page 124. Elateia 1. *For* 8 *read* X. 34,8.

Page 127. *For* 1881 *read* 1880.

Page 151. *For* I, 23 *read* I. 21,3.

Page 158. Tenea. *For* II.5,3 read II. 5,4.

Page 109. The recognition by the authors of the incorrect ascriptions of the coins minted by *"Asine"* to the city Asine in Argolis rather than the one in Messene does not alter the identification of the statue as Apollo Pythaeus. The existance of a cult in the shrine of Apollo Pythaeus in the ruins of the Argolic Asine is recognized, and the "ancient statue of Apollo" recorded by Pausanias *(IV. 39,9)* in "the temple of Apollo" in the Messenian Asine must be the statue of Apollo Pythaeus taken by the people when they were pressed by the Argives to migrate from Argolis to Messenia.

3.

2.

1. Bronze copy of Artemis Brauronia as found with other bronzes in Piraeus in 1959 (cf.page 82). Notice extended right arm which once held phiale. 2. Artemis Brauronia and priestess or suppliant (or Iphigeneia?). Marble pediment sculptures from Temple of Artemis at Brauron. N.Y. Metropolitan Museum of Art. 3. Dedicatory relief to Artemis found at excavations at Brauron, in Athens, National Museum. The Praxitelean statue is depicted standing before an altar and holds a libation phiale in her right hand (cf. fig.1) and a bow in her left.

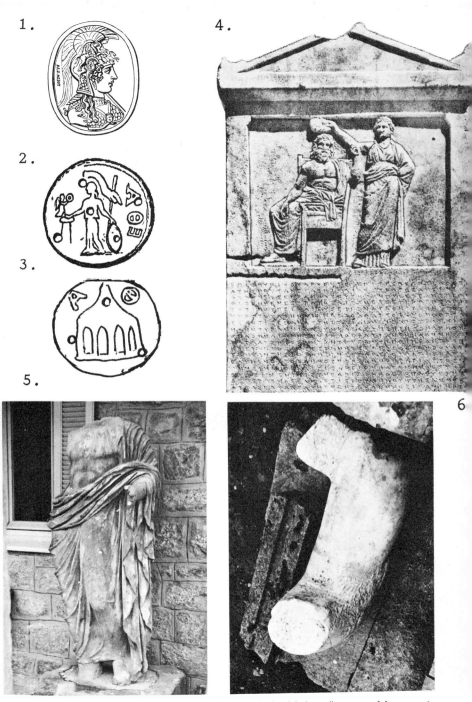

1. Athena Parthenos on Gem by Aspasios. Line drawing dated before discovery of Lenormant and Varvakeion Statuettes. 2. Athena Parthenos. Drawing from a tessera (theatre ticket). 3. Odeion of Pericles in Athens on tessera (theatre ticket). From private collection. 4. Demos and Demokratia on stele relief. Athens, Stoa of Attalos Museum. 5. Marble statue of Amphiaraos in museum of the excavations by Leonardos at the Amphiareion of Oropus. 6. Colossal left arm, from marble cult statue of Amphiaraos discovered by the Temple of Amphiaraos at Oropus.

A Numismatic Commentary on Pausanias

by

F. W. Imhoof-Blumer   Percy Gardner

Detail of bronze statue of Athena found in Piraeus in 1959. Athens, National Musuem.

NUMISMATIC COMMENTARY ON PAUSANIAS.

I.

BOOK I. 39–44.—MEGARICA.

BOOK II.—CORINTHIACA.

THE following paper is the first of a series of two or three which will bring into contact the extant coins of Greece and the text of Pausanias, thus furnishing to many passages of the traveller's writings a running numismatic commentary.

The main object we have set before us is to collect and set forth the numismatic reproductions of works of art mentioned by Pausanias; but we have not excluded any numismatic types which at all illustrate the cults and the legends mentioned by him as existing in the various cities of Peloponnesus.

The importance of the work cannot be doubted when we consider that in the case of many of the statues mentioned by Pausanias the only copies known are those upon coins; we may therefore hope to reconstruct from numismatic evidence, at least the general schemes of many great works of art wholly lost, and thus furnish very important material for recovering the history of Greek art; especially the history of the succession of types of the chief deities of Greece, which is a subject of great and increasing interest to archaeologists.

Generally speaking, the coins on which we can place the most reliance as sources of information as to the monuments are those of Hadrian and the Antonines. These coins are also the best in point of execution; and we may add that they are contemporary with the travels of Pausanias.

To discern whether the types of Greek coins of the Imperial
class, with which chiefly we shall have to do, are merely conventional representations of deities, or whether on the other
hand they are copies of statues, is not an easy task. But a few
rules may be laid down which may be safely used in judging
of this matter.

There is reason to suppose that the figure of a deity
on a coin is a copy of a cultus - statue in the following
cases :—

(1) When it is represented within a temple or shrine. This
is the surest of all indications of an intention to copy ; and few
or no instances will be found in which on coins a merely
conventional figure of a deity is placed in a temple. Of course
we cannot trust the small and careless representations on coins
for accuracy in such details as the number of pillars in a temple,
or the design of the pediment ; and even in representing the
cultus-statue, a die-sinker might take strange liberties. But
it seems that in every case he meant to copy so far as his
ability and memory served.

(2) When the figure stands on a pedestal, the intention
is obviously to represent a statue. By parity of reasoning,
when the figure on the coins leans on a pillar, or otherwise
is of a design fitted for the round but not for reliefs, it is
probably inspired by a statue.

(3) The presence of an altar on a coin is also an indication,
although a less trustworthy indication, of the intention to
portray a cultus-statue.

(4) So is also any indication of locality, such as a river-god
or acropolis-rock. But of course such proofs as these must not
be seriously relied on.

(5) When an identical type recurs unchanged on the coins
of a series of emperors stretching over a long period, then
there arises a presumption that such uniformity is caused by
the existence of a sculptural original, constantly under the
eyes of successive die-sinkers. They may in some cases
have copied the coins one of another, but this is less likely.

(6) Sometimes the language used by Pausanias enables us
to determine the connexion of a statue and a coin-type. For
instance, he may describe the statue in detail and the description
may apply to the coin-type ; or he may state the age and the

author of the statue, and these may completely suit the figure of the coin.

(7) In some cases, especially where archaic types are concerned, the figure on the coin may bear sufficient internal evidence of being copied from a statue, and we may in some cases be able to identify that statue from information otherwise gained.

The only previous writer who must be acknowledged as our predecessor is Panofka, who published in 1853-5, *Archæological Commentaries* on certain portions of Pausanias, more especially II. 24, which describes the citadel of Argos. Of course the material at our disposal is far more abundant than that which he could command.

A word must be said as to the share taken in this paper by the two compilers. They began the task independently; for the present article it was found advisable to use the numismatic lists of the Swiss colleague, which were more complete, as a basis: he has also furnished the casts used for illustration in the case of all coins not in England or Paris. The English colleague has added some material and put the article into final form, and is responsible for the comments added after the lists of coins.[1]

The text used is that of Schubring (Teubner 1881).

F. IMHOOF-BLUMER.
PERCY GARDNER.

[1] *Abbreviations.*

A I. II. &c., **B** I. II. &c., and so on to **M** are references to the accompanying plates.
Mion. Mionnet.
M. S. Mionnet, *Supplement.*
B. M. British Museum.
Arch. Z. Archäologische Zeitung.
Imh. Imhoof-Blumer's Collection.
Æ copper.
Æ silver.
Obv. Obverse.
Rev. Reverse.
Sup. Supplement.
Sancl. Museo Sanclementi.
Auton. Autonomous.

R. and F. Messrs. Rollin et Feuardent.
P. O. Count Prokesch-Osten.
Mus. Nap. Museum of Naples.
Arig. Arigoni *Catalogue.*
St. Flor. Museum des Stiftes St. Florian.
Mil. *Rec.* Millingen *Recueil de Monnaies,* &c.
Mil. *A. G. C.* Millingen, *Ancient Greek Coins.*
Overbeck *K. M. Kunstmythologie.*
Berl. Bl. Berliner Blätter für Münz-Siegel-u. Wappenkunde.
Ann. d. Inst. Annali dell' Inst. arch. di Roma.

MEGARA.

1.—Paus. I. 40, 2. Τῆς δὲ κρήνης οὐ πόρρω ταύτης ἀρχαῖόν
ἐστιν ἱερόν . . . . καὶ ἄγαλμά τε κεῖται χαλκοῦν Ἀρτέμιδος ἐπίκλησιν Σωτείρας . . . . τὴν δὲ Ἄρτεμιν αὐτὴν
Στρογγυλίων ἐποίησε. Cf. 44, 2, statue of Artemis in
temple of Apollo.

ARTEMIS running to the right in short chiton; holds torch
in each hand.

Æ Auton. *Obv.* Apollo-head. Neumann I. pl. VII. 4. Mion. II. 141, 319.
Auton. *Obv.* Head of Eucleides. B.M. Mion. II. 141, 318. (A I.).
Ant. Pius. Leake, p. 74. M. Aurel. M.S. III. 588, 377.
Commodus and Sept. Severus. B.M.

This type of Artemis recurs on coins of Pagae in exactly
similar form. It is, as we shall show in treating of that
city (*infra*) undoubtedly a copy of the work of Strongylion.
The head of Eucleides of Megara is very peculiar. The
philosopher, though bearded, wears the veil and the earring of
a woman. It has been suggested by Visconti that this is
obviously in allusion to the tale told about Eucleides, that he
came disguised as a woman, and veiled, from Megara, to attend
the lectures of Plato, at a time when access to Athens was
forbidden to the Megarians under pain of death. See Aulus
Gellius, *Noct. Att.* VI. 10.

2.—Paus. I. 41, 3. Οὐ πόρρω δὲ τοῦ Ὕλλου μνήματος . . . .
ναὸς . . . . Ἀπόλλωνός ἐστι καὶ Ἀρτέμιδος· . . . . Ἀλκά-
θουν τὸν Πέλοπος . . . . τὸ ἱερὸν ποιῆσαι τοῦτο Ἀγρο-
τέραν Ἄρτεμιν καὶ Ἀπόλλωνα Ἀγραῖον ἐπονομάσαντα.

Artemis Agrotera in long chiton running to the right, holds
bow in left hand, and with right draws an arrow from
her quiver.

Æ Caracalla. B. M. (A II.) *Revue Belge*, 1860, pl. II. 6.
Sept. Severus. B.M.

See also Apollo.

3.—Paus. I. 40, 4. Ἐς τὸ τοῦ Διὸς τέμενος ἐσελθοῦσι καλούμενον Ὀλυμπιεῖον ναός ἐστι θέας ἄξιος . . . . τῷ δὲ
ἀγάλματι τοῦ Διὸς πρόσωπον ἐλέφαντος καὶ χρυσοῦ, τὰ
δὲ λοιπὰ πηλοῦ τέ ἐστι καὶ γύψου· ποιῆσαι δὲ αὐτὸ
Θεόκοσμον λέγουσιν ἐπιχώριον, συνεργάσασθαι δέ οἱ
Φειδίαν.

ZEUS seated on throne, holds Victory.

Æ Ant. Pius. *Arch. Z.* 1843, p. 148, 16.
M. Aurel. B. M. (A III.) M. S. III. 588, 375.

Zeus seated, holds eagle.

Æ Sept. Sev.

The figure on the coins·is the usual conventional representation of a seated Zeus by Pheidias, such as that found on the
coins of Elis, of Alexander the Great, &c. It is curious that the
Zeus on the coins bears sometimes a Victory and sometimes an
eagle. The statues doubtless held a Victory, and it was the
natural instinct of Greek art in the good period, in engraving
so small a thing as a coin die, to substitute for the Victory a
simpler device of the same meaning, such as an eagle, the bird
of victory. Accordingly on Alexander's own coins, the Olympian
Zeus invariably carries an eagle; on the coins of his successors,
a figure of Victory is sometimes substituted.

4.—Cf. Paus. I. 43, 6. Καὶ ἐν τῷ ναῷ τῷ πλησίον Μούσας
καὶ χαλκοῦν Δία ἐποίησε Λύσιππος. Cf. 40, 6, Διὸς
Κονίου ναὸς οὐκ ἔχων ὄροφον.

Zeus striding to the right, naked, holds thunderbolt and eagle.
In some cases he seems to stand on a basis, and so to
represent a statue.

Æ Caracalla. M.S. III. 590, 384.
L. Verus. Imh. (A IV.)

5.—Paus. I. 40, 6. Ἐς τὴν ἀκρόπολιν ἀνελθοῦσι . . . . ἔστι
μὲν Διονύσου ναὸς Νυκτελίου. Cf. 43, 5, ᾠκοδόμησε
δὴ καὶ τῷ Διονύσῳ τὸ ἱερὸν Πολύειδος, καὶ ξόανον
ἀνέθηκεν ἀποκεκρυμμένον ἐφ᾿ ἡμῶν πλὴν τοῦ προσώπου.
. . . . τοῦτον μὲν δὴ Πατρῷον καλοῦσιν· ἕτερον δὲ
Διόνυσον Δασύλλιον ἐπονομάζοντες κ.τ.λ.

DIONYSUS standing, clad in short chiton, holds in right hand
kantharos, left rests on thyrsos.

Æ Sept. Sev. Imh. Mion. II. 142, 331 (A v.)

6.—Paus. I. 40, 6. Τοῦ δὲ Ἀσκληπιοῦ τὸ ἄγαλμα Βρύαξις
καὶ αὐτὸ καὶ τὴν Ὑγίειαν ἐποίησεν.

ASKLEPIOS and HYGIEIA, side by side, in usual attitudes.

Æ Sept. Sev. B. M. (A VI.)

Asklepios standing.

Æ Commodus. Imh. (A VII.)
Caracalla.

Hygieia standing, feeds serpent.

Æ M. Aurel.
Caracalla M. S. III. 590, 386. Leake, Sup. 134.

These figures are of quite conventional type; and as they do
not appear in a temple there is no strong reason to suppose that

they repeat the statues of Bryaxis. But at the same time there is nothing at all improbable in such a view. Mr. Wroth, who has made a most careful study of the artistic representations of Asklepios and Hygieia, states his opinion (*Journ. Hell. Stud.* v. p. 90) that the customary late schemes of the pair came into existence about the time of Scopas, and were possibly due to that artist. But the only figure of Asklepios by Scopas, of the details of which we know anything, was beardless (Overbeck, *G. P.* II. 11) : so that perhaps the claims of Bryaxis to the origination of the usual type are preferable to his, in the existing state of knowledge.

7.—Paus. I. 44, 2. Ἔστι δὲ ἐν τῷ γυμνασίῳ τῷ ἀρχαίῳ πλησίον πυλῶν καλουμένων Νυμφάδων λίθος παρεχόμενος πυραμίδος σχῆμα οὐ μεγάλης· τοῦτον Ἀπόλλωνα ὀνομάζουσι Καρινόν.

OBELISK between two dolphins.
Æ aut. B. M. (A VIII.) *Obv.* ΜΕΓ Prow.

For the Greek custom of representing deities in columnar form, Daremberg and Saglio s.v. *Baetylia*, Gardner, *Types*, &c., p. 77, &c. Apollo is thus represented on coins of Ambracia, and commonly in front of Greek houses, as Apollo Ἀγυιεύς.

8.—Paus. I. 42, 5. Τοῦ δὲ Ἀπόλλωνος πλίνθου μὲν ἦν ὁ ἀρχαῖος ναός· ὕστερον δὲ βασιλεὺς ᾠκοδόμησεν Ἀδριανὸς λίθου λευκοῦ· ὁ μὲν δὴ Πύθιος καλούμενος καὶ ὁ Δεκατηφόρος τοῖς Αἰγυπτίοις μάλιστα ἐοίκασι ξοάνοις, ὃν δὲ Ἀρχηγέτην ἐπονομάζουσιν Αἰγινητικοῖς ἔργοις ἐστὶν ὅμοιος. Cf. 44, 2. Ἀπόλλωνος ἱερόν ἐστιν ἐν δεξιᾷ Προστατηρίου . . . . Ἀπόλλων δὲ ἐν αὐτῷ κεῖται θέας ἄξιος καὶ Ἄρτεμις καὶ Λητώ, καὶ ἄλλα ἀγάλματά ἐστι Πραξιτέλους ποιήσαντος, Λητὼ καὶ οἱ παῖδες. 42, 2. Τότε δὲ αὐτῷ τειχίζοντι, ὥς φασιν οἱ Μεγαρεῖς, συνεργάζεταί τε Ἀπόλλων καὶ τὴν κιθάραν κατέθηκεν ἐπὶ τὸν λίθον· ἦν δὲ τύχῃ βαλών τις ψηφῖδι, κατὰ ταὐτὰ οὗτός τε ἤχησε καὶ κιθάρα κρουσθεῖσα.

Cf. also Apollo Agraeus, above.

Head of APOLLO. *Rev.* Lyre, tripod, dolphin or quiver.
Ꭺ Æ Auton. B. M.

Apollo standing, holds plectron and lyre.
Æ Ant. Pius. Mion. II. 142, 330 (holds branch instead of plectron).
    Carac. M. S. III. 590, 385.
    Geta. B. M. Beside Apollo omphalos surmounted by eagles, or altar on which ravens. (A IX.)

APOLLO ARTEMIS and LETO.

Æ Sept. Severus. Athens Mus. 3218. (A x.)

We have here a most important type, which should be a copy more or less free of the statues of Praxiteles. It merits a detailed description. To the left is Leto clad in long chiton; in her raised right hand she holds a long sceptre, her left hand hangs by her side. In the midst stands Apollo in citharoedic dress, holding in his right hand a plectrum, and in his left a lyre. To the right stands Artemis clad in long chiton with diploïs, holding in her left hand a plectrum, and with her right drawing an arrow from the quiver at her back. None of these schemes are in conflict with the style of Praxiteles.

9.—Paus. I. 42, 4. ᾠκοδόμηται δὲ ἐπὶ τῇ κορυφῇ τῆς ἀκρο-πόλεως ναὸς Ἀθηνᾶς, ἄγαλμα δέ ἐστιν ἐπίχρυσον πλὴν χειρῶν καὶ ἄκρων ποδῶν· ταῦτα δὲ καὶ τὸ πρόσωπόν ἐστιν ἐλέφαντος. καὶ ἕτερον ἐνταῦθα ἱερὸν Ἀθηνᾶς πεποίηται καλουμένης Νίκης, καὶ ἄλλο Αἰαντίδος.

ATHENE erect, spear in raised right hand, shield on left arm.

Æ L. Verus. Rev. Belge, 1860, Pl. II. 5.
S. Severus. R. and F.
Geta. B. M. (A xi.) Imh.

It would seem that this rather archaic and stiff type is most appropriate to Athene Aiantis.

10.—Paus. I. 40, 6. Ἐνταῦθα καὶ τῆς Δήμητρος τὸ καλούμενον Μέγαρον. Cf. 42, 6, ἔστι δὲ καὶ Δήμητρος ἱερὸν Θεσμοφόρου.

DEMETER standing veiled clad in chiton with diploïs, holds in either hand a torch ; before her, large torch fixed in the ground.

Æ M. Aurel. Imh. (A xii.) Verus Commodus. M. S. III. 376-9.
Sept. Severus. Geta. (A xiii.) B. M.

11.—Paus. I. 43, 6. Πλησίον δὲ τοῦ τῆς Ἀφροδίτης ναοῦ Τύχης ἐστὶν ἱερόν· Πραξιτέλους καὶ αὕτη τέχνη.

TYCHE wearing mural crown, holds patera and cornucopiae.

Æ Commodus. M. S. III. 589, 380.
Sept. Severus. B. M. Altar before her.
Domna. Mion. II. 143, 332.
Geta. B. M. (A xiv.) Tyche facing, altar beside her.

The mural crown, which is clear on some specimens, may be a mere later addition, but it is by no means unlikely that the scheme of the coin, though quite ordinary, may be copied from the statue of Praxiteles. It is said that Bupalus is the earliest sculptor who made a statue of Tyche; but Praxiteles and

Damophon of Messene set the fashion, so greatly followed in later times, of setting up cultus-statues of the goddess. In all probability the normal type, as represented on our coin, was the invention of one of them. The altar beside Tyche on the coin is an indication of locality which tells in favour of the view that we have to do with a copy of a statue.

12.—OTHER TYPES at Megara :

Herakles resting.

Æ Carac. P. O. Abh. 1845, pl. II. 32.
Sept. Sever. Sancl. II. XXV. 221.

Nemesis (?), right hand on her mouth, leaning on pillar (possibly Paregoros, statue by Praxiteles. Paus. I. 43, 6).

Æ Geta. M. S. III. 590, 389.

Terminal figure, with long hair, between pillars of a temple ; before it, a railing.

Æ Geta. Imh. (A XV.)

13.—Paus. I. 40, 3. Statues of twelve gods.
      41, 3. Temple of Isis.
      42, 7. Heroon of Ino.
      43, 5. Satyr of Praxiteles.
      43, 6. Temple and statue of Aphrodite Praxis ; in it, Peitho and Paregoros by Praxiteles ; Eros, Himeros, and Pothos, by Scopas.

PAGAE.

1.—Paus. I. 44, 4. Ἐν δὲ ταῖς Παγαῖς θέας ὑπελείπετο ἄξιον Ἀρτέμιδος Σωτείρας ἐπίκλησιν χαλκοῦν ἄγαλμα, μεγέθει τῷ παρὰ Μεγαρεῦσιν ἴσον καὶ σχῆμα οὐδὲν διαφόρως ἔχον.

ARTEMIS running, clad in short chiton, holds torch in each hand.

Æ M. Aurel. Sanclementi II. XXII. 175.
Commod. Mion. II. 143, 335. M. S. III. 592, 396.

Similar figure on basis, altar before her.

Æ M. Aurel. Arig. I. 81, 67.
Commod. Mus. Font. I. pl. V. 8. Imh. (A I.)
S. Severus. M. S. III. 593, 400 (Vienna). Leake, Suppl. 137.

Similar figure in temple : tree on either side.

Æ Commod. M. S. III. 592, 397. Munich. (A II.)

This figure of Artemis was (cf. Paus. I. 40, 2) a replica of that made by Strongylion, the contemporary of Pheidias, for the people of Megara. The coins of Megara and Pagae present us with figures of Artemis exactly alike. At Pagae this figure appears in a temple and on a basis. There can therefore be no doubt that it reproduces Strongylion's statue. This has been already stated by Streber, and accepted in Müller-Wieseler, *Denkmaeler*, II. 174 *b*. Pausanias gives (*l.c.*) an account of the tale which led to the erection of the statue, in which Artemis seems to be embodied as the goddess of night, and is assimilated to the Thessalian Hecate, who also is represented on coins of Pherae of the fourth and third centuries as bearing two torches.

2.—OTHER TYPES at Pagae.

Dionysus seated, holds kantharos and sceptre; panther before him.

Æ Sept. Sev. Turin. Panther at his feet. (**A** III.)

Cybele seated, holds patera and sceptre; lion beside her.

Æ Sept. Sev. B. M. (**A** IV.)

Isis in temple.

Bust of Tyche.

Gate with three doors, and figures over them.

Æ S. Sev. Vienna. (**A** V.) Athens. (**A** VI.)

Herakles on basis in building of two stories, surmounted by statues.

Æ S. Sev. Vienna. (**A** VII.)

AEGOSTHENA.

1. Paus. 1, 44, 5. Ἐν Αἰγοσθένοις δὲ Μελάμποδος τοῦ Ἀμυθάονός ἐστιν ἱερόν, καὶ ἀνὴρ οὐ μέγας ἐπειργασμένος ἐν στήλῃ.

Round BUILDING, whence rises a tree, entwined by a serpent.

Æ Geta. Athens. *Ann. dell' Inst.* 1866, 336.

Child suckled by she-goat. (MELAMPUS ?)

Æ Sept. Sev. B. M. (**A** I.)

The tree entwined by a serpent is a regular symbol of the grave, and this is sufficient proof that the building represented on the coin of Geta must be a well-known tomb; but as to details we have no information.

I am not aware that there is any record of the existence of a tradition that Melampus was suckled by a she-goat : but nothing is more likely. Such stories were told of highly-gifted men, and it is fairly certain that the type of the coin must refer to a noted native of Aegosthena, and so to Melampus, who was its only remarkable man.

2.—OTHER TYPES at Aegosthena.

Artemis as huntress.

Æ Sept. Sev.   *Ann. d. Inst.* 1866, 336.

CORINTH.

In criticising the types which we meet on the coins of
Corinth we must always bear in mind the words of Pausanias :
(II. 2, 6.) Λόγου δὲ ἄξια ἐν τῇ πόλει τὰ μὲν λειπόμενα ἔτι
τῶν ἀρχαίων ἐστίν, τὰ δὲ πολλὰ αὐτῶν ἐπὶ τῆς ἀκμῆς
ἐποιήθη τῆς ὕστερον.
It will seem unlikely that a sack, like that of Corinth in B.C
146, would spare any works of art existing in the city.   Yet it
appears, alike from the general statement of Pausanias just
quoted, and from the remarks which he makes as to various
temples and statues, that there were in Roman Corinth a great
number of works of early Greek art.   Of these some may have
been brought into Roman Corinth from neighbouring towns ;
but others are in character so local that we can scarcely doubt
that they belonged to the early city, whatever theory we may
form as to the manner of their survival.

The Roman colonists, entering on a wealth of Greek art and
legend, adopted both with enthusiasm, and were very proud of
both.   There is no other Greek city whereof the coins give us so
extensive information on the subject of temples and statues,
legends and cults.   The imperial series of Corinth furnishes a
very full archæological commentary on the text of Pausanias :
indeed the correspondences between the two are so many and so
close, that it seems rather the rule than the exception for coin-
types to be copies of works of art, more especially works of
early Greek art.

1.—Paus. II. 1, 3.   Προϊοῦσι δὲ ἡ πίτυς ἄχρι γε ἐμοῦ πεφύκει
παρὰ τὸν αἰγιαλόν, καὶ Μελικέρτου βωμὸς ἦν.   ἐς
τοῦτον τὸν τόπον ἐκκομισθῆναι τὸν παῖδα ὑπὸ δελφῖνος
λέγουσι . . . . . ἔστι δὲ ἐπὶ τοῦ Ἰσθμοῦ τῆς ἀρχῆς.

MELICERTES reclining on dolphin, under pine.   Cf. Stephani,
Compte Rendu, 1864, 209.

Æ Hadrian. B. M. Imh.
    M. Aurelius. Imh. (B I)
    Commodus. B. M. In field, wreath. (B II.)
    J. Domna. Imh. In field, two pines, wreath, and palm. (B III.)
    J. Domna. M. S. IV. 119, 816. Three trees.

Melicertes on dolphin on altar, under pine (Isthmus sometimes present *q. v.*).

Æ M. Aurel. Mus. Benkowitz. B. M. Isthmus standing by, holds rudder. (B IV.)

M. Aurel. B. M. Athlete by, holds palm. (B V.)

Domna. M. S. IV. 119, 817. Table, Triton, &c. in field.

M. Aurelius. Copenhagen. Poseidon standing by. (B VI.)

Melicertes lying on dolphin under pine : the whole on table.

Æ Ant. Pius. Mion. II. 181, 244. (B VII.)

Melicertes lying on dolphin, draped.

Æ Auton. Mus. Hunter. Imh.

Auton. *Obv.* Pegasus. *Rev.* Melicertes on dolphin, head raised. Munich. (B VIII.)

L. Verus. B. M., &c.

Paus. II. 1, 7.   Τῷ ναῷ δὲ ὄντι μέγεθος οὐ μείζονι ἐφεστήκασι Τρίτωνες χαλκοῖ. καὶ ἀγάλματά ἐστιν ἐν τῷ προνάῳ, δύο μὲν Ποσειδῶνος, τρίτον δὲ Ἀμφιτρίτης, καὶ Θάλασσα, καὶ αὕτη χαλκῆ. τὰ δὲ ἔνδον ἐφ' ἡμῶν ἀνέθηκεν Ἡρώδης Ἀθηναῖος, ἵππους τέσσαρας ἐπιχρύσους πλὴν τῶν ὁπλῶν· ὁπλαὶ δέ σφισίν εἰσιν ἐλέφαντος. καὶ Τρίτωνες δύο παρὰ τοὺς ἵππους εἰσὶ χρυσοῖ, τὰ μετ' ἰξὺν ἐλέφαντος καὶ οὗτοι· τῷ δὲ ἅρματι Ἀμφιτρίτη καὶ Ποσειδῶν ἐφεστήκασι, καὶ παῖς ὀρθός ἐστιν ἐπὶ δελφῖνος ὁ Παλαίμων· ἐλέφαντος δὲ καὶ χρυσοῦ καὶ οὗτοι πεποίηνται.

Palaemon standing on dolphin, draped.

Æ M. Aurel. M. S. IV. 98, 666.

Ant. Pius. Mion. II. 181, 245. Imh. (B IX.)

S. Severus. Mus. Arig. IV. pl. VII. 35. Isthmus seated by. Turin. (B X.)

Paus. II. 2, 1.   Τοῦ περιβόλου δέ ἐστιν ἐντὸς Παλαίμονος ἐν ἀριστερᾷ ναός, ἀγάλματα δὲ ἐν αὐτῷ Ποσειδῶν καὶ Λευκοθέα καὶ αὐτὸς ὁ Παλαίμων.

Round temple of Palaemon : within, sometimes Palaemon lying on dolphin.

Æ M. Aurel. B. M. Ox approaching for sacrifice. (B XI.)

L. Verus. B. M. Trees around. Imh. (B XII)

Geta. B. M. Ox approaching.

Caracalla. M. S. IV. 122, 837. In front priest and ox. B. M. (B XIII.)

Paus. II. 3, 4.   Μετὰ δὲ τὸ ἄγαλμα τοῦ Ἑρμοῦ Ποσειδῶν καὶ Λευκοθέα καὶ ἐπὶ δελφῖνός ἐστιν ὁ Παλαίμων.

Palaemon (or Melicertes *q. v.*) lying on dolphin.

Palaemon sitting on dolphin.

Æ Auton. M. S. IV. 50, 338. Imh. P. holds thyrsus.

M. Aurel. B. M.

L Verus. Mion. II. 185, 280. (B XIV.) Florence. (B XV.)

S. Severus. M. S. IV. 115, 784. P. holds wreath, Isthmus seated near.

Commodus.   Imh.   Group on altar.   (B xvi.)
Carac.   Parma.   Dolphin bridled.   (B xvii.)

It is evident from Pausanias' statements, confronted with the coins, that the one among the many stories as to the history of Ino and Melicertes or Palaemon which was accepted at Corinth was that which represented that Ino and Melicertes leaped into the sea at Megara, and Palaemon was borne by a dolphin to the part of the Isthmus where was the sanctuary of Poseidon; that he there died and was buried, and after death was worshipped as a hero, and honoured by funeral games.

It is not easy to reconcile this tale, and the peculiar artistic representation of Melicertes as a young boy which prevailed at Corinth, with the view of those who suppose Melicertes to be a form of the Tyrian god Melkarth.   But this matters little to the present purpose, for it is certain that the Corinthians knew nothing of the proposed identification.

On coins there are three schemes of Palaemon and the dolphin: sometimes he is sitting on it, sometimes standing, sometimes lying; the standing figure certainly belongs to the group of gold and ivory set up by Herodes Atticus in the temple of Poseidon; the lying figure is connected with the pine-tree and the altar under it, as well as with the round temple of Palaemon; the seated figure may perhaps be copied from the statue mentioned by Pausanias lower down (II. 3, 4).   But of course such distinctions are too nice to be strongly insisted on.

Figures of Ino and Melicertes, as of Poseidon and other types of Corinthian coins are to be found on the splendid cameo of Vienna (Overbeck, *Kunstmyth.* III., Gemmentafel II. 8), which presents us with an abridged picture of the region.

2.—Paus. II. 1, 9.   Ἀνάκειται Γαλήνης ἄγαλμα καὶ Θαλάσ-
σης, καὶ ἵππος εἰκασμένος κήτει τὰ μετὰ τὸ στέρνον,
Ἰνώ τε καὶ Βελλεροφόντης καὶ ὁ ἵππος ὁ Πήγασος.
(For Ino, cf. I. 44, 7 and 8.)

INO with her veil: beside her, hippocamp.

Æ Ant. Pius.   Imh.   *Choix*, pl. II. 50.   Vienna.   (B xviii.)
L. Verus.   Berlin.

Ino holding Melicertes in her arms.

Æ M. Aurel.   Imh.   (B xix.)
Domitian.   Berlin.   (B xx.)
Domitian.   M. II. 177, 218.   Isthmus seated on rock, *q.v.*   B. M.   (B xxi.)
Sept. Severus.   B. M.   Isthmus seated on rock.   Imh.   (B xxii.)
Sept. Severus.   M. II. 187, 292.   Ino on a rock; before her, dolphin.
Vienna.   (B xxiii.)

Caracalla. Imh. *Monn. Gr.* p. 160.
Ant. Pius. Mus. Nap. 7441. Ino and Melicertes : Sea deity holding out his arms to receive the child. (B xxiv.)

The presence of the hippocamp suggests that the type first described, which represents Ino without her child, may represent one of the anathemata of the temple of Poseidon, there set up in Roman times.

The second type, which appears full-face, represents Ino as holding her child on her left arm, and grasping with her right hand the end of her veil. In the third type she is in rapid motion towards the sea, which is represented on one coin by a marine deity, on others by a dolphin. Sometimes, however, the locality is changed, and in the place of the sea appears a seated figure of Isthmus. As this figure of Ino persists unchanged from the time of Domitian to that of Septimius Severus, it would seem to be based on some work of art.

3.—Cf. 2, 4. Κράνειον. ἐνταῦθα Βελλεροφόντου τέ ἐστι τέμενος καὶ, κ.τ.λ.

BELLEROPHON leading Pegasus : holds spear.
Æ Sep. Sev. Imh. (C xxv.)
Bellerophon taming Pegasus : holds shield.
Æ Nero. B. M. Imh. (C xxvi.)
Hadrian. Paris. (C xxvii.)
Caracalla. B. M.
Bellerophon seizing Pegasus near spring Peirene.
Æ Auton. B. M. (C xxviii.)
Bellerophon watering Pegasus : near by, Acropolis.
Æ Sept. Severus. B. M. (C xxix.)
Pegasus drinking.
Æ Aut. Imh. (C xxx.)

4.—Cf. Paus. ii. 3, 5. Κρῆναι. . . . θέας δὲ μάλιστα ἀξία ἡ παρὰ τὸ ἄγαλμα τὸ τῆς Ἀρτέμιδος, καὶ ὁ Βελλεροφόντης ἔπεστι, καὶ τὸ ὕδωρ οἱ δι' ὁπλῆς ἵππου ῥεῖ τοῦ Πηγάσου.

Bellerophon slaying Chimaera ; beside him seated Artemis who holds bow.
Æ Caracalla. *A. Z.* 1843, pl. ix. 13. B. M. (C xxxii.)
Bellerophon slaying Chimaera, on Corinthian column.
Æ Geta. Mion. ii. 189, 304.
Bellerophon slaying Chimaera, mounted on Pegasus.
Æ Auton. B. M. (C xxxi.)
Æ Hadrian. B. M.
L. Verus. B. M., &c.

[A list of Monuments on which the myth of Bellerophon is depicted, by Engelmann, in *Ann. d. Inst.* 1874, p. 1, pls. A—F.]

The presence of Artemis, and the use in some cases of a
column to support the group of Bellerophon and the Chimaera,
alike indicate that it is copied from the sculptured group of
the fountain. The water would flow from one of the forefeet of
Pegasus.

5.—Paus. II. 1, 6. Λέγουσι δὲ καὶ οἱ Κορίνθιοι Ποσειδῶνα
ἐλθεῖν Ἡλίῳ περὶ τῆς γῆς ἐς ἀμφισβήτησιν.

Coin with head of HELIOS on one side, Poseidon on the other.

Æ Aut.   Roman period.   B. M.   Imh.
Cf. Poseidon, below.

6.—Paus. II. 1, 5 and 6. Καθήκει δὲ ὁ τῶν Κορινθίων ἰσθμὸς
τῇ μὲν ἐς τὴν ἐπὶ Κεγχρέαις, τῇ δὲ ἐς τὴν ἐπὶ Λεχαίῳ
θάλασσαν.

ISTHMUS personified as a young male figure, standing, holding
rudders.

Æ Auton. Roman.   B. M.   (C XXXIII.) Imh.   (C XXXIV.)
Domitian.   B. M.   (C XXXV.)
M. Aurel.   Z. f. N. x. p. 75.
Sept. Sev.   St. Florian.   (C XXXVI.)

Isthmus seated, holds rudder.

Æ Hadrian.   Imh.   Isthmus seated in temple, right hand rests on head, left on
     rudder.   (C XXXVII.)
Sept. Severus.   B. M.   Similar, no temple.   (C XXXVIII.)
Hadrian.   Isthmus seated on rock, holds inverted rudder ; legend ISTHMVS.
     W. Froehner.   (C XXXIX.)
S. Severus.   Imh.   Isthmus seated left, holds rudder and palm ; before him
     Ino and Melicertes, q.v.
Domitian.   M. II. 177, 218.   Isthmus seated on rock, at his feet sea and
     dolphin ; opposite Ino with Melicertes in her arms.   (Millin. G.M. cx.
     400, B XXI.)

See also above, (B IV.) and (B X.)

The coin which represents Isthmus as seated within a temple
(C XXXVII.) repeats a Corinthian cultus-statue. No doubt Isthmus
was personified as a local hero ; and tradition must, as the coins
show, have connected him with the history of Ino and Melicertes.
In his temple he was represented as a young and naked man,
seated on a rock, resting his right hand on his head, and
supporting himself on his rudder, in an attitude of complete
repose. His face is turned backwards, implying probably that
Isthmus faced both the eastern and the western sea. Compare
a very similar figure of Haemus on the coins of Nicopolis.

If the standing figure of the coins represents a work of art,
it might well be a bronze statue erected in the neighbourhood
of the Isthmian temple ; such a statue is not mentioned by
Pausanias. The two rudders in the hands clearly refer to

the two harbours which existed, one on each side of the isthmus.

7.—The two harbours, LECHAEUM and CENCHREAE.

(1) As nymphs turned opposite ways, each holding a rudder.

Æ Hadrian. B. M. Inscribed **LECH, CENCH.** (**C** XL.)

(2) As reclining male figures.

Æ Sept. Sev. Mill. *Sylloge*, pl. II. 30. Acropolis; at the foot, on either side, male figure reclining, one holds rudder, one anchor. See below, (**G** CXXXIV.)

8.—Paus. II. 2, 2. Ὁ δὲ Ἰσθμικὸς ἀγών, κ.τ.λ.

ATHLETES : Two naked wrestlers or boxers.

Æ Ant. Roman. Imh. Wrestlers. (**C** XLI.)
Aut. Roman. Imh. Boxers. (**C** XLII.)
Aut. Imh. Boxer striking one who has fallen. (**C** XLIII.)

Runners.

Æ Auton. *Rev. Num.* 1851, p. 402. Armed runner.
Auton. Imh. Unarmed runner, holds palm. (**C** XLIV.)
Domitian. Imh. Unarmed runner, holds palm. (**C** XLV.)
Commod. M. S. IV. 111, 755. Armed runner.

Other Athletes.

Æ Auton. Imh. Athlete standing, holds palm.
M. Aurel. B. M. Athlete standing, holds palm, beside Melicertes and pine. See above, (**B** V.)

Conical building; perhaps a spring-house; possibly an obelisk within a stadium.

Æ Domitian. Arig. I. 67, 43. Berlin. (**C** XLVI.)
Hadrian. *Revue Belge*, 1860, pl. II. 7. Imh. (**C** XLVII.)

On the Berlin coin the representation varies. There is a door in the midst, flanked by standing figures, and surmounted by a horseman.

BUILDING, from the midst of which rises a column surmounted by a naked male figure, holding sceptre : and over each side an equestrian statue.

Æ M. Aurel. M. II. 184, 264. Leake, *Eur. Gr.* p. 41.
L. Verus. W. Froehner. (**C** XLVIII.)
S. Severus. Mion. IV. 117, 806 (where the equestrian statues are wrongly described as racing horses.)
Caracalla. Mion. IV. 124, 849.

This building may be meant for a stadium or a hippodrome ; the latter is not mentioned by Pausanias.

ISTHMIA in wreath.

Æ Nero. Imh. Anton. Pius and L. Verus. B. M. &c.

9.—Paus. II. 1, 7. Ἐλθόντι δὲ ἐς τοῦ θεοῦ τὸ ἱερὸν ......
πιτύων δένδρα ἐστὶ πεφυτευμένα ἐπὶ στοίχου, τὰ πολλὰ
ἐς εὐθὺ αὐτῶν ἀνήκοντα. τῷ ναῷ δὲ ὄντι μέγεθος οὐ
μείζονι ἐφεστήκασι Τρίτωνες χαλκοῖ.

Tetrastyle temple of POSEIDON surrounded by Tritons; tree
 beside it.

Æ L. Verus. M. S. IV. 103, 701.
 Geta. Imh. *Choix*, pl. II. 51. (**D** XLIX.) Vienna. (**D** L.)
Æ Aut. &c. Tetrastyle temple. (See **E** XCV.)

The details of architecture are among the matters as to
which the representations of coins are least trustworthy. But
in this particular case there is an obvious intention to represent
the temple of Poseidon as faithfully as space would allow. The
tree in front of the temple and the Tritons over the angles of
the pediment are certainly taken from the Poseidium. We may
therefore venture to accept the numismatic testimony that the
little temple of Poseidon was not peripteral but either prostyle
or amphiprostyle ; and we may even regard it as probable that
the temple was tetrastyle.

10.—Καὶ ἀγάλματά ἐστιν ἐν τῷ προνάῳ δύο μὲν Ποσειδῶνος,
 κ.τ.λ. Cf. 2, 3, ἐν Λεχαίῳ Ποσειδῶνος ἱερόν, καὶ ἄγαλμα
 χαλκοῦν. 2, 8, κρήνη καὶ Π. ἐπ' αὐτῇ χαλκοῦς.

Head of Poseidon, trident over shoulder.

Æ Auton. B. M. Imh.
 Hadrian. Imh. (**D** LI.)
 M. Aurel. Imh. &c. Overbeck, *K. M.*, Munzt. v. 14.

Poseidon, naked, seated on rock, holds trident.

Æ Auton. Imh. B. M. (**D** LII.)

Poseidon standing, holds dolphin and trident, one foot on rock.

Æ Domitian. B. M. Imh. (**D** LIII.)
 M. Aurel. Turin. Behind Poseidon, tree.
 Sept. Severus. Imh. Behind Poseidon, tree.

Poseidon standing, left foot on dolphin, in right hand trident.

Æ Domitian. Berlin.
Æ Domna. Aplustre in place of trident.

Poseidon seated, holds dolphin and trident.

Æ Trajan. B. M. (**D** LIV.)
 Hadrian. *St. Flor.* pl. II. 16.
 Commodus. Imh. B. M. Pallas standing before him. (**D** LV.)
 Verus. Imh. Victorious athlete before him. (**D** LVI.)

Poseidon standing, holds patera and trident, before altar of
 Melicertes *q. v.*

Æ M. Aurel. Copenhagen. Near by, tree.

Poseidon standing in chariot drawn by two Tritons.

Æ Domitian. Overb. *K. M.* III. pl. VI. 21. Imh. (**D** LVII.)
 Nero. B. M. (**D** LVIII.) Octavia. B. M.

Poseidon standing in chariot drawn by hippocamps.

Æ Nero. B. M. Domitian. Imh. (**D** LIX.)

These figures in chariots may be confronted with Pausanias'
description, II. 1, 7 above quoted, of the group of Poseidon and

Amphitrite in a chariot drawn by four horses. The coins cannot, however, embody a reminiscence of the group, as the date of Herodes is later than that at which they were struck. Of the various figures of Poseidon thus far mentioned the only one which can be regarded as a copy of a statue is that which figures Poseidon as seated (**D** LIV.–VI.), holding dolphin and trident. This type has the air of the cultus-statue of a temple ; but we cannot be sure of the particular temple, for on one coin the seated Poseidon is confronted with an athlete which seems to point to the Isthmus, in another with Pallas, which seems to indicate the market-place. (See below.)

11.—Paus. II. 2, 3. Ἐν δὲ Κεγχρέαις Ἀφροδίτης τέ ἐστι ναὸς καὶ ἄγαλμα λίθου, μετὰ δὲ αὐτὸν ἐπὶ τῷ ἐρύματι τῷ διὰ τῆς θαλάσσης Ποσειδῶνος χαλκοῦν· κατὰ δὲ τὸ ἕτερον πέρας τοῦ λιμένος Ἀσκληπιοῦ καὶ Ἴσιδος ἱερά.

Views of harbour of CENCHREAE, flanked on either side by temple, and containing standing colossus of Poseidon and three ships.

Æ Ant. Pius. Imh. Millingen, *Réc.* pl. II. 19. Vienna. (**D** LX.)

POSEIDON standing naked, holds dolphin and trident.

Æ Auton. B. M. *Obv.* Head of Helios. (**D** LXI.)
Commodus. B. M. At feet of Poseidon, second dolphin. (**D** LXII.)
Plautilla. Vienna. Opposite Poseidon armed Aphrodite. (**D** LXIII.)

ISIS Pharia, holds sail. Cf. II. 4, 6, Isis Pelagia and Aegyptia.
Æ Plotina. Mion. II. 179, 226.
L. Verus. Imh. (**D** LXIV.)

Head of APHRODITE : below, galley inscribed CENCRHEAE.
Æ Nero. B. M. (**D** LXV.)

The coin of Millingen (**D** LX.) is important, as it enables us to identify positively the type of Poseidon represented in the bronze statue of the mole. Poseidon stood erect and naked with a dolphin in one hand and a trident in the other, a figure well adapted for execution in bronze and for a statue of great size. The date of its erection must have been subsequent to the colony of Cæsar ; had it belonged to the old city Mummius would scarcely have spared such a mass of metal. In case of the B. M. coin (**D**. LXII), the second dolphin at the feet of the god may be held to stand for the water of the harbour which flowed at his feet.

The head of Aphrodite on the last coin cited must stand for an abbreviated representation of the temple dedicated to her.

12.—Paus. II. 2, 3. Τὴν δὲ ἐς Κεγχρέας ἰόντων ἐξ Ἰσθμοῦ ναὸς Ἀρτέμιδος καὶ ξόανον ἀρχαῖον. Cf. 3, 5, μετ' αὐτὸν (Poseidon) Ἄρτεμις θηρεύουσα ἔστηκε (in the baths of Eurycles).

ARTEMIS as huntress : holds torch and bow.

Æ Hadrian. Imh.
Hadrian. Arig. I. 95, 41. Dog and stag beside her.
L. Verus. M. II. 185, 271. B. M. Dog and stag beside her. (D LXVI.)
S. Severus. M. S. IV. 113, 770. B. M. Dog and stag beside her.
Commod. Imh. As before.
Hadrian. M. S. IV. 82, 549. Pillar and stag beside her.
Ant. Pius. B. M. Dog running beside her. (D LXVII.)

Artemis hunting, in temple, holds torch and bow.

Æ Sept. Severus. St. Flor. III. 1. Dog and stag beside her.
Plautilla. On either side of temple, tree. R. and F. (D LXVIII.)

Statue of Artemis, her right hand on her hip, in her left a bow ; opposite, Poseidon (?) ; before each a cippus, that of Poseidon surmounted by a dolphin.

Æ Commodus. Imh. (D LXIX.)

The hunting Artemis in **D** LXVIII. must be a copy of a statue in her temple ; not the archaic xoanon, but a later figure such as the Greeks from the fifth century onwards commonly set up in the cella in place of the early statues, still retaining the latter in the background.

The figure in **D** LXIX. would seem to be a copy of the statue which stood in the baths of Eurycles near a statue of Poseidon, and in the neighbourhood of his temple. On the coin the figure of Poseidon is nearly obliterated : it is not indeed certain that Poseidon is the deity represented : the figure seems to wear a long chiton.

13.—Paus. II. 2, 4. Πρὸ δὲ τῆς πόλεως κυπαρίσσων ἐστὶν ἄλσος ὀνομαζόμενον Κράνειον. ἐνταῦθα Βελλεροφόντου τέ ἐστι τέμενος καὶ Ἀφροδίτης ναὸς Μελανίδος. Cf. 2, 8, ἄγαλμα Ἀφροδίτης, Ἑρμογένους Κυθηρίου ποιήσαντος.

APHRODITE standing ; holds sceptre and apple.

Æ Auton. (Obv. Head of Lais ?) Munich.
Sabina. Imh.
Ant. Pius. Mion. II. 181, 242.
M. Aurel. Vienna. (D LXX.)
Caracalla. Imh.
L. Verus. B. M.

Aphrodite naked, her right hand raised to her hair.

Æ Carac. St. Florian. (D LXXI.)

Aphrodite in a biga drawn by Tritons.

Æ Nero. Munich. Holds mirror.
Agrippina, Jun. Turin. (D LXXII.)

Compare the figure of Poseidon in a similar biga mentioned above. In regard to Hermogenes, Brunn remarks (*Gr. Künstler,* I. p. 522) that he must be assigned to the period of Greek autonomy and not to the Roman age. The coins offer us no safe data for further conclusions.

14.—Paus. II. 2, 4. Καὶ τάφος Λαΐδος, ᾧ δὴ λέαινα ἐπίθημά ἐστι κριὸν ἔχουσα ἐν τοῖς προτέροις ποσίν.

The monument of LAÏS; a lioness standing over a prostrate ram, on Doric column.

Æ Auton. *Obv.* Head of Laïs or Aphrodite. B. M. Imh. (E LXXIII.)
  Copenhagen. (E LXXIV.)
  Brera. (E LXXV.)
  St. Florian. (E LXXVI.)
  Sept. Severus. Vienna.
  Geta. Imh.

This identification of the tomb of Laïs the Elder has long been accepted, and is so certain as to be beyond dispute. On a B. M. specimen not here figured Leake read on the capital of the column the letters E Y . . . which he supposes to be an artist's name (Leake, *Supp. Europe,* p. 121). I am inclined to think that the appearance of letters is fallacious, and due merely to the oxidation of the coin. But if we accept Leake's reading it is likely that the word beginning Eu is not an artist's name, for artists did not put their names in so conspicuous a position on monuments, but some heroic name by which Laïs may have been, so to speak, canonised after her death. The name ΕΥΦΡΟΣΥΝΑ would suit the space very well, and there is certainly at the end an appearence of the letters . . . N A, as well as of E Y . . . at the beginning.

The head on the obverse of the coin may be intended either for Aphrodite or for Laïs herself.

15.—Paus. II. 2, 6. Ἔστιν οὖν ἐπὶ τῆς ἀγορᾶς . . . . . . Ἄρτεμίς τε ἐπίκλησιν Ἐφεσία, καὶ κ.τ.λ.

ARTEMIS EPHESIA : archaic simulacrum.

Æ M. Aurel. M. S. IV. 92, 626.
Sep. Severus. M. S. IV. 112, 769. Beside her, Aphrodite holding shield.

16.—Paus. II. 2, 6. Καὶ Διονύσου ξόανα ἐπίχρυσα πλὴν τῶν προσώπων· τὰ δὲ πρόσωπα ἀλοιφῇ σφίσιν ἐρυθρᾷ κεκόσμηται· Λύσιον δέ, τὸν δὲ Βάκχειον ὀνομάζουσι. τὰ δὲ λεγόμενα ἐς τὰ ξόανα καὶ ἐγὼ γράφω.

Bearded DIONYSUS standing to right, fully clad, holds kantharos and thyrsos ; at his feet, panther.

Æ Hadr. Fox. (E LXXVII.)

Young Dionysus, clad in short chiton, holds bunch of grapes
and thyrsos ; at his feet, panther.

Æ Ant. Pius. B. M. (**E** LXXVIII.)

Young Dionysus wearing himation about his loins and leaning
on pillar: holds kantharos and thyrsos; at his feet, panther.

Æ Trajan. Copenhagen. (**E** LXXIX.)

Young Dionysus clad in short chiton ; holds kantharos and
thyrsos.

Æ Aut. *Obv.* Head of Kronos. Copenhagen. (**E** LXXX.)

Young Dionysus seated on throne, holds thyrsos erect.

Æ Ant. Pius. B. M. (**E** LXXXI.)

   Vienna. At his feet, panther. (**E** LXXXII.)

17.—Paus. II. 2, 8. Ἔστι δὲ καὶ Τύχης ναός. ἄγαλμα ὀρθὸν
Παρίου λίθου.

TYCHE standing, holding patera and cornucopiae, in hexastyle
temple ; before her, altar.

Æ Ant. Pius. *St. Florian,* pl. II. 19.

Tyche, holds patera, rudder, &c.

Æ Auton.   M. S. IV. 53, 358.   Holds rudder and patera over altar.
Hadrian.   M. S. IV. 83, 555.   Holds rudder and cornucopiae. ⌋
M. Aurel.   Mion. II. 183, 257.   Holds patera and rudder.
Commodus.   M. S. IV. 111, 756, &c.
Plautilla.   B. M.   Holds patera and cornucopiae. (**E** LXXXIII.)
Plautilla.   B. M.   Seated, holds patera and cornucopiae.
Sept. Sev.   Imh.   Seated. (**E** LXXXIV.)

Head of Tyche, turreted.

Æ Hadrian. Imh. (**E** LXXXV.)

Agathos Daemon : male figure holding cornucopiae.

GEN. COL. COR. Octavia. B. M. See below, (**G** CXLIII.)

The coin first described, that of the St. Florian Collection, is
unfortunately ill-preserved, and Dr. Kenner expresses doubts as
to the deity whom it is intended to represent. Arneth has
described it as Abundantia holding cornucopiae and patera ;
and this is the impression conveyed by the engraving in Kenner's
book. If · so, the figure must certainly be a copy of the statue
of Tyche in her temple. In consequence of the condition of
the coin we cannot be sure as to the attributes given to Tyche ;
they may even be rudder and patera or cornucopiae, as in the
succeeding specimens.

18.—Paus. II. 2, 8. Ἑρμοῦ τέ ἐστιν ἀγάλματα χαλκοῦ μὲν καὶ
ὀρθὰ ἀμφότερα, τῷ δὲ ἑτέρῳ καὶ ναὸς πεποίηται.

HERMES naked, standing.

Æ Hadrian. Six.   Right hand on head of ram, in left caduceus. (**E** LXXXVI.)
Anton. Pius. B. M. Left arm rests on tree, caduceus in right. Imh.
(**E** LXXXVII.)

M. Aurel. *Rev. Belge*, 1865, pl. XVII. 9. As last but one.
Sept. Severus. M. S. IV. 113, 777. Holds purse and caduceus : ram.
Caracalla. M. S. IV. 122, 834. Holds purse, caduceus, and chlamys : ram.
Hermes, clad in chlamys, carrying the child Dionysus on his left arm.
Æ Trajan. Mion. II. 179, 231. (**E** LXXXVIII.)

The coin of Antoninus (**E** LXXXVII.) seems to represent a statue, since the scheme of a figure resting on the trunk of a tree as a support is more appropriate to sculpture than to die-sinking. This figure is remarkable in being entirely nude.

The type of the first coin, (**E** LXXXVI.), is closely like the seated Hermes, of which we shall speak below ; indeed, so like that both would seem to be work of one artist or one school, probably of Imperial times.

19.—Paus. II. 2, 8. Τὰ δὲ (ἀγάλματα) τοῦ Διός, καὶ ταῦτα ὄντα ἐν ὑπαίθρῳ, τὸ μὲν ἐπίκλησιν οὐκ εἶχε, τὸν δὲ αὐτῶν Χθόνιον καὶ τὸν τρίτον καλοῦσιν "Ὕψιστον. Cf. 4, 5, ὑπὲρ δὲ τὸ θέατρόν ἐστιν ἱερὸν Διὸς Καπετωλίου, &c.

ZEUS standing naked : holds thunderbolt and eagle.
Æ Domitian.
Anton. Pius. Imh. (**E** LXXXIX.)
Cf. L. Verus. Mion. II. 184, 266.
Zeus running, naked, holds thunderbolt and eagle.
Æ Auton. B. M. (**E** XC.)
20.—Paus. II. 3, 1. Ἐν μέσῳ δὲ τῆς ἀγορᾶς ἐστὶν Ἀθηνᾶ χαλκῆ.

PALLAS standing, holds thunderbolt in right, shield in left.
Æ Auton. *Obv.* Head of Poseidon. Imh. B. M. (**E** XCI.)
Pallas holding Victory and spear ; shield and owl beside her.
Æ Hadrian. M. S. IV. 81, 543. Imh. (**E** XCII.)
Ant. Pius. M. S. IV. 86, 579/81. Arigoni, &c. Klagenfurt. (**E** XCIII.)
Sept. Sev. M. II. 187, 291. Altar before her.
Plautilla. B. M. Imh. Altar before her.
Sept. Sev. M. S. IV. 112, 767. Owl before her.
Commod. Imh. Pallas holding patera and spear, face to face with seated Poseidon. See above. (**D** LV.)
Head of Pallas, helmeted.
Æ Ant. Pius. M. S. IV. 86, 578. Copenh.

The altar placed before the figure of Pallas, who holds Victory and spear, seems to show that this figure is a copy of a statue.

This same figure in slightly varied form (patera for Victory) is placed on the coin of Commodus in near proximity to Poseidon, which may indicate for the original a locality near the Isthmus, rather than in the agora.

21.—Paus. II. 3, 1. Ὑπὲρ δὲ τὴν ἀγοράν ἐστιν Ὀκταβίας ναὸς ἀδελφῆς Ἀυγούστου.

TEMPLE, facing, inscribed on the frieze CAESAR, AVGVSTVS or GENT. IVLI.

Æ Augustus. Imh. Livia. B. M. Tiberius. B. M. (**E** xciv.) The same temple (?) not inscribed, in profile.

Æ Auton. Imh. (**E** xcv.) Livia or Octavia seated, holds sceptre and patera.

Æ Tiberius. B. M. (**E** xcvi.) Agrippa, Jun. B. M. Head of Roma, turreted.

Æ Aut. *Rev.* Temple, &c. B. M. &c.

It would seem probable from comparison of the coins that the temple described by Pausanias as that of Octavia was really of the Gens Julia. The seated lady holding sceptre and patera may be copied from the statue in this temple. In details it exactly resembles the figure on the coins of Tiberius commonly called Livia, but more probably really standing for a personification of the Gens Julia. Such a personification would naturally take the features of one of the imperial ladies, Livia or Julia or Octavia. If in the Corinthian temple the cultus-statue represented the Gens Julia in the likeness of Octavia, then it would be very natural for any visitor to suppose that the temple was dedicated to Octavia.

22.—Paus. 3, 2. Ἐκ δὲ τῆς ἀγορᾶς ἐξιόντων τὴν ἐπὶ Λεχαίου προπύλαιά ἐστι, καὶ ἐπ᾽ αὐτῶν ἅρματα ἐπίχρυσα, τὸ μὲν Φάεθοντα Ἡλίου παῖδα, τὸ δὲ Ἥλιον αὐτοὶ φέρον.

PROPYLAEA, surmounted by quadrigas, &c.

Æ Augustus.   Mion. II. 172, 185.
Domitian.   Munich.   (**F** xcvii.)
Hadrian.   Mion. II. 179, 230.   (**F** xcviii.)
Ant. Pius.   Imh.   (**F** xcix.)
Commodus.   Imh.   (**F** c.)
M. Aurel.   M. S. IV. 106, 682.   Surmounted by biga.

Helios in quadriga.

Æ Nero.   M. II. 176, 209.
Domitian.   B. M.   (**F** ci.)
L. Verus.   Vienna.   (**F** cii.)
Caracalla.   B. M.

Helios in long chiton, radiate, holds whip.

Æ Verus.   M. II. 184, 269.   Vaillant.

23.—Paus. II. 3, 2. Ἐν δεξιᾷ ἐστιν Ἡρακλῆς χαλκοῦς. Cf. 4, 5, ξόανον γυμνὸν Ἡρακλέους· Δαιδάλου δὲ αὐτό φασιν εἶναι τέχνην.

HERAKLES standing.

Æ M. Aurel. Mion. II. 182, 252, 253. M. S. IV. 96, 653.
Sept. Severus. Mion. II. 187, 253.
Caracalla. B. M. In attitude of Glycon's statue. (F CIII.)

Herakles naked, to left; club and skin in left; right hand raised; to his left, Aphrodite Urania with shield, and Poseidon.

Æ Commodus. Vienna. (F CIV.)

As two of the deities in this group, Poseidon and Aphrodite, are copied from statues, there is a presumption that the third is so also. The figure of Herakles is not very distinct, but it is unclad but for a lion's skin.

24.—Paus. II. 3, 2. Μετὰ δὲ αὐτὸν ἔσοδός ἐστι τῆς Πειρήνης ἐς τὸ ὕδωρ.

PEIRENE, personified as a seated nymph, rests left hand on rock, holds in right, pitcher.

Æ Plautilla. Vienna. (F CV.)
Sept. Severus. B. M. Imh. Behind her, snake erect.
Sept. Severus. Beside rock, dolphin.
Sept. Severus. B. M. Before her, fountain in form of Scylla. (F CVI.)
Plautilla. Vienna. Behind her, snake erect. (F CVII.)
Caracalla. Berlin. Behind her, snake erect.
L. Verus. Mill. Rec. II. 21. Vienna. Before her, Pegasus drinking from fountain; in background, Acrocorinthus. (F CVIII.)
Sept. Severus. B. M. Before her, Pegasus drinking from fountain; in background, Acrocorinthus.

As the figure of Peirene is repeated without variation during several reigns, it is likely that it is copied from a statue which adorned the spring.

25.—Paus. II. 3, 2. Ἔτι γε δὴ καὶ Ἀπόλλωνος ἄγαλμα πρὸς τῇ Πειρήνῃ καὶ περίβολός ἐστιν.

APOLLO, naked, on basis, right elbow rests on term; below, a basin.

Æ Commod. M. S. IV. 106, 721. Berlin. (F CIX.)

In this case there can be little doubt that we have the copy of a statue.

26.—Paus. II. 3, 4. Αὖθις δ' ἰοῦσιν ἐπὶ Λεχαίου τὴν εὐθεῖαν χαλκοῦς καθήμενός ἐστιν Ἑρμῆς, παρέστηκε δέ οἱ κριός.

HERMES SEATED on a rock, caduceus in left, right hand on head of ram beside him.

Æ M. Aurel. M. S. IV. 94, 639. B. M. (F CX.)
L. Verus. Mion. II. 186, 281.
Caracalla. Gréau, 1481.
Sev. Alexander. Rev. Belge, 1865, XVII. 10.

Hermes as above, seated in distyle temple.

Æ Ant. Pius. Mion. II. 181, 246. Imh. (F CXI.)

Hermes with caduceus, seated in round temple, on which
dolphins : on either side of temple a tree.
Æ Domna. Gréau, 1479.

In the coins first described we have an unmistakable copy of
the statue of Hermes. The details of the coin correspond
altogether to the description of Pausanias : and the representation of the temple in which the figure sits completes the
proof.

27.—Paus. II. 3, 5. Κρῆναι δὲ πολλαὶ μέν ἀνὰ τὴν πόλιν
πεποίηνται πᾶσαν . . . . . θέας δὲ μάλιστα ἀξία ἡ παρὰ
τὸ ἄγαλμα τὸ τῆς Ἀρτέμιδος, καὶ ὁ Βελλεροφόντης
ἔπεστι.

ARTEMIS SEATED on a rock, holds bow; before her Belle-
rophon on Pegasus slaying Chimaera. Cf. above, under
Bellerophon.
Æ Caracalla. A. Z. 1843, p'. IX. 13. B. M.

Statues of Artemis seated are quite or almost unknown. It
would therefore seem most reasonable to suppose that the
figure of Artemis on the coin is intended merely to mark the
locality. She is seated not on a throne but on a hill, just as we
should expect in a deity inserted to indicate locality.

28.—FOUNTAINS.
Æ Anton. Pius. M. S. IV. 88, 596. (*Fontana*, II. 2.)
  L. Verus. M. II. 185, 272. Fountain surmounted by Scylla. Imh.
  (F CXII.)
Commodus. Turin. Fountain surmounted by Scylla. (F CXIII.)
Sept. Severus. B. M. Fountain surmounted by Scylla. See above, under
  Peirene.
Domna. M. S. IV. 119, 813. Scylla between fountains.
Commodus. Imh. Basis on which dolphin, his tail supported by rudder.
  (F CXIV.)
  L. Verus. M. II. 185, 276. Seated lion (fountain or tomb). B. M. (F CXV.)

The coins furnish us with the designs of at least four of the
fountains of Corinth : (1) that surmounted by Bellerophon and
Pegasus (see above) ; (2) that surmounted by Scylla ; (3) that
surmounted by dolphin and rudder ; (4) that surmounted by
a lion. We may perhaps add to the list the fountain Peirene, if
it was surmounted by a figure of the nymph of that name.
Probably all these fountains were mere decorative works of
Roman times.

29.—Paus. II. 4, 1. Τοῦ μνήματος δέ ἐστιν οὐ πόρρω Χαλινί-
τιδος Ἀθηνᾶς ἱερόν . . . . . τὸ δὲ ἄγαλμά οἱ τοῦτο ξόανόν
ἐστι, πρόσωπον δὲ καὶ χεῖρες καὶ ἄκροι πόδες εἰσὶ
λευκοῦ λίθου.

NUMISMATIC COMMENTARY ON PAUSANIAS. 25

ATHENE CHALINITIS holding in right hand bridle, in left hand,
spear and shield.
Æ Hadrian.   Imh.   (F cxvi.)
Probably a copy of the temple-statue, Acrolithic statues do
not seem to have been peculiar to any age.
30.—Paus. II. 4, 5.   Πρὸς τούτῳ τῷ γυμνασίῳ (the ancient)
ναοὶ θεῶν εἰσίν, ὁ μὲν Διὸς ὁ δὲ ᾿Ασκληπιοῦ. τὰ δὲ ἀγάλ-
ματα, ᾿Ασκληπιὸς μὲν καὶ ῾Υγίεια λευκοῦ λίθου, κ.τ.λ.
ASKLEPIOS and HYGIEIA (together or separate).
Æ L. Verus.   B. M.   Imh.   Together.   (F cxvii.)
Sabina.   M. II. 180, 237.   Asklepios.
Commodus.   M. S. IV. 106, 724.   Theup.   B. M.   Asklepios.
L. Verus.   M. S. IV. 102, 693.   Hygieia.
Gordian.   M. II. 189, 308.
Asklepios (?) in a temple.
Æ Nero.   M. S. IV. 73, 487.
Temple, with steps ; below these, serpent.
Æ M. Aurel.   M. S. IV. 101, 686.   Arig. II. 7, 72.   Athens.   (F cxviii.)
It cannot be considered certain that this temple *in antis*
beneath which is a snake is that of Asklepios.   It may be
a heroon : indeed from its small size and the curious way in
which it is erected on a basis, this seems likely.   The figure in
the temple on the coin of Nero does not seem to be Asklepios
at all, but an emperor ; on similar coins of the B. M. a figure
clad in a toga is clearly depicted.
31.—Paus. II. 4, 6.   ᾿Ες δὴ τὸν ᾿Ακροκόρινθον τοῦτον ἀνιοῦσίν
ἐστιν ῎Ισιδος τεμένη.
ISIS holding sistrum and vase.
Æ Hadrian.   Arig. I. 95, 39.   Turin.   (F cxix.)
32.—Paus. II. 4, 7.   ῾Υπὲρ τοῦτο Μητρὸς θεῶν ναός ἐστι.
CYBELE seated, lion beside her.
Æ Anton. Pius.   M. S. IV. 85, 576.
M. Aurel.   Imh.   (F cxx.)
Domna.   Imh.
33.—Paus. II. 5, 1.   ᾿Ανελθοῦσι δὲ ἐς τὸν ᾿Ακροκόρινθον ναός
ἐστιν ᾿Αφροδίτης, ἀγάλματα δὲ αὐτή τε ὡπλισμένη καὶ
῎Ηλιος καὶ ῎Ερως ἔχων τόξον.
APHRODITE, naked to waist, holds shield, sometimes with Eros.
Æ Auton.   *Obv.* Head of Aphrodite.   B. M.   Eros behind her.   (G cxxi.)
Hadrian.   M. II. 179, 232.   Without Eros.
M. Aurel.   Imh.   Without Eros.
M. Aurel.   M. S. IV. 94, 635.   Arig.   Eros beside her.
L. Verus.   M. II. 185, 273.   Imh.   Eros beside her.   (G cxxii.)
Commodus.   B. M.   Imh.   Eros beside her.   (G cxxiii.)
Commodus.   M. S. IV. 107, 725.   Two Erotes by her.
Plautilla.   B. M.   Two Erotes by her.   (G cxxiv.)

Aphrodite on ACROCORINTHUS, without temple.

Æ Plautilla. B. M. Laynes. (**G** cxxv.)

Aphrodite in temple on Acrocorinthus.

Æ Anton. Pius. M. S. IV. 87, 588. Arig. Tetrastyle temple.
Hadrian. Parma. Tetrastyle temple.
L. Verus. B. M. (**G** cxxvi.) S. Severus. B. M. Tetrastyle temple.
M. Aurel. M. II. 182, 255. Distyle temple.
M. Aurel. M. S. IV. 94, 634—636. Distyle temple, with Eros.
S. Severus. M. S. IV. 113, 773. Arig. Distyle temple.

Acropolis rock ; Pegasus flying above it.

Æ Claudius. M. II. 175, 202. (**G** cxxvii.)

Temple on Acrocorinthus.

Æ Claudius. M. II. 172, 187. Imh. (**G** cxxviii.)
Hadrian. M. II. 179, 229. B. M. (**G** cxxix.)
M. Aurel. M. S. IV. 101, 687. B. M. At foot, buildings and trees.
(**G** cxxx.) Arolsen. (**G** cxxxi.)
L. Verus. M. S. IV. 104, 710. Mill. *Réc.* II. 20. At foot, tree ; Pegasus
flying. Naples. (**G** cxxxii.)
Commodus. M. S. IV. 102, 765. Imh. At foot, tree ; Pegasus flying.
(**G** cxxxiii.)

Aphrodite on Acrocorinthus, between two harbours (cf. above).

Æ S. Severus. B. M. Vienna. (**G** cxxxiv.)

Aphrodite Urania and Poseidon. See Poseidon.

Æ M. Aurel. M. S. IV. 94, 637.
Plautilla. Vienna.

Aphrodite and Herakles.

Æ M. Aurel. M. S. IV. 94, 638. Arig.
Commodus. M. S. IV. 109, 739. Arig. Eros between them. *St. Flor.* I. 18.

Aphrodite, Poseidon, and Herakles (see above).

Æ Commodus. M. S. IV. 107, 728. Theup. Vienna.

This important series of coins furnishes complete proof, as
Imhoof has pointed out more than once (see *Monn. Grec.* p. 158),
of the type of the statue of Aphrodite which stood on the
Corinthian acropolis. The figure of armed Aphrodite which
existed there under the Empire was no archaic figure of
an armed goddess, such as the Syrian Astarte, but an unmistakable Greek Aphrodite, using the shield of Ares as a
mirror. This is a motive natural to Roman rather than to
Greek art, and we may be almost sure that the statue does not
date from an earlier period than that of Julius Cæsar. Indeed
to his time it would be peculiarly appropriate, considering his
descent and pretensions.

Imhoof has also observed that Lenormant's idea that the
helmeted head on the early autonomous coins of Corinth is that
of the armed Aphrodite must be given up, seeing that
Pausanias is the only writer who speaks of a statue of armed

Aphrodite at Corinth, and it is certain that the figure seen by him was not helmeted : there is, therefore, no evidence of the existence at Corinth of a helmeted Aphrodite.

The type of Aphrodite herself is fixed and scarcely varies ; no doubt it reproduces the exact scheme of the statue. But the figure or figures of Eros which appear beside her seem to be mere attributes, as they hold wreaths and not bows.

The temple of Aphrodite is represented sometimes as tetrastyle sometimes as hexastyle, sometimes as prostyle and sometimes as peripteral : all of which proves that in matters of architectural detail coins are not trustworthy.

34.—OTHER TYPES at Corinth.

Kronos standing, holds sickle.

Ant. Pius. Paris. (G cxxxv.)

Head of Kronos, sickle over shoulder.

Auton. Copenhagen.

Hephaestus, naked to waist, tongs in left hand.

M. Aur. Imh. (G cxxxvi.)

Ares to right, holding spear and trophy.

M. Aur. Copenhagen. (G cxxxvii.)

Triptolemus on winged car drawn by serpents.

Auton. M. ii. 169, 162. (G cxxxviii.)

Male figure seated (Populus), clad in himation, inscribed POPVL . COL . COR.

Verus. Paris. (G cxxxix.)

Military female figure (Achaia ?) seated on rock, holds spear and sword ; in front, ears of corn.

Geta. Imh. (G cxl.)

Victory flying to left.

M. Aurel. Récanier. (G cxli.)

Victory facing.

Augustus. Imh. (G cxlii.)

Male figure, Genius, holds patera and cornucopiae, inscribed GEN . COL . COR.

Auton. B. M. (G cxliii.)

Palm tree within inclosure.

Ant. Pius. Munich. Imh. L. Verus. B. M. (G cxliv.)

The following in Mionnet seem to be some of the above types wrongly described; Eros in quadriga; Pan holding pedum; Pharos and ship ; Head of Indian Dionysus; Cadmus attacking serpent, (see under Argos—Opheltes.)

Some of the types proper to Corinth are repeated on the
coins of other cities. For instance, the seated Hermes, and
the Aphrodite of the Acropolis, are repeated on the coins of
Patrae. In the same way the Corinthian coins repeat the
Argive type of Opheltes.

SICYON.

1.—Paus. II. 7, 2. Αὐτοὶ δὲ Σικυώνιοι τὰ πολλὰ ἐοικότι
τρόπῳ θάπτουσι. τὸ μὲν σῶμα γῇ κρύπτουοι, λίθου δὲ
ἐποικοδομήσαντες κρηπῖδα κίονας ἐφιστᾶσι, καὶ ἐπ᾽
αὐτοῖς ἐπίθημα ποιοῦσι κατὰ τοὺς ἀετοὺς μάλιστα τοὺς
ἐν τοῖς ναοῖς.

TOMB (ναΐδιον) on basis, between two terminal figures and two
cypresses.

Æ S. Severus.   Mion. S. IV. 169, 1123.
  Caracalla.   Imh.
  Plautilla.   Allier, pl. VI. 15.   B. M.   (**H** I.)
  Caracalla (without and with cypresses).   Imh.   (**H** II.)

The design of the coin illustrates very well the words of
Pausanias. Below, we see a basis or pedestal, apparently round ;
on it, four pillars erected, supporting an aëtoma. In the midst
there seems to be a statue. It does not appear, either from
Pausanias' words, or from the coin, that the ναΐδιον on the
pedestal had walls : rather it would seem that the roof rested
on pillars only. The terminal figures on the coin may represent
smaller tombs, or they may define the bounds of a temenos. The
cypress was sacred to Hades : see Lajard, *Culte du Cyprès*,
p. 231.

2.—Paus. II. 7, 5. Ἐν δὲ τῇ νῦν ἀκροπόλει Τύχης ἱερόν ἐστιν
Ἀκραίας, μετὰ δὲ αὐτὸ Διοσκούρων. ξόανα δὲ οὗτοί τε
καὶ τὸ ἄγαλμα τῆς Τύχης ἐστί.

TYCHE AKRAIA, standing, with patera and cornucopiae.

Æ J. Domna.   M. S. IV. 170, 1127.
  Plautilla.   B. M.   (**H** III.)
  Geta.   M. S. IV. 173, 1146.   Imh.   (With altar.)

3.—Paus. II. 7, 5. Μετὰ δὲ τὸ θέατρον Διονύσου ναός ἐστι·
χρυσοῦ μὲν καὶ ἐλέφαντος ὁ θεός, παρὰ δὲ αὐτὸν Βάκχαι
λίθου λευκοῦ.

DIONYSUS standing, holds kantharos and thyrsus, panther at
his feet.

Æ Domitian.   M. S. IV. 169, 1122.
  S. Severus.   (**H** IV.)
  Domna.   B. M.   (**H** V.)
  Caracalla.   M. S. IV. 170, 1133.   Wiczay.

BACCHA or Maenad in attitude of ecstasy, holds knife.

Æ J. Domna. B. M. (H vi.) Imh. (H vii.)

4.—Paus. II. 7, 8. Οἱ δὲ παῖδας ἑπτὰ καὶ ἴσας παρθένους
ἐπὶ τὸν Σύθαν ποταμὸν ἀποστέλλουσιν ἱκετεύοντας
(yearly ceremony).

SUPPLIANT BOY (?) with raised hands, holding stemma.

Æ Autonomous. B. M. ℛ Alexander the Great. B. M.
J. Domna. Turin. (H viii.)
Plautilla. B. M. (H ix.)

This figure, the attribution of which is doubtful, has greatly
perplexed numismatists. It has been called hitherto a bird
catcher, or, as by Müller (Alex. le Gr. p. 219), Apollo in dancing
attitude, holding up taenia. In numismatics the type is
peculiar to Sicyon: and as it recurs without variation from
the time of Alexander the Great to that of Plautilla, it must
almost certainly repeat a Sicyonian work of art.

5.—Paus. II. 7, 9. Τῷ Ἀπόλλωνι . . . . . τὸν δὲ ἐπ᾽ ἐμοῦ
ναὸν καὶ τὸ ἄγαλμα Πυθοκλῆς ἀνέθηκεν (cf. 9, 7, ruined
temple of Apollo Lycius: 10, 2, adytum of Apollo
Carneius).

APOLLO in citharoedic dress, holding lyre.

Æ Domna. Leake, Suppl. 145.
Plautilla. M. II. 200, 381.
Caracalla. M. S. IV. 171, 1135. Theup. and Sestini.

It seems not improbable that the Pythocles here mentioned,
who is evidently regarded by Pausanias as a well-known man,
is the same as the Pythocles mentioned by Pliny (N. H. XXXIV.
51) as a famous artist of the period after Ol. 156. This clue
would be of value if we could be sure that the coin reproduced
a statue of Pythocles : but this cannot be proved.

6.—Paus. II. 9, 6. Τῆς δὲ ἀγορᾶς ἐστὶν ἐν τῷ ὑπαίθρῳ Ζεὺς
χαλκοῦς, τέχνη Λυσίππου. Cf. ἔστι δὲ Ζεὺς Μειλίχιος
. . . . σὺν τέχνῃ πεποιημένα οὐδεμιᾷ.

ZEUS standing, undraped ; holds thunderbolt and sceptre.

Æ Caracalla. B. M. (H x.)

Zeus seated, holding patera and sceptre.

Æ Geta. M. S. IV. 172, 1143. Vaillant.

The standing figure of Zeus would certainly well suit the
school of Lysippus : it belongs to group 11 of Overbeck's
arrangement (Kunstmyth., II. p. 151). Zeus is entirely undraped,
and of a scheme which especially befits bronze. If the Sicyonian
statue of Zeus Meilichius was a copy of that of Argos, it must

have been seated, like the second type here cited. See below under Argos.

7.—Paus. II. 10, 1. Ἐν δὲ τῷ γυμνασίῳ τῆς ἀγορᾶς ὄντι οὐ μακρὰν Ἡρακλῆς ἀνάκειται λίθου, Σκόπα ποίημα. Ἔστι δὲ καὶ ἑτέρωθι ἱερὸν Ἡρακλέους.

HERAKLES standing, holds apples (?) and club ; lion's skin over left arm.

Æ Geta. B. M. (**H** XI.)

The figure of Herakles on the coin is unfortunately indistinct : but the deity seems to be unbearded, and of somewhat slight build.

8.—Paus. II. 10, 2. Ἐς δὲ τὸ Ἀσκληπιεῖον ἐσιοῦσι . . . . . . τῇ μὲν Πανὸς καθήμενον ἄγαλμά ἐστι (cf. 11, 1, βωμὸς Πανὸς).

PAN walking, holds goblet, and goat by the horns.

Æ Plautilla. Imh. (**H** XII.)

9.—Paus. II. 10, 2. Τὸ Ἀσκληπιεῖον . . . . . . ἐσελθοῦσι δὲ ὁ θεός ἐστιν οὐκ ἔχων γένεια, χρυσοῦ καὶ ἐλέφαντος, Καλάμιδος δὲ ἔργον· ἔχει δὲ καὶ σκῆπτρον, καὶ ἐπὶ τῆς ἑτέρας χειρὸς πίτυος καρπὸν τῆς ἡμέρου. Cf. 11, 6, Statue of Hygieia (archaic).

ASKLEPIOS standing, with usual attributes.

Æ Caracalla. M. S. IV. 170, 1131. (Vaill.)
Domna. (**H** XIII.)

Hygieia standing.

Æ Geta. M. II. 201, 382. B. M. (**H** XIV.)

10.—Paus. II. 10, 4. Μετὰ τοῦτο ἤδη τὸ τῆς Ἀφροδίτης ἐστὶν ἱερόν . . . . . . τὸ μὲν δὴ ἄγαλμα καθήμενον Κάναχος Σικυώνιος ἐποίησεν . . . . . πεποίηνται δὲ ἔκ τε χρυσοῦ καὶ ἐλέφαντος, φέρουσα ἐπὶ τῇ κεφαλῇ πόλον· τῶν χειρῶν δε ἔχει τῇ μὲν μήκωνα τῇ δὲ ἑτέρᾳ μῆλον.

APHRODITE standing, in attitude of Venus de' Medici.

Æ S. Severus. Bologna. Beside her Eros on basis, holding torch. (**H** XV.)
Domna. Arch. Z. 1869. pl. XXIII. 7. Imh. Beside her dolphin. (**H** XVI.)

DOVE.

Æ Auton. B. M.

11.—Paus. II. 10, 7. Ἐν δεξιᾷ Φεραίας ἱερὸν Ἀρτέμιδος· κομισθῆναι δὲ τὸ ξόανον λέγουσιν ἐκ Φερῶν. Cf. 9, 6, Artemis Patroa ; 7, 6, Artemis Limnaea ; 10, 2, τῇ δὲ Ἄρτεμις ἔστηκεν.

ARTEMIS, clad in long chiton and mantle, with torches in her raised hands.

Æ Geta. Dresden. (**H** XVII.) Imh. (**H** XVIII.)

Similar figure, in temple.

Æ Caracalla. Paris. (**H** xix.)

There can be little doubt that we have in this figure a copy of the statue which stood in the temple of Artemis Pheraea. We are told that it was brought from Pherae. The coins of Pherae, from the fourth century onwards, present us with a female figure holding two torches or one torch, which may be meant for Artemis, but more probably represents Hecate, a deity greatly worshipped in the south of Thessaly. But the distinction is not important, as the torch-bearing Artemis and Hecate are closely allied.

12.—Paus. II. 11, 2. Καταβαίνουσι δὲ ὡς ἐπὶ τὸ πεδίον ἱερόν ἐστιν ἐνταῦθα Δήμητρος· ἱδρῦσαι δέ φασιν αὐτὸ Πλημναῖον.

DEMETER seated on throne, wears polos, holds ears of corn in each hand.

Æ Sep. Severus. Imh. (**H** xx.)

The throned figure of the coins has much of the air of the cultus statue of a temple.

13.—Paus. II. 11, 1. Ναός ἐστιν Ἀθηνᾶς (cf. 12, 1, Temple of Athene at Titane).

PALLAS standing ; holds lance and buckler.

Æ Caracalla. M. S. IV. 170, 1130. Vaill.

14.—OTHER TYPES :

Serapis and Cerberus.
Eros with torch.
Nike.

PHLIUS.

1.—Paus. II. 12, 4. Ἀσωπὸς .... ἐξεῦρε τοῦ ποταμοῦ τὶ ὕδωρ.

Butting BULL (type of river or of Dionysus, see below).

Ӕ Auton. B. M. (**H** i.)

2.—Paus. II. 13, 3. Τὴν δὲ θεὸν ἧς ἐστὶ τὸ ἱερὸν οἱ μὲν ἀρχαιότατοι Φλιασίων Γανυμήδαν, οἱ δὲ ὕστερον Ἥβην ὀνομάζουσιν.

Head of HEBE (?), hair rolled.

Ӕ Auton. B. M. (**H** i.)

This attribution is not certain, but highly probable. The character of Hebe's head is not unlike that of Hera, but younger and less dignified. She wears no ornaments, but her hair is simply rolled at the back.

3.—Paus. II. 13, 5. Ἔστι γὰρ καὶ Ἀρτέμιδος ἐνταῦθα χαλκοῦν
    ἄγαλμα, ὃ ἐφαίνετο ἀρχαῖον εἶναί μοι.
ARTEMIS hunting, with dog.
Æ Geta.   Rev. Belge, 1860, pl. II. 9.
4.—Paus. II. 13, 5. Κατιόντων δὲ ἐκ τῆς ἀκροπόλεώς ἐστιν
    Ἀσκληπιοῦ ναὸς ἐν δεξιᾷ, καὶ ἄγαλμα οὐκ ἔχον πω γένεια.
ASKLEPIOS standing, bearded, with attributes.
Æ S. Severus.   M. S. IV. 159, 1044.   Journ. of Hell. Stud. iv. 50.
Caracalla.   M. II. 198, 368.
5.—Paus. II. 13, 7. Διονύσου σφίσιν ἱερόν ἐστιν ἀρχαῖον.
Bull butting (Dionysus ?). Ivy : grapes.
Æ Auton.   B. M.
Head of Dionysos.   Rev., Bull butting and thyrsos.
Æ Auton.   Imh.
6.—OTHER TYPE.   Tyche sacrificing at altar : holds patera and
    cornucopiae.
Æ Plautilla.   B. M.   Sept. Sev.   Geta.

CLEONAE.

1.—Paus. II. 15, 1.   Ἐνταῦθά ἐστιν ἱερὸν Ἀθηνᾶς, τὸ δὲ
    ἄγαλμα Σκύλλιδος τέχνη καὶ Διποίνου.
ATHENE standing, holds lance and shield (archaic).
Æ Geta.   M. II. 237, 58.   B. M.   (H I.)   Cf. Caved. Spic. 105.

The Athene of the coin seems an interesting record of the
archaic statue of Dipoenus and Scyllis, whom Pliny gives to the
50th Olympiad, and who were among the first to produce
national Greek types of various divinities.   The present coin-
type represents a figure of Athene retaining the pose of the still
older Palladia, but far more refined in detail.   The helmet is
larger, the aegis on the breast worked out ; folds appear in the
chiton, and the feet are articulate.

2.—OTHER TYPES :
            Eagle on altar.   (See Argos.)
            Asklepios seated with dog (cf. Epidaurus).
            Isis, holds sistrum and vase.
            Plautilla.   B. M.
            Isis Pharia.
            Carac.   St. Flor. pl. III. 19.
            Tyche, holds patera and cornucopiae, at altar.
            Plautilla.   B. M.   (H II.)
            Artemis accompanied by hound.
            Horse ridden by human head.
            Domna.   B. M.

NEMEA. (Coins of Argos.)

1.—Paus. II. 15, 2. Ἐν τούτοις τοῖς ὄρεσι τὸ σπήλαιον ἔτι δείκνυται τοῦ λέοντος.

HERAKLES strangling the Nemean lion.

Æ Trajan. M. S. IV. 240, 27.
Sept. Severus. M. II. 235, 48.
Domna. Leake, p. 20. (I I.)

2.—Paus. II. 15, 2. Τὸν Ὀφέλτην ἐνταῦθα ὑπὸ τῆς τροφοῦ τεθέντα ἐς τὴν πόαν διαφθαρῆναι λέγουσιν ὑπό τοῦ δράκοντος . . . . . .ἐνταῦθα ἔστι μὲν Ὀφέλτου τάφος.

OPHELTES, the serpent, and Hypsipyle.

Æ Hadrian. Arch. Z. 1869, pl. XXIII. 12. Hypsipyle, and serpent twined around Opheltes.
Anton. Pius. Imh. Opheltes in coils of serpent. (I II.)
L. Verus. L.c. No. 13. Nurse, a hero, and Opheltes lying dead ; also serpent.
S. Severus. M. Fontana, I. pl. II. 18. Hero fighting snake, Opheltes on the ground. B. Turin. (I III.)
J. Domna. B. M. Hypsipyle flying, snake twined around Opheltes. (I IV.)
Plautilla. A. Z. 1869, No. 11. Serpent coiled over dead Opheltes. Imh. (I V.)
Domna. Munich. Naked male figure, facing ; at his feet Opheltes, to right, snake. (I VI.)
Also Æ of CORINTH. Domitian. Mill. An. G. C. pl. IV. 14. Hero fighting serpent, who holds Opheltes in mouth. Imh. (I VII.)
S. Severus. Mill. An. G. C. pl. IV. 16. Similar. Imh. (I VIII.)
Caracalla. Fox. Hero fighting snake, beneath whom Opheltes, Hypsipyle fleeing. (I IX.)

The variety in the types representing the fate of Opheltes is remarkable, and seems to prove that at Argos the subject was a favourite one with artists. For illustrations of the subject from vases, &c., see Overbeck's *Heroische Bildwerke*. Some of the above-described coins are published by Dr. Friedlander in the *Archäol. Zeitung* for 1869.

3.—Paus. II. 15, 3. Καὶ δὴ καὶ δρόμου προτιθέασιν ἀγῶνα ἀνδράσιν ὡπλισμένοις Νεμείων πανηγύρει τῶν χειμερινῶν.

Symbols of NEMEAN GAMES (also Heraea, cf. Paus. II. 24, 2).

Æ Anton. Pius. M. II. 234, 44. Imh. NEMEIA HPAIA. Table, peacock, and eagle.

Anton. Pius. Leake, *Suppl.* 114. NEMEIA in parsley crown.
M. Aurelius. Verus. Commodus. S. Severus. Domna. As last.
Domna. Table, on which eagle, wreath, and owl.

4.—Paus. II. 15, 3. Ὄρος Ἀπέσας ἐστὶν ὑπὲρ τὴν Νεμέαν, ἔνθα Περσέα πρῶτον Διὶ θῦσαι λέγουσιν Ἀπεσαντίῳ.

Symbol of Zeus on MOUNT APESAS. (Coins of CLEONAE.)

Æ S. Severus. Hill, on which a cippus or altar, surmounted by an eagle. *Mus. Sanclem.* N. S. II. pl. xxv. No. 219.

Domna.   Mus. Arig. I. *Impp.* VIII. 13.   Similar.
Geta.   Mus. Arig. I. *Impp.* IX. 137.   Similar.
Herakles clad in lion's skin, resting at the foot of Mount Apesas,
on the summit of which is an eagle.   (Coin of ARGOS.)
Æ Sept. Sev.   Berlin.   (I x.)

HERAEUM near Argos.   (Argive coins.)

5.—Paus. II. 17, 3.   'Εν δὲ τῷ προνάῳ τῇ μὲν Χάριτες ἀγάλματά ἐστιν ἀρχαῖα.
The three CHARITES, naked, embracing one another (conventional group).
Æ Sept. Severus.   Imh.   (I xi.)

6.—Paus. II. 17, 4.   Τὸ δὲ ἄγαλμα τῆς "Ηρας ἐπὶ θρόνου
κάθηται μεγέθει μέγα, χρυσοῦ μὲν καὶ ἐλέφαντος,
Πολυκλείτου δὲ ἔργον· ἔπεστι δὲ οἱ στέφανος Χάριτας
ἔχων καὶ "Ωρας ἐπειργασμένας, καὶ τῶν χειρῶν τῇ μὲν
καρπὸν φέρει ῥοιᾶς, τῇ δὲ σκῆπτρον . . . . . κόκκυγα δὲ
ἐπὶ τῷ σκήπτρῳ καθῆσθαί φασι, κ.τ.λ.
HERA SITTING, holds pomegranate and sceptre, turreted.
Æ Anton. Pius.   B. M.   Mion. S. IV. 242, 43.   (I xii.)
L. Verus.   B. M.   Also Sept. Severus and Caracalla.
Domna.   Overbeck, *K. M. Hera,* pl. III. 3.   Imh.   (I xiii.)
Head of Hera, wearing stephanos adorned with flowers.
R Æ Autonomous.   B. M.   Imh.   (I xiv.)

Paus. II. 17, 5.   Λέγεται δὲ παρεστηκέναι τῇ "Ηρᾳ τέχνη
Ναυκύδους ἄγαλμα "Ηβης.
HERA and HEBE, peacock between them (cf. below).
Æ Anton. Pius.   Overbeck, *Hera,* pl. III. 1.   Imh.   (I xv.)
The coins reproduce faithfully the details of the statue of
Polycleitus, even, in some instances, to the cuckoo on her sceptre
(I xii.).   They are fully discussed in Overbeck's *Kunstmythologie*
(II. p. 43).   It is elsewhere suggested (Gardner, *Coins of Elis,*
p. 19) that the flowers with which the stephanos of Hera is
adorned on I xiv. are an abridged symbol of the Horae and
Charites whose figures were introduced in the same place by
Polycleitus.
The statue of Naucydes is also repeated on the coin, a
standing figure with one hand advanced, clad in long chiton.

7.—Paus. II. 17, 6.   Χρυσοῦ δὲ καὶ λίθων λαμπόντων Ἀδριανὸς
βασιλεὺς ταὼν ἀνέθηκεν.
PEACOCK (see above).
Æ Hadrian.   B. M.   Peacock facing, tail spread.   (I xvi.)
Gordian III.   Salonina.   B. M.   Imh.   Peacock to right.

G 2

The peacock on Hadrian's coin is probably a copy of his anathema: that on the later coin may be a merely conventional representation.

ARGOS.

8.—Paus. II. 18, 1, Ἐκ Μυκηνῶν δὲ ἐς "Αργος ἐρχομένοις ἐν ἀριστερᾷ Περσέως παρὰ τὴν ὁδόν ἐστιν ἡρῷον.

PERSEUS standing, holding Gorgoneion in right, harpa and chlamys in left.

Æ Hadrian. Imh. (**I** XVII.)
L. Verus. B. M. (**I** XVIII.) Also Mion. *S.* IV. 246, 66.
Sept. Severus. B. M. Also Mion. *S.* IV. 249, 86.
Valerianus. M. S. IV. 255, 124.

Perseus facing, holds in right harpa, in left Gorgoneion, above shield, which rests on cippus.

S. Severus. Imh. (**I** XIX.)
S. Severus. Imh. *Choix*, pl. II. 67. To right, Pallas turning away. (**I** XX.)

Head of Perseus, winged ; in front, harpa.

Æ Ant. Pius. Venice. (**I** XXI.)

The type of Perseus (**I** XVII. XVIII), which is repeated without variation from the time of Hadrian to that of Severus, should be copied from a statue.

9.—Paus. 19, 3. Ἀργείοις δ᾽ τῶν ἐν τῇ πόλει τὸ ἐπιφανέστατόν ἐστιν Ἀπόλλωνος ἱερὸν Λυκίου· τὸ μὲν οὖν ἄγαλμα τὸ ἐφ᾽ ἡμῶν Ἀττάλου ποίημα ἦν Ἀθηναίου (cf. Brunn, *Gr. Künstler*, I. p. 558 ; Attalus' date is unknown).

APOLLO, naked, left arm resting on pillar, in right, twig (Lycius ?)

Æ Verus. M. S. IV. 245, 63.

Cf. Paus. II. 19, 8. Ἐπὶ τούτοις ἐστὶν Ἀπόλλων Ἀγυιεύς.

24, 1. Ναὸς Ἀπόλλωνος .... τὸ δὲ ἄγαλμα τὸ νῦν χαλκοῦν ἐστιν ὀρθὸν, Δειραδιώτης Ἀπόλλων καλούμενος.

Apollo advancing, naked, drawing arrow from quiver.

Æ M. Aurel. M. II. 235, 45.

Apollo in Citharoedic costume.

Æ Verus. B. M. Holds lyre and patera. (**I** XXII.)
S. Severus. M. S. IV. 247, 76. Holds lyre and plectrum.
Caracalla. Imh. Holds lyre and plectrum. (**I** XXIII)
Plautilla. Sest. *Mus. Hed.* p. 137, 40. Holds lyre and plectrum.
J. Domna. M. S. IV. 251, 102. Holds lyre and patera.
Plautilla. Imh. Holds lyre and patera. (**I** XXIV.)

Head of Apollo : Wolf : tripod.

Æ Auton. B. M.

10.—Paus. II. 19, 4-7. Βόθρος, πεποιημένα ἐν τύπῳ ταύρου μάχην ἔχων καὶ λύκου, σὺν δὲ αὐτοῖς παρθένον ἀφιεῖσαν πέτραν ἐπὶ τὸν ταῦρον.

Battle of bull and wolf.

Æ Auton. Imh. *Böotien u. Argos*, p. 55, No. 17.

11.—Paus. II. 20, 1. Ἄγαλμά ἐστι καθήμενον Διὸς Μειλιχίου, λίθου λευκοῦ, Πολυκλείτου δὲ ἔργον. Cf. 19, 7. Διὸς ξόανον. 19, 8. Βωμὸς Ὑετίου Διός. 20, 6. Διὸς ἱερὸν Σωτῆρος. 21, 2. Δι᾽ς Φυξίου βωμός. 22, 2. Ἄγαλμα ἀρχαῖον Διός. 24, 3. Ἐπ᾽ ἄκρᾳ δὲ ἐστι τῇ Λαρίσῃ Διὸς ἐπίκλησιν Λαρισαίου ναός . . . . τὸ δε ἄγαλμα ξύλου, κ.τ.λ. . . . . ἐνταῦθα ἀναθήματα κεῖται καὶ ἄλλα καὶ Ζεὺς ξόανον, δύο μὲν ᾗ πεφύκαμεν ἔχον ὀφθαλμούς, τρίτον δὲ ἐπὶ τοῦ μετώπου.

ZEUS seated, holds patera and sceptre.

Æ Anton. Pius.   M. S. IV. 242, 42.
M. Aurelius.   M. S. IV. 244, 55.
L. Verus.   (**K** XXV.)

Zeus seated, holds eagle or Victory.

Æ Sept. Severus.   Holds eagle.
Plautilla.   Holds victory.   Mion. II. 235, 50.   (**K** XXVI.)

Zeus striding, naked, holds eagle and thunderbolt.

Æ Plautilla.   M. S. IV. 253, 112.   Sestini.

Head of Zeus.

Æ Hadrian.   M. S. IV. 240, 28.   Imh.   (**K** XXVII.)
L. Verus.   M. S. IV. 245, 58.

Paus. II. 20, 3. Τούτων δ᾽ ἀπαντικρὺ Νεμείου Διός ἐστιν ἱερὸν, ἄγαλμα ὀρθὸν χαλκοῦν, τέχνη Λυσίππου.

Zeus, naked, standing, sceptre in right hand : eagle at his feet.

Æ Hadrian.   B. M.
M. Aurelius.   Imh.   (**K** XXVIII.)
Sept. Severus.   B. M. &c.
J. Domna.   M. S. IV. 251, 99.   Plautilla.   M. S. IV. 253, 113.

The number of statues of Zeus at Argos is so large that it is not possible to be sure whether we have copies of any of them on coins. It is possible that the type first described (**K** XXV.) may reproduce the figure of the Zeus Meilichius; and the type of the head of Zeus is decidedly fine and early; we may suspect it to be a reminiscence of the head of Polycleitus' statue. With more confidence we may suppose that the standing Zeus of the coins (**K** XXVIII.) is a copy of Lysippus' statue; for in this case the coin-type persists practically unchanged through several reigns.

But in all these cases the evidence of copying is internal rather than external; we therefore prefer to leave the matter for future discussion.

12.—Paus. II. 20, 3. Πέραν δὲ τοῦ Νεμείου Διὸς Τύχης ἐστὶν ἐκ παλαιοτάτου ναός, εἰ δὴ, &c.

TYCHE standing, holds cornucopiae.

Æ Auton. Third century, B.C. B. M. Holds patera and cornucopiae. (K xxix.)
M. Aurelius. Imh. Holds patera and cornucopiae.
L. Verus. M. S. IV. 246, 65. Holds patera and cornucopiae.
S. Severus. M. II. 235, 47. Holds patera and cornucopiae. At her feet altar.
Domna. Imh. Geta. M. II. 236, 51. Holds patera and cornucopiae.
Domna. Rev. Belge, 1860, pl. II. 12. Holds rudder and cornucopiae.
Caracalla. Imh. Turreted, holding sceptre and cornucopiae. (K xxx.)

Head of Tyche, turreted.

Æ Ant. Pius. M. II. 234, 41. (K xxxi.)
M. Aurelius. M. S. IV. 244, 57.

13.—Paus. II. 19, 6. Τὰ δὲ ξόανα Ἀφροδίτης καὶ Ἑρμοῦ, τὸ μὲν Ἐπειοῦ λέγουσιν ἔργον εἶναι, κ.τ.λ. Cf. 19, 7. Καὶ Ἑρμῆς ἐς λύρας ποίησιν χελώνην ἡρκώς.

HERMES standing, right arm resting on trunk of tree, in left caduceus and chlamys.

Æ Sept. Severus. Imh. (K xxxii.) Florence. (K xxxiii.)

Apparently a copy of a statue.

14.—Paus. II. 20, 3. Πλησίον δέ εἰσιν ἐπειργασμένοι λίθῳ Κλέοβις καὶ Βίτων, αὐτοί τε ἕλκοντες τὴν ἅμαξαν καὶ ἐπ' αὐτῇ ἄγοντες τὴν μητέρα ἐς τὸ Ἡραῖον.

CLEOBIS and BITON drawing their mother in a chariot.

Æ Domna. Copenhagen. (K xxxiv.)
Plautilla. Arch. Z. 1869, pl. 23, 9.

Dr. Friedländer has already (Archäol. Zeit. 1869, p. 98) brought this numismatic type into connexion with the words of Pausanias. But various treatments of the group may, of course, have been familiar to the die-sinker, and there is nothing to prove that he copied the relief seen by the Traveller.

15.—Paus. II. 21, 1. Ἔστι δὲ ναὸς Ἀσκληπιοῦ. Cf. 23, 4 below.

ASKLEPIOS standing, with usual attributes.

Æ Sept. Severus. Imh. (K xxxv.)

16.—Paus. II. 21, 9. Τὸ δὲ ἱερὸν τῆς Λητοῦς ἔστι μὲν οὐ μακρὰν τοῦ τροπαίου, τέχνη δὲ τὸ ἄγαλμα Πραξιτέλους· τὴν δὲ εἰκόνα παρὰ τῇ θεῷ τῆς παρθένου Χλῶριν ὀνομάζουσι.

LETO, right hand raised to shoulder, the left extended over small figure of CHLORIS.

Æ M. Aurelius. Imh. (**K** xxxvi.)
Sept. Severus. Imh. *Choix*, pl. II. 68. (**K** xxxvii.)
J. Domna. B. M. (**K** xxxviii.) Millingen, *Syll.* pl. III. 32.
Caracalla. *Rev. Belge*, 1860, pl. III. 1.

The same group in a temple.

Æ Anton. Pius. M. S. IV. 243, 48. Wiczay, xvii. 379.

This is a clear instance of the copying on coins of a statue, and very instructive. One coin figured (**K** xxxvii.) differently represents the action of Leto's right hand, which clearly, on the later coins, seems raised to a quiver on her shoulder. On this coin also the head of Leto is turned to the left, on the other coins to the right. But it is easy to see that these slight variations only arise from the fact that in the case of the first coin the artist made an attempt to represent the statue from the front, while in the case of the later coins it is depicted in profile. Combining our representations we can form a fairly complete notion of the statue of Praxiteles. Leto stood clad in a long chiton with diplois, holding some object (a torch?) in her left hand, and raising her right to her shoulder. The small figure of Chloris was close to her elbow, clad like the goddess herself.

17.—Paus. II. 22, 1. Ἀντικρὺ δὲ τοῦ μνήματος τῶν γυναικῶν Δήμητρός ἐστιν ἱερὸν ἐπίκλησιν Πελασγίδος. Cf. 18, 3. Δήμητρος Μυσίας ἱερόν. 21, 4. Κεῖται τοῦ Πύρρου τὰ ὀστᾶ ἐν τῷ ἱερῷ τῆς Δήμητρος.

DEMETER standing.

Æ Hadrian. M. S. IV. 241, 34. Wiczay, pl. XVII. 378. Holds sceptre and ears of corn.
Hadrian. M. S. IV. 241, 33. Holds sceptre and poppy head.
Ant. Pius. M. S. IV. 243, 49. Paris. Holds in both hands ears of corn and poppy heads.
L. Verus. M. S. IV. 245, 64. Vaillant. Holds in both hands ears of corn and poppy heads.
S. Severus. M. S. IV. 247, 77. Mus. Font. Holds in both hands ears of corn and poppy heads.
J. Domna. M. S. IV. 251, 104 .Turin. Holds in both hands ears of corn and poppy heads. (**K** xxxix.)
Plautilla. M. S. IV. 253, 114. Holds in both hands ears of corn and poppy heads.
M. Aurelius. Imh. Holds in both hands ears of corn and poppy heads.

18.—Paus. II. 22, 5. Μετὰ δὲ ταῦτα Διοσκούρων ναός.

The DIOSCURI on horseback.

Æ S. Severus. Mion. S. IV. 248, 85. Wiczay, pl. XVII. 382.

19.—Paus. II. 22, 6. Πλησίον δὲ τῶν Ἀνάκτων Εἰληθυίας ἐστὶν ἱερὸν ἀνάθημα Ἑλένης. (cf. 18, 3. Ἱερόν ἐστιν Εἰλειθυίας).

EILEITHUIA, holding in each hand a torch, one raised, one lowered.
Æ Commodus. M. S. IV. 246, 71. (Arig. II. 31, 210.)
M. Aurelius. Berlin. Two such figures, each with quiver at back, an altar between them. (K XL.)

The reason for supposing this type to represent Eileithuia lies in the fact that there is a type almost identical at Aegium in Achaia, which reproduces a statue of Eileithuia accurately described by Pausanias (VII. 23, 5), ταῖς χερσὶ τῇ μὲν ἐς εὐθὺ ἐκτέταται, τῇ δὲ ἀνέχει δᾷδα. The quiver might seem more appropriate to Artemis; but she could scarcely be, like Eileithuia, duplicated.

20.—Paus. II. 22, 7. Πέραν ἐστὶν Ἑκάτης ναός, Σκόπα δὲ τὸ ἄγαλμα ἔργον· τοῦτο μὲν λίθου, τὰ δ' ἀπαντικρὺ χαλκᾶ Ἑκάτης καὶ ταῦτα ἀγάλματα, τὸ μὲν Πολύκλειτος ἐποίησε, τὸ δὲ ἀδελφὸς Πολυκλείτου Ναυκύδης Μόθωνος.

HECATE triformis.
Æ Hadrian. Leake, Eur. Gr. p. 20.
Sabina. M. S. IV. 242, 41. (Mus. Font. pl. II. 17.) Munich. (K XLI.)

21.—Paus. II. 22, 9. Ἐν δὲ τῷ γυμνασίῳ τῷ Κυλαράβου Καπανεία ἐστὶν Ἀθηνᾶ. Cf. 21, 3. Ἀθηνᾶς δὲ ἰδρύσασθαι Σάλπιγγος ἱερόν φασιν Ἡγέλεων.

ATHENE standing, holding patera, shield, and spear.
Æ Hadrian. M. S. IV. 240, 27.

Athene with Perseus. See Perseus.

22.—Paus. II. 24, 3. Ἐπ ἄκρᾳ δὲ ἐστι τῇ Λαρίσῃ . . . . . . καὶ Ἀθηνᾶς δὲ ναός ἐστι θέας ἄξιος. Cf. 24, 2. Τοῦ Δειραδιώτου δὲ Ἀπόλλωνος ἔχεται μὲν ἱερὸν Ἀθηνᾶς Ὀξυδερκοῦς καλουμένης Διομήδους ἀνάθημα. 23, 5. Λέγουσι . . . . . ἄγαλμα κεῖσθαι παρὰ σφίσιν Ἀθηνᾶς τὸ ἐκκομισθὲν ἐξ Ἰλίου.

Archaic PALLADIUM.
Æ Æ Auton. Fourth century. B. M.
Æ Verus. M. S. IV. 245, 60. Arig. IV. 50, 9.

Palladium in temple on the Larissa.
Æ Antoninus Pius. Imh. B. M. (K XLII.)
Sept. Severus. B. M.
Domna. M. S. IV. 251, 100. Arig.

DIOMEDES advancing, holds sword and Palladium.
Æ Auton. Fourth century. B. M. Imh. (K XLIII.)
Auton. Fourth century. B. M. At his feet swan.
Æ Anton. Pius. Imh. (K XLIV.) M. S. IV. 244, 52, 53.

Diomedes, sword in hand, standing before statue of Pallas, on which he lays hands.
Æ Sept. Severus. Mus. Font. I. p. 66, 21.

Diomedes seated on altar, his leg bent under him, holds sword and Palladium.

Æ Hadrian. B. M. (**K** xlv.)

It would seem from the not very clear language of Pausanias, that there was a temple of Athene Oxyderkes on the slope of the Acropolis-hill, and another of Athene on the summit. In one of these temples would be probably the statue supposed to have been brought by Diomedes from Ilium. *A priori* one would naturally suppose this statue to have been in the temple first mentioned, said to have been dedicated by Diomedes. But the coins appear to prove that this was not the case ; but that the Ilian Palladium was set up in the temple on the summit of the hill. For the archaic image of Pallas, which on some coins (**K** xliii.) Diomedes carries, is identical in details with the image represented on other coins (**K** xlii.) as occupying the temple on the Acropolis. In form it is an ordinary archaic Palladium, representing the goddess as stiff and erect, holding a spear in her raised right hand, and a shield on her left arm. Below, the figure passes into a mere column.

23.—Paus. ii. 23, 1.　Ναός ἐστιν ἐν δεξιᾷ Διονύσου· τὸ δὲ ἄγαλμα εἶναι λέγουσιν ἐξ Εὐβοίας (ancient). Cf. 23, 7. Διονύσου ναὸς Κρησίου, and 24, 7.

DIONYSUS standing ; holds kantharos and thyrsos.

Æ Hadrian. M. ii. 234, 40. (**K** xlvi.)
Hadrian. M. S. iv. 241, 35. With panther.
Commodus. M. S. iv. 246, 68.
Caracalla. M. S. iv. 252, 107.

This representation of Dionysus is of a very unusual type. The god appears to be beardless, though this is not certain. He is enveloped in the folds of an ample himation, and holds an upright thyrsos in his left hand.

24.—Paus. ii. 23, 4.　Τὸ δ' ἐπιφανέστατον Ἀργείοις τῶν Ἀσκληπιείων ἄγαλμα ἐφ' ἡμῶν ἔχει καθήμενον Ἀσκληπιὸν λίθου λευκοῦ, καὶ παρ' αὐτὸν ἔστηκεν Ὑγίεια· κάθηνται δὲ καὶ οἱ ποιήσαντες τὰ ἀγάλματα, Ξενόφιλος καὶ Στράτων.

ASKLEPIOS seated on throne ; in front of him, snake.

Æ Sept. Severus. B. M. (**K** xlvii.)
Domna. M. S. iv. 251, 103. Wiczay, xvii. 387.
Valerian. M. S. iv. 255, 125.

HYGIEIA standing, her right hand extended over an altar, around which twines a snake; in her left, patera. Cf. Tyche above.

Æ Geta. Imh. M. S. iv. 253, 116. (**K** xlviii.)

Xenophilus and Strato lived probably late in the third
century B.C., if we may judge from a tablet bearing their names
published by Ross, *Inscr. Ined.* I. No. 58, in which we find the
forms Λ and Ο. There seems every probability that the coins
reproduce their types of the Asklepios and Hygieia. Both are
very unusual. The Asklepios is apparently a copy of the statue
of Thrasymedes at Epidaurus, and is of thoroughly Pheidian
type. The Hygieia is an interesting and remarkable type, differ-
ing, I think, from all known statues of the goddess. She is
clad in a long chiton, and wears an overdress, of which the end
hangs over her left arm.

25.—Paus. II. 23, 7. Κατάγεων οἰκοδόμημα, ἐπ᾽ αὐτῷ δὲ ἦν
ὁ χαλκοῦς θάλαμος, ὃν ᾿Ακρίσιός ποτε ἐπὶ φρουρᾷ τῆς
θυγατρὸς ἐποίησε.

DANAE receiving the golden shower, seated on throne.
Æ Hadrian. B. M. (L XLIX.)

Although this is probably the only appearance of Danae on
coins, the attribution is fairly certain. Danae's face is turned
upwards ; her bosom is bare, her extended hands grasp the ends
of her garment. Parallel representations on vases and in wall
paintings may be found in Overbeck, *Kunstmyth.*, II. p. 406.

26.—Paus. II. 24, 1. ᾿Ανιόντων δὲ ἐς τὴν ᾿Ακρόπολιν ἔστι μὲν
τῆς ᾿Ακραίας ῞Ηρας τὸ ἱερόν.

Head of JUNO Lanuvina in goat-skin (?).
Æ Sept. Severus. Mus. Font. II. pl. v. 14.

27.—Paus. II. 24, 2. Τὸ στάδιον, ἐν ᾧ τὸν ἀγῶνα τῷ Νεμείῳ
Διὶ καὶ τὰ ῾Ηραῖα ἄγουσιν.

Wreath of HERAEA. See also Nemea.
Æ Sept. Severus. Leake, Add. 157. *Arch. Z.* 1843, p. 151. (HPAIA, palm.)
Sept. Severus. Kenner, St. Florian, pl. III. 6. (HPAIA, shield.)
Domna. M. S. IV. 252, 106. HPEA.
Geta. M. S. IV. 254, 117. Arigoni (?)

28.—Paus. II. 24, 2. Τῶν Αἰγύπτου παίδων .... μνῆμα. χωρὶς
μὲν γὰρ ἀπὸ τῶν σωμάτων ἐνταῦθα αἱ κεφαλαί.

A DAUGHTER of DANAUS, holding in each hand a head.
Æ Ant. Pius. M. S. IV. 243, 46.

This description is scarcely to be relied on ; the figure may be
a Maenad, or Demeter, holding ears of corn in each hand.

29.—Paus. II. 25, 1. Κατὰ μὲν δὴ τοῦτο ᾿Αφροδίτης κεῖται
ξόανον, πρὸς δὲ ἡλίου δυσμὰς ῎Αρεως. εἶναι δὲ τὰ
ἀγάλματα Πολυνείκους λέγουσιν ἀναθήματα.

ARES standing to right helmeted ; holds in left hand, branch (?).

Æ Hadrian. Leake, *Eur.* p. 20.
Antinous. M. S. IV. 242, 40. (Gotha.)
S. Severus. (**L** L.)

APHRODITE standing to left, in long drapery; with right hand drawing forward her veil; before her, dolphin.

Æ Ant. Pius. Verus. Imh. (**L** LI.)

The dolphin may refer to the river Charadrus which flowed close to the temple.   The figure of Aphrodite is stiff and archaic, and closely draped.

30.—OTHER TYPES at Argos :

Isis standing, holds sistrum and vessel.

Æ Hadrian. Munich.
Mamaea. Imh.

Isis seated, suckling Horus (?)

Æ Hadrian. B. M. (**L** LII.)

Female figure with wheel on hand (Nemesis ?).

Æ Sep. Severus. M. S. IV. 248, 79/80.
Caracalla. Wicz. XVII. 386.

Female figure holding wheel on basis.

Æ Sep. Severus. Imh. (**L** LIII.) M. Font. II. 15.

Shrine ; Herakles in it.

Æ S. Severus. Imh. M. S. IV. 249, 91.

Female figure seated to left, on rock ; male figure approaching her with hand raised.   (Phaedra and Hippolytus ?)

Æ Hadrian. St. Florian. (**L** LIV.)

Poet (Homer ?) seated, a scroll in his hand.

Æ M. Aurel. M. S. IV. 244, 55.
Verus. M. II. 235, 46. Imh. (**L** LV.)

Draped male figure holding by the throats two serpents.

Æ Hadrian. B. M. Imh. (**L** LVI.)

Terminal figure, male.

Æ Hadrian. Imh. Cf. Verus. B M.

Temple key : Symbol **Ꮔ**.

Ꭱ Æ Auton. B. M. Imh. &c.

Head of Faustina the Elder, wearing Phrygian cap.

Æ M. Aur. Imh.

Head of Julia Domna, wearing Phrygian cap.

Æ S. Sev. Turin.

EPIDAURUS.

1.—Paus. II. 26.   Ἀσκληπιοῦ δὲ ἱερὰν μάλιστα εἶναι τὴν γῆν ἐπὶ λόγῳ συμβέβηκε τοιῷδε ... (Coronis) .... ἐκτίθησι τὸν παῖδα .... ἐκκειμένῳ δὲ ἐδίδου μὲν οἱ γάλα μία τῶν

περὶ τὸ ὄρος ποιμαινομένων αἰγῶν, ἐφύλασσε δὲ ὁ κύων
ὁ τοῦ αἰπολίου φρουρός.....'Αρεσθάναν εὑρόντα ἐπι-
θυμῆσαι τὸν παῖδα ἀνελέσθαι καὶ, κ.τ.λ.
SHEPHERD finding ASKLEPIOS suckled by a goat, among trees.
Æ Ant. Pius. Imh. (L I.) Panofka, *Asklepios, &c.* pl. I. 2.
Caracalla. Panofka, *l.c.* I. 1. Vienna. Müller, *D. M.* II. 759.
Head of Asklepios.
Æ Æ Auton. B. M. (L II.) Imh.

2.—Paus. II. 27, 2. Τοῦ δὲ 'Ασκληπιοῦ τὸ ἄγαλμα ....
πεποίηται ἐλέφαντος καὶ χρυσοῦ· μηνύει δὲ ἐπίγραμμα
τὸν εἰργασμένον εἶναι Θρασυμήδην 'Αριγνώτου Πάριον·
κάθηται δὲ ἐπὶ θρόνου βακτηρίαν κρατῶν, τὴν δὲ ἑτέραν
τῶν χειρῶν ὑπὲρ κεφαλῆς ἔχει τοῦ δράκοντος, καὶ οἱ καὶ
κύων παρακατακείμενος πεποίηται.
ASKLEPIOS SEATED, with dog and snake.
Æ Auton. Fourth century. *Berlin. Bl.* 1866, pl. xxx. 3, &c. B. M.
Munich. (L III.) Imh. &c.
Æ Auton. Athens, 4431, *B.* (Dog behind seat.)
Hadrian. *Berlin. Bl.* 1870, p. 15, 9. (Dog behind seat.)
Ant. Pius. B. M. Imh. Leake, p. 51. (No dog.)
M. Aurel. Athens, No. 4481, *b.* Dog behind. (L IV.)
Asklepios as above, in temple.
Æ Ant. Pius. B. M. (L V.) *Mus. Fontana,* I. iii. 2. No dog.
Dog reclining.
Æ Auton. B. M. Imh.
Paus. II. 27, 6. Ἔστι μὲν 'Ασκληπιοῦ λουτρόν.
Cupping-vases and thymiaterion.
Æ Auton. B. M. Imh.
Cupping-vase on coins of Achaean league.
These coins, which have been repeatedly published, and are
discussed in the histories of ancient sculpture, are generally
allowed to repeat the statue by Thrasymedes. They agree with
the words of Pausanias, even to the attitude of the dog, παρακατακείμενος. They thus furnish a strong argument that in
other cases also we may expect to find on coins fairly exact
copies of works of sculpture. For the connexion of the dog
with the Epidaurian worship, see *Rev. Arch.* 1884, II. pp. 78,
129, 217.

3.—Paus. II. 27, 6. 'Αντωνῖνος ..... ἐποίησε δὲ καὶ Ὑγιείᾳ
ναὸν καὶ 'Ασκληπιῷ καὶ 'Απόλλωνι ἐπίκλησιν Αἰγυπτίοις. Cf. 27, 5. Ἐντὸς δὲ τοῦ ἄλσους ..... ἐστιν
..... ἄγαλμα 'Ηπιόνης. 29, 1. Τέμενος δή ἐστιν
'Ασκληπιοῦ, καὶ ἀγάλματα ὁ θεὸς αὐτὸς καὶ 'Ηπιόνη·

γυναῖκα δὲ εἶναι τὴν Ἠπιόνην Ἀσκληπιοῦ φασί.   ταῦτά
ἐστιν ἐν ὑπαίθρῳ λίθου Παρίου.

Standing figure of Asklepios.

Æ J. Maesa.   Mion. II. 239, 72.   *Mus. Farnese.*

HYGIEIA standing in round temple.

Æ Ant. Pius.   M. S. IV. 265, 155.   *M. Fontana*, p. 67, 2 and 3.   Munich.
(L VI.)

Hygieia or EPIONE standing, feeds serpent from patera, clad
in long drapery.

Æ Auton. Fourth century. *M. Hunter*, XXVI. 12. B. M. (L VII.) Imh. &c.
Ant. Pius. Mion. II. 239, 71. Holds sceptre and patera.

It is unfortunate that the coin which represents Hygieia in
her temple is so indistinct that the details cannot be with
certainty recovered. Her right hand appears to be extended,
and to hold a patera ; and a serpent is visible to left.

The figure which I have termed Hygieia or Epione occurs on
early coins. Epione is the more likely attribution, as that deity
was from early times acknowledged at Epidaurus as the wife of
Asklepios, whereas Hygieia does not seem to have been there
recognised publicly until the times of the Antonines.

4.—Paus. II. 27, 7.   Ὄρος ὀνομαζόμενον Κυνόρτιον, Μαλεάτου
δὲ Ἀπόλλωνος ἱερὸν ἐν αὐτῷ. τοῦτο μὲν δὴ τῶν ἀρχαίων.

APOLLO Citharoedus.

Æ Auton. Copenhagen.

Head of Apollo, laur.

Æ Æ Auton. B. M. &c.

5.—Paus. II. 28, 1.   Δράκοντες δὲ οἱ λοιποὶ καὶ ἕτερον γένος ἐς
τὸ ξανθότερον ῥέπον τῆς χρόας ἱεροὶ μὲν τοῦ Ἀσκληπιοῦ
νομίζονται.

SERPENT.

Æ Auton. B. M. Imh. *M. Hunter*, XXXVI. 13.
Sev. Alexander. M. S. IV. 261, 157. D'Ennery.

6.—OTHER TYPES :

Poseidon naked, standing to left ; holds in right, dolphin ; in
left trident.

Æ Caracalla. B. M. (L VIII.)

The figure is identical with that of the standing Poseidon on
the coins of Corinth, which we have shown to be a copy of the
colossus which stood in the harbour at Cenchreae.

AEGINA.

1.—Paus. II. 29, 6.   Πλησίον δὲ τοῦ λιμένος ἐν ᾧ μάλιστα
ὁρμίζονται ναός ἐστιν Ἀφροδίτης.

Semi-circular PORT, within it, ship; above, hexastyle temple
or colonnade, in the midst of it a door, up to which
steps lead.

Æ J. Domna. Sestini, *M. Fontana*, p. 49, 4.   Imh.   (L I.)
APHRODITE draped, holds branch and apple (Venus Victrix).
Æ Plautilla. Sestini, *M. Fontana*, p. 50, No. 7.
Tortoise.
Ɍ Æ Auton. B. M. &c.
There still exist at Aegina remains of two harbours (Leake,
Morea, II. 436), both of which are inclosed by two moles, and
either of which would correspond to the representation on the
coin. Pausanias mentions both, one as the general harbour,
near which was the temple of Aphrodite, the other as the secret
harbour, near which was a large theatre. On the coin the
building in the background looks less like a temple than a
theatre, market, or wharf.

2.—Paus. II. 29, 6. Ἐν ἐπιφανεστάτῳ δὲ τῆς πόλεως τὸ
Αἰάκειον καλούμενον.
AEACUS seated as judge of the dead.
Æ Imperial of *uncertain city.*
Friedländer, *Arch. Z.* 1871, p. 79.

3.—Paus. II. 30, 1. Ἀπόλλωνι μὲν δὴ ξόανον γυμνόν ἐστι
τέχνης τῆς ἐπιχωρίου.
Archaic nude figure of APOLLO right, holds bow and branch.
Æ Auton. B. M. (L II.)
In this case the coins furnish us with a copy of an early
work of Aeginetan art. It is distinctive that the legs are
represented one in advance of the other: and the anatomy
seems to be clearly marked.

4.—Paus. II. 30, 2. Θεῶν δὲ Αἰγινῆται τιμῶσιν Ἑκάτην
μάλιστα . . . . . . ξόανον δὲ ἔργον Μύρωνος, ὁμοίως ἐν
πρόσωπόν τε καὶ τὸ λοιπὸν σῶμα.
HECATE with three bodies.
Æ Sept. Severus. *Arch. Z.* 1843, pl. IX. 6. Imh. (L III.)
Plautilla. *St. Florian*, pl. II. 7. B. M.

5.—Paus. II. 30, 3. Πρὸς τὸ ὄρος τοῦ Πανελληνίου Διὸς ἰοῦσίν
ἐστιν Ἀφαίας ἱερόν.
APHAIA (Britomartis) standing by Zeus; holds arrow and torch.
Æ Caracalla. Sestini, *Mus. Fontana*, pl. II. 7.
This engraving and the description of Sestini are not to be
trusted implicitly, especially as Aphaia is represented with a
turreted crown, and carries an arrow in a very unusual way.

6.—Paus. II. 30, 4. Τὸ δὲ Πανελλήνιον, ὅτι μὴ τοῦ Διὸς τὸ
ἱερὸν ἄλλο τὸ ὄρος ἀξιόλογον εἶχεν οὐδέν. τοῦτο δὲ τὸ
ἱερὸν λέγουσιν Αἰακὸν ποιῆσαι τῷ Διί.

ZEUS standing by Aphaia, holds thunderbolt and sceptre.
Æ Caracalla. l.c.
Zeus striding, holding eagle and thunderbolt.
Æ Sept. Severus. M. S. III. 600, 52.
Domna. B. M. (L IV.)
Caracalla. Mion. II. 148, 38.
7.—OTHER TYPES at Aegina :
Hermes carrying ram, facing.
Sept. Sev. Athens. (L V.)
Hermes carrying ram to right.
Plautilla. Vienna. (L VI.)
Small temple, tetrastyle, prostyle.
Sept. Sev. Munich. (L VII.)
Demeter.
Pallas. (The temple of Athene is mentioned by Herodotus,
but not by Pausanias.)
Nike.
Two female figures standing.
M. S. III. 601, 56.
Nemesis (?) with cornucopiae.
Poseidon standing.
Bearded terminal figure.
Plautilla. B. M. (L VIII.)
Prow of ship.
B. M.

The type of Hermes carrying a ram (L V. VI.) must almost certainly be a copy of some work of Aeginetan art, such as the statue
of the same subject by Onatas, preserved at Olympia: the
Olympian statue, however, wore a chlamys and a chiton,
whereas the figure on the coins is altogether naked, like that
on the coins of Tanagra, which represents the Hermes Criophorus of Calamis. The stretching of arms and legs on the coin
VI. is quite characteristic of Aeginetan art.

TROEZEN.

1.—Paus. II. 30, 6. Ἀθηνᾶν τε σέβουσι Πολιάδα καὶ Σθενιάδα
ὀνομάζοντες τὴν αὐτήν, καὶ Ποσειδῶνα Βασιλέα ἐπί-
κλησιν· καὶ δὴ καὶ νόμισμα αὐτοῖς τὸ ἀρχαῖον ἐπίσημα
ἔχει τρίαιναν καὶ Ἀθηνᾶς πρόσωπον.

Coin, *obv.* head of ATHENE bound with taenia only ; *rev.* trident.
Æ Auton. B. M. &c. (M I. II.)
Æ with helmeted head of Pallas. B. M.
The identification of the head on the figured coins as Athene
may be disputed, and is doubted by Imhoof. But Pausanias in
his statement as to the coins of Troezen must be repeating
matter of common notoriety ; and he must refer to the coins
of the autonomous series, before one side was occupied by the
head of an emperor. The head on the silver, **M** I. II., is so bold
and strong that it has been taken for that of Apollo ; but in
some cases it wears an earring, which seems conclusive as to its
feminine character. And, if it be feminine, it is more likely,
even apart from Pausanias' express statement, to belong to
Athene, rather than any other goddess. The absence of the
helmet is not unusual in case of early representations of Athene.

2.—Cf. 32, 5. Ἐν δὲ τῇ ἀκροπόλει τῆς Σθενιάδος καλουμένης ναός ἐστιν Ἀθηνᾶς. αὐτὸ δὲ εἰργάσατο τῆς θεοῦ
τὸ ξόανον Κάλλων Αἰγινήτης.

CITADEL surmounted by temple (tetrastyle).
Æ Commodus. Arigoni IV. 51, 3. Turin. (**M** III.)
Sept. Severus. B. M. On either side olive and cypress. (**M** IV.)
Domna. M. S. IV. 271, 208. On either side olive and cypress.

The olive is spoken of by Pausanias, 31, 10 ; laurel, 31, 8 ;
myrtle, 32, 3 : all sacred trees with histories.

Athene (archaic) resembling a Palladium.
Æ Commodus. B. M. (**M** V.)
This figure of Pallas may be described in the very words
already used in describing that at Cleonae, which we supposed
to be copied from the work of Dipoenus and Scyllis. This is
evidence, so far as it goes, that Callon adhered to the same
general scheme as the Cretan artists ; although, of course, we
must not press the argument, as the die-sinkers may have
intended merely to portray the general type of an archaic
Athene, as in **A** XI.

3.—Paus. II. 31, 1. Ἐν τῇ ἀγορᾷ Τροιζηνίων ναὸς καὶ ἀγάλματα Ἀρτέμιδός ἐστι Σωτείρας. Cf. 30, 7. Οὗτος
(Saron) τῇ Σαρωνίδι τὸ ἱερὸν Ἀρτέμιδι ᾠκοδόμησεν.
31, 4. Πλησίον δὲ τοῦ θεάτρου Λυκείας ναὸν Ἀρτέμιδος
ἐποίησεν Ἱππόλυτος.

ARTEMIS as a huntress.
Æ Sept. Severus. Imh. Holds torch and bow, dog by her pursuing stag.
(**M** VI.)

Sept. Severus. M. S. IV. 268, 200. Holds torch, dog by her, pursuing stag.
Sept. Severus. M. S. IV. 201. Draws arrow from quiver.
Caracalla. Arig. I. 115, 185. Holds arrow and bow, dog pursuing stag.

4.—Paus. II. 31, 6. Τὸ μὲν ἱερὸν τοῦ Ἀπόλλωνος τοῦ Θεαρίου κατασκευάσαι μὲν Πιτθέα ἔφασαν. Cf. 32, 2. Ἐντὸς τοῦ περιβόλου ναός ἐστιν Ἀπόλλωνος Ἐπιβατηρίου, Διομήδους ἀνάθημα.

APOLLO holding an arrow and leaning on a tripod, around which is twined a serpent.

Æ Sept. Severus. M. S. IV. 268, 199.

5.—Paus. II. 31, 6. Τοῦ δὲ Ἕρμωνος τούτου καὶ τὰ τῶν Διοσκούρων ξόανά ἐστι.

Archaic figures of the DIOSCURI facing, altar between them.

Æ Commodus. Imh. (**M** VII.)

This coin-type is valuable as furnishing evidence—probably the only extant evidence—of the style and date of the artist Hermon of Troezen. The Dioscuri stand naked, with long hair, both arms extended before them, not unlike, in attitude, to the Apollo of Canachus, but more primitive. Their proportions seem to be decidedly slight.

6.—Paus. II. 31, 10. Ἔστι δὲ καὶ Διὸς ἱερὸν ἐπίκλησιν Σωτῆρος.

ZEUS standing, holds eagle and sceptre.

Æ Sept. Severus. M. S. IV. 268, 198. Vaillant.

7.—Paus. II. 32, 1. Ἱππολύτῳ δὲ τῷ Θησέως τέμενός τε ἐπιφανέστατον ἀνεῖται, καὶ ναὸς ἐν αὐτῷ καὶ ἄγαλμά ἐστιν ἀρχαῖον.

HIPPOLYTUS as a hunter, on foot, holding spear, and leaning on tree; dog beside him.

Æ Commodus. Fox, Uned. Coins, IX. 100; Leake, Eur. Gr. add. 165. (**M** VIII.)

Hippolytus leading a horse, accompanied by a dog.

Æ Commodus. M. S. IV. 268, 195. Arigoni, II. 32, 228.

Hippolytus with spear and sword before Phaedra (or her nurse), who approaches him in attitude of supplication.

Æ Sept. Severus. M. S. IV. 269, 204. Milling. 1831, pl. IV. 22 (who regards the pair as Theseus and Aethra).

8.—Paus. II. 32, 3. Καὶ ναὸς ὑπὲρ αὐτοῦ Ἀφροδίτης Κατασκοπίας. Cf. 32, 6. Ναὸν . . . . . Ἀφροδίτης Ἀκραίας. 32, 7. Ἀφροδίτης ἐστὶν ἱερὸν Νυμφίας.

APHRODITE standing, holds apple in left hand, and lifts her veil with right.

Æ Commodus. Imh. (**M** IX.)
Domna. M. S. IV. 270, 209. Theup.

This type, the idea of which is taken from statues of Roman times, perhaps that of Arcesilaus, seems to represent Aphrodite Nymphia.

9.—Paus. II. 32, 4.   Τοῦ δὲ Ἀσκληπιοῦ τὸ ἄγαλμα ἐποίησε μὲν Τιμόθεος, Τροιζήνιοι δὲ οὐκ Ἀσκληπιὸν ἀλλὰ εἰκόνα Ἱππολύτου φασὶν εἶναι.

ASKLEPIOS standing at altar, snake-entwined staff in left hand.
Æ Commodus.   M. S. IV. 268, 196.   Arig. II. 18, 227.

The figure of Asklepios seems, so far as can be judged from the unsatisfactory engraving, to be of the ordinary conventional type; and, therefore, to offer no explanation of Pausanias' curious statement.

10.—Paus. II. 32, 4.   Καὶ οἰκίαν ἰδὼν οἶδα Ἱππολύτου· πρὸ δὲ αὐτῆς ἐστὶν Ἡράκλειος καλουμένη κρήνη.

FOUNTAIN, a pillar with lion sitting thereon, water flowing into basin from between his feet.
Æ Commodus.   M. Athens, 4475.δ.   (M x.)

11.—Paus. II. 32, 7.   Πέτρα Θησέως ὀνομαζομένη, μεταβαλοῦσα καὶ αὐτὴ τὸ ὄνομα ἀνελομένου Θησέως ὑπ' αὐτῇ κρηπῖδας τὰς Αἰγέως καὶ ξίφος.   Cf. 31, 1.   Θησεὺς . . . . . ἡνίκα Ἀστερίωνα τὸν Μίνω καταγωνισάμενος ἀνέστρεψεν.

THESEUS, naked, lifting the rock.
Æ Commodus.   B. M.   (M XI.)
Sept. Severus.   M. S. IV. 269, 205.   Wiczay, XXXI. 698.
Geta.   B. M.
Philippus, Jun.   B. M.

The identity of this type through several reigns may indicate for it an origin in sculpture.
Theseus slaying the Minotaur.
Æ Commodus.   M. II. 242, 87.   Turin.

12.—OTHER TYPES :
Tyche at altar : holds patera and cornucopiae.
Æ Commodus.   B. M.   (M XII.)

METHANA.

1.—Paus. II. 34, 1.   Τοῦ δὲ πολίσματος τριάκοντά που στάδια ἀπέχει λουτρὰ θερμά. φασὶ δὲ Ἀντιγόνου τοῦ Δημητρίου Μακεδόνων βασιλεύοντος, τότε πρῶτον τὸ ὕδωρ φανῆναι.

Head of HEPHAESTUS in pileus.
Æ Auton.   Third century.   B. M.   Imh.

The connexion of Hephaestus with volcanic phenomena such as that recorded in the text is well known.

Other types:
Artemis to left, hunting.
Geta. B. M. (**M** I.)
Artemis about to discharge an arrow.
Sept. Sev. B. M. (**M** II.)
Poseidon.
Pallas standing, holds Victory and sceptre; at her feet, altar.
M. Aurel. Imh. (**M** III.)
Zeus.
Tyche.
Aphrodite, facing, naked to waist, holds tresses with both hands.
Caracalla. Paris. (**M** IV.)
N.B.—It is curious that Isis was worshipped at Methana, and appears on coins of Mothone; Artemis was worshipped at Mothone, and appears commonly on coins of Methana.

HERMIONE.

1.—Paus. II. 34, 10. Ἔστι δέ σφισι καὶ νῦν ἔτι ἱερὰ αὐτόθι, Ποσειδῶνος μὲν ἐπὶ τῆς ἀκτῆς τῇ ἀρχῇ, προελθοῦσι δὲ, κ.τ.λ. Cf. 35, 1. Καὶ Ποσειδῶν χαλκοῦς τὸν ἕτερον πόδα ἔχων ἐπὶ δελφῖνος.
POSEIDON standing, holds trident, his foot on a dolphin.
Æ J. Domna. M. S. IV. 262, 159, 160. (*M. Fontana*, 69, 2, 3.)

2.—Paus. II. 34, 11. Ἀφροδίτης ναός ἐστιν ἐπίκλησιν Ποντίας καὶ Λιμενίας τῆς αὐτῆς, ἄγαλμα δὲ λευκοῦ λίθου, μεγέθει τε μέγα καὶ ἐπὶ τῇ τέχνῃ θέας ἄξιον. καὶ ναὸς ἕτερός ἐστιν Ἀφροδίτης.
APHRODITE standing, with Eros.
Æ Caracalla. M. S. IV. 263, 162. *M. Fontana*, 68, 1.

3.—Paus. II. 35, 1. Πλησίον δὲ αὐτοῦ Διονύσου ναὸς Μελαναίγιδος.
DIONYSUS standing, holds kantharos and sceptre.
Æ Plautilla. B. M. Dionysus naked.
Geta. B. M. Dionysus draped. (**M** I.)

4.—Paus. II. 35, 3. Τὸ δὲ ἱερὸν τῆς Τύχης νεώτατον μὲν λέγουσιν Ἑρμιονεῖς τῶν παρὰ σφίσιν εἶναι, λίθου δὲ Παρίου κολοσσὸς ἕστηκεν.
TYCHE standing, holds rudder and cornucopiae.
Æ Plautilla. B. M. (**M** II.) Imh. M. S. IV. 263, 167.
Tyche standing, holding patera and cornucopiae, at an altar.
Æ Plautilla. M. S. IV. 264, 168. (Arigoni.)

H 2

Tyche (?) seated, crowned by male figure, who holds lance.
Æ Caracalla. M. S. IV. 262, 161. Copenhagen.
Plautilla. M. S. IV. 263, 165. Sest. *Molt. med. gr.* XII. 18.
5.—Paus. II. 35, 4. Τὸ δὲ λόγου μάλιστα ἄξιον ἱερὸν
Δήμητρός ἐστιν ἐπὶ τοῦ Πρωνός. Cf. also 35, 6, 8, 11.
Head of DEMETER crowned with corn.
Æ Æ Auton. B. M.
Also ears of corn, and torch.
6.—Paus. II. 35, 6. Τοῖς δὲ τὴν πομπὴν πέμπουσιν ἕπονται
τελείαν ἐξ ἀγέλης βοῦν ἄγοντες διειλημμένην δεσμοῖς τε
καὶ ὑβρίζουσαν ἔτι ὑπὸ ἀγριότητος, κ.τ.λ. (Description
of the Chthonia.)
Cow led by attendant with a rope.
Æ Plautilla. B. M. (**M** III.)
OTHER TYPES :
Hermes standing.
Æ J. Domna. Mion. II. 239, 74.
Zeus Nikephoros ?
Æ Plautilla. M. S. IV. 263, 163.
Cybele.
Æ Plautilla.

ASINE.

1.—Paus. II. 36, 5. Πυθαέως τε 'Απόλλωνος ὑπέλιπον το
ἱερόν, καὶ νῦν ἐτὶ δῆλόν ἐστι.
APOLLO PYTHAEUS clad in himation, a laurel twig in his right
hand, leaning on pillar.
Æ Sept. Severus. Munich. (**M** I.)
Plautilla. Mion. II. 224, 75.
2.—OTHER TYPES :
Asklepios.
Snake.
Hermes (?).
Draped female figure ?
Fortuna, holds rudder and cornucopiae.
Æ Imh. (**M** II.)

LERNA and NAUPLIA, Coins of Argos.

1.—Paus. II. 37, 2. 'Αφροδίτης ἄγαλμα ἐπὶ θαλάσσῃ λίθου.
Cf. II. 19, 6 ; 19, 7 ; 20, 8 ; 23, 8 ; 25, 1 ; 38, 1.
APHRODITE standing, holds in right hand a fold of her garment;
before her, a dolphin.
Æ Anton. Pius. Imh.
L. Verus. Imh. (**L** LI.) (Above cited under Argos.)

2.—Paus. II. 37, 4.   Τῆς δὲ 'Αμυμώνης πέφυκεν' ἐπὶ τῇ πηγῇ πλάτανος· ὑπὸ ταύτῃ τὴν ὕδραν τραφῆναι τῇ πλατάνῳ φασίν, κ.τ.λ.

HERAKLES slaying the Lernaean hydra.

Æ Hadrian.   Imh.   (**M** I.)

3.—Paus. II. 38, 2.   Οἰκιστὴς δὲ ἐγένετο᾽ αὐτῆς (of Nauplia) Ναύπλιος Ποσειδῶνος λεγόμενος καὶ 'Αμυμώνης εἶναι ... καὶ Ποσειδῶνος ἱερὸν καὶ λιμένες εἰσὶν ἐν Ναυπλίᾳ. Cf. above, also 37, 1.

AMYMONE pursued by Poseidon.

Æ Anton. Pius.   Imh.   (**M** II.)   *Choix*, pl. II. 6.   Overbeck, *Poseidon*, VI. 32.

NUMISMATIC COMMENTARY ON PAUSANIAS.

II.

BOOKS III., IV., V., VI., VII., VIII.

[PLATES LXV.—LXVIII.]

IN the present paper we continue the commentary begun in last year's *Journal*, and set forth the numismatic facts which run parallel to those books of Pausanias which deal with the remainder of Peloponnesus; Laconia, Messenia, Elis, Achaia, and Arcadia. Athens, Phocis, and Boeotia still remain for future treatment.

In spite of our efforts to be complete, we have already discovered a number of coins of Corinth and Argos and the neighbouring cities which had escaped us, and which present new types, or important varieties of the types which appear in our plates. This will necessitate the publication of a supplement to our first paper. While this is in preparation numismatists will be doing the greatest service if they will let us have casts of any types in their possession which are omitted in the descriptions or the plates of this paper or the last. Casts of unusual coins of imperial times of Phocis or Boeotia will also be most welcome.

For the purposes of the present paper, in addition to the material already laid up by the editors, the authorities of the Bibliothèque Nationale at Paris have kindly allowed us to have casts of all the coins in that collection selected as desirable; and Dr. von Sallet, of the Royal Museum of Berlin, has sent to London, with the utmost friendliness and liberality, casts of all important coins of Peloponnesus of imperial times in his keeping.

In this instalment of the work, the numismatic lists and comments have alike been compiled by the English colleague ; the Swiss colleague has supplied casts and carefully revised the whole. The text used is that of Schubart, not of Schubring, as stated by a *lapsus pennae* in the first article. The method of numbering in the plates has been modified for reasons of convenience.

LACEDAEMON.

1.—Paus. III. 10, 7. Τρίτη δὲ ἐκ τῆς ὁδοῦ τῆς εὐθείας ἐκβολὴ κατὰ τὰ δεξιὰ ἐς Καρύας ἄγει καὶ ἐς τὸ ἱερὸν τῆς Ἀρτέμιδος. τὸ γὰρ χωρίον Ἀρτέμιδος καὶ Νυμφῶν ἐστὶν αἱ Κάρυαι, καὶ ἄγαλμα ἔστηκεν Ἀρτέμιδος ἐν ὑπαίθρῳ Καρυάτιδος.

III. 14, 2. Θεῶν δὲ ἱερὰ Ποσειδῶνός ἐστιν Ἱπποκουρίου καὶ Ἀρτέμιδος Αἰγιναίας. ἐπανελθοῦσι δὲ ὀπίσω πρὸς τὴν λέσχην ἐστὶν Ἀρτέμιδος Ἰσσώρας ἱερόν· ἐπονομάζουσι δὲ αὐτὴν καὶ Λιμναίαν, οὖσαν οὐκ Ἄρτεμιν, Βριτόμαρτιν δὲ τὴν Κρητῶν· τὰ δὲ ἐς αὐτὴν ὁ Αἰγιναῖος ἔχει μοι λόγος.

III. 18, 4. Τὰ δὲ ἐς τὴν Κναγίαν Ἄρτεμίν ἐστιν οὕτω λεγόμενα. Κναγέα ἄνδρα ἐπιχώριον κ.τ.λ.

III. 20, 7. Οὐ πόρρω Δέρειον, ἔνθα Ἀρτέμιδος ἄγαλμα ἐν ὑπαίθρῳ Δερεάτιδος.

ARTEMIS standing left, in short chiton, right extended, in left, spear ; beside her, dog.

Æ Aut.   B. M.   (**N** I.)   Mion. S. IV. 221.

Artemis running right, holding torch in both hands, dog beside her.

Æ Aut.   B. M.   (**N** II.)   Mion. S. IV. 223.

Paus. III. 25, 3. Θεῶν δὲ ἐν τῇ γῇ σφίσιν ἱερά ἐστιν Ἀρτέμιδός τε ἐπίκλησιν Ἀστρατείας, ὅτι τῆς ἐς τὸ πρόσω στρατείας ἐνταῦθα ἐπαύσαντο Ἀμαζόνες, καὶ Ἀπόλλων Ἀμαζόνιος· ξόανα μὲν ἀμφότερα, ἀναθεῖναι δὲ λέγουσιν αὐτὰ τὰς ἀπὸ Θερμώδοντος γυναῖκας.

ARTEMIS Astrateia ? laur. clad in short chiton and endromides, holds out in right, bow ? in left, shield and spear.

Æ Caracalla.   B. M.   (**N** III.)

This attribution is anything but certain.   The figure on the coin is, however, apparently female, fully armed, but in an attitude of rest. The object in the right hand seems to have a cord attached, and may be either bow or whip. As to a shield as an attribute of Artemis, see below **N** XI., XII.

Artemis clad in short chiton, holds branch in right, quiver at shoulder, inscription **KYΠAPICCIA**. (*Obv.* Head of Rome.)

Æ Auton. B. M. Berlin. (**N** IV.) Imh., *Carlsruhe Mus.* p. 19.

This coin was not struck at Cyparissia, but probably at Lacedaemon, on occasion of an agonistic festival.

2.—Paus. III. 11, 11. Ἔστι δὲ καὶ Ἑρμῆς Ἀγοραῖος Διόνυσον φέρων παῖδα.

HERMES Agoraeus, wearing chlamys, to right, holds in left hand caduceus, on left arm infant Dionysus, who raises left hand.

Æ Domna. Imh. *Mon. Gr.* p. 173. (**N** V.)
Plautilla. Berlin. *Mon. Gr.* p. 173. (**N** VI.)

Hermes Agoraeus, wearing chlamys, to right, holds in right staff resting against shoulder, in left, infant Dionysus and caduceus.

Æ Gallienus. Imh. *Mon. Gr.* p. 174.
Salonina. Imh. Berlin. (**N** VII.)

The staff, which is quite clear on **N** VII., is not to be so clearly seen on V. and VI. But the action of the right hand is the same, and the staff may be there. If so, all the representations would be practically identical, and almost certainly copies of the statue mentioned by Pausanias. The staff which Hermes is carrying in his right hand is probably a thyrsus, towards which the child Dionysus stretches out his hand.

3.—Paus. III. 12, 8. Λακεδαιμονίοις δὲ ἔστι μὲν Ἀπόλλωνος Ἀκρείτα βωμός, ἔστι δ' ἐπονομαζόμενον Γάσηπτον ἱερὸν Γῆς· Ἀπόλλων δὲ ὑπὲρ αὐτὸ ἵδρυται Μαλεάτης.

III. 13, 3. Ὁ δὲ Κάρνειος, ὃν Οἰκέταν ἐπονομάζουσι, τιμὰς εἶχεν ἐν Σπάρτῃ καὶ πρὶν Ἡρακλείδας κατελθεῖν, ἵδρυτο δὲ ἐν οἰκίᾳ Κρίου τοῦ Θεοκλέους, ἀνδρὸς μάντεως. Cf. 14, 6.

APOLLO naked, facing, right hand rests on head, in left, bow.

Æ Commodus. B. M.
Gallienus. Loebbecke. (**N** VIII.)
Salonina. B. M. Imh.

Apollo in long drapery, holds plectrum and lyre.

Æ Ant. Pius. Mion. S. IV. 224, 35. Paris. (**N** IX.)

A comparison with the coins of Gytheium, **N** XXIII., XXIV., seems to show that the naked Apollo, **N** VIII., is Carneius. On **N** IX. we seem to have rather the Pythian form of the god.

4.—Paus. III. 14, 6. Προελθόντι δὲ ἀπὸ τοῦ Δρόμου Διοσκούρων ἱερὸν καὶ Χαρίτων. Cf. III. 20, 1.

The DIOSCURI on horseback, charging with couched lances.

Æ Aut. B. M. &c.
Hadrian. B. M. Berlin. Imh.
Commod. Mion. S. IV. 225, 39.
Geta. Berlin.

The Dioscuri standing beside their horses.

Æ Gallienus. Imh.

The Dioscuri standing side by side, each holding spear and sword.

Æ Aut. B. M. &c.
Ant. Pius. Mion. II. 223, 68.
M. Aurel. Munich.
Caracalla. Imh.
Plautilla. B. M.

Heads of the Dioscuri; their pilei; two amphorae.

Æ Aut. B. M. &c.

5.—Paus. III. 16, 3. Ἑλένης δὲ ἱερὰ καὶ Ἡρακλέους, τῆς μὲν πλησίον τοῦ τάφου τοῦ Ἀλκμᾶνος, τῷ δὲ ἐγγυτάτω τοῦ τείχους, ἐν αὐτῷ δὲ ἄγαλμα Ἡρακλέους ἐστὶν ὡπλισμένον (and passim).

HERAKLES naked, resting, leaning on club, much in the attitude of Glycon's statue.

Æ Ant. Pius. Paris.
Domna. B. M. (**N** x.)

6.—Paus. III. 16, 6. Λακεδαιμόνιοι δὲ καὶ Λυκούργῳ τῷ θεμένῳ τοὺς νόμους, οἷα δὴ θεῷ πεποιήκασι καὶ τούτῳ ἱερόν.

Head of LYCURGUS, bearded, diad., inscribed ΛΥΚΟΥΡΓΟC.

Æ Auton. B. M. Mion. II. 217, &c.

7.—PAUS. III. 16, 7. Τὸ δὲ χωρίον τὸ ἐπονομαζόμενον Λιμναῖον Ὀρθίας ἱερόν ἐστιν Ἀρτέμιδος. τὸ ξόανον δὲ ἐκεῖνο εἶναι λέγουσιν ὅ ποτε Ὀρέστης καὶ Ἰφιγένεια ἐκ τῆς Ταυρικῆς ἐκκλέπτουσιν· ἐς δὲ τὴν σφετέραν Λακεδαιμόνιοι κομισθῆναί φασιν Ὀρέστου καὶ ἐνταῦθα βασιλεύοντος. καί μοι εἰκότα λέγειν μᾶλλόν τι δοκοῦσιν ἢ Ἀθηναῖοι.

Ἀθηναίοις δὲ ἄρα παρώφθη γενόμενον λάφυρον τῷ Μήδῳ· τὸ γὰρ ἐκ Βραυρῶνος ἐκομίσθη τε ἐς Σοῦσα, καὶ ὕστερον Σελεύκου δόντος Σύροι Λαοδικεῖς ἐφ᾽ ἡμῶν ἔχουσι.

Archaic figure of ARTEMIS, wears polos, long chiton and over-
dress ; holds in raised right hand, axe, in left, buckler,
on either side, stag.

(Coins of Laodicea in Syria.)

Æ Elagabalus. Mion. v. 260, 795.
  Philip Sen. Mion. v. 262, 806.
  Gallus. Mion. v. 263, 810. B. M. (**N** XI.)

The same figure, turned the other way.   (At Laodicea.)

Æ Philip Sen. B. M. (**N** XII.)

The same figure, holding axe in right, shield in left, in presence
of seated Tyche of city. (At Laodicea.)

Æ Elagabalus. Mion. S. VIII. 177, 252. (Sestini, *Mus. Hed.* III. 61, 45.)

In his Attica (I. 33, 1) Pausanias says that in the temple of
Artemis at Brauron there was an archaic xoanon ; but in his
opinion this was not the original. In the above-quoted passage,
he says further that the original statue was still extant at
Laodicea in Syria. That the figure on the coins of Laodicea is
a copy of this original, carried off from Attica, is sufficiently
evident. Pausanias seems to have thought that the Spartan
statue of Artemis Orthia had a better claim to have been brought
from Taurica than even the Laodicean statue. However that
be, there can be no doubt that the statue represented on the
Laodicean coins is very original and interesting.

The goddess wears on her head a modius ; in one hand she
carries not a bipennis but an axe of the form of a socketed celt ;
she is clad in long drapery, in the disposition of which, as well
as in the pose of her legs, but little archaism is visible. Beside
her are two stags, which make the identification certain.

The shield is an attribute unusual in the case of Artemis, but
not unheard of. Pausanias (IV. 13, 1) heard at Messene of an
ancient statue of Artemis, which had on one occasion let fall
its shield ; and Iphigeneia is sometimes represented as carrying
a statue, which in any hands but hers might pass for a Palladium.
See Gerhard in *Arch. Zeitung*, 1849, pl. VII. p. 70. Compare
also **N** III. The form of the axe is very noteworthy.

On the silver coins issued at Athens by Eubulides and
Agathocles (Beulé, *Monn. d'Ath.* p. 287) occurs an archaic figure
of Artemis, veiled, wearing modius, holding patera and bow,
which has been by some taken for a copy of the statue existing
at the time at Brauron, or (as by Beulé) for a copy of an imitation of that statue by Praxiteles, which was preserved on the

Athenian acropolis (Paus. I. 23, 7). If either of these views be
correct, there were decided differences between the statue
carried off by the Persians and that made by the Athenians to
replace it.

8.—Paus. III. 17, 2. Λακεδαιμόνιοι πολλοῖς ἔτεσιν ὕστερον
τόν τε ναὸν ὁμοίως καὶ τὸ ἄγαλμα ἐποιήσαντο ᾿Αθηνᾶς
χαλκοῦν· Γιτιάδας δὲ εἰργάσατο ἀνὴρ ἐπιχώριος. ἐποίησε
δὲ καὶ ᾄσματα Δώρια ὁ Γιτιάδας ἄλλα τε καὶ ὕμνον ἐς
τὴν θεόν. ἐπείργασται δὲ τῷ χαλκῷ πολλὰ μὲν τῶν
ἄθλων ῾Ηρακλέους κ.τ.λ.

The PALLAS of Gitiadas, helmeted, holding lance and shield,
the lower part of the body arranged in bands adorned
with reliefs.

Æ Gallienus.   B. M.   Imh.   Munich.   (N XIII.)
Gallienus.   Sestini, *Mus. Hed.* II. 131, 37.
Gallienus.   Cadalvène, *Recueil*, pl. II. 35.

Head of Pallas, helmeted.

Æ Domna.   Paris.   (N XIV.)

This identification is advocated by Koner (*Zeitschr. f. Münzk.*
1845, p. 2) and Jahn, but doubted by Overbeck (*Gr. Plast.*
I. p. 124), who also considers it improbable that the reliefs were
on the person of the goddess. It is, however, not easy to explain
the words of Pausanias, except on the supposition that the
reliefs were on the goddess herself, that is, on her close-fitting
chiton, and the representation on the coin, which is quite *sui
generis*, and can scarcely be interpreted except as it is by Koner,
seems to clinch the argument. In the upper part of the body
we may trace something of womanly form; the shape of the
lower part seems to be sacrificed to the exigencies of the
reliefs.

The head on No. XIV. must almost certainly be copied from a
statue, for the head of a deity, unless so copied, seldom or never
appears on imperial coins of Peloponnesus. It is probably a
free copy of the head of the statue of Gitiadas. The form of
the helmet, half way between the close-fitting and the Corinthian
types, is notable; but unfortunately the coin is badly preserved,
and the details obscure.

Coins of Melos (Paris Coll. and *Br. Mus. Cat., Islands*, pl.
xxiv. 13) bear a type which seems to reproduce the same statue;
the details, however, are not clear. Melos was a Laconian
colony. Of the head of this statue we have also a record on

Melian coins of imperial times, which bear a head of Pallas distinctly archaic, with long straight tresses falling behind the ear, in a close-fitting helmet (**N** xv.).

9.—Paus. III. 19, 1. Καὶ τὸ ἄγαλμα ἐνταῦθα ἐνέστηκε. μέγεθος δὲ αὐτοῦ μέτρῳ μὲν οὐδένα ἀνευρόντα οἶδα, εἰκάζοντι δὲ καὶ τριάκοντα εἶναι φαίνοιντο ἂν πήχεις. ἔργον δὲ οὐ Βαθυκλέους ἐστίν, ἀλλὰ ἀρχαῖον καὶ οὐ σὺν τέχνῃ πεποιημένον· ὅτι γὰρ μὴ πρόσωπον αὐτῷ καὶ πόδες εἰσὶν ἄκροι καὶ χεῖρες, τὸ λοιπὸν χαλκῷ κίονί ἐστιν εἰκασμένον. ἔχει δὲ ἐπὶ τῇ κεφαλῇ κράνος, λόγχην δὲ ἐν ταῖς χερσὶ καὶ τόξον. τοῦ δὲ ἀγάλματος τὸ βάθρον παρέχεται μὲν βωμοῦ σχῆμα, τεθάφθαι δὲ τὸν Ὑάκινθον λέγουσιν ἐν αὐτῷ. A copy of this statue as Pythaeus at Thornax, III. 10, 8, cf. 11, 9.

Statue of APOLLO Amyclaeus clad in long chiton and aegis, helmeted, holding lance and bow, body in form of a pillar.

Æ of a king third century B.C. Beside Apollo goat, and aplustre surmounted by cock, wreath in field. B. M. Berlin. Bompois. (**N** xvi.) Paris &c. Cf. Bompois, *Portraits attrib. à Cléomène*, pl. I.

Similar figure without chiton.

Æ Commodus. B. M. (**N** xvii.)
Gallienus. Imh.

Leake has shown (*Num. Hellen., Europe*, p. 55) that the figure on these coins is a copy of the colossus of Apollo at Amyclae. The work seems to be of the same school as the statue of Athene already mentioned, but ruder and earlier, the body showing no approach to the human form. As to the exact form of the body, however, the coins differ: the earlier make it clad and conical, the later like a term. We can scarcely doubt that the later representation (**N** xvii.) is more faithful, since it belongs to a time when the die cutter took smaller liberties with his model. On it the body of the deity is divided by crossing lines into lozenge-shaped divisions, no doubt representing the plates of bronze; one can even detect on the coin the nails by which these are secured. The head of the deity is archaic, with long curl falling on to the neck, and a queue behind. The whole is let into a stand or basis.

10.—OTHER TYPES at Lacedaemon :—

Male figure, bearded, seated on cippus, looking back, holds knotted staff.

Æ Ant. Pius. B. M. Imh.
Geta. Imh. *Mon. Gr.* p. 174. (**N** xviii.)

Veiled female figure seated left on cippus, in attitude of
grief.

Æ Geta.   B. M.   (N xix.)

The pose of this figure is strikingly like that of the so-called
Penelope of the Vatican.

Nike, holds wreath and palm.

Æ Geta.   Imh.

Female head, left, diad. : inscription ΣΠΑΡΤΗ.

Æ Aut.   B. M.   Imh.   Paris.

GYTHEIUM.

1.—Paus. III. 21, 7.   Γυθεᾶται δὲ τῆς πόλεως ἀνθρώπων μὲν
οὐδένα οἰκιστὴν γενέσθαι λέγουσιν, Ἡρακλέα δὲ καὶ
Ἀπόλλωνα ὑπὲρ τοῦ τρίποδος ἐς ἀγῶνα ἐλθόντας, ὡς
διηλλάγησαν, μετὰ τὴν ἔριν οἰκίσαι κοινῇ τὴν πόλιν·
καὶ ἐν τῇ ἀγορᾷ σφίσιν Ἀπόλλωνος καὶ Ἡρακλέους
ἐστὶν ἀγάλματα.

APOLLO facing, clad in long chiton, right hand extended, in
left, lyre.

Æ Domna.   Imh.
Carac.   Paris.   (N xx.)
Geta.   B. M.

Apollo facing, naked, holds branch and bow.

Æ Sept. Sev.   Mion. S. iv. 230, 55.   Paris.   (N xxi.)   (Eckhel, *Num. Vet.*
    ix. 1.)

Bearded HERAKLES standing, holds club, which rests on the
ground, and lion's skin.

Æ Sept. Sev.   B. M.   (N xxii.)
Domna.   Mion. ii. 226, 83.   Paris.
Geta.   B. M.   Mion. ii. 227, 87.

Herakles in attitude of Glycon's figure.

Æ Geta.   Paris.

The branch in the hand of the Apollo (N xxi.) reminds one
of that which Herakles holds on the coin of Croton, where he
is specially described as ΟΙΚΙΣΤΑΣ (Carelli, *Num. Ital. Vet.*
pl. clxxxiii. 21 ; Gardner, *Types*, pl. v. 2).   It may refer to his
office as founder ; with the other hand he seems to be laying
aside his bow.   Herakles (N xxii.) is also in an attitude of
conciliation ; whether the two figures can be reasonably regarded
as belonging to one group is a question.

2.—Paus. III. 21, 7.   Ἑτέρωθι δὲ Ἀπόλλων Κάρνειος.

APOLLO naked, right hand raised over his head, in left, which
rests on trunk of tree, leaf ? beside him on a basis

horned Pan, holding pedum and nebris in right hand,
syrinx in left.

Æ Sept. Sev. Bibl. Turin.
Geta. B. M. (**N** xxiii.)

Similar, without Pan.

Æ Sept. Sev. *Mus. Sancl.* ii. pl. 24, 210, B.
Carac. Mion. S. iv. 232, 65. Paris.
Carac. Berlin. (**N** xxiv.)

In the first of these coins the object in the hand of Apollo
appears not to be an arrow, but a trefoil leaf; in the other coins
it is not clear. The presence of Pan seems to show that Apollo
Carneius is here intended; and the Pan and Apollo alike should
be, according to the usual tests, copies of statues, as one stands
on a basis, the other leans on a pillar.

3.—Paus. iii. 21, 7. Πλησίον δὲ αὐτῶν Διόνυσος. Cf. 22, 2,
Διονύσου δὲ ὄρος ἱερὸν Λαρύσιον καλούμενόν ἐστιν
κ.τ.λ.

Dionysus standing, holds in right grapes or kantharos, in left,
thyrsos ; wears nebris.

Æ Sept. Sev. Mion. S. iv. 230, 56, 57.

(Possibly a Hermes wrongly described ; see below under
section 9 : **O** vii.)

4.—Paus. iii. 21, 7. Καὶ Ἀσκληπιοῦ χαλκοῦν ἄγαλμά ἐστιν,
οὐκ ἐπόντος ὀρόφου τῷ ναῷ, καὶ πηγὴ τοῦ θεοῦ.

Asklepios facing, clad in himation, right hand extended, in
left, serpent-staff; before him, snake-entwined altar.

Æ Sept. Sev. B. M. Paris. (**O** i.)
J. Domna. Sest. *Let. Cont.* ix. 10, 1.
Geta. Sest. *Let. Cont.* ix. 10, 2.

Similar figure, with altar, in a temple : roof only over opisthodomos, not over naos.

Æ Sept. Sev. B. M. (**O** ii.)
Geta. *Mus. Arig.* ii. 25, 354.

This is a clear instance of the copy of a statue on coins ; the
type of the statue is, however, quite ordinary. It seems that
the temple is rendered on the coin with some exactness. It is
seen nearly in profile from its left side. To the extreme left are
two pillars, which stand for the front of the temple ; next an
unroofed space, ναός, in which stands the statue; and furthest
to the right an opisthodomos with roof. That this is what is
intended seems to be proved by the fact that the corner of the
aëtoma does not reach to the furthest pillar ; but aëtoma and
pillars and the deity himself are all represented in a perspective

which is not correct, too much facing the spectator. The pillars
are fluted in their upper, plain in their lower half.

5.—Paus. III. 21, 7. . . . Καὶ Δήμητρος ἱερὸν ἅγιον.
DEMETER seated, holds ears of corn and sceptre.
Æ Geta. *Mus. Arig.* I. 9, 134.

6.—Paus. III. 21, 7. . . . Καὶ Ποσειδῶνος ἄγαλμα Γαιαόχου.
POSEIDON naked, standing, holds dolphin and trident.
Æ Caracalla. (O III.)
This is a pose in which Poseidon often appears on coins of
Corinth (D LX.–LXII.) and other cities of Peloponnesus.

7.—Paus. III. 21, 9.   Καλοῦνται δὲ ἐνταῦθα καὶ πύλαι Καστο-
ρίδες.
The DIOSCURI standing, each holding his horse ; between them
a tree.
Æ Geta. Mion. S. IV. 233, 75.
    Leake, *Sup.* p. 127.
The Dioscuri standing, each holds spear and sword; between
them altar entwined by snake.
Æ Sept. Sev. Imh. (O IV.)

8.—Paus. III. 21, 9.   Καὶ ἐν τῇ ἀκροπόλει ναὸς καὶ ἄγαλμα
Ἀθηνᾶς πεποίηται.
PALLAS standing, holds in her right hand a spear.
Æ Geta. Mion. S. IV. 233, 72.

9.—Paus. III. 22, 1.   Κατὰ δὲ τὴν νῆσον ἱερόν ἐστιν Ἀφρο-
δίτης ἐν τῇ ἠπείρῳ Μιγωνίτιδος, καὶ ὁ τόπος οὗτος ἅπας
καλεῖται Μιγώνιον.   τοῦτο μὲν δὴ τὸ ἱερὸν ποιῆσαι
λέγουσιν Ἀλέξανδρον.
APHRODITE standing, draped, holds apple and sceptre.
Æ Domna. Wiczay, *Mus. Hed.* I. pl. XVII. 374.
  Plautilla. Paris. R. & F. (O V.)
  Geta. Löbbecke.

10.—OTHER TYPES at Gytheium.
Zeus seated, holds thunderbolt and sceptre.
Æ Sept. Sev. Caracalla. B. M.
  Geta. Munich.
Zeus standing, holds Victory and sceptre, chlamys over
shoulders.
Æ Geta. Mion. II. 227, 86. Paris. (O VI.)
  Plautilla. Mion. S. IV. 233, 70.
Hermes standing at altar, holds purse and caduceus, chlamys
over shoulders.
Æ Sept. Sev. Paris.
  Caracalla. Mion. S. IV. 232, 68.
  Geta. B. M.

Same type, without altar.
Æ Sept. Sev. Berlin.
Caracalla. Vienna. (O VII.)

Two wrestlers.
Æ Geta. Leake, *Supp.* p. 127.

Artemis, left, clad in long chiton; holds in right hand, bow inverted, in left, long sceptre.
Æ Plautilla. Imh. (O VIII.)

Artemis, left, clad in long chiton, with quiver at shoulder, leaning right elbow on pillar; in left hand, bow.
Æ Plautilla. Berlin. Munich.

Artemis, as above, leaning left elbow on pillar, bow in right.
Æ Plautilla. (O IX.)

ASOPUS.

1.—Paus. III. 22, 9. Καὶ Ἀθηνᾶς ἱερόν ἐστιν ἐν τῇ ἀκροπόλει Κυπαρισσίας ἐπίκλησιν.

ATHENE standing, left, helmeted? clad in long chiton ; holds in raised right, spear, in left, cypress-branch.
Æ Sept. Sev. Paris. (O x.)

This coin is in so poor preservation that the description cannot be relied on.

2. OTHER TYPES at Asopus.

Zeus facing, clad in himation, sceptre in raised right hand.
Æ Sept. Sev. Paris. (O XI.)

Artemis hunting.
Æ Sept. Sev.

Dionysus standing, naked, holds kantharos and thyrsos; panther beside him.
Æ Carac. Munich. (O XII.)

Poseidon standing.
Æ Carac.

Nemesis ; a wheel at her feet; holds end of her veil,
Æ Plautilla. Berlin. (O XIII.)

(All in Mion. *S.* IV. p. 228.)

BOEAE.

1.—Paus. III. 22, 12. Μάντευμα ἦν αὐτοῖς Ἄρτεμιν ἔνθα οἰκήσουσιν ἐπιδείξειν. . . Ἄρτεμιν ὀνομάζουσι Σώτειραν.

Bust of ARTEMIS.
Æ Geta. Mion. *Sup.* IV. 230, 54.

2.—Paus. III. 22, 13. Καὶ ἑτέρωθι Ἀσκληπιοῦ καὶ Σαράπιδός τε καὶ Ἴσιδος.

F 2

ASKLEPIOS standing as usual.

Æ Caracalla. Paris. (O xiv.) Plautilla.
Mion. *Sup.* iv. 229, 53.

ISIS, holds sistrum and vase, usual ornament on her head.

Æ Domna. Munich. (O xv.)

3.—Paus. III. 23, 2. Πλέοντι δὲ ἐκ Βοιῶν τὴν ἐπὶ τὴν ἄκραν τῆς Μαλέας λιμήν ἐστιν ὀνομαζόμενον Νύμφαιον, καὶ Ποσειδῶνος ἄγαλμα ὀρθόν.

POSEIDON naked, standing, holds in right hand dolphin, in left trident.

Æ Domna. B. M. (O xvi.)

4.—OTHER TYPES at Boeae.

Eros walking, holds bow and torch.

Caracalla, Geta. (Paris.)

[Cf. 22, 11, Aphrodisias, a small town, was incorporated in Boeae.]

(See Mion. *Sup.* iv. p. 229.)

Athene standing, holds shield resting on the ground, and spear.

Æ Geta. Leake, *Sup.* p. 117.

LAS.

1.—Paus. III. 24, 6. Καὶ νῦν ἔτι τῆς πόλεώς ἐστι τῆς ἀρχαίας ἐρείπια, καὶ πρὸ τῶν τειχῶν ἄγαλμα ʿΗρακλέους.

HERAKLES standing, holds club and lion's skin.

Æ Sept. Sev. Mion. S. iv. 234, 77. Copenhagen.
Carac. Imh. (O xvii.)
Geta. Mion. S. iv. 235, 81. Copenhagen.

2.—Paus. III. 24, 7. Ἔστι δὲ ἐν τοῖς ἐρειπίοις ναὸς ᾿Αθηνᾶς ἐπίκλησιν ᾿Ασίας, ποιῆσαι δὲ Πολυδεύκην καὶ Κάστορά φασιν ἀνασωθέντας ἐκ Κόλχων.

ATHENE standing, in raised right, spear, left resting on shield placed on the ground.

Æ Caracalla. Munich. Athens.
Geta. Mion. II. 228, 88. Paris. (O xviii.)

This representation of Athene is in general aspect not unlike the Brauronian statue of Artemis (N XII.), which was supposed to be of Colchian origin ; but it has no appearance of extreme antiquity.

3.—Paus. III. 24, 8. Τῶν δὲ ὀρῶν ἐπὶ μὲν τοῦ ᾿Ιλίου Διονύσου τέ ἐστι καὶ ἐπ᾿ ἄκρας τῆς κορυφῆς ᾿Ασκληπιοῦ ναός.

ASKLEPIOS standing, as usual.

Æ Caracalla. Mion. S. iv. 234, 78. Paris.
Plautilla. B. M. (O xix.)

Stiff and apparently early figure of Hygieia standing, feeding serpent, which she holds in left hand on fruit which she holds in right hand.

Æ Caracalla.   B. M. &c.   (O xx.)
Sept. Sev.   Imh.   Occupation of hands reversed.

4.—Paus. III. 24, 9.   Πρὸς θαλάσσῃ δὲ ἐπὶ ἄκρας ναός ἐστι Δικτύννης Ἀρτέμιδος, καὶ οἱ κατὰ ἔτος ἕκαστον ἑορτὴν ἄγουσι.

ARTEMIS Dictynna standing drawing an arrow from quiver with right, in left, bow; beside her, dog and stag.
Æ Sept. Sev.   Leake, *Eur. Gr.* p. 60.   (O xxi.)

5.—OTHER TYPES at Las.

Tyche sacrificing at altar.
Æ Carac.   B. M., &c.

THURIA.

See Paus. IV. 31, 2.

TYPES ON COINS.

Athene standing, holds spear and shield which rests on the ground.
Æ Auton., Sep. Sev., Carac., &c.

In an inscription from Thuria (Le Bas and Wad., part II., no. 301), mention is made of a priest of Athene.

Athene standing, holds patera and spear.
Æ Sept. Sev., Carac.   Loebbecke.   (O xxii.)

This is apparently a type borrowed from that of Athena Panachaia at Patrae, Q XIV.

Zeus striding, holds thunderbolt and eagle (type of Messene).
Æ Auton.   Mion. S. IV. 216, 56.

Zeus standing, holds eagle and sceptre.
Æ Sept. Sev.
Geta.   Munich.

The letters ΛΑ[κεδαιμονίων] in the field of many coins of Thuria confirm the saying of Paus. IV. 31, 1.   Λακεδαιμονίοις δὲ ἔχειν τοῖς ἐν Σπάρτῃ τὴν Θουρίαν ἔδωκεν Αὔγουστος.   Cf. Weil in *Mittheil. d. I.* VII. 217.

Asklepios facing, leans on serpent-entwined staff.
Æ Geta.

Artemis, in long chiton, holds in both hands long torch.
Æ Domna.   Berlin.   (O xxiii.)

Apollo standing, clad in long chiton, holds in right, tripod, in left, sceptre.

Æ Domna.   Imh.   (O xxiv.)
Carac.   Berlin.

66   NUMISMATIC COMMENTARY ON PAUSANIAS.

TYCHE turreted, holds patera and cornucopiae.
Æ Sept. Sev.
  Carac., &c.
  Geta.
Tyche, holds rudder and cornucopiae.
Æ Sept. Sev.
Domna.

MESSENE.

1.—Paus. IV. 31, 9. Καὶ Δήμητρος ἱερὸν Μεσσηνίοις ἐστὶν
ἅγιον.
Head of DEMETER bound with corn.
Æ, Æ Auton.
2.—Paus. IV. 31, 10. Πλεῖστα δέ σφισι καὶ θέας μάλιστα
[ἀγάλματα] ἄξια τοῦ Ἀσκληπιοῦ παρέχεται τὸ ἱερόν.
χωρὶς μὲν γὰρ τοῦ θεοῦ καὶ τῶν παίδων ἐστὶν ἀγάλματα
κ.τ.λ., works of Damophon of Messene.
ASKLEPIOS with usual attributes; in field wreath.
Æ Auton. (Obv. Bust of City.) B. M. (P I.)
  Geta. Paris.
Hygieia standing.
Æ Domna. M.S. IV. 208, 15.
IV. 31, 10. Πόλις τε ἡ Θηβαίων καὶ Ἐπαμεινώνδας ὁ
Κλεόμμιδος, Τύχη τε καὶ τ. λ. Ἔστι δὲ καὶ Μεσσήνης
τῆς Τριόπα ναὸς καὶ ἄγαλμα χρυσοῦ καὶ λίθου Παρίου.
Bust of CITY of Messene wearing turreted crown and veil.
Æ Auton. B. M. (P II.) Mion. II. 211, &c.
  [Cf. however 31, 6. ἄγαλμα Μητρὸς θεῶν λίθου Παρίου,
  Δαμοφῶντος δὲ ἔργον.]
P I. and P II. are the two sides of one coin, issued probably
in imperial times. The wreath in the field may indicate that
it, like most of the autonomous coins issued in Greece during
Roman domination, was struck on the occasion of a festival. As
to the head on the obverse, we cannot be sure whether it is
meant for Messene or Tyche, or the Mother of the Gods. There
is something in its aspect which seems to show that it is meant
for the copy of a work of art. Almost all the great statues at
Messene were made by Damophon at the time of the restoration
of the city by Epaminondas, B.C. 370. Our coins enable us to
restore the outlines of several of the statues of this interesting
artist, of whom apart from coins and the statements of Pausanias
we know nothing.
3.—Paus. IV. 31, 10. Καὶ Ἡρακλέους (ἄγαλμα) . . . cf. 32, 1.

HERAKLES resting, in the attitude of Glycon's statue.
Æ Sept. Sev. Paris.

4.—Paus. IV. 31, 7. Δαμοφῶντος δέ ἐστι τούτου καὶ ἡ Λαφρία καλουμένη παρὰ Μεσσηνίοις.

ARTEMIS Laphria standing, clad in short chiton, spear in right, left elbow resting on column ; beside her, dog.
Æ Auton. Paris. (P III.)

A comparison of this figure with that of Artemis Laphria on the coins of Patrae (Q VII.—XI.), which reproduces the statue of Menaechmus and Soidas, furnishes sufficient reason for calling this figure also Laphria. It is probably, as the pillar indicates, a copy of a statue, therefore of the statue of Damophon. Damophon was doubtless familiar with the earlier statue of Laphria, which in his time stood not at Patrae but at Calydon in Aetolia, not far from Naupactus, where the Messenians were settled before their city was rebuilt by Epaminondas. The chief variety introduced by him on the older type seems to have been to make the goddess grasp a spear instead of placing her hand on her side.

5.—Paus. IV. 33, 2. Τοῦ Διὸς τοῦ Ἰθωμάτα τὸ ἱερόν. Τὸ δὲ ἄγαλμα τοῦ Διὸς Ἀγελάδα μέν ἐστιν ἔργον, ἐποιήθη δὲ ἐξ ἀρχῆς τοῖς οἰκήσασιν ἐν Ναυπάκτῳ Μεσσηνίων.

The ZEUS of Ageladas striding to right; in right hand, fulmen, on left wrist, eagle.
Ꝛ Auton. Fourth century. B. M. (P IV.) Third century. B. M. (P V.)
Ꝛ Æ (Tripod in front.) Auton.
Æ (Tripod behind.) Auton.

Cf. 31, 6. ἐν τῇ ἀγορᾷ Διός ἐστιν ἄγαλμα Σωτῆρος.

Zeus naked, standing to right; in right hand, sceptre, in extended left, eagle.
Æ Auton. (Tripod in field.) B. M.
Geta. (Sceptre surmounted by eagle.) Berlin. (P VI.)

Zeus standing, holds sceptre and thunderbolt.
Æ Sept. Sev. M.S. IV. 208, 14. Paris.

Zeus Nikephoros seated.
Æ Carac. Postol. Cat. 1884, p. 23.

The coins (P IV. V.), as might be expected from their date, give us only very free copies of the statue of Ageladas ; copies from which we can only judge of its pose and general composition ; in details they conform to the ideas of the times when the coins were severally struck. As to the statue itself, see Overbeck,

Kunstmythologie II. 12. The usual opinion that the head was beardless seems to be not well-founded.

6.—OTHER TYPES at Messene.

Athene standing, holds in raised right hand, lance, in left, shield.

Æ Sept. Sev.   *Stift St. Flor.* pl. III. 3.
Domna. Imh.   (P VII.)

CORONE.

1.—Paus. IV. 34, 7.   Χαλκοῦν δὲ καὶ ἐν ἀκροπόλει τῆς Ἀθηνᾶς τὸ ἄγαλμά ἐστιν ἐν ὑπαίθρῳ, κορώνην ἐν τῇ χειρὶ ἔχουσα —cf. 34, 6. καὶ Διονύσου ναός.

Head of ATHENE helmeted. *Rev.* grapes.

Æ Æ Auton. B. M., &c.

COLONIDES.

Paus. IV. 34, 8.

TYPES on coins.

Asklepios standing.

Æ Sept. Sev.

Aphrodite facing, holds apple and sceptre.

Æ Geta. Imh. (P X.)

Poseidon, holds dolphin and trident.

Æ Sept. Sev.

Tyche at altar, right hand advanced, in left, sceptre.

Æ Sept. Sev. B. M.

Pallas standing, holds patera and spear.

Æ Geta. Athens.

MOTHONE.

1.—Paus. IV. 35, 1.   Δόξῃ δὲ ἐμῇ δέδωκε τῷ χωρίῳ τὸ ὄνομα ὁ Μόθων λίθος. οὗτος δέ σφισι καὶ ὁ ποιῶν τὸν λιμένα ἐστί· τόν τε γὰρ ἔσπλουν στενώτερον ταῖς ναυσὶν ἐργάζεται παρήκων ὕφαλος, καὶ ἅμα μὴ ἐκ βυθοῦ ταράσσεσθαι τὸν κλύδωνα ἔρυμα ἔστηκεν.

PORT in form of an amphitheatre ; in the entrance a ship with sail.

Æ Carac. *Mus. Sancl.* III. p. 17 and 1.
Imh.   Statue in entrance. (P VIII.)

2.—Paus. IV. 35.   Ἐν Μοθώνῃ δὲ ναός ἐστιν Ἀθηνᾶς Ἀνεμώ-τιδος· Διομήδην δὲ τὸ ἄγαλμα ἀναθεῖναι καὶ τὸ ὄνομα τῇ θεῷ φασὶ θέσθαι.

PALLAS standing, helmeted, in right hand, patera, in left, spear.

Æ Domna. Mion. II. 213, 34.
Geta. B. M.
Plautilla. Mion. II. 213, 35. Lübbecke. (P XI.) Altar at her feet.

PYLOS. 69

Pallas standing, left hand extended, in right spear, against
which leans shield.
Æ Domna. B. M. (**P** xii.)
This type of Athene is by no means archaic ; it is a copy of
the Athene at Patrae (*q. v.*) **Q** xiv.
3.—Paus. iv. 35, 8. Καὶ ᾿Αρτέμιδος δ᾽ ἱερόν ἐστιν ἐνταῦθα.
ARTEMIS standing, her right hand resting on a spear : a stag
and a dog on either side of her.
Æ Geta. Mion. ii. 214, 36. Imh. (**P** xiii.)
Artemis hunting, holds arrow and bow.
Æ Domna. Mion. S. iv. 212, 34.
Geta. Mion. S. iv. 213, 36.
4.—OTHER TYPES at Mothone.
Isis.
Æ Domna. Plautilla. B. M.
Two female figures face to face, one has right hand raised, the
other right hand advanced, sceptre in left.
Æ Geta. Paris.
Poseidon, naked, holds dolphin and trident.
Æ Sept. Sev.
Asklepios.
Æ Geta.
Hephaestus running, holds torch in both hands.
Æ Auton. Imh. *M.G.* pl. D. 2. (**P** ix.)
Female figure holding out both hands.
Æ Plautilla. B. M. (**P** xiv.)

PYLOS.
1.—Paus. iv. 36, 2. ᾿Ενταῦθα ἱερόν ἐστιν ᾿Αθηνᾶς ἐπίκλησιν
Κορυφασίας.
PALLAS standing, holds patera and spear.
Æ Sept. Sev. Paris. B. M. Imh.
Caracalla. Berlin. (**P** xv.)
Plautilla. Mion. S. iv. 215, 52, &c.
Pallas, holds owl and spear.
Æ Domna. Mion. S. iv. 215, 48.
2.—OTHER TYPES at Pylos.
Asklepios.
Æ Caracalla.
Terminal female figure veiled and closely draped, holds in right
end of her garment.
Æ Carac. Paris.
Geta. Copenhagen. (**P** xvi.)
Dionysus, holds kantharos and thyrsos.
Æ Geta.

Goat reclining on basis.
Æ Sept. Sev., Geta.   B. M., &c.
Carac.   Munich.

CYPARISSIA.

1.—Paus. IV. 36, 7. ᾿Αφικομένων δὲ ἐς Κυπαρισσιὰς ἐκ Πύλου
σφίσι πηγὴ ὑπὸ τῇ πόλει πλησίον θαλάσσης ἐστί·
ῥυῆναι δὲ Διονύσῳ τὸ ὕδωρ λέγουσι θύρσῳ πλήξαντι
ἐς τὴν γῆν, καὶ ἐπὶ τούτῳ Διονυσιάδα ὀνομάζουσι τὴν
πηγήν.

DIONYSUS standing, in short chiton, holds kantharos and
thyrsos.
Æ Sept. Sev.   B. M.   Imh.   (P XVII.)
Domna, Caracalla.   Paris, &c.

2.—Paus. IV. 36, 7. ῎Εστι δὲ καὶ ᾿Απόλλωνος ἐν Κυπαρισσιαῖς
ἱερὸν καὶ ᾿Αθηνᾶς ἐπίκλησιν Κυπαρισσίας.

ATHENE standing, holds patera and spear, against which, some-
times, leans a shield.
Æ Sept. Sev.   Berlin.
Domna.   Mion S. 210, 20, 23.
Caracalla.   (P XVIII.)
Plautilla.   B. M.
Geta.   Munich.

APOLLO facing, naked, holds in right, branch, in left, lyre which
rests on pillar.
Æ Sept. Sev.   Berlin.   (P XIX.)

3.—Paus. IV. 36, 5. ᾿Εν δὲ Αὐλῶνι καλουμένῳ ναὸς ᾿Ασκληπιοῦ
καὶ ἄγαλμά ἐστιν Αὐλωνίου.

ASKLEPIOS standing; usual type.
Æ Sept. Sev.   Paris.   B. M.
Domna.   Loebbecke.
Caracalla, Geta.   B. M.

Hygieia standing; feeds serpent from patera.
Æ Domna.   Loebbecke.

4.—OTHER TYPES at Cyparissia.

Athlete, holding urn in which is a palm, and a staff.
Æ Domna.   Vaillant, Num. Gr. p. 92.

Poseidon naked, standing left; holds dolphin and trident.
Æ Caracalla.   Carlsruhe.

Tyche, holds cornucopiae and sceptre.
Æ Caracalla.   Munich.

ELIS.

The coins of Elis present us unfortunately in but very few
instances with copies of the numberless works of art which
existed at Olympia. There are, however, extant a very few

important pieces struck in the reign of Hadrian, and in that of Septimius Severus, which are clearly intended as medals to perpetuate certain works of art, and on them we have some of the most satisfactory reproductions of ancient statues extant on coins. Among the statues thus reproduced are the Olympian Zeus of Pheidias, the Aphrodite Pandemos of Scopas, and the Dionysus of Praxiteles. In the recent excavations at Olympia a large number of coins of Elis of the Imperial age were found, and are now in the Athenian coin-cabinet. See Postolacca's *Catalogue* of coins presented in 1883–4.

1.—Paus. v. 10, 7. Καὶ αὖθις ὁ ἀετὸς κάτεισιν ἐς στενόν, καὶ κατὰ τοῦτο Ἀλφειὸς ἐπ᾽ αὐτοῦ πεποίηται.

v. 14, 6. Μετὰ δὲ τοὺς κατειλεγμένους Ἀλφειῷ καὶ Ἀρτέμιδι θύουσιν ἐπὶ ἑνὸς βωμοῦ· τούτου δὲ οὐ πόρρω καὶ ἄλλος τῷ Ἀλφειῷ βωμὸς πεποίηται.

ALPHEIUS beardless reclining in waves, holds wreath and reed; before him, vessel.

Æ Hadrian. M.S. iv. 180, 49. Postol. *Cat.* 1884, p. 20.
Sept. Sev., Caracalla. Postolacca. *l. c.* pl. ii. 12.

Alpheius reclining, bearded, holds cornucopiae and reed.

Æ Hadrian. Sest. *Fontana Mus.* p. 58, 1.

See also below.

2.—Paus. v. 11. Καθέζεται μὲν δὴ ὁ θεὸς ἐν θρόνῳ χρυσοῦ πεποιημένος καὶ ἐλέφαντος· στέφανος δὲ ἐπίκειταί οἱ τῇ κεφαλῇ μεμιμημένος ἐλαίας κλῶνας. ἐν μὲν δὴ τῇ δεξιᾷ φέρει Νίκην ἐξ ἐλέφαντος καὶ ταύτην καὶ χρυσοῦ, ταινίαν τε ἔχουσαν καὶ ἐπὶ τῇ κεφαλῇ στέφανον· τῇ δὲ ἀριστερᾷ τοῦ θεοῦ χειρὶ ἔνεστι σκῆπτρον μετάλλοις τοῖς πᾶσι διηνθισμένον. ὁ δὲ ὄρνις ὁ ἐπὶ τῷ σκήπτρῳ καθήμενός ἐστιν ὁ ἀετός.

ZEUS Olympius seated on throne, holds Nike and sceptre.

Æ Hadrian. Florence. (P xx.) Berlin. (P xxi.) Athens. *Fontana*, pl. vi. 1.
Caracalla. Athens. Paris. Imh. *Mus. Hedcrv.*
Geta. B. M. Athens. Postolacca. *Cat.* 1884, p. 22.
Compare Stephani; *Compte rendu* 1876, plate, Nos. 3 and 4.

Head of Zeus Olympius laur.

Æ Hadr. Paris. (P xxii.)
Sept. Sev. Vaill. *Gr.* p. 82. Paris. (P xxiii.)

Head of Zeus.

Æ Auton. B. M.

Cf. v. 24, 1. Ἀπὸ δὲ τοῦ βουλευτηρίου πρὸς τὸν ναὸν ἐρχομένῳ τὸν μέγαν ἔστιν ἄγαλμα ἐν ἀριστερᾷ Διός,

ἐστεφανωμένον δὲ οἷα δὴ ἄνθεσι, καὶ ἐν τῇ δεξιᾷ χειρὶ
αὐτοῦ κεραυνὸς πεποίηται.

Zeus striding, hurls fulmen, eagle on extended right.

Æ (archaic) Auton.   Photiades Coll.
Æ Auton.   B. M.
  Hadr.   B. M.   Postol. *Cat.* 1884, pl. I. 6.

Zeus standing, resting on right leg, in sunk right hand, fulmen,
on left wrist, eagle.

Æ Hadr.   Postol. *Cat.* 1884, pl. I. 5, 7, 8.

Zeus seated, eagle flying from him.

Æ Auton.   Early.   B. M.

Nike winged, standing and running; thunderbolt; eagle tearing
serpent.

Æ Auton.

The reproductions, statue and head, of the colossus of Pheidias
are so fully discussed in the histories of sculpture that no more
need here be said about them.   See also Gardner, *Coins of Elis,*
p. 48.   The statues of Zeus in the Altis must have been numberless; we cannot venture therefore more closely to identify any
of the other coin-types.

3.—Paus. V. 13.   Ἔστι δὲ ἐντὸς τῆς Ἄλτεως καὶ Πέλοπι
ἀποτετμημένον τέμενος· ἡρώων δὲ τῶν ἐν Ὀλυμπίᾳ
τοσοῦτον προτετιμημένος ἐστὶν ὁ Πέλοψ ὑπὸ Ἠλείων
ὅσον Ζεὺς θεῶν τῶν ἄλλων.

PELOPS? clad in short chiton, leading horse by the bridle.

Æ Hadr.   Postol. *Cat.* 1884, p. 20.   Milan.
    Mus. Sancl. II. 19, 127.

4.—Paus. V. 17, 1.   Τὸ δὲ Ἥρας ἄγαλμα καθήμενόν ἐστιν ἐπὶ
θρόνῳ.

Head of HERA wearing stephanos.

Æ Auton.   B. M.

5.—Paus. VI. 25, 2.   Κρηπὶς δὲ ἐντὸς τοῦ τεμένους πεποίηται,
καὶ ἐπὶ τῇ κρηπῖδι ἄγαλμα Ἀφροδίτης χαλκοῦν ἐπὶ
τράγῳ κάθηται χαλκῷ· Σκόπα τοῦτο ἔργον, Ἀφροδίτην
δὲ Πάνδημον ὀνομάζουσι.

APHRODITE clad in long chiton and full over-garment, seated
sideways on goat galloping to right.

Æ Hadr.   B. M.   (P XXIV.)
  Sept. Sev.   Postol. *Cat.* 1884, p. 21.
  Carac.   Postol. *Cat.* 1884, pl. II. 11.

This identification is due to R. Weil (*Archäol. Aufsätze
E. Curtius gewidmet,* 1884), who publishes the coin of Severus,
of which a cut is here added.

The coin of the British Museum, **P** XXIV, though unfortunately in a very poor state of preservation, is in a better style than this, and apparently more faithful to the original. The attitude is less stiff, and more graceful. The mantle of Aphrodite seems to envelop her sides and back completely, and the chiton reaches to her feet; only her head and arms appear; in the treatment of these and of the drapery the charm of the statue must have consisted.

6.—Paus. VI. 26, 1. Θέατρον δὲ ἀρχαῖον μεταξὺ τῆς ἀγορᾶς καὶ τοῦ Μηνίου τὸ θέατρόν τε καὶ ἱερόν ἐστι Διονύσου· τέχνη τὸ ἄγαλμα Πραξιτέλους. θεῶν δὲ ἐν τοῖς μάλιστα Διόνυσον σέβουσιν Ἠλεῖοι, καὶ τὸν θεόν σφισιν ἐπιφοιτᾶν ἐς τῶν Θυίων τὴν ἑορτὴν λέγουσιν.

DIONYSUS facing; in raised right hand rhyton, in left thyrsus; on one side panther, on the other tympanum.

Æ Hadr.   Postol. *Cat.* 1884, pl. II. 9.   Berlin.   *Zeitschr. f. Num.* 13, 384.

Satyr, holds bunch of grapes and pedum.

Æ Hadr.   Mion. S. IV. 180, 46.

Cf. V. 19, 6. Διόνυσος δὲ ἐν ἄντρῳ κατακείμενος, γένεια ἔχων καὶ ἔκπωμα χρυσοῦν, ἐνδεδυκώς ἐστι ποδήρη χιτῶνα· δένδρα δὲ ἄμπελοι περὶ αὐτὸ καὶ μηλέαι τε εἰσὶ καὶ ῥοιαί.

Head of. Dionysus bearded, crowned with ivy.

Æ Sept. Sev.   Mion. S. IV. 181, 57.

[This is a mistake; the head is really of the Olympian Zeus, **P** XXIII.]

Dr. Weil has ably shown that the figure of Dionysus on the coin of Hadrian is very probably a copy of the statue of Praxiteles. In addition to internal evidence, the fact that the other coins of Hadrian bear copies of statues points in this direction. We reproduce Weil's cut, made under his direction from the coins.

The forms of the god are rather effeminate; his garment, fastened at his neck, falls round his lower limbs in full folds; the left leg is crossed over the right. His left elbow rests on a prop over which also hangs his upper garment. Beside him is on one side a panther, on the other his thyrsus and tympanum. In his left hand is a cup, in his right he lifts aloft a rhyton.

7.—OTHER TYPES at Elis.

Female figure (Olympia ?) facing, holds eagle and palm branch ; at her feet two rivers reclining.

Æ Hadr.   Postol. *Cat.* 1884, pl. II. 10.

Head of Olympia ; inscription ΟΛΥΜΠΙΑ.

Æ Auton.   B. M.

DYME.

1.—Paus. VII. 17, 5.   Ποταμός τε Λάρισος καὶ Ἀθηνᾶς ἐπὶ τῷ ποταμῷ ναός ἐστι Λαρισαίας, καὶ Ἀχαιῶν πόλις Δύμη σταδίους ὅσον τε τριάκοντα ἀπέχουσα τοῦ Λαρίσου.

VII. 17, 9.   Δυμαίοις δὲ ἔστι μὲν Ἀθηνᾶς ναὸς καὶ ἄγαλμα ἐς τὰ μάλιστα ἀρχαῖον.

Head of PALLAS, helmeted.

Æ Auton.   Leake, *Eur. Sup.* p. 124.

Auton.   Imh.   *M. G.* p. 163.

FISH.

Æ Auton.

2.—OTHER TYPES at Dyme.

Veiled female head, perhaps of Demeter, possibly of **Mater Dindymene** (Paus. VII. 17, 9).

Æ Auton.

PATRAE.

1.—Paus. VII. 18, 2.   Πατρέων ἡ πόλις· οὐ πόρρω δὲ αὐτῆς ποταμὸς Γλαῦκος ἐκδίδωσιν ἐς θάλασσαν.

VII. 19, 5. Ταύτης μὲν δὴ τῆς θυσίας ἕνεκα ὁ ποταμὸς ὁ πρὸς τῷ ἱερῷ τῆς Τρικλαρίας ᾿Αμείλιχος ἐκλήθη· τέως δὲ ὄνομα εἶχεν οὐδέν. Cf. 19, 9. τό τε ὄνομα ἐτέθη τὸ νῦν τῷ ποταμῷ Μείλιχος.

RIVER-GOD reclining.
Æ Ant. Pius. *Mus. Arig.* II. 7. 67.

2.—Paus. VII. 19, 6. ᾿Ιλίου δὲ ἁλούσης καὶ νεμομένων τὰ λάφυρα τῶν Ἑλλήνων, Εὐρύπυλος ὁ Εὐαίμονος λαμβάνει λάρνακα· Διονύσου δὲ ἄγαλμα ἦν ἐν τῇ λάρνακι, ἔργον μέν, ὥς φασιν, Ἡφαίστου, δῶρον δὲ ὑπὸ Διὸς ἐδόθη Δαρδάνῳ, κ.τ.λ.

(Box and statue in it brought by Eurypylus to Patrae.)
Man running to altar, clad in chlamys, holds a box in his hand.
Æ Hadrian. Berlin. (Q I.)
   Sabina. Sest. *Lit. Num,* IX. pl. I. 5.

The altar is probably that of Artemis Triclaria, on approaching which Eurypylus was healed of his insanity.

Genius of Patrae, naked, facing, one arm extended over altar, one rests on box raised on pedestal.
Æ M. Aurel. Imh. (Q II.) Berlin.
  L. Verus. Paris.
  Commodus. Paris.

Altar surmounted by box, in front of it some temple-officers; behind, spectators; in exergue, river-god reclining.
Æ Sept. Sev. Munich. (Q IV.)

Round box with conical cover, wreathed with ivy, within ivy wreath, sometimes between ears of corn.
Æ Auton. Paris. Imh. (Q III.) Leake, *Eur.* p. 83.
  Auton. *St. Flor.* p. 74, pl. II. 21.

Similar box; thyrsus and bunch of grapes.
Æ Auton. Paris.

This type has perplexed many writers: it has been termed Mons Panachaïcus, or (by Leake) the tomb of Patreus; but Kenner's view (*St. Flor.* p. 74) is preferable, according to which it represents the casket in which the statue of Bacchus was kept.

On the reverse of the coins above described appears a figure clad in a short chiton, holding in one hand a torch, in the other a short thyrsus or spear. This appears in our plates, Q XII. Leake supposes it to be a representation of the figure of Dionysus contained in the chest. A Dionysus it may be, but it can

scarcely stand for a statue supposed to have been brought from
Ilium, and so, presumably, of archaic type. There is something
to be said for the view of Kenner (*St. Flor., l. c.*), that the
deity represented is rather Artemis Triclaria, with whose cultus
the box containing the Dionysus was closely connected.

21, 1. Καὶ Διονύσου κατὰ τοῦτο τῆς πόλεώς ἐστιν ἱερὸν
ἐπίκλησιν Καλυδωνίου· μετεκομίσθη γὰρ καὶ τοῦ Διονύσου τὸ ἄγαλμα ἐκ Καλυδῶνος.

21, 6. Διονύσου δέ ἐστιν ἐνταῦθα ἀγάλματα, ἴσοι τε τοῖς
ἀρχαίοις πολίσμασι καὶ ὁμώνυμοι· Μεσατεὺς γὰρ καὶ
Ἀνθεύς τε καὶ Ἀροεύς ἐστιν αὐτοῖς τὰ ὀνόματα.

Dionysus? radiate, holds in right, bunch of grapes, over left arm,
nebris.

Æ Elagabalus ? Paris. (Q v.)

DIONYSUS standing, himation wrapped round loins, holds in
right hand kantharos, left rests on column.

Æ M. Aurel. *Mus. Arig.* I. 6, 86.

Dionysus, and Satyrs, one of whom supports him, and one
follows; also panther.

Æ Sept. Sev. Ramus, *Cat. Num. Dan.* I. IV. 1.

3.—Paus. VII. 18, 9. Πατρεῦσι δὲ ὁ Αὔγουστος ἄλλα τε τῶν
ἐκ Καλυδῶνος λαφύρων καὶ δὴ καὶ τῆς Λαφρίας ἔδωκε
τὸ ἄγαλμα, ὁ δὴ καὶ ἐς ἐμὲ ἔτι ἐν τῇ ἀκροπόλει τῇ
Πατρέων εἶχε τιμάς.

18, 10. Τὸ μὲν σχῆμα τοῦ ἀγάλματος θηρεύουσά ἐστιν,
ἐλέφαντος δὲ καὶ χρυσοῦ πεποίηται, Ναυπάκτιοι δὲ Μέ-
ναιχμος καὶ Σοΐδας εἰργάσαντο· τεκμαίρονται δὲ σφᾶς
Κανάχου τοῦ Σικυωνίου καὶ τοῦ Αἰγινήτου Κάλλωνος
οὐ πολλῷ γενέσθαι τινὶ ἡλικίαν ὑστέρους.

ARTEMIS Laphria facing, clad in short chiton which leaves
right breast bare, a quiver at her shoulder, right hand
rests on hip, in left bow, chlamys falling over left arm;
to left a dog, to right a pedestal, on which the bow rests.

Æ Galba.   Berlin.   Inscr. DIANA LAPHRIA.
Domitian. B. M.
Hadr. Imh. Loebbecke. (Q VI.)
L. Verus. B. M.   Stuttgart.   (Q VII.)
Commod. *Mus. Arig.* I. 7, 111.
Carac. B. M.

Artemis facing, clad in short chiton, right on hip, left rests on
bow which is supported by low pedestal; beside her,
dog.

Æ Carac.   Berlin.   Imh.   (Q VIII.)

Similar figure turned to right, bow rests on ground.

Æ Nero. Paris. ' (**Q** IX.) Inscr. DIANA LAPHRIA.

Artemis Laphria and Aphrodite of Corinth side by side.

Æ Commodus. B. M. Paris. Imh. (**Q** X.)

Artemis, carrying bow, in chariot drawn by four stags.

Æ Sept. Sev. *Mus. Arig.* II. 9, 98.

(It may be doubted if this supposed figure of Artemis be not her priestess as in **Q** XIII.)

Quiver with strap and hound.

Æ Nero. Bibl. Turin. Inscr. DEANA LAPHRIA.

The figure of Artemis Laphria on coins VI.–X. is almost unvaried ; the only marked variation being that the bow rests in some cases on a high pedestal, in some cases on a low pedestal, in some cases on the ground. The goddess stands, her head slightly turned to her left, clad in a short chiton with diplois which leaves the right breast bare, a chlamys hanging over her left shoulder, high cothurni on her feet. Her hair is in a knot at the back ; a quiver is at her shoulder. Her attitude is one of ease, yet not quite free from stiffness ; the left knee slightly advanced, the right hand resting on her side ; in the left hand a bow. The type is clearly a copy of the cultus-statue of Artemis Laphria ; this is even proved to demonstration by coin No. X. where it appears side by side with the Aphrodite of the Corinthian acropolis. We thus arrive at an interesting result. It is distinctly stated by Pausanias that the cultus-image at Patrae was the work of Menaechmus and Soidas of Naupactus. On this Brunn (*Gr. K.* I. 112) remarks that its date must be earlier than the settlement of Naupactus by the Messenians at the beginning of the Peloponnesian war. And Pausanias says that the sculptors must have lived not much after the archaic sculptors Callon of Aegina, and Canachus of Sicyon. But the statement of Pausanias seems exaggerated in view of the style of the figure on the coins, which may perhaps be assigned to the middle of the fifth century, but can with difficulty be given to an earlier date. In any case this will be one of the earliest statues which represent Artemis in Amazonian form, earlier than the statue of Strongylion (**A** I. II.), and as early as the rude relief from Asopus, *Arch. Zeitung* 1882, pl. VI. 1.

4.—Paus. VII. 19, 1. Ἰώνων τοῖς Ἀρόην καὶ Ἄνθειαν καὶ
Μεσάτιν οἰκοῦσιν ἦν ἐν κοινῷ τέμενος καὶ ναὸς Ἀρτέμιδος

Τρικλαρίας ἐπίκλησιν, καὶ ἑορτὴν οἱ Ἴωνες αὐτῇ καὶ
παννυχίδα ἦγον ἀνὰ πᾶν ἔτος.
20, 7.   Τῆς δὲ ἀγορᾶς ἄντικρυς κατ᾽ αὐτὴν τὴν διέξοδον
τέμενός ἐστιν Ἀρτέμιδος καὶ ναὸς Λιμνάτιδος.

Artemis running, holds torch and spear.

Æ Hadrian.   Imh.   Stag beside her.   (Q XI.)
    M. Aur.   M. S. IV. 144, ?60.   Paris.
    L. Verus.   B. M.   Dog at her feet.
    Commodus.   Vienna.   Stag and dog at her feet.

Artemis? standing in short chiton, holds torch and spear or
thyrsus.

Æ Auton.   St. Flor. p. 75, pl. II. 21.   Leake.   Paris.   Imh.   (Q XII.)

The same figure which Leake (Eur. p. 83) calls Bacchus; it
is not possible to say with certainty which of these deities is
intended.   See above.

Artemis on horse, with inflated veil, riding right; before her,
Pan holding pedum, seated on rock.

Æ M. Aur.   Sest. Let. Num. V. I. 13.

Sestini states that this coin, in the Cabinet de Chaudoir, is in
poor preservation.   The description cannot therefore be relied on.

5.—Paus. VII. 18, 12.   Πομπὴν μεγαλοπρεπεστάτην τῇ Ἀρτέμιδι
πομπεύουσι, καὶ ἡ ἱερωμένη παρθένος ὀχεῖται τελευταία
τῆς πομπῆς ἐπὶ ἐλάφων ὑπὸ τὸ ἅρμα ἐζευγμένων.

PRIESTESS in chariot drawn by two stags.

Æ M. Aur.   B. M.   Loebbecke.   (Q XIII.)
    Elagabalus.   Mion. II. 197, 364.

6.—Paus. VII. 20, 2.   Τοῦ περιβόλου δέ ἐστιν ἐντὸς τῆς
Λαφρίας καὶ Ἀθηνᾶς ναὸς ἐπίκλησιν Παναχαΐδος·
ἐλέφαντος τὸ ἄγαλμα καὶ χρυσοῦ.   Cf. 20, 6; 20, 9.

PALLAS standing in distyle temple, owl beside her : holds patera
and lance, against which rests a shield.

Æ M. Aur.   Mion. II. 195, 347.   Paris.   (Q XIV.)
    M. Aur.   M. S. IV. 143, 958.
    Commod.   M. S. IV. 146, 976, 977.   Paris.

Pallas standing, holds spear and Victory.

Æ Hadr.   M. S. IV. 141, 947.

Pallas standing, holds spear advanced and shield.

Æ Hadr.   Leake, Eur. p. 84.
    Hadr.   Berlin.   (Q XV.)
    Sabina.   B. M.

Pallas charging, holds spear and shield.

Æ Auton.   (Obv. Head of Herakles.)   B. M., &c.

Coin Q XIV. is particularly valuable.   The image on it is
shewn by the temple in which it is enclosed to be a copy of a

cultus-image, probably of that of Athena Panachaïs. The figure of Atheue holding in one hand a patera, in the other a spear appears on the coins of many of the cities of Peloponnesus, whether they had an ancient cult of Athena or not. We may account for this fact in either of two ways : (1) we may suppose that the various cities produced on their coins the widely-known type of the statue at Patrae, or (2) we may suppose that the cities commonly established within their own walls a shrine of Athena Panachaïs with a statue copied from the metropolitan statue of Patrae ; and that these local imitations were again imitated on the coins. It may count against the second view that Pausanias mentions no other temples of Athena Panachaïs.

7.—Paus. VII. 20, 3. Ἐρχομένῳ δὲ ἐς τὴν κάτω πόλιν Μητρὸς Δινδυμήνης ἐστὶν ἱερὸν, ἐν δὲ αὐτῷ καὶ ᾿Αττης ἔχει τιμάς· τούτου μὲν δὴ ἄγαλμα οὐδὲν ἀποφαίνουσι· τὸ δὲ τῆς Μητρὸς λίθου πεποίηται.

KYBELE seated ; holds patera and sceptre ; lion beside her.
Æ Commodus. Paris.

Female figure draped and turreted, holding a bunch of grapes in right hand and something in left, standing on cippus ; on either side of her a similar figure appearing to grasp her, and to be dancing or leaping.
Æ Geta. Berlin. (Q XVI.)

This type, the details of which are somewhat obscure, seems clearly to refer to the orgiastic rites connected with the worship of Mater Dindymene.

8.—Paus. VII. 20, 3. Ἔστι δὲ ἐν τῇ ἀγορᾷ Διὸς ναος ᾿Ολυμ-πίου, αὐτός τε ἐπὶ θρόνου καὶ ἑστῶσα ᾿Αθηνᾶ παρὰ τὸν θρόνον.

ZEUS seated in temple of six columns.
Æ Hadr. Mion. II. 194, 343.
Zeus seated, holds Victory and sceptre.
Æ Hadr. M. S. IV. 141, 946.
Commod. Mion. II. 196, 354. Imh. (Q XVII.)
Zeus seated, holds patera.
Æ M. Aur. Mus. Arig. I. 6, 87.

The Zeus on No. XVII. is of the usual Olympian type ; compare. the coins of Elis, P XX. XXI.

9.—Paus. VII. 20, 3. Τῆς τε ῞Ηρας ἄγαλμα τοῦ ᾿Ολυμπίου πέραν πεποίηται.

HERA ? veiled, seated on throne with high back ; right hand
advanced, in left pomegranate ?

Æ Hadr. B. M.
Aelius. Imh. (Q XVIII.)

The presence of the throne sufficiently proves that we
have in this case a copy of a statue. That the figure is
of Hera is however not certain. In the statue itself the
arms would be both stretched forward, the backward turning
of the left hand on the coin is probably only an attempt at
perspective.

10.—Paus. VII. 20, 3. Ἱερόν τε Ἀπόλλωνος πεποίηται, καὶ
Ἀπόλλων χαλκοῦς γυμνὸς ἐσθῆτος·

20, 6. Ἔχεται δὲ τῆς ἀγορᾶς τὸ ᾠδεῖον, καὶ Ἀπόλλων
ἐνταῦθα ἀνάκειται θέας ἄξιος· ἐποιήθη δὲ ἀπὸ λαφύρων,
ἡνίκα ἐπὶ τὸν στρατὸν τῶν Γαλατῶν οἱ Πατρεῖς ἤμυναν
Αἰτωλοῖς Ἀχαιῶν μόνοι.

20, 9. Ἐν τούτῳ τῷ ἄλσει καὶ ναοὶ θεῶν, Ἀπόλλωνος,
ὁ δὲ Ἀφροδίτης· πεποίηται λίθου καὶ τούτοις τὰ ἀγάλματα.

APOLLO naked, standing, his right hand extended, his left
holding lyre which rests on base.

Æ Ant. Pius.   Mion. II. 195, 344.
L. Verus.   Mus. Arig. IV. No. 34, pl. VI.   (Altar before him.)

Apollo seated, holds in raised right lyre, behind him cippus on
which a bird.

Æ Domit.   Mus. Arig. IV. pl. IV. 34.

The engraving in this work is inaccurately drawn and not
trustworthy.

Apollo standing on basis, holds in right hand Victory, in left
branch.

Æ M. Aur.   M. S. IV. 143, 959.
Commod.   M. S. IV. 149, 992.

It is unfortunate that we have been unable to procure a cast
of the coin last mentioned, which might perhaps be a copy of
the statue set up at the time of the Gaulish invasion. It is also
not impossible, though such conjectures are very dangerous, that
the Apollo γυμνὸς ἐσθῆτος of Pausanias may be represented by
the type of Apollo first mentioned, the naked Apollo with the
lyre resting on a basis.

11.—Paus. VII. 21, 7. Πρὸς δὲ τῷ λιμένι Ποσειδῶνός τε ναὸς
καὶ ἄγαλμά ἐστιν ὀρθὸν λίθου.

POSEIDON standing with one foot resting on rock ; holds dolphin
and trident.

Æ Domit. Paris. Inscribed NEPTVNO.
Hadrian. Imh. (No dolphin.) (Q XIX.)
Commod. M. S. IV. 147, 983.
Sept. Sev. Paris. (Holds figure of Pallas and trident, but the coin is
tooled and the figure of Pallas added.)

This type is shown by Q XXI. to be a copy of the statue
mentioned in the text. No. XIX is varied in the omission of
the dolphin, but otherwise is like the rest.

Poseidon standing, naked, thrusts with trident ; dolphin on
extended left arm.

Æ Auton. (*Obv.* Head of Pallas.) B. M. (Q XX.)

Obv. Owl ; *Rev.* Trident.
Æ Auton.

View of harbour of Patrae ; in the foreground, vessels ; in the
background figure of Poseidon (as above) in temple, and
another temple.

Æ Sept. Sev. Sest. *Fontana*, pl. II. 16. Berlin. (Q XXI.)
Geta. *St. Flor.* pl. II. 22. Paris.

View of same harbour : in the foreground vessels and statue
of Emperor ; in the background arcades surmounted by
temples.

Æ Commod. Mion. II. 197, 359. Imh. (Q XXII.)
Gordian. III. M. S. IV. 156, 1035.
Gordian. III. Gessner, *Imp.* pl. 176.

View of same harbour from the land ; temples in foreground ;
in background vessels and mole surmounted by tower
and equestrian statue.

Æ Sept. Sev. Sest. *Fontana*, pl. II. 11. Vienna (Q XXIII.)

All these coins are discussed by Kenner, *St. Flor.* p. 78.

12.—Paus. VII. 20, 9. Τὸ μὲν δὴ ἄγαλμα τοῦ Ἀσκληπιοῦ,
πλὴν ἐσθῆτος, λίθου τὰ ἄλλα.

VII. 21, 14. Ἔστι δὲ καὶ ἱερὸν Πατρεῦσιν Ἀσκληπιοῦ·
τοῦτο τὸ ἱερὸν ὑπὲρ τὴν ἀκρόπολιν τῶν πυλῶν ἐστιν
ἐγγὺς αἱ ἐπὶ Μεσάτιν ἄγουσιν.

ASKLEPIUS standing, resting, as usual, on serpent-staff.
Æ Sabina. Berlin.
M. Aur. M. S. IV. 144, 962. Paris.
Commod. B. M. Berlin. (Q XXIV.)

13.—Paus. VII. 21, 10. Ἐν Πάτραις δὲ οὐ πολὺ ἀπωτέρω τοῦ
Ποσειδῶνος ἱερά ἐστιν Ἀφροδίτης.

Head of APHRODITE.
Æ Aut. B. M.

Eros embracing Psyche.

Æ Commod. Imh. *M. G.* p. 166.

14.—Paus. VII. 21, 10. Ἔστι δὲ καὶ ἀγάλματα τοῦ λιμένος ἐγγυτάτω χαλκοῦ πεποιημένα Ἄρεως, τὸ δὲ Ἀπόλλωνος. ARES standing, helmeted, holds spear and shield.

Æ M. Aur. Paris. (No shield.)
Sept. Sev. M. S. IV. 151, 1009.

15.—Paus. VII. 21, 13. Ἐν Πάτραις δὲ πρὸς τῷ ἄλσει καὶ ἱερὰ δύο ἐστὶ Σαράπιδος· ἐν δὲ τῷ ἑτέρῳ πεποίηται μνῆμα Αἰγύπτου τοῦ Βήλου.
Head-dress of ISIS.

Æ Cleopatra. B. M. Imh.

16.—OTHER TYPES at Patrae.

Male figure naked, standing on a column in a circular enclosure.

Æ Galba. Berlin.
Domit. Naples. Paris.
Hadr. M.S. Loebbecke. (R I.)

Rome seated, holding standard, crowned by a warrior wearing helmet and holding spear.

Æ Domitian. Froehner. (R II.)
M. Aur., Commodus. Paris, &c.

Genius of the City; holds patera and cornucopiae at altar. (Sometimes inscribed GEN[ius].)

Æ Nero. Imh. B. M. Domit., &c.

Tyche of the city, turreted, holding cornucopiae.

Æ Verus, Commodus, &c.

Head of Tyche, with cornucopiae.

Herakles resting on club.

Æ Nero. Imh. Inscr. HERCVLI AVGVSTO.
M. Aur. B. M., &c.

Herakles holding club in both hands, lion's skin on left arm.

Æ Commodus. Bibl. Turin. (R III.)

Hermes seated, ram at his feet; holds purse and caduceus.

Æ Carac. B. M. Imh. Berlin.

Similar figure in temple.

Æ Commod. Mion. Berl. Carac. Imh. (R IV.) B. M. Berlin.

Hermes standing, ram at his feet; behind him, term.

Æ Verus. Berlin. (R V.)
Commod., Severus.

Juppiter Liberator (so inscribed) :—

Zeus standing, holds eagle and sceptre.

Æ Nero. Paris.

Libertas, &c.

The figure of Hermes seated (**R** IV.) is closely similar to a type of Corinth (**F** CX., CXI.), but not identical, for at Patrae the god holds a purse in his right hand, which he does not at Corinth. In this case it is clear that either the people of Patrae copied their cultus-statue from that of the Corinthians, or the people of Corinth from the Patreans. The standing figure of Hermes (**R** v.) also nearly resembles one on a coin of Corinth (**E** LXXXVI.).

AEGIUM.

1.—Paus. VII. 23, 5. Αἰγιεῦσι δὲ Εἰλειθυίας ἱερόν ἐστιν ἀρχαῖον, καὶ ἡ Εἰλείθυια ἐς ἄκρους ἐκ κεφαλῆς τοὺς πόδας ὑφάσματι κεκάλυπται λεπτῷ, ξόανον πλὴν προσ- ώπου τε καὶ χειρῶν ἄκρων καὶ ποδῶν· ταῦτα δὲ τοῦ Πεντελησίου λίθου πεποίηται· καὶ ταῖς χερσὶ τῇ μὲν ἐς εὐθὺ ἐκτέταται, τῇ δὲ ἀνέχει δᾷδα. . . . . . . ἔργον δὲ τοῦ Μεσσηνίου Δαμοφῶντός ἐστι τὸ ἄγαλμα.

EILEITHUIA facing, clad in long chiton with diploïs, head wears polos; holds in raised right torch, in extended left hand another torch.

Æ Ant. Pius.　B. M.　*Mus. Arig.* II. 14, 155.　Bibl. Turin.　(**R** VI.)
L. Verus.　*Mus. Arig.* I. 5, 76.
S. Sev.　Sest. *Mus. Font.* p. 51, 4.　Berlin.
Carac.　Imh.　(Position of arms transposed.)

Geta.　Paris.　(Figure turreted.)　Inscr. ΑΙΓΙΕΩΝ ΑϹΙ (**R** VII.).

The identification of the figure on **R** VI., VII., as Eileithuia cannot be regarded as certain. If we accept the identification we must suppose that the word δᾷς has fallen out after ἐκτέταται, 'in one hand she holds out a torch, in the other holds up a torch': and in support of this emendation we may cite the occurrence of δᾷδας in the plural in the next line. On the other hand the Paris coin (**R** VII.) presents in this view difficulties. On it the head of the goddess wears a turreted crown, which seems inappropriate to Eileithuia. The final letters of the inscription on this coin are uncertain; all that is visible is ΑϹΙ which may stand for 10 assaria, but may also be the beginning of some explanatory word like the ΖΕΥϹ ΜΕΓΑϹ, which occurs at Aegium beside the figure of Zeus. Nearly similar are the two figures on a coin of Argos, **K** XL., which are explained in the text as two Eileithuiae.

The following may, perhaps, be a representation of Eileithuia:—

Female figure, hair in knot, and clad in long chiton with
diploïs; holds in extended right an object which may be
a torch, her left hand hangs by her side.

Æ Auton.   *Obv.* head of Artemis.   B. M.   Klagenfurt.   (R VIII.)

Engraved in Wieseler's *Denkmaeler* (II. 57, 729) and Gerhard,
Ant. Bildw. CCCIX., 1, is a figure of Eileithuia professedly taken
from a coin of Aegium.   It is, however, evidently badly drawn,
and appears to be rather a copy of a figure of Eileithuia or
Demeter at Bura.

2.—Paus. VII. 23, 7.   Τῆς δὲ Εἰλειθυίας οὐ μακρὰν Ἀσκληπιοῦ
τέ ἐστι τέμενος καὶ ἀγάλματα Ὑγιείας καὶ Ἀσκληπιοῦ.
ἰαμβεῖον δὲ ἐπὶ τῷ βάθρῳ τὸν Μεσσήνιον Δαμοφῶντα
εἶναι τὸν εἰργασμένον φησίν.

ASKLEPIOS seated to right, on throne, himation falling from
shoulder, holds in right hand sceptre ; before him, serpent
twined round altar.

Æ M. Aurel.   M. S. IV. 25, 146.   Paris.   (Said to hold Victory, but wrongly.)
Commodus.   Berlin.   (R IX.)
Sept. Sev.   M. S. IV. 27, 158.

Hygieia standing ; her right hand over altar, round which
snake twines ; in her left, patera.

Æ M. Aurel.   Vienna.
Sept. Sev.   Loebbecke.   (R x.)

Asklepios seated, and Hygieia standing ; between them, altar
entwined by serpent.

Æ Commod.   M. S. IV. 26, 152, 154.   Paris.   (R XI.)

There can be scarcely a doubt that these figures reproduce
the group of Damophon ; on all the coins the snake-entwined
altar appears as a sort of identification ; and the separate figures
on IX. and X. are exactly reproduced in the group on XI.   We
thus gain definite and welcome information as to the style of
Damophon, information which seems to show that in representing Asklepios he followed the type of the Zeus of Pheidias.
In his Hygieia, also, which is of noble and majestic type, he
seems to have followed the traditions of the best school.   This
confirms the view of Brunn (*Gr. K.*, I. 291), 'we shall not err
in recognising in Damophon one of the most religious artists
of his time, who endeavoured to retain art at that level of
moral elevation to which it had been raised, principally by
Pheidias.'

3.—Paus. VII. 23, 9.   Ἔστι δὲ καὶ Διὸς ἐπίκλησιν Σωτῆρος
ἐν τῇ ἀγορᾷ τέμενος, καὶ ἀγάλματα ἐσελθόντων ἐν

ἀριστερᾷ χαλκοῦ μὲν ἀμφότερα, τὸ δὲ οὐκ ἔχον πω γένεια
ἐφαίνετο ἀρχαιότερον εἶναί μοι.

24, 4. Ἔστι δὲ καὶ ἄλλα Αἰγιεῦσιν ἀγάλματα χαλκοῦ
πεποιημένα, Ζεύς τε ἡλικίαν παῖς καὶ Ἡρακλῆς, οὐδὲ
οὗτος ἔχων πω γένεια, Ἀγελάδα τέχνη τοῦ Ἀργείου.

Archaic statue of ZEUS on basis, naked, without beard, holds
in raised right, thunderbolt, on extended left arm, eagle.

Æ Auton.　Obv. Head of bearded Zeus.　B. M.　(R xii.) &c.
Ant. Pius.　B. M.　Paris.
Ant. Pius.　Sest. Mus. Font. pl. iv. 2.
M. Aur.　Mion. S. iv. 25, 144.　Paris.　(R xiii.)
Sept. Sev.　Leake, Eur. p. 5.

The British Museum coin (R xii.) bears the inscription
HMIOBEΛIN (ἡμιωβόλιον), shewing its current value. The
inscription on the Fontana coin is in the engraving in the
Mus. Font., ZEYC MEΓAC, the second word being indistinct,
so that there stood on the coin either ZEYC MEΓAC or,
perhaps, ZEYC CωTHP. On the Paris coin (R xiii.) the
reading seems to be ΛIΓIEωN ΠAIC, 'the child of the people
of Aegae.' The figure of Zeus on both the coins on our plate
is beardless. There can be no question that this striding archaic
figure is intended to represent a statue; this is proved by the
basis or plinth, sometimes hung with wreaths, on which he
stands. A doubt may, however, be entertained which of the
statues of Zeus mentioned by Pausanias is here intended: he
speaks of two, both archaic, and both beardless. He seems to
ascribe one of the two to Ageladas of Argos, and our coin-type
is in attitude just like that which reproduces the statue by
Ageladas preserved at Messene (P v.). It is not important to
decide the question, as the attitude of the figure of Zeus on the
coins is quite conventional. The hinder foot does not rest flat
on the ground, but the heel is raised; and the anatomy of the
body is well rendered, but the treatment of the hair, which falls
in long curls, is archaic.

There seems insufficient foundation for Jahn's theory that
Zeus under this form is regularly Polieus.

Zeus as an infant suckled by the she-goat Amaltheia; on
either side, tree; above, eagle with spread wings.

Æ Auton.　Bull. dell' I. 1843, p. 109. (Streber, Denkschr. d. K. Acad. zu Münch.
vii. pl. ii. 26.)　Bibl. Turin.　(R xiv.)

The proper home of the myth of Amaltheia was in Crete;
but there was probably at Aegium a local legend which in

some way connected the name of the city with her, Αἴγιον
with αἴξ.

4.—Paus. VII. 24, 2. Καὶ τέταρτον Ὁμαγυρίῳ Διί. ἐνταῦθα
Διὸς καὶ ᾿Αφροδίτης ἐστὶ καὶ ᾿Αθηνᾶς ἀγάλματα.
Ὁμαγύριος δὲ ἐγένετο τῷ Διὶ ἐπίκλησις, ὅτι ᾿Αγαμέμνων
ἤθροισεν, κ.τ.λ.
24, 3. ᾿Εφεξῆς δὲ τῷ Ὁμαγυρίῳ Διὶ Παναχαιᾶς ἐστὶ
Δήμητρος.

Æ of Achaean League :—

Obv. Zeus standing, naked ; holds Nike and long sceptre (**R** XV.).
Rev. Female figure seated, holds wreath and long sceptre
(**R** XVI.).

Æ Geta. Zeus as above. M. S. IV. 30, 168.

As all the bronze coins of the Achaean League bear these
types, they would seem to represent the principal deities of the
place of meeting of the League. After the destruction of
Helice, this was Aegium, and solemn sacrifices were offered to
the principal deities of that city. It seems that the historical
associations connected with Zeus Homagyrius made him a
peculiarly suitable patron-deity for the League.

The figure on the coin, a naked Zeus, holding Victory in his
hand, may well be a copy of a statue set up in this temple in
the days of the revival of the League, or possibly at an earlier
period. The figure of the reverse may, perhaps, be Demeter
Panachaia, but it certainly has none of the attributes of Demeter.
It would therefore be preferable to regard it as representing not
Demeter but Achaia personified. Similarly Aetolia appears on
coins of the Aetolian League, Bithynia on those of the Bithynian
kings, Roma on those of Rome, &c.

The following is certainly Demeter :—

Demeter standing, holds in right hand poppies and corn, in
left hand, sceptre.

Æ L. Verus. Leake, *Suppl. Eur.* p. 111. (**R** XVII.)

Zeus naked, standing, holds eagle and long sceptre, held
transversely, garment over left arm.

Æ L. Verus. *Arig.* I. Imp. v. 76.
Carac. M. S. IV. 28, 159. Paris. (**R** XVIII.)

Zeus seated, holds Victory and sceptre.

Æ Plautilla. Pellerin, *Mélanges*, I. pl. 1, 8.

Head of Zeus, right, laur.

Æ Auton. Vienna. (**R** XIX.) Imh. B. M. Inscribed **HMIOBEΛIN.**

A very unusual type of head for Zeus.

5.—Paus. VII. 23, 9. Αἰγιεῦσι δὲ ᾿Αθηνᾶς τε ναὸς καὶ ῞Ηρας ἐστὶν ἄλλος. ᾿Αθηνᾶς μὲν δὴ δύο ἀγάλματα λευκοῦ λίθου. Cf. 23, 10. ῎Εστι μὲν Ποσειδῶν καὶ ῾Ηρακλῆς, ἔστι δὲ Ζεύς τε καὶ ᾿Αθηνᾶ, θεοὺς δὲ σφᾶς καλοῦσιν ἐξ ῎Αργους.

PALLAS standing, holds spear and shield which rests on the ground.

Æ M. Aurel. *Mus. Arig.* II. 14, 154. (Pallas unhelmeted ?)
Commod. Sest. *Princ. Danimarca*, 18, 1.
Carac. Berlin. (R xx.)

This type of Athene is not usual in Peloponnese; it is quite different from the usual Athene Panachaea (Q xiv.).

6.—Paus. VII. 24, 1. Αἰγιεῦσι δὲ ἔστι μὲν πρὸς τῇ ἀγορᾷ ναὸς ᾿Απόλλωνι καὶ ᾿Αρτέμιδι ἐν κοινῷ· ἔστι δὲ ἐν τῇ ἀγορᾷ ἱερὸν ᾿Αρτέμιδος, τοξευούσῃ δὲ εἴκασται.

Artemis clad in short chiton; in her raised right, torch; in her left, which rests on pillar, a bow; dog at her feet.

Æ Ant. Pius. Imh. (R xxi.)
Sept. Sev. Berlin.

Artemis running, her veil floating round her head; holds torch in each hand : at her feet, dog (which, however, looks more like a peacock).

Æ Domna. Imh. (R xxii.)

Τοξευούσῃ δὲ εἴκασται reminds us of the phrase used by Pausanias of Artemis Laphria at Patrae; and the figure on R xxi. is apparently a variation on the archaic Laphria of Menaechmus and Soidas, the goddess holding a torch in her right hand, instead of resting it on her side.

7.—Paus. VII. 24, 2. Πρὸς θαλάσσῃ δὲ ᾿Αφροδίτης ἱερὸν ἐν Αἰγίῳ, καὶ μετ᾽ αὐτὸ Ποσειδῶνος.

POSEIDON standing, his right foot on a rock, his right hand resting on trident.

Æ Commodus. M. S. IV. 27, 155.

APHRODITE naked, arranging her tresses; at her feet, dolphin.

Æ Faustina Jun. Griolet at Geneva. (R xxiii.)

8.—OTHER TYPES at Aegium.

Phthia advancing right, her peplum flying, before her, dove of colossal size.

Æ Auton. B. M. (R xxiv.) Eckhel, *N. V.* p. 118.

For the story of Phthia and the dove, see Athenaeus, p. 395a.

This is, with one doubtful exception (Overbeck, *Kunstmyth.*

II. p. 415), the only representation of the myth of Phthia.   It
has already been rightly explained by Khell and Eckhel.
River-god reclining; holds vase and reed.

Æ Auton.   Eckhel, *N. V.* 118.   Vienna.

Head of Aegium turreted, inscribed ΑΙΓΙΟΝ.

Æ Auton.   Vienna.

Sarapis and Fortune, side by side.

Æ M. Aur.   Kenner, *St. Flor.* p. 59, pl. II. 8.

Turreted female figure, holds sceptre and cornucopiae.

Æ M. Aur.   Sept. Sev.   Plautilla.
   Carac.   Loebbecke.

HELICE.

1.—Paus. VII. 24, 5.   Ἐνταῦθα ᾤκητο Ἑλίκη πόλις, καὶ Ἰωσιν
   ἱερὸν ἁγιώτατον Ποσειδῶνος ἦν Ἑλικωνίου.

Obv.   Head of POSEIDON in circle of waves.

Rev.   Trident between fishes in wreath.

Æ Auton.   Fourth century.   *Z. f. N.* VII. pl. VIII. 6.

BURA.

1.—Paus. VII. 25, 9.   Τῆς Βούρας ἐγένοντο οἰκισταί.   Ναὸς
   ἐνταῦθα Δήμητρος, ὁ δὲ Ἀφροδίτης Διονύσου τέ ἐστι,
   καὶ ἄλλος Εἰλειθυίας.   Λίθου τοῦ Πεντελησίου τὰ
   ἀγάλματα, Ἀθηναίου δὲ ἔργα Εὐκλείδου· καὶ τῇ Δήμητρί
   ἐστιν ἐσθής.

DEMETER or EILEITHUIA, clad in long chiton and himation ;
   right hand raised ; in left, torch.

Æ Caracalla.   Munich.
   Geta.   B. M.   (S I.)

APHRODITE partly nude ; holds sceptre.

Æ Domna.   Mion. II. 165, 128.   (Vaillant.)

It is not certain whether the figure on S I. is of Demeter or
of Eileithuia.   The outstretched right hand would tell rather
in favour of the latter attribution, it being very usual to
find on vases figures of Eileithuia with outstretched hands,
a gesture intended to indicate a smooth course in child-
birth.   The phrase of Pausanias strictly taken would seem to
assert that the figure of Demeter alone was draped, those of
Aphrodite, Dionysus, and Eileithuia all undraped ; but it can
scarcely be supposed that Eileithuia would be nude.   As to
Eucleides of Athens see Brunn (*Gr. K.* I. p. 274), who conjectures that he worked for the people of Bura when they
restored their city soon after its destruction in B.C. 373.   In

that case he would be a contemporary of Damophon, a period which will very well suit the figure on **S** I. We shall return to Eucleides under Aegira.

2.—Paus. VIII. 25, 10. Καταβάντων δὲ ἐκ Βούρας ὡς ἐπὶ θάλασσαν ποταμός τε Βουραϊκὸς ὀνομαζόμενος καὶ Ἡρακλῆς οὐ μέγας ἐστὶν ἐν σπηλαίῳ· ἐπίκλησις μὲν καὶ τούτου Βουραϊκός.

Temple on a hill, in the side of which is a portico, and a cave within which statue of Herakles, spear? in raised right hand ; below, a vase.

Æ Geta. Prok.-Osten, *A. Z.* 1843, pl. IX. 14.
Athens. (**S** II.) Vienna.

HERAKLES bearded, standing ; raised club in right hand, lion's skin in left; behind him, bow.

Æ Geta. Mion. II. 166, 129.
Geta. Vienna. (**S** III.)

There is an apparent discrepancy between the type of the figure in the shrine or cave on **S** II. and the figure of Herakles on **S** III. The former seems to hold a spear, and is so described by v. Duhn in *Mittheil. d. d. Inst. Ath.* III. 62 ; the latter clearly holds a club. But considering the very small size of the figure on **S** II. we can scarcely insist upon this apparent difference. It is likely that in both cases a figure of Herakles is intended, of which figure **S** III. gives us, of course, the best idea. This figure is of stiff and decidedly archaic type, dating from not later than the middle of the fifth century. The antiquity of the Buraic cultus of Herakles is shewn by its seat being in a cave, and by the survival in connection with it of a primitive oracle by lot. Beside the cave on **S** II. is a portico, and above it, on the top of the hill, a temple, no doubt of one of the deities mentioned by Pausanias in the passage above quoted.

AEGIRA.

1.—Paus. VII. 26, 3. Ἀρτέμιδος Ἀγροτέρας ἐποιήσαντο ἱερόν, τὸ σόφισμα ἐς τοὺς Σικυωνίους οὐκ ἄνευ τῆς Ἀρτέμιδος σφισιν ἐπελθεῖν νομίζοντες. . . . . . Ἀρτέμιδός τε ναὸς καὶ ἄγαλμα τέχνης τῆς ἐφ᾽ ἡμῶν.

VII. 26, 11. Θεῶν δὲ ἱερὰ Διονύσου καὶ Ἀρτέμιδός ἐστιν· ἡ μὲν χαλκοῦ πεποίηται, βέλος δὲ ἐκ φαρέτρας λαμβάνουσα.

ARTEMIS as huntress, standing ; holds in left, bow, and with right hand draws arrow from quiver; at her feet, dog looking up.

Æ Plautilla.   B. M.   Munich.   (S IV.)   M. S. IV. 22, 128.

In Sett. *Lett. Num. Cont.* v. p. 11 Artemis is said to hold a torch in place of the bow on coins of Plautilla.

Similar figure of Artemis running.

Æ Plautilla.   Berlin.   (S v.)

The phrase τέχνης τῆς ἐφ᾽ ἡμῶν would well characterize either of these figures.

Deer.

Æ Auton.   B. M.

2.—Paus. vII. 26, 4.   Παρείχετο δὲ ἡ Αἴγειρα ἐς συγγραφὴν ἱερὸν Διὸς καὶ ἄγαλμα καθήμενον, λίθου τοῦ Πεντελησίου, Ἀθηναίου δὲ ἔργον Εὐκλείδου.

ZEUS seated, in attitude of the Olympian deity ; holds Victory and sceptre.

Æ Sep. Sev.   Sest. *Lett. Num. Cont.* VIII. p. 2, No. 2.
Plautilla.   B. M.   (S VI.)   Sest. *l.c.* No. 4.
Plautilla.   Leake, *Eur. Sup.* p. 111.

This representation, though of very ordinary character, yet, if we suppose it a copy of Eucleides' work, has interest as shewing that Eucleides adhered to the Pheidian school in his statue of Zeus, as indeed we might suppose from his representing a seated Zeus at all. Eucleides was probably a contemporary of Damophon, and he seems, if we may judge from the very slight evidence which remains (see under Bura), to have followed the same tendencies.

3.—Paus. VII. 26, 4.   Ἐν τούτῳ τῷ ἱερῷ καὶ Ἀθηνᾶς ἄγαλμα ἕστηκε· πρόσωπόν τε καὶ ἄκραι χεῖρες ἐλέφαντος καὶ οἱ πόδες, τὸ δὲ ἄλλο ξόανον χρυσῷ τε ἐπιπολῆς διηνθισμένον ἐστὶ καὶ φαρμάκοις.

PALLAS standing, holds spear, and shield which rests on the ground.

Æ Sept. Sev.   Paris.   Loebbecke.   (S VII.)
Plautilla.   *Mus. Arig.* IV. pl. XIII. No. 54.

Compare R XX. and our remarks on it.

4.—Paus. VII. 26, 7.   Ἀσκληπιοῦ δὲ ἀγάλματα ὀρθά ἐστιν ἐν ναῷ, καὶ Σαράπιδος ἑτέρωθι καὶ Ἴσιδος, λίθου καὶ ταῦτα Πεντελησίου.

ASKLEPIUS standing as usual.

Æ Plautilla.   M. S. IV. 22, 129 ; 29, 166.   Paris.

Head of Asklepius.

Æ Auton. Mion. II. 164, 118.

ACKΛH in wreath (Asklepieia, the Games).

Æ Auton. Sest. *Let. Num.* IX. pl. I. 32.

Hygieia standing.

Geta. *St. Flor.* p. 61, pl. II. 9.

5.—Paus. VII. 26, 8. Οἶδα καὶ οἴκημα ἐν Αἰγείρᾳ θεασάμενος· ἄγαλμα ἦν ἐν τῷ οἰκήματι Τύχης, τὸ κέρας φέρουσα τὸ Ἀμαλθείας· παρὰ δὲ αὐτὴν Ἔρως πτερὰ ἔχων ἐστίν.

TYCHE turreted ; holds sceptre and cornucopiae.

Æ Plautilla. M. S. IV. 22, 131. Paris.
Plautilla. Berlin. Loebbecke. (S VIII.)

Tyche as above, face to face with Eros winged, who stands with legs crossed leaning on a long torch or staff : between them, altar entwined by serpent ?

Æ Plautilla. Berlin. (S IX.)

In this case, the juxtaposition of Tyche with Eros shews that both figures are intended as copies of the statues.

PELLENE.

1.—Paus. VII. 27, 2. Κατὰ δὲ τὴν ὁδὸν ἐς αὐτὴν τὴν πόλιν ἐστὶν Ἀθηνᾶς λίθου μὲν ἐπιχωρίου ναός, ἐλέφαντος δὲ τὸ ἄγαλμα καὶ χρυσοῦ· Φειδίαν δὲ εἶναι τὸν εἰργασμένον φασί, πρότερον ἔτι ἢ ἐν τῇ ἀκροπόλει τε αὐτὸν τῇ Ἀθηναίων καὶ ἐν Πλαταιαῖς ποιῆσαι τῆς Ἀθηνᾶς τὰ ἀγάλματα.

PALLAS clad in long chiton, thrusting with lance, and holding before her oval shield.

Æ Sept. Sev. Bibl. Turin. (S x.) *Mus. Arig.* IV. No. 52, pl. XI.
Domna. Paris.
Plautilla. *St. Flor.* p. 79.

This is a most interesting illustration of what 'Pausanias considered to be the early style of Pheidias. The character of the figure on our coin is far earlier than the Athenian statues of Pallas by Pheidias, and in type approaches such figures as the Athene Chalcioecus **N** XIII., or the statue by Dipoenus and Scyllis at Cleonae **H** I. The device on the shield of the goddess is on our coin (**S** x.) not clear, it looks like the upper part of a human figure ; in the *Arigoni Cat.* it is drawn as the upper part of a Giant or Triton. It may very probably be only a winged Gorgoneion. The hair of the goddess seems to fall in a queue behind ; her closely-fitting chiton is divided into a set of vertical bands, which bands may possibly have been adorned with scenes in relief, as in the case of the Pallas of Gitiadas ; her aegis falls over her bosom as a breast-plate. The type is fully discussed by Kenner (*St. Flor.* p. 79).

2.—Paus. VII. 27, 3. Τοῦ δὲ ἄλσους τῆς Σωτείρας ἱερὸν ἀπαν- τικρὺ Διονύσου Λαμπτῆρός ἐστιν ἐπίκλησιν· τούτῳ καὶ Λαμπτήρια ἑορτὴν ἄγουσι, καὶ δᾳδάς τε ἐς τὸ ἱερὸν κομίζουσιν ἐν νυκτί, καὶ οἴνου κρατῆρας ἱστᾶσιν ἀνὰ τὴν πόλιν πᾶσαν.

DIONYSUS clad only in cothurni, standing ; holds in right, wine-cup, in left, long thyrsos or torch, bound with fillet.

Æ Sept. Sev. B. M. (S XI.) *Mus. Sancl.* N. S. II. 25, 222.

3.—Paus. VII. 27, 4. Ἔστι καὶ Ἀπόλλωνος Θεοξενίου Πελ- λήνευσιν ἱερόν, τὸ δὲ ἄγαλμα χαλκοῦ πεποίηται· Πλησίον δὲ τοῦ Ἀπόλλωνος ναός ἐστιν Ἀρτέμιδος· τοξευούσης δὲ ἡ θεὸς παρέχεται σχῆμα. Cf. 27, 3.

Head of APOLLO.

Æ Auton.

ARTEMIS clad in short chiton, running, holds arrow or torch and bow, quiver at shoulder ; in front, stag, behind, dog.

Æ Sept. Sev. *Mus. Sancl.* N. S. II. p. 288.
Carac. B. M. (S XII.)

This precise type of Artemis, and the stag and dog on either side of her, forming as it were supporters, appears also on the coins of Corinth, D LXVI.–LXVIII. ; and at that city is proved to be a copy of a statue by its appearance on coins in a temple.

4.—Paus. VII. 27, 11. Ἀπωτέρω δὲ οὐ πολὺ ἀπὸ τοῦ Μυσαίου ἱερόν ἐστιν Ἀσκληπιοῦ καλούμενον Κῦρος, καὶ ἰάματα ἀνθρώποις παρὰ τοῦ θεοῦ γίνεται.

ASKLEPIUS standing : holds serpent-staff, left hand wrapped in himation.

Æ S. Sev. *Mus. Arig.* IV. No. 55, pl. XIV.
Domna. M. S. IV. 158, 1041. Paris.
Domna. Munich. (S XIII.)

This is a variety of the usual representations of Asklepius : the deity holds the serpent-staff differently.

OTHER TYPES at Pellene.

Zeus standing, naked, holds in right, long sceptre.

Æ Sept. Sev. Berlin. (S XIV.)
Carac. B. M. (Cf. Paus. VII. 27, 8.)

Tyche, holds patera and cornucopiae.

Æ Sept. Sev. B. M. Loebbecke.
 Geta. B. M.

Nike.

Æ Caracalla. Imh.

The Zeus is like the standing figure of that deity at Argos,
K XXVIII.

ARCADIA.

1.—Paus. VIII. 2, 6. Ὁ Πελασγός· ὁ δὲ τὸν καρπὸν τῶν
δρυῶν οὔτι που πασῶν, ἀλλὰ τὰς βαλάνους τῆς φηγοῦ
τροφὴν ἐξεῦρεν εἶναι.

ACORN. (Coins of Mantineia.)

Æ Auton. Fifth century. B. M. &c.

2.—Paus. VIII. 3, 6. Ἐποίησεν ἄρκτον τὴν Καλλιστώ, Ἄρτεμις δὲ ἐς χάριν τῆς Ἥρας κατετόξευσεν αὐτήν. καὶ ὁ
Ζεὺς Ἑρμῆν πέμπει σῶσαι τὸν παῖδά οἱ προστάξας, ὃν
ἐν τῇ γαστρὶ εἶχεν ἡ Καλλιστώ.

ARCAS. See below, under Mantineia.

BEAR. See below, under Mantineia.

CALLISTO. See Orchomenus, Methydrion.

HERMES AND ARCAS. See Pheneus.

MANTINEIA.

1.—Paus. VIII. 9, 1. Ἔστι δὲ Μαντινεῦσι ναὸς διπλοῦς μάλιστά
που κατὰ μέσον τοίχῳ διειργόμενος· τοῦ ναοῦ δὲ τῇ μὲν
ἄγαλμά ἐστιν Ἀσκληπιοῦ, τέχνη Ἀλκαμένους.

ASKLEPIUS standing, serpent-staff under left shoulder.

Æ S. Sev. and Carac. M. II. 249, 33, 35.
Domna. Loebbecke. (S XV.)
Plautilla. B. M.

Hygieia standing.

Æ Domna. M. II. 249, 34.

The figure of Asklepius is of the usual conventional character,
just like the Megarean type A VI. We should naturally expect
the statue of Alcamenes to be seated; and there is no special
reason to suppose that the figure on the coin reproduces a statue.

2.—Paus. VIII. 9, 1. Τὸ δὲ ἕτερον Λητοῦς ἐστιν ἱερὸν καὶ
τῶν παίδων· Πραξιτέλης δὲ τὰ. ἀγάλματα εἰργάσατο
τρίτῃ μετὰ Ἀλκαμένην ὕστερον γενεᾷ. Cf. 54, 5. Μετὰ
δὲ ἐκτραπεῖσιν ἐς ἀριστερὰ ὅσον στάδιον Ἀπόλλωνος
ἐπίκλησιν Πυθίου καταλελυμένον ἐστὶν ἱερὸν καὶ ἐρείπια
ἐς ἅπαν.

APOLLO clad in long chiton and himation, holds in right, plectrum, in left, lyre which rests on column.

Æ Domna. B. M.
Plautilla. B. M. (S xvi.) Munich.
Head of Apollo.
Ꞧ Auton.

ARTEMIS advancing, accompanied by her dog.

Æ Sept. Sev. M. S. iv. 280, 47.
Plautilla. M. S. iv. 280, 52.

Artemis clad in short chiton, holds torch in each hand.

Æ Plautilla. M. S. iv. 280, 53. Paris. (S xvii.)
Plautilla. Leake, *Eur. Sup.* p. 132.

We can scarcely venture to connect these types with the statues of Praxiteles.

3.—Paus. VIII. 9, 2. Μαντινεῦσι δέ ἐστι καὶ ἄλλα ἱερά, τὸ μὲν Σωτῆρος Διός, τὸ δὲ ᾿Επιδώτου καλουμένου.

ZEUS naked facing, in right, long sceptre, left hand on hip.

Æ Geta. Paris.

4.—Paus. VIII. 9, 2. ῎Εστι δὲ καὶ Διοσκούρων . . . ἱερόν.

Altar or edifice; over the top of which appear the heads and shoulders of the DIOSCURI wearing pilei, one hand raised, spears over shoulders.

Ꞧ Auton. Fourth century. B. M.
Imh. *Mon. Gr.* p. 199. (S xviii.)

The obverse of this coin is as follows :—

Fisherman? wearing conical pileus, clothes girt round waist, and boots with toes turned up ; carries two lances.

Ꞧ Auton. Fourth century. B. M. Photiades Coll. (S xix.)
Imh. *Mon. Gr.* pp. 199, 200.
Æ Auton. Ibid.

Both of these types are, on coins of so early a period, of unexampled singularity. They are discussed by Imhoof *l.c.* One of the most curious features of the supposed fisherman are his boots, which are not merely turned up, but seem to end in serpents; his clothes too are girt up in an extraordinary fashion.

5.—Paus. VIII. 9, 3. Πρὸς δὲ τῆς ῞Ηρας τῷ βωμῷ καὶ ᾿Αρκάδος τάφος τοῦ Καλλιστοῦς ἐστι.

Bearded head of warrior, ARCAS?

Ꞧ Auton.

Arcas as an infant, seated.

Ꞧ Auton. Photiades Coll.

Arcas? standing; rests right hand on bearded Term; in left, spear.

Æ Sept. Sev. Berlin. (S xx.)

The terminal figure may signify a tomb, as on coins of Sicyon
H I. II. And in that case the hero standing may well be
Arcas. Local heroes of the *Ktistes* class are very frequently
represented on coins of Peloponnesus.

6.—Paus. VIII. 9, 7. Σέβουσι δὲ καὶ 'Αθηνᾶν 'Αλέαν, καὶ
ἱερόν τε καὶ ἄγαλμα 'Αθηνᾶς ἐστὶν 'Αλέας αὐτοῖς.
Head of PALLAS, helmeted.
Æ Æ Auton.

7.—Paus. VIII. 9, 7. 'Ενομίσθη δὲ καὶ 'Αντίνους σφίσιν εἶναι
θεός· ναῶν δὲ ἐν Μαντινείᾳ νεώτατός ἐστιν ὁ τοῦ 'Αντίνου
ναός. . . . . . . τιμὰς δὲ ἐν Μαντινείᾳ κατὰ τοιόνδε
ἔσχηκε. γένος ἦν ὁ 'Αντίνους ἐκ (Βιθυνίου πόλεώς)
Βιθυνίας τῆς ὑπὲρ Σαγγαρίου ποταμοῦ· οἱ δὲ Βιθυνιεῖς
'Αρκάδες τέ εἰσι καὶ Μαντινεῖς τὰ ἄνωθεν.
Æ Obv. Bust of ANTINOUS.
Rev. Free horse.
Inscribed ΒΕΤΟΥΡΙΟC ΤΟΙC ΑΡΚΑCΙ.
The horse is a symbol of the heroic honours paid to
Antinous.
Bridled horse.
Æ Caracalla. Berlin.

8.—Paus. VIII. 10, 2. Παρὰ δὲ τοῦ ὄρους τὰ ἔσχατα τοῦ
Ποσειδῶνός ἐστι τοῦ 'Ιππίου τὸ ἱερόν, οὐ πρόσω σταδίου
Μαντινείας· τὸ μὲν δὴ ἱερὸν τὸ ἐφ' ἡμῶν ᾠκοδομήσατο
'Αδριανὸς βασιλεύς.
POSEIDON seated left, on rock, holds dolphin and trident.
Æ Auton. B. M.
Poseidon naked, striding with trident; sometimes a dragon
before him.
Æ Auton. B. M.
Trident.
Æ Æ Auton.

9.—OTHER TYPES at Mantineia.
Tyche; holds patera and cornucopiae, at altar.
Æ Plautilla. Imh. &c.
Nike running: holds wreath.
Æ Plautilla. Berlin.

ORCHOMENUS.

1.—Paus. VIII. 13, 1. 'Εν ἀριστερᾷ τῆς ὁδοῦ τῆς ἀπὸ 'Αγχι-
σιῶν, ἐν ὑπτίῳ τοῦ ὄρους τὸ ἱερόν ἐστι τῆς 'Υμνίας
'Αρτέμιδος.

13, 2. Πρὸς δὲ τῇ πόλει ξόανόν ἐστιν Ἀρτέμιδος· ἵδρυται
δὲ ἐν κέδρῳ μεγάλῃ, καὶ τὴν θεὸν ὀνομάζουσιν ἀπὸ τῆς
κέδρου Κεδρεᾶτιν.

ARTEMIS standing, clad in long chiton, shooting arrow from bow.
Æ Auton. B. M. (S xxi.)

Obv. Artemis wearing petasus and short chiton, kneeling;
right rests on the ground, in left hand, bow, from which
she has just discharged an arrow; behind her, dog
seated (S XXII.).

Rev. CALLISTO with bosom bare, seated, and falling backward;
in her bosom an arrow; beside her, Arcas playing.
Æ Auton. B. M. &c.   (S XXIII.)
   Imh. *Mon. Gr.* p. 203.   (Arcas lying.)

Cf. below, VIII. 35, 8.

Artemis clad in short chiton; holds in either hand a torch;
dog at her feet.
Æ Sept. Sev.   *Mus. Arig.* I. Imp. 7, 104.
Domna.   *Mus. Arig.* II. Imp. 21, 289, 290.
Domna.   Imh.   (S xxiv.)   Munich.   (Artemis turned the other way.)

Artemis? seated on throne; her right hand resting on throne;
in her left a parazonium.
Æ Auton.   Prok.-Osten, *Ined.* 1854, p. 45.   Imh.

We cannot venture to identify the various types of Artemis.
The figure holding two torches (S XXIV.) nearly resembles that
at Mantineia (S XVII.), and that at Caphyae (T XIV.). The
figure described by Prokesch-Osten as a seated Artemis must
almost certainly be a personification of Arcadia.

2.—Paus. VIII. 13, 2. . . . . . Καὶ Ποσειδῶνός ἐστι καὶ
Ἀφροδίτης ἱερά· λίθου δὲ τὰ ἀγάλματα.

POSEIDON standing, holds dolphin and trident.
Æ Domna.   M. S. IV. 284, 70.

Female figure draped, resting right arm on column, holds in
left, apple or helmet? (Venus Victrix?)
Æ Domna.   M. S. IV. 284, 69.
Domna.   Leake, *Eur. Sup.* p. 136.   Loebbecke.   (T I.)

3.—OTHER TYPES at Orchomenus.

Dionysus standing, holding wine-cup; beneath the left arm,
stump of tree, panther at his feet.
Æ Sept. Sev.   B. M.   Paris.   (T II.)   Munich (Without tree).

Apollo in long drapery, leaning on tripod.
Æ Sept. Sev.

Asklepius standing.
Æ Sept. Sev., Carac.

Tyche, holds patera and cornucopiae.
Æ Carac.

Two Satyrs facing; one holds grapes and pedum, the other krater over shoulder.
Æ Sept. Sev. B. M. (T III.)

Hero, holding spear and shield.
Æ Auton.

PHENEUS.

1.—Paus. VIII. 14, 5. . . . . 'Οδυσσέα ἔφασαν . . . . ἱδρύσασθαι μὲν ἱερὸν ἐνταῦθα 'Αρτέμιδος, καὶ Εὐρίππαν ὀνομάσαι τὴν θεὸν, ἔνθα τῆς Φενεατικῆς χώρας εὗρε τὰς ἵππους.

Obv. Head of Artemis.
Rev. Horse feeding.
Æ Auton. B. M.

2.—Paus. VIII. 14, 10. Θεῶν δὲ τιμῶσιν 'Ερμῆν Φενεᾶται μάλιστα, καὶ ἀγῶνα ἄγουσιν "Ερμαια, καὶ ναός ἐστιν 'Ερμοῦ σφισι καὶ ἄγαλμα λίθου· τοῦτο ἐποίησεν ἀνὴρ 'Αθηναῖος, Εὔχειρ Εὐβουλίδου.

HERMES naked, carrying in one hand, caduceus, in the other, young Arcas; inscr. ΑΡΚΑΣ.
Æ Auton. Fourth century. B. M. Loebbecke. (T IV.) Berlin. (T V.)

Hermes wearing petasos and chlamys, seated on rock; holds in right, caduceus, left rests on rock.
Æ Auton. Fourth century. B. M. Imh. Paris.

Hermes standing: holds purse and caduceus; wears chlamys; before him, term.
Æ Carac. M. S. 286, 83. Berlin. Imh. (T VI.)
    Plautilla. M. S. 287, 88.
    Geta. Loebbecke.

Head of Hermes; caduceus.
Æ Æ Auton.

The autonomous coins (T IV. and V.) give us no doubt a group invented by the die-sinker, and not a copy of any sculptural work. T VI., on the other hand, seems, from the presence of the Term, to be a reproduction of a statue, very possibly that of Eucheir, who was, as Brunn (*Gr. Kün.*, I. 551) maintains, an artist of early imperial times, or thereabouts. The general type is not unlike that of the Hermes on the Ephesian Column, a type widely spread in Roman times (*Journ. Hell. Stud.* III. 96).

3.—Paus. VIII. 15. Φενεάταις δὲ καὶ Δήμητρός ἐστιν ἱερὸν
ἐπίκλησιν Ἐλευσινίας, καὶ ἄγουσι τῇ θεῷ τελετήν, τὰ
Ἐλευσῖνι δρώμενα καὶ παρὰ σφίσι τὰ αὐτὰ φάσκοντες
καθεστηκέναι.

Head of DEMETER.

Æ Æ Auton.   Fourth century.

HADES seated, Cerberus at his feet.

Æ Carac.   Mion. II. 252, 55.   M. S. IV. 286, 82.
    Plautilla.   Paris.

Hades standing, Cerberus beside him.

Æ Plautilla.   M. S. IV. 287, 86.

DIONYSUS standing, naked, holds wine-cup and grapes, rests
left arm on tree : beside him, panther.

Æ Carac.   Munich.   (T VII.)   Paris.
    Plautilla.   B. M.   St. Flor. p. 96.

Dionysus ; holds kantharos and thyrsos.

Æ Carac.   M. S. IV. 287, 85.
    Mion. II. 252, 54.
Geta.   M. S. IV. 228, 89.   Paris.

Bearded Satyr, Marsyas ? naked, right hand raised.

Æ S. Severus.   Rhousopoulos.   (T VIII.)   Paris.

CLEITOR.

1.—Paus. VIII. 21, 3.   Κλειτορίοις δὲ ἱερὰ τὰ ἐπιφανέστατα
Δήμητρος, τὸ δὲ Ἀσκληπιοῦ.

DEMETER ? standing ; holds patera and long sceptre.

Æ Domna.   B. M.   (T IX.)

On obv. Head of Domna as Demeter, holding cornucopiae.

ASKLEPIOS standing.

Æ Domna.   M. S. IV. 277, 35.

2.—Paus. VIII. 21, 4.   Κλειτορίοις δὲ καὶ Διοσκούρων καλουμένων δὲ Θεῶν Μεγάλων ἐστὶν ἱερόν, ὅσον τέσσαρα
ἀπέχον στάδια ἀπὸ τῆς πόλεως, καὶ ἀγάλματά ἐστιν
αὐτοῖς χαλκᾶ.

Naked HORSEMAN on horse galloping.

Æ Auton.   Fifth century.

This horseman may be intended for one of the Dioscuri.

3.—Paus. VIII. 21, 4.   Πεποίηται δὲ καὶ ἐπὶ ὄρους κορυφῆς
σταδίοις τριάκοντα ἀπωτέρω τῆς πόλεως ναὸς καὶ
ἄγαλμα Ἀθηνᾶς Κορίας.

Head of ATHENE.

Æ Æ Auton.

4.—OTHER TYPES at Cleitor.

Head of Helios.

Ɍ Æ Auton.

Tyche standing at altar; holds patera and cornucopiae.

Æ Plautilla.

STYMPHALUS.

1.—Paus. VIII. 22, 7. Ἐν Στυμφήλῳ δὲ καὶ ἱερὸν Ἀρτέμιδός ἐστιν ἀρχαῖον Στυμφηλίας· τὸ δὲ ἄγαλμα ξόανόν ἐστι τὰ πολλὰ ἐπίχρυσον. πρὸς δὲ τοῦ ναοῦ τῷ ὀρόφῳ πεποιημέναι καὶ αἱ Στυμφηλίδες εἰσὶν ὄρνιθες· σαφῶς μὲν οὖν χαλεπὸν ἦν διαγνῶναι πότερον ξύλου ποίημα ἦν ἢ γύψου, τεκμαιρομένοις δὲ ἡμῖν ἐφαίνετο εἶναι ξύλου μᾶλλον ἢ γύψου.

VIII. 22, 5. Αὗται μέγεθος μὲν κατὰ γέρανόν εἰσιν αἱ ὄρνιθες, ἐοίκασι δὲ ἴβεσι, ῥάμφη δὲ ἀλκιμώτερα φέρουσι καὶ οὐ σκολιά, ὥσπερ αἱ ἴβεις.

Head of ARTEMIS Stymphalia crowned with laurel.

Ɍ Æ Auton. Fourth century.

Head of Stymphalian bird.

Ɍ Auton. Fourth century. B. M. &c. Imh. (T x.)

Same head emerging from reeds.

Ɍ Auton. B. M. (T xi.) &c.

HERAKLES naked, striking with club; in his left hand, bow and lion's skin.

Ɍ Auton. B. M. (T xii.) &c.

Head of Herakles.

Ɍ Auton.

It is interesting to compare the birds' heads on the coins T x., xi., with the exact description of Pausanias. They are an extreme instance of the dislike of the Greeks for monstrous forms, reducing the terrible Stymphalian birds of the tale to mere ordinary water-fowl. It is very curious, too, that Herakles should be represented as attacking these birds with club rather than bow.

ALEA.

1.—Paus. VIII. 23, 1. Θεῶν δὲ ἱερὰ αὐτόθι Ἀρτέμιδός ἐστιν Ἐφεσίας καὶ Ἀθηνᾶς Ἀλέας.

Obv. Head of ARTEMIS.

Rev. ΑΛ Strung bow.

Ɍ and Æ Auton. B. M. Imh.

Obv. Head of ATHENA.

Rev. ΑΛΕΑ in wreath.

Æ Auton. Paris.

CAPHYAE.

1.—Paus. VIII. 23, 3. Καφυάταις δὲ ἱερὰ θεῶν Ποσειδῶνός ἐστι καὶ ἐπίκλησιν Κνακαλησίας Ἀρτέμιδος. ἔστι δὲ αὐτοῖς καὶ ὄρος Κνάκαλος, ἔνθα ἐπέτειον τελετὴν ἄγουσι τῇ Ἀρτέμιδι. POSEIDON standing, holds dolphin, and trident transversely, himation wrapped round waist.

Æ Domna. Paris. Berlin. (T XIII.) M. S. IV. 275, 27.

2.—Paus. 23, 6. Καφυῶν δὲ ἀφέστηκεν ὅσον στάδιον Κονδυλέα χωρίον, καὶ Ἀρτέμιδος ἄλσος καὶ ναός ἐστιν ἐνταῦθα καλουμένης Κονδυλεάτιδος τὸ ἀρχαῖον. ARTEMIS facing, clad in short chiton, a quiver at her shoulder, holds torch in each hand.

Æ Auton. M. S. IV. 275, 24.
Sept. Sev. B. M. Leake, Eur. Sup. p. 119.
Domna. M. S. IV. 276, 29. Imh. (T XIV.)

3.—OTHER TYPES at Caphyae.
Demeter standing, holds poppy-head and corn-ears.

Æ Auton. Imh. (T XV.) Prok.-Ost. Inedita 1854, p. 44.

Demeter, or Artemis, clad in long chiton, holds a torch in right hand.

Æ Carac. M. S. IV. 276, 31.

Female figure, indistinct, running, a serpent arched over her head; holds in right, head of serpent.

Æ Domna. Paris. (T XVI.)

Apollo naked, facing, holds in right hand, branch; in left, which rests on tripod, a scroll.

Æ Sept. Sev. B. M. Loebbecke. (T XVII.)

Asklepios standing.

Æ Geta. Berlin.

Tyche, holds patera and cornucopiae, at altar.

Æ Sept. Sev., Plautilla. Paris, &c.

PSOPHIS.

1.—Paus. VIII. 24, 1. Ψωφῖδος δὲ οἱ μέν φασιν οἰκιστὴν γενέσθαι Ψώφιδα τὸν Ἄρρωνος τοῦ Ἐρυμάνθου τοῦ Ἀρίστα τοῦ Παρθάονος τοῦ Περιφήτου τοῦ Νυκτίμου· τοῖς δέ ἐστιν εἰρημένα θυγατέρα Ψωφῖδα εἶναι Ξάνθου τοῦ Ἐρυμάνθου τοῦ Ἀρκάδος. Bust of nymph PSOPHIS wearing wreath, sceptre on shoulder.

Æ Geta. Mus. Sanclem. III. pl. 27, 263.

2.—Paus. VIII. 24, 5. Λεγεται δὲ ὡς Ἡρακλῆς κατὰ πρόσ-
ταγμα Εὐρυσθέως παρὰ τῷ Ἐρυμάνθῳ θηράσειεν ὖν
μεγέθει καὶ ἀλκῇ τοὺς ἄλλους ὑπερηρκότα.
Obv. Head of HERAKLES bearded, laur.
Rev. Boar running.
Æ Auton. Paris. Imh. Sest., *Mus. Font.* pl. I. 16.

3.—Paus. VIII. 24, 12. Ψωφιδίοις δὲ καὶ παρὰ τῷ Ἐρυμάνθῳ
ναός ἐστιν Ἐρυμάνθου καὶ ἄγαλμα.
River-god Erymanthus reclining, naked to waist, holds in
right, branch, rests left elbow on vase; below, fish.
Æ Domna. M. S. IV. 291, 106. Imh. (T XVIII.)

4.—Paus. VIII. 21, 2. Εἰσὶ δὲ ἰχθῦς ἐν τῷ Ἀροανίῳ καὶ ἄλλοι
καὶ οἱ ποικιλίαι καλούμενοι· τούτους λέγουσι τοὺς
ποικιλίας φθέγγεσθαι κίχλῃ τῇ ὄρνιθι ἐοικός.
Fish.
Æ Auton. Fifth century.

5.—Paus. VIII. 23, 8. Ἐπὶ δρυμὸν ἀφίξῃ Σόρωνα διά τε
Ἀργεαθῶν καὶ Λυκούντων καλουμένων καὶ Σκοτάνης.
ἄγει μὲν δὴ ὁ Σόρων τὴν ἐπὶ Ψωφῖδος· θηρία δὲ οὗτός
τε καὶ ὅσοι δρυμοὶ τοῖς Ἀρκάσιν εἰσὶν ἄλλοι παρέχονται
τοσάδε, ἀγρίους ὖς καὶ ἄρκτους καὶ χελώνας μεγίστας
μεγέθει.
Stag: forepart of doe.
Æ Auton. Fifth century.
ARTEMIS clad in short chiton, her right hand on her side, her
left on a spear, quiver at shoulder.
Æ Sept. Sev. M. S. IV. 291, 105.
Sept. Sev. Lcake, *Eur. Sup.* p. 143. (T XIX.)
Domna. Leake, *l. c.* (Position of arms reversed.) (T XX.)

6.—Paus. VIII. 24, 4. Ἔχει δὲ τὰς πηγὰς ὁ Ἐρύμανθος ἐν
ὄρει Λαμπείᾳ· τὸ δὲ ὄρος τοῦτο ἱερὸν εἶναι Πανὸς
λέγεται.
Pan standing, holds in his hands human head (mask or
syrinx?).
Æ Geta. Vaill. *Num. Gr.* p. 120.
Naples. *Cat.* No. 7578.

7.—OTHER TYPE at Psophis.
Dionysus clad in short chiton; holds wine-cup and long
thyrsus.
Æ Sept. Sev. B. M.
Domna. Munich. (T XXI.)

THELPUSA.

1.—Paus. VIII. 25, 4. Μετὰ δὲ Θέλπουσαν ἐπὶ τὸ ἱερὸν τῆς Δήμητρος ὁ Λάδων κάτεισι τὸ ἐν 'Ογκείῳ· καλοῦσι δὲ 'Ερινὺν οἱ Θελπούσιοι τὴν θεόν, κ.τ.λ.

VIII. 25, 7. Τὴν δὲ Δήμητρα τεκεῖν φασὶν ἐκ τοῦ Ποσειδῶνος θυγατέρα, ἧς τὸ ὄνομα ἐς ἀτελέστους λέγειν οὐ νομίζουσι, καὶ ἵππον τὸν 'Αρείονα.

Obv. Head of DEMETER, adorned with necklace ending in horse's head.

Rev. ΕΡΙΩΝ. The horse ARION, running, bridled.

Æ and Æ Auton. Paris. Imh. (T XXII., XXIII.) *Mon. Gr.* p. 209.

2.—OTHER TYPES at Thelpusa.

PAN horned, wearing nebris over shoulders and holding pedum, touching with his left hand the top of a reed (Syrinx).

Æ Sept. Sev. B. M.
Plautilla. Imh.
Geta. Vienna. (T XXIV.)

See *Zeitschr. f. Num.* I. p. 125. The love of Pan for Syrinx and her transformation into a reed is related by several ancient writers. Pausanias VIII. 38, 11, mentions Melpeia in Arcadia as the place where the syrinx was invented by Pan.

Female head, radiate, possibly of Demeter Erinnys.
Æ Auton.

Isis.
Æ Sept. Sev.

Artemis hunting.
Æ Geta.

Dionysos naked, holds wine-cup and thyrsus.
Æ Sept. Sev.

Hermes, holds purse and caduceus.
Æ Geta. Berlin.

Tyche ; holds patera and cornucopiae.
Æ Geta. Loebbecke.

HERAEA.

1.—Paus. VIII. 26, 1. 'Ηραιεῦσι δὲ οἰκιστὴς μὲν γέγονεν 'Ηραιεὺς ὁ Λυκάονος κεῖται δὲ ἡ πόλις ἐν δεξιᾷ τοῦ 'Αλφειοῦ.

River god ALPHEIUS reclining, before him an ox standing ; below, fishes.
Æ Carac. Mion. II. 248, 30. Paris.

The ox may bear allusion to the sacrifices brought to Alpheius in Peloponnese, especially at Olympia.

2.—Paus. VIII. 26, 1. Εἰσὶ δὲ καὶ Διονύσῳ ναοί· τὸν μὲν καλοῦσιν αὐτῶν Πολίτην, τὸν δὲ Αὐξίτην. καὶ οἴκημά ἐστί σφισιν ἔνθα τῷ Διονύσῳ τὰ ὄργια ἄγουσιν.

DIONYSUS standing; in both hands grapes, left elbow resting on column ; beside him, panther.
Æ Carac. Leake, *Eur. Sup.* p. 128. (T xxv.)
Dionysus in short chiton ; holds in each hand grapes.
Æ Carac. Leake, *l. c.* (T xxvi.)
The former of these types is characteristic, and clearly the copy of a statue.

3.—Paus. VIII. 26, 2. Ἔστι καὶ ναὸς ἐν τῇ Ἡραίᾳ Πανὸς ἄτε τοῖς Ἀρκάσιν ἐπιχωρίου. τῆς δὲ Ἥρας τοῦ ναοῦ καὶ ἄλλα ἐρείπια καὶ οἱ κίονες ἔτι ἐλείποντο.

PAN standing, left foot resting on rock, holds in left hand spear, chlamys over shoulder.
Æ Auton. Fifth century.
HERA standing, holds in right hand sceptre.
Æ Sept. Sev. M. S. iv. 278, 39.
Head of Hera, veiled.
Æ Auton. Sixth century.

4.—OTHER TYPES at Heraea,
Head of Pallas.
Head of Artemis.
Æ Auton.
Artemis kneeling, discharging arrow.
Æ Auton. Imh. Photiades Coll.
Tyche, holds patera and cornucopiae.
Æ Sept. Sev. Paris.

MEGALOPOLIS.

1.—Paus. VIII. 30, 2. Περίβολος δέ ἐστιν ἐν ταύτῃ λίθων καὶ ἱερὸν Λυκαίου Διός. ἔσοδος δ᾽ ἐς αὐτὸ οὐκ ἔστι.

30, 10. Ταύτης τῆς στοᾶς ἐστιν ἐγγυτάτω ὡς πρὸς ἥλιον ἀνίσχοντα ἱερὸν Σωτῆρος ἐπίκλησιν Διός· κεκόσμηται δὲ πέριξ κίοσι. καθεζομένῳ δὲ τῷ Διὶ ἐν θρόνῳ παρεστήκασι τῇ μὲν ἡ Μεγάλη πόλις, ἐν ἀριστερᾷ δὲ Ἀρτέμιδος Σωτείρας ἄγαλμα. ταῦτα μὲν λίθου τοῦ Πεντελησίου Ἀθηναῖοι Κηφισόδοτος καὶ Ξενοφῶν εἰργάσαντο.

ZEUS seated facing, on throne ; holds in raised right, sceptre ; himation over left shoulder.
Æ Sept. Sev. B. M. (V i.) Paris.
Head of Zeus.
Æ Æ Auton. B. M. &c.

We can scarcely hesitate to consider the facing Zeus (**V** I.) as a reminiscence of the statue by Cephisodotus and Xenophon, set up soon after B.C. 370. The figure seems to be of the noble Attic type. What Zeus holds in his left hand it is unfortunately not possible to distinguish.

ARTEMIS ? standing to left clad in short chiton ; spear in raised right hand, in left the end of her over-dress.

Æ Sept. Sev. Paris.
Domna. M. S. IV. 282, 59. Berlin. (**V** II.)
Carac. M. S. IV. 282, 61. (?)

Cf. VIII. 32, 4. Ἔστι δὲ ἐν τῇ μοίρᾳ ταύτῃ λόφος πρὸς ἀνίσχοντα ἥλιον, καὶ Ἀγροτέρας ἐν αὐτῷ ναὸς Ἀρτέμιδος, ἀνάθημα Ἀριστοδήμου καὶ τοῦτο.

In the Brunswick cabinet is a coin of Sept. Severus, on which is a figure in attitude and dress resembling **V** II. but the head bearded and turned to the right. It is therefore very doubtful if the figure in the plate be of Artemis.

2.—Paus. VIII. 38, 5. Ἔστι δὲ ἐν τῷ Λυκαίῳ Πανός τε ἱερὸν καὶ περὶ αὐτὸ ἄλσος δένδρων, καὶ ἱππόδρομός τε καὶ πρὸ αὐτοῦ στάδιον.

30, 3. Καὶ ἄγαλμα Πανὸς λίθου πεποιημένον· ἐπίκλησις δὲ Οἰνόεις ἐστὶν αὐτῷ.

PAN horned naked, seated on rock, over which is spread his garment, holds in right hand pedum ; below, syrinx.

Æ Auton. Fourth century. B. M. &c.
Klagenfurt, X A P I on rock. Loebbecke, O Λ Y M on rock. (**V** III.)

Pan horned seated on rock, right hand raised, in left pedum.

Æ Auton. Sometimes eagle before him. B. M. &c.

Pan naked seated on rock, holds in right hand pedum which rests on the ground, left rests on rock ; all in wreath.

Æ Auton. B. M. (**V** IV.)

Pan walking, spear in right hand, in left pedum.

Æ Sept. Sev. M. S. IV. 281, 58. Paris.

(Probably an incorrect description of the type **V** II.)

3.—Paus. VIII. 30, 3. Ἔστι δὲ πρὸ τοῦ τεμένους τούτου χαλκοῦν ἄγαλμα Ἀπόλλωνος θέας ἄξιον, μέγεθος μὲν ἐς πόδας δώδεκα, ἐκομίσθη δὲ ἐκ τῆς Φιγαλέων συντέλεια ἐς κόσμον τῇ Μεγάλῃ πόλει.

APOLLO naked, laur., standing, leaning on column, holds branch in right, and bow in left.

Æ Sept. Sev. Paris. (**V** v.)
Carac. M. S. IV. 282, 60.

The coin probably reproduces the pose of the colossal figure mentioned in the text. On the coin figured branch and bow are not clearly distinguishable.

4.—Paus. VIII. 30, 7. Τῶν ἀρχαίων δὲ ὄπισθε ναὸς Τύχης καὶ ἄγαλμα λίθου πεποίηται ποδῶν πέντε οὐκ ἀποδέον.

TYCHE, holds rudder and cornucopiae.

Æ Sept. Sev. Paris.

5.—Paus. VIII. 31, 3. Ἔστι δὲ καὶ Ἡρακλῆς παρὰ τῇ Δήμητρι μέγεθος μάλιστα πῆχυν· τοῦτον τὸν Ἡρακλέα εἶναι τῶν Ἰδαίων καλουμένων Δακτύλων Ὀνομάκριτός φησιν ἐν τοῖς ἔπεσι. κεῖται δὲ τράπεζα ἔμπροσθεν. Cf. 31, 7.

HERAKLES bearded, in form of term, lion's skin wrapped about him, the head visible under his left arm.

Æ Carac. Paris. (V VI.)

Herakles bearded in form of term; no lion's skin.

Geta. Berlin. (V VII.)

6.—Paus. VIII. 31, 5. Ἔστι δὲ ἐντὸς τοῦ περιβόλου . . . . . Ἀφροδίτης ἱερόν. Cf. 32, 2, ἐρείπια δὲ καὶ τῆς Ἀφροδίτης ἦν τὸ ἱερόν, πλὴν ὅσον πρόναός τε ἐλείπετο ἔτι καὶ ἀγάλματα ἀριθμὸν τρία, ἐπίκλησις δὲ Οὐρανία, τῇδ᾽ ἔστι Πάνδημος, τῇ τρίτῃ δὲ οὐδὲν ἐτίθεντο.

APHRODITE naked facing, in attitude of Medicean Venus; beside her, dolphin.

Æ Sept. Sev. Paris. (V VIII.)

METHYDRION.

1.—Paus. VIII. 35, 8. Σταδίους δὲ ὡς τριάκοντα καταβάντι ἐκ Κρουνῶν τάφος ἐστὶ Καλλιστοῦς, χῶμα γῆς ὑψηλόν, δένδρα ἔχον πολλὰ μὲν τῶν ἀκάρπων, πολλὰ δὲ καὶ ἥμερα. ἐπὶ δὲ ἄκρῳ τῷ χώματι ἱερόν ἐστιν Ἀρτέμιδος ἐπίκλησιν Καλλίστης.

CALLISTO, falling back, pierced with an arrow, her arms extended; beside her, the infant Arcas lying.

Æ Auton. Obv. Head of Zeus.
Imh. M. G. p. 200, pl. E. 9.

LYCOSURA.

1.—Paus. VIII. 38, 5. Ἔστι δὲ ἐν τῷ Λυκαίῳ . . . . στάδιον· τὸ δὲ ἀρχαῖον τῶν Λυκαίων ἦγον τὸν ἀγῶνα ἐνταῦθα.

ΛΥΚΑΙΑ on coins of Sept. Severus. Athens.

The early silver coins of the Arcadians, having on the obverse a seated figure of Zeus and on the reverse a female head, were formerly attributed to Lycosura and regarded as illustrative of the cultus of Zeus Lycaeus, and of Despoena. It is, however, shewn in Imhoof's *Monnaies Grecques*, p. 196, that they were probably issued at Heraea, and have reference to the cultus of Zeus at Olympia and that of Artemis at Heraea.

PHIGALEIA.

1.—Paus. VIII. 39, 5. "Εστι δὲ Σωτείρας τε ἱερὸν ἐνταῦθα 'Αρτέμιδος καὶ ἄγαλμα ὀρθὸν λίθου· ἐκ τούτου δὲ τοῦ ἱεροῦ καὶ τὰς πομπὰς σφίσι πέμπειν κατέστη.

ARTEMIS standing, clad in short chiton with diploïs, holds bipennis and lance.

Æ Sept. Sev.   Leake, *Eur. Sup.* p. 140.
Æ Carac.   B. M.   Imh.   (V IX.)

Artemis as huntress.

Æ Sept. Sev.   M. S. IV. 288, 91.

Artemis holding a torch in right hand.

Æ Plautilla.   M. S. IV. 290, 102.

Artemis (or Demeter) in long chiton, holding out a torch in each hand.

Æ S. Severus.   Lambros.   (V X.)
Domna.   M. S. IV. 289, 95.
Carac.   Paris.

Artemis Soteira sometimes bears torches (Megara **A** I.).

2.—Paus. VIII. 39, 6. 'Εν δὲ τῷ γυμνασίῳ τὸ ἄγαλμα τοῦ 'Ερμοῦ ἀμπεχομένῳ μὲν ἔοικεν ἱμάτιον, καταλήγει δὲ οὐκ ἐς πόδας, ἀλλὰ ἐς τὸ τετράγωνον σχῆμα.

Term-like figure of HERMES, clad in himation, and holding caduceus in right hand ; end of garment wrapped round left arm.

Æ Sept. Sev.   Leake, *Eur. Sup.* p. 140.   Berlin.   (V XII.)
Carac.   M. S. IV. 290, 100.
Geta.   Leake, *Eur.* p. 90.

Similar figure, caduceus not visible, placed in arched niche between columns.

Æ Domna.   Munich.   (V XI.)
Carac.   M. S. IV. 290, 101.

3.—Paus. VIII. 39, 6. Πεποίηται δὲ καὶ Διονύσου ναός· ἐπίκλησις μέν ἐστιν αὐτῷ παρὰ τῶν ἐπιχωρίων 'Ακρατοφόρος.

DIONYSUS standing, holds wine-cup and thyrsus.

Æ Sept. Sev.   Naples.

4.—Paus. VIII. 41, 2. Ποταμὸς δὲ ὁ καλούμενος Λύμαξ ἐκδίδωσι μὲν ἐς τὴν Νέδαν παρ' αὐτὴν ῥέων Φιγαλίαν, γενέσθαι δὲ τοὔνομά φασι τῷ ποταμῷ καθαρσίων τῶν 'Ρέας ἔνεκα.

RIVER-GOD seated on rock looking back, himation over one
shoulder; holds in right, vessel from which he pours, in
left, branch.
Æ Plautilla. Paris.
Geta. Munich. (V XIII.)
5.—Paus. VIII. 41, 10. Ἀφροδίτη δέ ἐστιν ἐν Κωτίλῳ· καὶ
αὐτῇ ναός τε ἦν οὐκ ἔχων ἔτι ὄροφον καὶ ἄγαλμα
ἐπεποίητο.
APHRODITE naked, leans her right elbow on a pillar, with left
hand grasps her hair; head turned to left.
Æ Plautilla. Loebbecke. (V XIV.)
6.—Paus. VIII. 42, 1. Τὸ δὲ ἕτερον τῶν ὁρῶν τὸ Ἐλάϊον ἀπωτέρω
μὲν Φιγαλίας ὅσον τε σταδίοις τριάκοντά ἐστι, Δήμητρος
δὲ ἄντρον αὐτόθι ἱερὸν ἐπίκλησιν Μελαίνης, cf. 42, 4;
see also above under Thelpusa.
DEMETER? holding a torch in each hand. See above under
Artemis.
Demeter veiled, facing, right hand extended, in left sceptre;
over-dress over both arms.
Æ Domna. Munich. (V XV.)
Demeter veiled standing left, holds in right hand poppy-head?
left rests on her side.
Æ Carac. Munich. (V XVI.)
Demeter standing veiled, holds in right long sceptre, left
wrapped in mantle.
ÆM. Aurel. Paris. (V XVII.)
Demeter facing, veiled and clad in chiton, holds in each hand
ears of corn?.
Æ Domna. Paris. (V XVIII.)
7.—OTHER TYPES at Phigaleia.
Pallas standing, holds patera and sceptre.
Æ Domna. Paris. Carac. &c.
Pallas, holds olive-branch and spear.
Æ Carac.
Pallas, holds spear and shield.
Æ Sept. Sev. Paris.
Pallas, holds Victory and spear.
Æ Carac. Domna.
Pallas, leaning on spear and another figure with both hands
extended, probably Demeter; behind the latter, altar.
Æ Domna. B. M. (V XIX.)
Asklepius standing.
Æ Sept. Sev. Paris &c.

TEGEA.

1.—Paus. VIII. 45, 6. Τὰ δὲ ἐν τοῖς ἀετοῖς, ἔστιν ἔμπροσθεν ἡ θήρα τοῦ ὑὸς τοῦ Καλυδωνίου· πεποιημένου δὲ κατὰ μέσον μάλιστα τοῦ ὑὸς τῇ μέν ἐστιν 'Αταλάντη καὶ τ. λ.

47, 2. ἐν τῷ ναῷ τὰ ἀξιολογώτατα, ἔστι μὲν τὸ δέρμα ὑὸς τοῦ Καλυδωνίου.

ATALANTA as a huntress, quiver at shoulder, spearing the Calydonian boar, who stands under a tree.

Æ Domna. Mion. II. 256, 75. Paris. Bibl. Turin. (V xx.)
M. S. IV. 294, 120.

2.—Paus. VIII. 45, 4. Τεγεάταις δὲ 'Αθηνᾶς τῆς 'Αλέας τὸ ἱερὸν τὸ ἀρχαῖον ἐποίησεν "Αλεος.

46, 4. Τῆς 'Αθηνᾶς τὸ ἄγαλμα . . . . . ἐλέφαντος διὰ παντὸς πεποιημένον, τέχνη δὲ 'Ενδοίου.

47, 1. Τὸ δὲ ἄγαλμα ἐν Τεγέᾳ τὸ ἐφ᾽ ἡμῶν ἐκομίσθη μὲν ἐκ δήμου τοῦ Μανθουρέων, 'Ιππία δὲ παρὰ τοῖς Μανθουρεῦσιν εἶχεν ἐπίκλησιν.

ATHENE, fighting.

Æ Auton. Leake, Eur. p. 98.

Athene, in long chiton ; holds raised spear and shield.

Æ Sept. Sev. Leake, Eur. Sup. p. 147. (V xxi.)

It may, perhaps, be doubted whether the statue which served as model for the coin **V** xxi. was the statue by Endoeus, removed to Rome by Augustus, or the later statue called Hippia brought to supply its place. Brunn (G. K. I. 118) has shewn that the date of Endoeus must be brought down to about B.C. 500, and the type of statue on our coin is not inappropriate to such a time ; but on the other hand it is unlikely that the die-cutters of Tegea would attempt in the time of Severus to reproduce a statue removed to Rome, rather than one which remained among them, and the attitude on the coin is well suited to Athene Hippia if we suppose her driving in her chariot against the Giants. There is a likeness between the type on this coin and that which at Pellene probably reproduces an early statue by Pheidias, **S** x.

Obv. Head of Pallas.

Rev. Owl: inscribed **AΘANA AΛEA**.

Æ Auton. Leake, *l. c.*

Head of ALEUS ; inscribed **AΛEOΣ**.

Æ Auton. Leake, *l. c.* Imh.

3.—Paus. VIII. 47, 5. Λέγοντες ὡς Κηφεῖ τῷ 'Αλέου γένοιτο
δωρεὰ παρὰ 'Αθηνᾶς ἀνάλωτον ἐς τὸν πάντα χρόνον
εἶναι Τεγέαν· καὶ αὐτῷ φασὶν ἐς φυλακὴν τῆς πόλεως
ἀποτεμοῦσαν τὴν θεὸν δοῦναι τριχῶν τῶν Μεδούσης.
ATHENE handing to Sterope as priestess the hair of Medusa,
which the latter receives in a vessel.
Æ Auton. B. M. Imh. (V xxii.)
Same scene in the presence of CEPHEUS, who receives the hair
from the goddess.
Æ Auton. B. M. Imh. (V xxiii.)
Head of Medusa.
Æ Auton.
Obv. Head of Athene.
Rev. Cepheus or other hero charging.
Æ Æ Auton.
Cepheus ? naked, standing; holds shield and spear.
Æ Sept. Sev. Paris.
Carac. M. S. iv. 294, 121.
4.—Paus. VIII. 48, 7. Καὶ ἐκτεθῆναι τὸν Τήλεφον λέγοντι ἐς
τὸ ὄρος τὸ Παρθένιον, καὶ τῷ παιδὶ ἐκκειμένῳ διδόναι
γάλα ἔλαφον.
TELEPHUS suckled by a doe.
Æ Auton.
5.—Paus. VIII. 48, 7. Τὴν δὲ Εἰλείθυιαν οἱ Τεγεᾶται, καὶ γὰρ
ταύτης ἔχουσιν ἐν τῇ ἀγορᾷ ναὸν καὶ ἄγαλμα, ἐπονομά-
ζουσιν Αὔγην ἐν γόνασι.
Head of EILEITHUIA, torch over shoulder.
Æ Auton. B. M.
6.—OTHER TYPES at Tegea.
Herakles as term; lion's skin wrapped about him.
Æ Geta. Imh. M. G. p. 209. (V xxiv.)
Cf. VIII. 48, 6. Ἄγαλμα τετράγωνον· περισσῶς γὰρ δή
τι τῷ σχήματι τούτῳ φαίνονταί μοι χαίρειν οἱ 'Αρκάδες.
This figure of Herakles is closely like that on the coins of
Megalopolis (V vi.). Megalopolis being a new city built B.C. 370
had to borrow the forms of its deities from its neighbours.
Hera ? seated, holds sceptre and pomegranate ?
Æ Sept. Sev. Naples, Cat. No. 7580.

P.S.—The coins of Asine in Messenia were in the first paper
incorrectly ascribed to Asine in Argolis, a city of which in
historical times only ruins remained.

NUMISMATIC COMMENTARY ON PAUSANIAS.

III.

BOOKS IX. X., I. 1–38.

AND SUPPLEMENT.

[PLATES LXXIV—VIII.]

WITH this third part our *Numismatic Commentary* is completed.
It consists of three sections :—
(1) Boeotia and Phocis (Paus. IX. X.)
(2) Athens (Paus. I. 1–38.)
(3) Supplement ; containing coins of Peloponnesus omitted
in parts I. and II. of the *Commentary*.

The Athenian section of the work involved great difficulties,
especially in view of the fact that it was difficult to treat of the
Athenian coins without reference to reliefs and other works of
art of Athens. This difficulty the compilers have met as best
they could : the Athenian coin-lists were drawn up in the first
instance by the Swiss colleague.

Special thanks are due to Herr Arthur Loebbecke and
Professor Rhousopoulos of Athens for most liberal *envois* of
casts : also to Professor Michaelis for valuable hints and cor-
rections in the Athenian section.

F. IMHOOF-BLUMER.
PERCY GARDNER.

PLATAEA.

1.—Paus. IX. 2, 7. Πλαταιεῦσι δὲ ναός ἐστιν Ἥρας, θέας ἄξιος·
.... τὴν δὲ Ἥραν Τελείαν καλοῦσι, πεποίηται δὲ ὀρθὸν
μεγέθει ἄγαλμα μέγα· λίθου δὲ ἀμφότερα τοῦ Πεντελησίου, Πραξιτέλους δέ ἐστιν ἔργα. ἐνταῦθα καὶ ἄλλο
Ἥρας ἄγαλμα καθήμενον Καλλίμαχος ἐποίησε· Νυμ-
φευομένην δὲ τὴν θεὸν ἐπὶ λόγῳ τοιῷδε ὀνομάζουσιν.

Head of HERA to right wearing stephanos.
Æ Auton.   Fourth century.   Imh.   Photiades.   Paris.
  B. M. Cat. pl. IX. 3.

Similar head, facing.
Æ Auton.   Fourth century.   Vienna.   Imh.
  B. M. Cat. pl. IX. 4.

Head of Hera in profile, wearing pointed stephane.
Æ Auton.   Fourth century.   Imh.
Æ Auton.   Imh.   *Num. Zeit.* III. pl. IX. 12.

The reverse of the bronze coin is a cow, which was sacrificed to Hera, as a bull to Zeus. See Paus. IX. 3, 8. An ox was a dedicatory offering of the Plataeans at Delphi: Paus. X. 15, 1, and 16, 6.

The two silver coins with the head of Hera are fixed by Mr. Head (*B. M. Cat.* l.c.) to B.C. 387–374. They are thus contemporary with the earlier activities of Praxiteles. We cannot with confidence assert that they are in any sense copied from his statue, but they will illustrate it as works of contemporary art.

THEBES.

1.—Paus. IX. 11, 7.   Ὑπὲρ δὲ τὸν Σωφρονιστῆρα λίθον βωμός ἐστιν Ἀπόλλωνος ἐπίκλησιν Σποδίου, πεποίηται δὲ ἀπὸ τῆς τέφρας τῶν ἱερείων.

IX. 17, 2.   Statue of Apollo Boedromius.
10, 2.   Statue like that at Branchidae.

APOLLO seated on cippus, naked, holding bow; behind him, on the cippus, his tripod.
Æ Auton.   Coin of Boeotia struck at Thebes.   *B. M. Cat.*   Pl. VI. 5.

2.—Paus. IX. 11, 4.   Ἐνταῦθα Ἡράκλειόν ἐστιν, ἄγαλμα δὲ τὸ μὲν λίθου λευκοῦ Πρόμαχος καλούμενον, ἔργον δὲ Ξενοκρίτου καὶ Εὐβίου Θηβαίων· τὸ δὲ ξόανον τὸ ἀρχαῖον Θηβαῖοί τε εἶναι Δαιδάλου νενομίκασι καὶ αὐτῷ μοι παρίστατο ἔχειν οὕτω . . . . Θηβαίοις δὲ τὰ ἐν τοῖς ἀετοῖς Πραξιτέλης ἐποίησε τὰ πολλὰ τῶν δώδεκα καλουμένων ἄθλων.

25, 4.   Herakles Rhinocolustes.
26, 1.   Temple of Herakles Hippodetus.

HERAKLES advancing with club and bow; carrying off tripod; shooting; stringing bow; or strangling serpents.
Æ Auton.   Fifth century.
  B. M. Cat.   Pl. XII. 1–8.   *Num. Zeit.* 1877.   Pl. II.

These types, representing the exploits of Herakles, are given

in the *B. M. Cat.* to B.C. 446–426. In any case they are much
earlier than the time of Praxiteles, and can have nothing to do
with his pediments. The Herakles holding club and bow is the
most interesting figure, and seems clearly to stand for the Herakles Promachos ascribed to Daedalus. But it can resemble that
statue only in pose and attributes ; in the execution the die-
cutter followed the ideas and customs of his own time. Compare
the Messenian coin **P** IV.

3.—Paus. IX. 12, 4.   πλησίον δὲ Διονύσου ἄγαλμα, καὶ τοῦτο
'Ονασιμήδης ἐποίησε δι' ὅλου πλῆρες ὑπὸ τοῦ χαλκοῦ·
τὸν βωμὸν δὲ οἱ παῖδες εἰργάσαντο οἱ Πραξιτέλους.

IX. 16, 6.   καὶ ἐγγυτάτω τοῦ θεάτρου Διονύσου ναός
ἐστιν ἐπίκλησιν Λυσίου.

Bearded DIONYSUS, in long chiton, standing, kantharos in
right hand.
Æ Auton.   First century, A.D.   Photiades.   (**X** I.)
Head, *Coinage of Boeotia*, p. 95.

Head of bearded Dionysus.
El. Æ Auton.   Fifth and fourth centuries.
B. M. Cat.   Pl. XIII. 5–9, &c.   *Num. Zeit.* 1877, pl. II.

Head of young Dionysus.
Æ Auton.   Third century B.C.
B. M. Cat.   Pl. VI. 5.

The reading in the passage first cited is corrupt : Kayser has
suggested ἐπιχώριος in the place of πλῆρες ὑπὸ τοῦ. See Brunn,
G.K. I. 297. The date of Onasimedes is unknown. The figure
on the coin is certainly archaic, as is proved not merely by the
beard and the long drapery, but by a certain stiffness of pose
and hardness in the outline of the back. We may compare the
Athenian coin **CC** VI.

4.—Paus. IX. 16, 1.   Temple of Tyche ;
25, 3 of Mater Dindymene.

Female head laureate and turreted, TYCHE or CYBELE ; pro-
bably the former.
Æ late Auton.   Photiades.   (**X** II.)
Head, *Boeotia*, p. 95.

We may compare the head probably of Messene, on the Messenian coin **P** II. At Messene there was a statue of Thebes of
the time of Epaminondas.

5.—Paus. IX. 16, 5.   Temple of Demeter Thesmophoros.
25, 5.   Grove of the Cabeiri, Demeter and Cora.

Head of DEMETER facing, crowned with corn.
Æ Æ Auton.   *B. M. Cat.*   Pl. VI. 6–8.   Imh.

6.—OTHER TYPES at Thebes (see *B. M. Cat.*)
Poseidon seated and standing.
Head of Poseidon.
Head of Zeus.
Nike.
Athene standing, winged. See Imh. Flügelgestalten, *Num.*
Zeit. III. pp. 1-50.   This type must represent rather Athene
Nike than Athene Zosteria (Paus. IX. 17, 3): the only Athene
mentioned by Pausanias at Thebes.

TANAGRA.

1.—Paus. IX. 19, 6.   Τοῦ δὲ Εὐρίπου τὴν Εὔβοιαν κατὰ τοῦτο
ἀπὸ τῆς Βοιωτῶν διείργοντος. . . . Ναὸς δὲ 'Αρτέμιδός
ἐστιν ἐνταῦθα καὶ ἀγάλματα λίθου λευκοῦ, τὸ μὲν
δᾷδας φέρον, τὸ δὲ ἔοικε τοξευούσῃ. . . . φοίνικες δὲ πρὸ
τοῦ ἱεροῦ πεφύκασιν.

ARTEMIS huntress in a tetrastyle temple, spear in raised right
hand, torch in left ; on each side of it a palm-tree ; below
ship with sailors.
Æ Anton. Pius. Paris. (**X** III.)
   M. S. III. 522, 110.
Artemis as above, without temple.
Æ Anton. Pius. Imh. (**X** IV.)
   Mion. S. III. 522, 111 (dog beside her).
In a distyle shrine, Artemis on a basis advancing to right ;
holds spear and torch.
Æ Commodus. B. M. (**X** V.)
Artemis advancing to right, holding burning torches in both
hands.
Æ Auton. Imh. *Num. Zeit.* 1877, p. 29, 104.
The temple of **X** III. containing a statue of the hunting
Artemis and flanked by palm-trees is clearly the temple by the
Euripus.   The statue **X** v. is not greatly different from that on
X III., and the difference in the number of pillars is not
essential.

2.—Paus. IX. 20, 1.   Ταναγραῖοι δὲ οἰκιστήν σφισι Ποίμανδρον
γενέσθαι λέγουσι. . . . Ποίμανδρον δὲ γυναῖκά φασιν
ἀγαγέσθαι Τάναγραν θυγατέρα Αἰόλου· Κορίννη δέ
ἐστιν ἐς αὐτὴν πεποιημένα 'Ασωποῦ παῖδα εἶναι.
Head of POEMANDER : inscribed ΠΟΙΜΑΝΔΡΟC.
Æ Auton. Imh.
   Num. Zeit. 1877 ; 29, 106.

Head of Asopus: inscribed ΑϹΩΠΟϹ.

Æ Auton. Imh. (**X** vi.)
Num. Zeit, 1877 : 30, 108.

The head of Asopus is bearded ; it does not appear to be horned, or present the distinctive type of a river-god.

3.—Paus. IX. 20, 4. Ἐν δὲ τοῦ Διονύσου τῷ ναῷ θέας μὲν καὶ τὸ ἄγαλμα ἄξιον, λίθου τε ὂν Παρίου καὶ ἔργον Καλά-μιδος, θαῦμα δὲ παρέχεται μεῖζον ἔτι ὁ Τρίτων.

Under a roof, supported by two Atlantes on pillars, young Dionysus wearing nebris and boots; holds kantharos and thyrsos : below Triton swimming to left looking back.

Æ Anton. Pius. B. M. (**X** vii.)
M. Aurel. Imh. (**X** viii.) Berlin.
Commodus. Rhousopoulos.
Num. Zeit. 1877 ; p. 32, 111. E. Curtius. *Arch. Zeit.* 1883, 255.
P. Wolters. *Arch. Zeit.* 1885, 263.

Imhoof, followed by Curtius, published this coin as giving a representation of the statue by Calamis, as well as of the Triton in the temple. Wolters, however, maintains (1) that the Triton at Tanagra was no work of art but a specimen preserved by pickling ; (2) that the type of Dionysus on the coin is certainly not earlier than the time of Pheidias, and cannot represent a work of Calamis. There is force in these observations : perhaps a solution of the difficulty may be found in this direction ; the Triton may be introduced as a sort of mint-mark or local symbol of the city of Tanagra of which the pickled Triton was the chief boast. And the building represented on the coin may not be the temple of Dionysus, but a shrine with roof supported by two Atlantes, and containing not the statue by Calamis, but one of later date.

The following may be a figure of Dionysus :—

Male figure standing to right, in raised right, sceptre or thyrsus, in left an object which looks like a huge ear of corn or bunch of grapes.

Æ Augustus. Imh. (**X** ix.)

This figure is on so small a scale that the details are obscure. The god seems to wear a chlamys or nebris over the shoulders : whether he is bearded or beardless is uncertain. This figure should from the analogy of the other small coins of Tanagra represent a statue ; and it is more like what we should expect in a Dionysus of Calamis than the figure of the previous coin.

TANAGRA. 115

4.—Paus. IX. 22, 1. Ἐν Τανάγρᾳ δὲ παρὰ τὸ ἱερὸν τοῦ Διονύσου Θέμιδός ἐστιν, ὁ δὲ Ἀφροδίτης, καὶ ὁ τρίτος τῶν ναῶν Ἀπόλλωνος, ὁμοῦ δὲ αὐτῷ [καὶ] Ἄρτεμίς τε καὶ Λητώ.

X. 28, 6. Apollo at Delium. ἐδήλωσε δὲ καὶ ὁ Μῆδος Δᾶτις λόγοις τε, οὓς εἶπε πρὸς Δηλίους, καὶ τῷ ἔργῳ, ἡνίκα ἐν Φοινίσσῃ νηὶ ἄγαλμα εὑρὼν Ἀπόλλωνος ἀπέδωκεν αὖθις Ταναγραίοις ἐς Δήλιον.

Archaic APOLLO facing; holds in right hand a branch, in left a bow : hair in formal curls.

Æ Germanicus. Imh. (**X** x.) B. M. Eckhel, *Sylloge* pl. III. 10. Commodus (Germanicus?) *Mus. Sanclem.*, pl. 24, 201.

This figure is of the usual archaic type, much like the Apollo of Tectaeus and Angelion at Delos (**CC** XI.—XIV.) and decidedly more archaic than that of Canachus at Miletus, since the legs seem to be parallel to each other as well as the arms. On the coin the hard outlines of chest and hips are conspicuous. This figure may be a copy of the statue at Delium, traditionally said to have come out of a Phoenician ship.

5.—Paus. IX. 22, 1. Ἐς δὲ τοῦ Ἑρμοῦ τὰ ἱερὰ τοῦ τε Κριοφόρου καὶ ὃν Πρόμαχον καλοῦσι, τοῦ μὲν ἐς τὴν ἐπίκλησιν λέγουσιν ὡς ὁ Ἑρμῆς σφίσιν ἀποτρέψαι νόσον λοιμώδη περὶ τὸ τεῖχος κριὸν περιενεγκών, καὶ ἐπὶ τούτῳ Κάλαμις ἐποίησεν ἄγαλμα Ἑρμοῦ φέροντα κριὸν ἐπὶ τῶν ὤμων.... Τὸν δὲ Ἑρμῆν λέγουσι τὸν Πρόμαχον Ἐρετριέων ναυσὶν ἐξ Εὐβοίας ἐς τὴν Ταναγραίαν σχόντων τούς τε ἐφήβους ἐξαγαγεῖν ἐπὶ τὴν μάχην, καὶ αὐτὸν ἅτε ἔφηβον στλεγγίδι ἀμυνόμενον μάλιστα ἐργάσασθαι τῶν Εὐβοέων τροπήν. Κεῖται δὲ ἐν τοῦ Προμάχου τῷ ἱερῷ τῆς [τε] ἀνδράχνου τὸ ὑπόλοιπον· τραφῆναι δὲ ὑπὸ τῷ δένδρῳ τὸν Ἑρμῆν τούτῳ νομίζουσιν.

HERMES Criophorus; naked, facing.

Æ Auton. Imh. *Num. Zeit.* 1877, 29, 106-7.
B. M. (**X** XI.) *Cat.* Pl. X. 12. Berlin. Imh. (**X** XII.)
Prokesch-Osten, *Inedita* 1854, II. 62.

Hermes Promachus facing, holds in right hand a strigil, in left a caduceus (?)

Æ Trajan. B. M. (**X** XIII.) See however *B. M. Cat.* p. 66.

Hermes naked, his feet winged, standing to right, caduceus in left hand ; beside him a tree on which sits an eagle ; right hand rests on hip, left on tree.

Æ Trajan and Ant. Pius. (**X** xiv.) Rhousopoulos.
M. Aurel. Imh. (**X** xv.) Vienna (**X** xvi.)
Num. Zeit. 1877, 32, 110.

The first of these types (xi., xii.) clearly reproduces the Hermes of Calamis. One arm of the god passes round the fore-feet and one round the hindfeet of the ram; on one coin the hands seem to meet on the breast as in the well-known Athenian statue of Hermes carrying a bull, on the other coin one hand seems to be higher than the other. The pose of the god is stiff and his legs rigid: he is naked. He is also beardless, but whether his feet are winged, the scale of the coin makes it impossible to say.

The second type (xiii.) is identified by means of the strigil, if it be a strigil, with Hermes Promachos. This type seems to represent an original of the fifth century. The hair of the god is long, his left leg is advanced and bent, but he can scarcely be said to lounge.

The third type (xiv.—xvi.) is connected with the temple of Hermes Promachus by the tree whereon the eagle sits, which is doubtless the andrachnus of the story. At the foot of the tree is a curved object which may be a strigil. The figure is youthful and wears short hair, but the pose is somewhat stiff.

6.—OTHER TYPES at Tanagra.

Three nymphs draped, hand in hand.

Æ Augustus. *B. M. Cat.* Pl. x. 13. Vienna. (**X** xvii.)
Cf. the Athenian coin (**EE** vi.)

HALIARTUS.

1.—Paus. ix. 26, 5. 'Από δὲ τοῦ ὄρους τούτου πέντε ἀπέχει καὶ δέκα σταδίους πόλεως ἐρείπια Ὀγχηστοῦ. φασὶ δὲ ἐνταῦθα οἰκῆσαι Ποσειδῶνος παῖδα Ὀγχηστόν. ἐπ' ἐμοῦ δὲ ναός τε καὶ ἄγαλμα Ποσειδῶνος ἐλείπετο Ὀγχηστίου καὶ τὸ ἄλσος, ὃ δὴ καὶ Ὅμηρος ἐπῄνεσε.

POSEIDON naked, charging to right with raised trident.

Æ Auton. Fifth century Imh. B. M.
Num. Zeit. 1871, 335, 19.

Onchestus was in the territory of Haliartus.

THESPIAE.

1.—Paus. ix. 26, 8. τὸ δὲ ἄγαλμα τὸ Διονύσου καὶ αὖθις Τύχης.

TYCHE standing : holds patera and cornucopiae.

Æ Domitian. *B. M. Cat.* pl. xvi. 15. (**X** xviii.)
Mion. S. iii. 533, 189 (turreted).

THESPIAE. 117

2.—Paus. IX. 27, 5. ἔστι δὲ καὶ ἑτέρωθι Ἀφροδίτης Μελαινίδος
ἱερόν, καὶ θέατρόν τε καὶ ἀγορὰ θέας ἄξια· ἐνταῦθα
Ἡσιόδος ἀνάκειται χαλκοῦς.

Head of APHRODITE, with one or two crescents in the field.
Æ Auton. Fourth century B.C. Florence.
B. M. Cat. pl. XVI. 8–10. Imh.

Aphrodite standing draped; the end of her himation falling
over her left arm, her right hand outstretched over a
draped figure, apparently female, who holds flower and
lifts her dress.
Æ Domitian. Imh. (**X** XIX.)

One is tempted to bring this group into connexion with the
statues of Athene Ergane and of Plutus standing by her, mentioned by Pausanias (26, 8). But the taller figure has none of
the attributes of Athene, and the shorter figure is clearly a
draped goddess and no representation of Plutus. The statues
of Aphrodite resting on a draped archaic female figure are
collected by Gerhard in his paper *Venere Proserpina*, plates
vii.–xii. See also R. Schneider, *Statuette der Artemis*, Vienna,
1886.

3. OTHER TYPES at Thespiae.

Apollo with hair in queue seated to right on cippus, in
citharoedic costume; holds lyre.
Æ Domitian. B. M. (**X** XX.) Rhousopoulos.

Here again we are at first sight tempted to see a copy of a
monument described by Pausanias, the seated statue of Hesiod
thus described by Pausanias (30, 3): Κάθηται δὲ καὶ Ἡσίοδος
κιθάραν ἐπὶ τοῖς γόνασιν ἔχων, οὐδέν τι οἰκεῖον Ἡσιόδῳ φόρημα.
But the figure is clearly beardless, which we can scarcely
suppose Hesiod to have been. It is, however, open to question
whether Pausanias may not have taken an Apcllo Citharoedus
for a Hesiod.

Apollo draped, facing, holds plectrum and lyre.
Æ Domitian. B. M. (**X** XXI.) Rhousopoulos.

Veiled female head, wears calathos.
Æ Auton. B. M. Cat. pl. XVI. 12–13.

Veiled female figure, right hand raised.
Æ Domitian. B. M.

CORONEIA.

1.—Paus. IX. 34, 1. Πρὶν δὲ ἐς Κορώνειαν ἐξ Ἀλαλκομενῶν
ἀφικέσθαι, τῆς Ἰτωνίας Ἀθηνᾶς ἐστὶ τὸ ἱερόν. ... Ἐν δὲ
τῷ ναῷ χαλκοῦ πεποιημένα Ἀθηνᾶς Ἰτωνίας καὶ Διός

ἐστιν ἀγάλματα· τέχνη δὲ 'Αγορακρίτου, μαθητοῦ τε καὶ
ἐρωμένου Φειδίου. ἀνέθεσαν δὲ καὶ Χαρίτων ἀγάλματα
ἐπ' ἐμοῦ. Λέγεται δὲ καὶ τοιόνδε, 'Ιοδάμαν ἱερωμένην τῇ
θεῷ νύκτωρ ἐς τὸ τέμενος ἐσελθεῖν, καὶ αὐτῇ τὴν 'Αθηνᾶν
φανῆναι, τῷ χιτῶνι δὲ τῆς θεοῦ τὴν Μεδούσης ἐπεῖναι
τῆς Γοργόνος κεφαλήν.
Head of ATHENE facing, and in profile.
Æ Auton.   B. M. Cat.   Pl. VII. 10-11.
Imh.   Num. Zeit. 1877, 20, 57.
Gorgoneion.
Æ Auton.   B. M. Cat. pl. VII. 6-9.
Imh.   Num. Zeit. 1877, 19, 56-57.

PHOCIS.

1.—Paus. X. 2, 5–7.   Mention of Onomarchus and Phalaecus.
Both names are found on autonomous copper of Phocis
B. M. Cat. p. 23, &c.

DELPHI.

1.—Paus. X. 5, 1.   "Εστι δὲ καὶ ἄνοδος διὰ τῆς Δαυλίδος ἐς
τὰ ἄκρα τοῦ Παρνασοῦ, μακροτέρα τῆς ἐκ Δελφῶν, οὐ
μέντοι καὶ κατὰ ταὐτὰ χαλεπή.
PARNASSUS within wreath; inscribed ΠΥΘΙΑ.
Æ Auton.   Millingen, Récueil II. 11.   Mus. Sanclem. I. 179.

In the engraving of Millingen, Parnassus appears to be
depicted on the coin much in the style of modern landscape-
painting, a mountain with three summits. This is for Greek
art a most unusual mode of representation, the nearest parallel
being the type of Mons Argaeus on the coins of Caesareia in
Cappadocia, and the mountains on two coins of Amisus, struck
by Trajan and Hadrian (Imh.)

2.—Paus. X. 5, 13.   τὸν δ' ἐφ' ἡμῶν τῷ θεῷ ναὸν ᾠκοδόμησαν
μὲν ἀπὸ τῶν ἱερῶν οἱ 'Αμφικτυόνες χρημάτων, ἀρχι-
τέκτων δέ [τις] Σπίνθαρος ἐγένετο αὐτοῦ Κορίνθιος.
X. 19, 4.   Τὰ δὲ ἐν τοῖς ἀετοῖς, ἔστιν "Αρτεμις καὶ Λητὼ
καὶ 'Απόλλων καὶ Μοῦσαι. . . . . τὰ μὲν δὴ πρῶτα αὐτῶν
'Αθηναῖος Πραξίας μαθητὴς Καλάμιδός ἐστιν ἐργασά-
μενος.
24, 1.   'Εν δὲ τῷ προνάῳ τῷ ἐν Δελφοῖς γεγραμμένα
ἐστὶν ὠφελήματα ἀνθρώποις ἐς βίον· ἐγράφη δὲ ὑπὸ
ἀνδρῶν οὓς γενέσθαι σοφοὺς λέγουσιν "Ελληνες.
24, 4.   ἔστηκε δὲ καὶ ἀγάλματα Μοιρῶν δύο· ἀντὶ δὲ

αὐτῶν τῆς τρίτης Ζεύς τε Μοιραγέτης καί Ἀπόλλων
σφίσι παρέστηκε Μοιραγέτης.

24, 5. Ἐς δὲ τοῦ ναοῦ τὸ ἐσωτάτω παρίασί τε ἐς αὐτὸ
ὀλίγοι, καὶ χρυσοῦν Ἀπόλλωνος ἕτερον ἄγαλμα ἀνάκειται.

Front of tetrastyle temple, with pediment containing standing
figures : E (Delphic EI) between pillars.

Æ Hadrian. Copenhagen. (X xxiii.)
Faustina Sen. Imh. (X xxii.)   *Zeitschr. f. Num.* i. 115 (hexastyle).

The pediment is variously represented on these two coins :
on No. xxii. there seems to be a standing figure with hand
raised between two crouching animals ; on No. xxiii. there
seem to be several figures.

TEMPLE OF APOLLO with six columns at side : in the entry
statue of Apollo naked, standing, resting left elbow on
a pillar, his right hand advanced ; at his feet omphalos
or altar.

Æ Faustina Sen. B. M. (X xxiv.) Rhousopoulos (X xxv.) cf. M. S. iii. 500, 49.

Similar figure of Apollo without temple or omphalos—
Æ Hadrian. Mus. Parma (X xxvi.) Paris. Rhousopoulos.

Apollo naked, standing to left, his right foot supported on a
square basis, holds in right hand lyre which rests on
knee, in raised left branch of laurel, left elbow rests on
tripod, on the basis of which is inscribed ΠΥΘΙΑ.

Æ Hadrian. Sestini, *Mus. Hederv.* pl. x. 2.

For this coin our only authority is the plate of Sestini's work,
which is not altogether trustworthy ; the lyre seems impossibly
small, and the letters ΠΥΘΙΑ may be suspected ; in fact it is
not unlikely that the figure described by Sestini may be
identical with that in the next description.

Apollo naked, standing, in his right hand a branch, his left
hand raised ; behind him, tripod on basis : at his feet,
river-god (Pleistus, Paus. x. 8, 8).

Æ Hadrian. Berlin (Y i.)
Berl. Blätter, v. pl. lvi. 8. *Zeit. f. Num.* vii. 217.

There is an appearance of a staff in the left hand of Apollo.
Tripod on stand.

Æ Hadrian. *Ramus.* i. pl. iii. 12.
Antinous. Photiades (Y ii.) Cf. *Zeit. f. Num.* xiii. pl. iv. 3, where the
tripod is inverted.

Altar bound with laurel.
Æ Hadrian. B. M.

Apollo standing; in right hand branch or patera; left arm
resting on pillar and holding lyre.

Æ Hadrian. Mion. S. III. 499, 38 (Vaillant).
Caracalla. Mion. II. 98, 31 (Vaillant).

The types thus far described are such as can with reasonable
probability be supposed really to represent the temple at Delphi
and objects contained in it. First we have the front of the
temple (**X** XXII.) supported by six Ionic columns and surmounted by a pediment, in which may be discerned a standing
figure with arm raised as if to strike, and two animals crouching
in the corners. Steps lead up to the temple. The letter **E**,
which occupies the intercolumniation, is no doubt the mysterious
Delphic εἶ as to which Plutarch has written : it here stands, in the
shorthand usual in Greek art, for all the wise and witty sayings
set up in the pronaüs. Next comes a side view of the same
temple (**X** XXIV.), the pediment occupied by a mere disk. In
the front appears a naked standing figure of Apollo, his elbow
resting on a column. This figure repeated in **X** XXVI. would
seem to be the principal statue of Apollo in the Temple. Two
other sets of coins present to us a figure in general pose closely
like this, but varied in attribute and detail. Of one set, only
known from the descriptions of Vaillant, we are unable to figure
a specimen. The other type appears as **Y** I. Here the figure
of Apollo is doubly localised, by the presence of the river-god,
and by the tripod on a stand in the background, which tripod
is the type of **Y** II. It has been wrongly supposed that this
tripod stands for that dedicated by the Greeks after Plataea and
placed on the brazen serpents still preserved at Constantinople
(cf. Paus. x. 13, 9), wrongly, since in Pausanias' time the tripod
had already disappeared and only the stand remained. Rather
it stands for the sacred tripod whereon the soothsaying priestess,
the Pythia, sat to deliver her oracles. On the coin published
by Sestini it is inscribed ΠYΘIA ; this inscription, supposing it
really to exist, is somewhat ambiguous : it may indicate that
the tripod was dedicated in memory of a victory in the Pythian
games, or it may have a more local signification.

When we reach the question in what part of the temple the
statues copied on these coins existed we land in great difficulties.
The two statues mentioned by Pausanias are that of Apollo
Moeragetes, and a golden statue undescribed, kept in the

adytum. The latter statue is mentioned by various writers, but not described. Wieseler (*Denkm.* II. 134) observes that the statue probably held a lyre, but even this is not completely established by the passages he cites, Plutarch, *de Pyth. orac.* 16, *Sulla* 12. It is therefore not improbable that the figure on the coins above mentioned may be the Apollo of the adytum, though we must mention as an alternative possibility that that statue is repeated rather on some of the coins mentioned below which bear the type of a Citharoedic Apollo. .

The golden statue can scarcely be supposed to be of earlier date than the times of Onomarchus, or it would probably have been seized by him.

Paus. X. 16, 3.   Τὸν δὲ ὑπὸ Δελφῶν καλούμενον ὀμφαλόν, λίθου πεποιημένον λευκοῦ, τοῦτο εἶναι τὸ ἐν μέσῳ γῆς πάσης αὐτοί τε λέγουσιν οἱ Δελφοί, κ.τ.λ.

Obv. Tripod.

Rev. Omphalos ; thus represented ☉.

Æ early Auton.   Imh.   B. M.   &c.   *Zeit. f. Num.* I. 294.
Æ Auton.   Ramus, I. pl. III. 12.
 Faustina Sen.   B. M.

Omphalos, entwined by snake, and covered with net-work.
Æ Auton.   Berlin.   *Rev. Num.* 1860, pl. XII. 8.
Æ Hadrian.

Omphalos on basis.
Æ Hadrian.   Imh.

Omphalos on rock.
Æ Hadrian.   *B. M. Cat.* pl. IV. 20.

Apollo naked, standing, right hand resting on head, left hand half raised.
Æ Hadrian.   B. M.   (Y III.)

Apollo Citharoedus, in long chiton, advancing to right, playing on lyre.
Æ Auton.   Millingen, *Récueil,* II. 10 and 11.
 Hadrian.   B. M.   Copenhagen (Y IV.) Berlin.   Rhousopoulos.
 Overbeck, *Berichte der Kais. Sächs. Ges. der Wissensch.* 1886.

Apollo Citharoedus facing, clad in long chiton, holds plectrum and lyre.
Æ Faustina Sen.   Rhousopoulos.

Apollo, wearing himation, seated on omphalos; right hand raised.
Æ Hadrian.   Berlin.   (Y v.)

Apollo laur., naked to waist, seated to left on rock, on which lyre; his right hand rests on his head.
Æ Faustina Sen.   Vienna, Schottenstift (Y vi.)

Coin struck by Amphictyons (x. 8, 1). *Obv.* Head of Demeter veiled and crowned with corn. *Rev.* Apollo, laur., clad in long chiton, seated to left on omphalos; right hand raised to his chin, in left, laurel-branch; lyre beside him. Æ Fourth cent. B. M. (Y vii.) Imh. Berlin.

Inscription ΠΡΟΠΟΛΟΙ ΑΜΦΙΚΤΥΟΝΕϹ. Æ Antinous. Imh. *Zeit. f. Num.* xiii. pl. iv. 3.

Head of Apollo, laureate. Æ Æ Auton. Berlin. (Bow before head.) Æ Faustina Sen. B. M. (Y viii.) Rhousopoulos. (Y ix.) Imh.

We have here a large group of types of Apollo the origin of which we cannot refer to any known statue at Delphi. The first type (Y iii.) certainly has a statuesque appearance, and Y iv. belongs to that class of representations of Apollo Citharoedus of which the origin is attributed to Scopas. As to these see Overbeck in the *Berichte* of the Saxon Academy, 1886. Wieseler (*Denkmaeler,* ii. 134*a*) regards the figure on the coin as a copy of a statue in the theatre of Delphi. The seated figures of Apollo cannot be traced back to a sculptural original: one of them (Y vii.) belongs to a period when we should expect the die-sinker to invent a type for himself, and not to copy a statue; the other two are of imperial times, but cannot be identified. The latter of the two heads of Apollo (Y viii., ix.) is probably copied from a statue; the queue falling on the neck of the god behind, and the severe features seem to indicate a work of early art.

Laurel wreath inscribed ΠΥΘΙΑ (Paus. x. 7, 8). Æ Auton. Hadrian. Anton. Pius. Faustina Sen. Caracalla.

Tripod with ΠΥΘΙΑ. Æ Auton. Bröndsted, *Reisen* i. p. vi. (*Obv.* Apollo Citharoedus.)

Table with ΠΥΘΙΑ. Æ Faustina Sen. B. M. Mus. Civico, Venice.

3.—Paus. x. 8, 6. Ἐσελθόντι δὲ ἐς τὴν πόλιν εἰσὶν ἐφεξῆς ναοί· . . . . ὁ τέταρτος δὲ Ἀθηνᾶς καλεῖται Προνοίας. Τῶν δὲ ἀγαλμάτων τὸ ἐν τῷ προνάῳ Μασσαλιωτῶν ἀνάθημά ἐστι, μεγέθει τοῦ ἔνδον ἀγάλματος μεῖζον.

ATHENE standing; spear in her raised right hand, shield on left arm. Æ Hadrian. Paris. (Y x.) Faustina Sen. Imh. (Y xi.) Mion. S. iii. 500, 50-51.

This type may be compared with those of Athens (**AA** xv., xvi.). The pose and attributes of the goddess belong to the time when the stiff archaic Palladia had been superseded by statues of softer outline and gentler movement, but before Pheidias had entirely recreated the ideal of the deity.

4.—Paus. x. 32, 7.

Τὸ δὲ ἄντρον τὸ Κωρύκιον μεγέθει τε ὑπερβάλλει τὰ εἰρημένα, καὶ ἔστιν ἐπὶ πλεῖστον ὁδεῦσαι δι' αὐτοῦ καὶ ἄνευ λαμπτήρων· ὅ τε ὄροφος ἐς αὔταρκες ἀπὸ τοῦ ἐδάφους ἀνέστηκε, καὶ ὕδωρ τὸ μὲν ἀνερχόμενον ἐκ πηγῶν, πλέον δὲ ἔτι ἀπὸ τοῦ ὀρόφου στάζει, ὥστε καὶ δῆλα ἐν τῷ ἐδάφει σταλαγμῶν τὰ ἴχνη διὰ παντὸς ἐστι τοῦ ἄντρου. Ἱερὸν δὲ αὐτὸ οἱ περὶ τὸν Παρνασὸν Κωρυκίων τε εἶναι Νυμφῶν καὶ Πανὸς μάλιστα ἥγηνται.

PAN naked, in human form, seated on rock, in right hand pedum, which rests on another rock.

Æ Hadrian. B. M. (**Y** xii.)

Pan seated to left in Corycian cave.

Æ Hadrian. Imh. (**Y** xiii.) *Zeit. f. Num.* i. pl. iv. 9a.
Baumeister, *Denkmaeler der Cl. Alt.* p. 961.

Pausanias does not speak of a statue of Pan: the representations on the coins seem to be rather of the class which indicate the presence of deities at certain localities than of the class which reproduce works of art.

6.—OTHER TYPES at Delphi:

Altar wreathed, on basis.

Æ Hadrian. Imh. B. M.

Raven on olive-branch.

Æ Hadrian. B. M. Paris.

Lyre on rock.

Æ Hadrian. Munich.

Artemis as huntress, clad in short chiton.

Æ Faustina Sen. Paris. (**Y** xiv.)
Mion. ii. 97, 30 : Sup. iii. 501, 55.

Several figures of Artemis are mentioned among the *donaria* at Delphi.

ELATEIA.

1.—Paus. x. 34, 6. Ἐπὶ τῷ πέρατι δὲ τῷ ἐν δεξιᾷ τῆς πόλεως θέατρόν τέ ἐστι καὶ χαλκοῦν Ἀθηνᾶς ἄγαλμα ἀρχαῖον· ταύτην τὴν θεὸν λέγουσιν ἀμῦναί σφισιν ἐπὶ τοὺς ὁμοῦ Ταξίλῳ βαρβάρους.

Ἐλατείας δὲ ὅσον σταδίους εἴκοσιν ἀφέστηκεν Ἀθηνᾶς ἐπίκλησιν Κραναίας ἱερόν.

8. Τὸ δὲ ἄγαλμα ἐποίησαν μὲν καὶ τοῦτο οἱ Πολυκλέους παῖδες, ἔστι δὲ ἐσκευασμένον ὡς ἐς μάχην, καὶ ἐπείργασται τῇ ἀσπίδι τῶν Ἀθήνῃσι μίμημα ἐπὶ τῇ ἀσπίδι τῆς καλουμένης ὑπὸ Ἀθηναίων Παρθένου.

ATHENE in form of Palladium.
Æ Auton. B. M. (Υ xvi.) &c.
Similar; in field, tripod.
Æ Auton. B. M. Imh.
Athene charging to right with spear advanced, shield on left arm.
Æ Auton. B. M. (Υ xv.)
Head of Athene.
Æ Auton. Paris.

We meet here with a difficulty : Pallas appears fighting in two different attitudes ; and it is impossible to say with certainty which is nearer to the sculptural work of the sons of Polycles, Timocles and Timarchides. But the date of these artists is later than that of the coins, 3rd century B.C.

ANTICYRA.

1.—Paus. x. 36, 8. Ἔστι δέ σφισιν ἐπὶ τῷ λιμένι Ποσειδῶνι οὐ μέγα ἱερόν, λογάσιν ᾠκοδομημένον λίθοις· κεκονίαται δὲ τὰ ἐντός. τὸ δὲ ἄγαλμα ὀρθὸν χαλκοῦ πεποιημένον, βέβηκε δὲ ἐπὶ δελφῖνι τῷ ἑτέρῳ τῶν ποδῶν· κατὰ τοῦτο δὲ ἔχει καὶ τὴν χεῖρα ἐπὶ τῷ μηρῷ, ἐν δὲ τῇ ἑτέρᾳ χειρὶ τρίαινά ἐστιν αὐτῷ.

Head of POSEIDON.
Æ Auton. Berlin.
Zeit. f. Num. vi. 15. Rev. Num. 1843, pl. x. 3.

2.—Paus. x. 37, 1. Τῆς πόλεως δὲ ἐν δεξιᾷ, δύο μάλιστα προελθόντι ἀπ' αὐτῆς σταδίους, πέτρα τέ ἐστιν ὑψηλή, μοῖρα ὄρους ἡ πέτρα, καὶ ἱερὸν ἐπ' αὐτῆς πεποιημένον ἐστὶν Ἀρτέμιδος· ἔργον τῶν Πραξιτέλους, δᾷδα ἔχουσα τῇ δεξιᾷ καὶ ὑπὲρ τῶν ὤμων φαρέτραν· παρὰ δὲ αὐτὴν κύων ἐν ἀριστερᾷ· μέγεθος δὲ ὑπὲρ τὴν μεγίστην γυναῖκα τὸ ἄγαλμα.

ARTEMIS clad in short chiton advancing to right, quiver at shoulder; in her right hand bow, in her left torch ; dog beside her.
Æ Auton. Berlin. (Υ xvii.)
Zeit. f. Num. l.c. Rev. Num. l.c.

This type and the head of Poseidon are two sides of the same coin. The torch borne by Artemis is distinctive, and gives us reason to think that the figure of the coin is, if not exactly a copy, at all events a free reproduction of the Anticyran statue of Artemis by the sons of Praxiteles, Cephisodotus and Timarchus. The old reading was ἔργων τῶν Πραξιτέλους, and the statue is cited by Brunn (*G. K.*) and other writers as a work of Praxiteles himself. And in fact the reading of our text does not exclude Praxiteles as the artist, cf. the phrase ἔργον τῶν Μύρωνος (ix. 30, 1) and compare *Arch. Zeit.* 1876, p. 167.

ATHENS.

1. (*a*) Paus. I. 1, 1. Athene Sunias: temple on the top of the promontory of Sunium.

(*b*) I. 1, 3. Athene in Piraeus, bronze statue holding lance.

(*c*) I. 1, 4 and 36, 4. At Phalerum. Temple of Athene Sciras.

(*d*) I. 2, 5. Near Cerameicus. Statue of Athene Paeonia.

(*e*) I. 8, 4. In the temple of Ares, statue of Athene by Locrus of Paros.

(*f*) I. 14, 6. In or near the temple of Hephaestus. Statue of Athene with blue eyes, γλαυκοὺς ἔχον τοὺς ὀφθαλμούς.

(*g*) I. 23, 4. On the Acropolis. Statue of Athene Hygieia (by Pyrrhus of Athens).

(*h*) I. 24, 1. On the Acropolis. Athene striking Marsyas, for picking up the flutes thrown away by her.

(*i*) I. 24, 2. On the Acropolis. Athene springing from the head of Zeus.

(*j*) I. 24, 3. On the Acropolis. Athene producing the olive, and Poseidon waves.

(*k*) I. 24, 5. The Parthenon. Subject of west pediment birth of Athene, of east pediment contest of Athene and Poseidon for the land.

(*l*) I. 24, 5-7. In the Parthenon. Chryselephantine statue, standing, in long chiton; on her breast, Medusa-head; holding Nike and spear, shield at her feet, by her spear, snake.

(*m*) I. 26, 4. On the Acropolis. Seated statue by Endoeus.

(*n*) I. 26, 6. On the Acropolis. Athene Polias, very sacred statue said to have fallen from heaven.

(*o*) I. 28, 2. On the Acropolis. Bronze statue by Pheidias (Promachos). Lance-point and helmet visible on the way from Sunium: shield decorated by Mys.

(*p*) I. 28, 2. On the Acropolis. Athene Lemnia, most remarkable of Pheidias' works.

(*q*) I. 30, 4; 31, 6. At Colonus. Altar of Athene Hippia, also at Acharnae.

(*r*) I. 32, 2. On Pentelicus. Statue of Athene.

(*s*) I. 37, 2. Temple of Demeter on sacred way. Athene and Poseidon honoured there.

(*t*) I. 37, 6. Temple of Apollo on sacred way. Statue of Athene.

In the following classification of the various types of Athene we would not be understood positively to endorse the identifications inserted in the text of coin-types with ancient works of art. But for the identifications there is, in each case, much to be said, and as we have not space to discuss them at length, we accept them provisionally in order to obtain a basis for arrangement. If any of them be hereafter disproved, it will not destroy the value of our work.

1. ATHENE PARTHENOS (*l*).

Athene standing, aegis on her breast; holds in right hand Nike, in left, spear; left hand rests on shield represented in profile.

Æ Imh. B. M. Loebbecke. (Y XVIII.)
Hunter Coll. Pl. x. 36, 37.

As last, shield bearing Gorgoneion partly conceals her body.

Æ B. M. (Y XIX.) Beulé 258, 1.

As last but one; snake at her feet.

Æ B. M. (Y XX.) Beulé 258.
Æ B. M. (Y XXI.) Beulé 258.

With these coins we may compare the following type on a Cilician coin of the fourth century B.C. which seems also a reproduction of the Athenian Parthenos.

Athene facing, holds in right hand Nike, left hand rests on shield, right elbow supported by trunk of tree.

Æ B. M. Gardner, *Types*, pl. x. 28. De Luynes' coll. (Y XXII.)

Also tetradrachms of Alexander I. and Antiochus VII., Euergetes, of Syria (Wieseler, *Denkm.* II. 203; *Br. Mus. Cat.* Seleucidae, pl. XV. 5; pl. XX. 6, &c.).

Paus. I. 24, 5. Μέσῳ μὲν οὖν ἐπίκειται οἱ τῷ κράνει Σφιγγὸς εἰκών, ... καθ᾽ ἑκάτερον δὲ τοῦ κράνους γρῦπές εἰσιν ἐπειργασμένοι.

Head of Athene in three-crested Athenian helmet; on the

side of it Pegasus running; over the forehead foreparts
of horses.

Æ Auton. B. M. (Y xxiii.)

Bust of Athene in crested Athenian helmet, of which the
ornamentation is obscure, but there seems to be an owl (?)
on the neck-piece; wears necklace and aegis.

Æ Auton. Loebbecke. Parma. (Y xxiv.) Berlin.

With these may be compared coins of Alexandria struck
under Julia Mammaea.

Bust of Athene in three-crested Athenian helmet: on the top,
sphinx, on the side a Pegasus or griffin, over the forehead
heads of four horses.

Potin. B. M. (Y xxv.)

The literature which treats of the Parthenos statue of Pheidias
and its reproductions in statuette relief and coin is so extensive
that it is quite impossible here to summarise the results which
it establishes. The coins add little to our knowledge; but on
one or two points their testimony is important :—

(1) the prop which on the Athenian statuette discovered in
1881 supported the right hand of Athene does not appear on
the Athenian coins; but it does on a leaden tessera at Berlin,
which bears the inscription A⊙E and reproduces the Parthenos
statue (v. Sallet, *Zeit. f. Num.* x. p. 152.) On the Cilician coin
above cited, the stump of a tree is similarly introduced as a
support. In our plates will be found several instances in which
a prop appears to have been placed under the arm of a statue,
see **E** LXXXVII., **N** XXIV., **O** IX., **T** VII., and more particularly
the reproductions of the early statue of Artemis Laphria at
Patrae on pl. **Q**, and the seated female figure, pl. **EE** XVI, XVII.,
who rests her hand on a column.

(2) The animal on the side of the helmet of Athene on late
silver coins of Athens is generally quite clearly a Pegasus (as
in XXIII.) but sometimes, though rarely, certainly a griffin.
The coin of Imperial times (XXIV.) gives us a nobler, and in
some respects truer, representation of the original, but the
details cannot be made out. The coin of Alexandria (XXV.)
adds the Sphinx as a support of the crest, and distinctly confirms the probability, established by coins and gems, that the
visor of Athene's helmet was adorned with foreparts of four
horses. Schreiber (*Arch. Zeit.* 1884, p. 196) remarks that
owls are sometimes found on the coins in the place of the fore-

parts of horses; such coins are entirely unknown to us; the foreparts of horses are universal, and it can scarcely be doubted that they represent something which existed over the forehead of the Parthenos statue. A curious variant, however, occurs in the gold reliefs of St. Petersburg which give the head of the Parthenos (*Athen. Mittheil.* 1883, pl. xv., p. 291). In this case a sphinx supports the crest, flanked by Pegasus on each side ; but over the forehead, in the place of the foreparts of horses, are foreparts of griffins and stags alternately.

2. ATHENE PROMACHOS (*o*).

Athene facing, head left, spear transversely in right hand, shield on left arm, aegis on breast.

Æ B. M. (**Z** I.) Imh.   Loebbecke (**Z** II.)
Beulé 390, 7.   Lange in *Arch. Zeit.* 1881, 147.

Similar ; before her, snake.

Æ Hunter, pl. x. 39.

On the whole Lange's identification of this type as a reproduction of the Promachos of Pheidias seems sound. He maintains that the turn of the head visible on the coin reproduces a turn of the statue's head which was directed towards its right shoulder. He considers that the relief and statues published by von Sybel in the Athenian *Mittheil.* 1880, p. 102, also represent Athene Promachos.

3. THE ACROPOLIS.

The Acropolis-rock ; on it to the left the Parthenon, to the right a staircase leading up to the Propylaea ; between these, figure of Athene on basis ; below, cave in which Pan seated to left.

Æ B. M. (**Z** III.) Imh. (**Z** IV.) Paris (**Z** V.)
Beulé, 394.   Lange in *Arch. Zeit.* 1881, p. 197.

Similar ; Propylaea lower down, and type of Athene different.

Æ Vienna (**Z** VI.) Rhousopoulos.

Similar, right and left transposed.

Æ Beulé, 394, 2.   Berlin.   Michaelis *Paus. descr. arcis*, p. 1, 3.
Loebbecke (**Z** VII.)

III. IV. and V. of the plate represent roughly the Acropolis as seen from the north-west angle, in which aspect the marble staircase leading up to the Propylaea would appear on the extreme right, next, the Propylaea themselves, next, the bronze Athene, and next, the Parthenon ; the Paneion being somewhat to the left of the staircase. The staircase is the principal feature of the view, this ἔργον τῆς ἀναβάσεως was executed in the reign of Caius (*C.I.A.* iii. 1284–85). The coins are all of the age of the Antonines. When, however, we come to a consideration of details we find much want of exactness. The Propylaea are very inadequately represented, and the orientation of the Parthenon is incorrect. M. Beulé thinks that Pan is in the act of playing on the flute ; but this is very doubtful.

But the most important point is the type and attitude of Athene. It is clear from the position of the statue that the intention of the die-cutter was to represent the bronze colossus of Pheidias which stood in the midst of the Acropolis, and we ought thus to gain some evidence as to the details of that colossus. But any such hope is destined to failure. On some of the coins such as **Z** IV., as Lange has already observed, the type represented is clearly that of the Parthenos. On others (as **Z** III.) she clearly holds Nike in her right hand, but her left seems to be raised. It is further a doubtful point whether the apparent differences between **Z** III, and **Z** IV. do not arise from mere oxidation.

4. ATHENE IN PEDIMENTS (*k*).

Athene running to right; in left shield and spear; right hand extended, beneath it olive entwined by snake; in front, owl.

Æ B. M. &c.   Imh. (**Z** VIII.)
Beulé, 390, 12.   *Arch. Zeit.* 1870, pl. xxx. 3.
E. A. Gardner in *Journ. Hell. Stud.* III. 252.
Schneider, *Die Geburt der Athena*, 1880, pl. I.

Similar figure ; no olive, but to right snake or snakes.

Æ Loebbecke (**Z** IX.) Rhousopoulos.
Beulé, 390, 10 and 11.

Similar figure ; no olive, but to left snake.

Æ Loebbecke (**Z** X.)

With these we may compare the following :—

Similar figure, plucking with right hand twig from olive ; under olive, owl on pillar ; to right, altar.

Æ Roman medallion of Commodus.   B. M. (**Z** XIII.)
Fröhner, p. 137.

Similar figure, holding in right hand Nike.

Æ of Tarsus : Balbinus, &c.

R. Schneider (*op. cit.*) discusses the origin of this type which is widely copied in sculpture (*e.g.* Clarac. pl. 462A, No. 858*a*, a small statue of Pentelic marble in the Capitoline Museum) and in reliefs, as well as on coins and gems. By the aid of a puteal discovered at Madrid (engraved also in L. Mitchell's *History of Sculpture*, p. 350) he traces the running figure of Athene back to the east pediment of the Parthenon, where the birth of the goddess is depicted. The resemblance of the coin-type to Athene on the puteal is very striking; but on the other hand we lack any satisfactory proof that the design on the puteal closely reproduces that of the pediment. Other writers, as Friederichs (*Bausteine*, 401) and Mr. Ernest Gardner (*Journ. Hell. Stud.* III. 252) have seen in the type reproduced in statues and coins of this group Athene from the west pediment. Certainly she is closely like the goddess in Carrey's drawing of that pediment, only turned in the opposite direction. The attitude of the right hand is enigmatic. Mr. E. Gardner sees in it a gesture of triumph as the goddess points to the olive of her creation, but on the Roman medallion the goddess is distinctly plucking an olive-spray from the tree.

Thus it cannot be considered certain which of the pediments has furnished the prototype of this running Pallas; but it is not improbable that she may be traced to one or the other; her likeness to the extant figure called Iris in the eastern pediment strengthens the presumption.

A figure closely similar occurs in a round temple on a gem, in Wieseler, *Denkmäler*, II. 216c. This may be regarded as telling against the identification here proposed, but not with great force.

4. Athene and Poseidon (*k* and *j*).

Olive-tree entwined by snake, owl seated in the branches. To left of it Poseidon, in whose raised right hand trident pointed to the ground, and on whose left arm chlamys; at his feet dolphin. To right of it Athene, right hand advanced, in left shield and spear.

Æ B. M.   Rhousopoulos (Z XI.)   Vienna (Z XII.)   Paris.   Loebbecke (Z XIV.)
Stephani, *Compte Rendu*, 1872, p. 5, 3 ; p. 135, 1.

Similar, owl and dolphin wanting.

Æ Imh. (Z XVI.)

Athene standing to right; shield behind her, her left stretched towards olive, round which snake twines; owl on olive. On the other side of the tree Poseidon standing to left, his right foot resting on a rock, left hand resting on trident, right hand advanced.

Æ Loebbecke (Z XVII.) Rhousopoulos.
  cf. Wieseler, *Denkmäler*, No. 234.

Athene standing to left, grasping with right hand olive-tree, against which her spear leans, behind her shield and snake : on the other side of the tree Poseidon to right, his left foot resting on rock, right hand resting on trident, left hand advanced.

Æ Roman medallion of M. Aurelius.
  Prov. Museum, Bonn (Z XV.)
  cf. the relief published by Robert in the Athens *Mittheilungen* for 1882.

We have here two entirely distinct groups, each comprising Athene, Poseidon, and an olive-tree entwined by a snake. The first group (XI., XII., XIV., XVI.) is closely like the celebrated group on the vase of St. Petersburg published by Stephani (*C.R.* 1872) and repeated in this Journal (III. p. 245), where some account is given of the various interpretations to which the group has given rise. In the other group (XV. XVII.) Athene and Poseidon are not in conflict but at rest, and apparently engaged in colloquy. One is naturally tempted to bring the former group into connexion with the west pediment of the Parthenon, and to regard the latter group as connected with the anathema on the Acropolis mentioned by Pausanias in passage *j.* A noticeable point in the coins of the first group is that the snake is in all cases distinctly hostile to Poseidon.

5. ATHENE STANDING BY OLIVE.

Athene standing to left before olive-tree ; in her right hand spear held transversely, in her left shield which rests on the ground.

Æ B. M. Rhousopoulos. Bibl. Turin. (Z XVIII.) Snake twined round tree.
  B. M. (Z XIX.) Owl perched in tree.
  Loebbecke. Owl at foot of tree.
  Beulé, 390, 3. Owl in tree, snake at foot.

This Athene may perhaps be part of a group, which, when complete, would include Poseidon on the other side of the tree. On one specimen (Z XVIII. B. M.) the snake which is twined round the tree seems to be looking at an enemy, who can scarcely be other than Poseidon. On the other ·hand the Athene of these coins is not exactly like the Athene of the groups above cited ; more, however, like the goddess in the second than in the first group.

6. OLIVE-TREE.

Paus. I. 27, 2.—Olive-tree in temple of Athene Polias:—

Περὶ δὲ τῆς ἐλαίας οὐδὲν ἔχουσιν ἄλλο εἰπεῖν ἢ τῇ θεῷ
μαρτύριον γενέσθαι τοῦτο ἐς τὸν ἀγῶνα τὸν ἐπὶ τῇ
χώρᾳ.

Olive-tree with snake and owl.
Æ B. M. &c.
Beulé, 391, 7-11.
Olive-tree with owl and amphora.
Æ B. M. Loebbecke, &c.
Beulé, 391, 10.
Olive-tree, owl, amphora, palm-tree.
Æ Rhousopoulos.
Ramus, I. pl. III. 18.
Olive-tree, snake, and dice-box.
Æ
Beulé, 392, 2.
Olive-tree, snake, owl, and dice-box.
Æ
Beulé, 154.

7. ATHENE AND MARSYAS (h.)

Athene standing, dropping the flutes; before her Marsyas in
an attitude of surprise.
Æ Athens Mus. Rhousopoulos (Z xx.)
Beulé, p. 393. Z. f. Num. VII. 216.
Overbeck, Gr. Plastik. I. p. 209.
Wieseler, Denkmäler, No. 239b.
Athene to left, right hand advanced, at her feet serpent;
before her Marsyas in an attitude of surprise.
Æ Bibl. Turin (Z xxI.)

This is an interesting group, and we find in it traces of
sculptural origin, although Athene is not, as in the group
described by Pausanias, striking Marsyas. Wieseler suggests
(Nachrichten der k. Gesellsch. d. Wis. Göttingen, 1885, p. 324)
that the reading Μαρσύαν παίουσα is corrupt, and that a
better would be Μαρσύαν αὐλοῦντα ἀναπαύουσα. Cf. however
Michaelis, Paus. descr. arcis, p. 9, and Petersen, Arch. Zeit. 1880,
who explains the phrase of the text.

Several writers whose opinions are summed up by Overbeck
(Gr. Plastik. I. 209, and note 165) agree in regarding the
Marsyas of the coin, which is like a marble statue in the
Lateran and a bronze statuette in the British Museum, as
copied from the Marsyas of Myron. The attitude of Athene is
on the two coins different, and as they are too ill-preserved for

us to judge of it in detail, we must content ourselves with saying that she is in a quiet attitude, indicating neither anger nor hostility. Pliny speaks of a group by Myron thus, (*fecit*) *satyrum admirantem tibias et Minervam*, which phrase applies far better to the group of the coin than the phrase of Pausanias; it thus appears not unlikely that we may have here a reproduction of the group of Myron, which may have been preserved at Athens.

We next reach a number of types of Athene which cannot be definitely traced back to a sculptural original : some are mere varieties of the types already described, some are new, and offer a field to investigation in future.

8. ATHENE NIKEPHOROS.

Athene standing to right; spear in raised right hand, Nike in left, himation round waist.

Æ B. M. Loebbecke. Paris (**Z** xxii.)
Furtwängler in Roscher's *Lexicon*, p. 702.
Beulé, 290, 6.

Athene standing to left ; holds in right Nike, in left spear, shield slung on left arm.

Æ Loebbecke (**Z** xxiii.)

Athene standing to right; in right hand Nike, in left spear; at her feet snake to right ; behind her, owl on pillar.

Æ Naples (*Cat.* No. 7156) (**AA** i.)

The first coin under head 8 belongs to the class of figures of which the Pallas of Velletri is the most noteworthy specimen. Furtwängler in Roscher's *Lexicon*, p. 702 describes the class, which seems to have originated in the fourth century.

9. ATHENE HOLDING OWL.

Athene standing to right; owl in left hand, patera (?) in right; clad in long chiton.

Æ Imh. B. M. Loebbecke (**AA** ii.)
Beulé, p. 387, 1, 2.
(*Obv.* Head of Zeus or Head of Artemis.)

Athene standing to left ; owl in right hand, spear in raised left; himation over shoulders.

Æ B. M. (**AA** iii.)

Athene standing to right ; owl in her right hand, in her left spear held transversely ; coiled snake at her feet.

Æ Imh. Loebbecke. Rhousopoulos (**AA** iv.)
Hunter, pl. x. 33.

Athene standing to right; owl in right hand, spear in left hand, shield on left arm, himation over shoulders.

Æ B. M. (**AA** v.)

Athene standing to right; in raised right hand owl; behind her owl on pillar.

Æ Rhousopoulos. Loebbecke.

cf. Müller-Wieseler, *Denkmäler*, ii. No. 221, where the object in the hand of Pallas is identified as a pomegranate.

The first described of these types is the most important, and seems clearly to portray a sculptural original of the early period; there is in the pose something of archaic stiffness. Beulé suggests that it may portray the Athene Archegetis, of which the scholiast to Aristophanes (*Aves*, l. 515) says γλαῦκα εἶχεν ἐν τῇ χειρί. But this phrase is not distinctive, the owl being a usual attribute of Athene: we are equally likely to be right in considering the present type as Athene Paeonia. Athene Hygieia it cannot be, as that statue held a spear in the left hand : cf. Michaelis in Athenian *Mittheil.* i. 289.

10. ATHENE HOLDING PATERA.

Athene facing, head to left; patera in right hand, spear in left ; shield on left arm.

Æ Loebbecke. Rhousopoulos (**AA** vi.)

Athene facing, head to left ; in right holds patera over altar, in left spear; shield on left arm.

Æ Hunter, pl. xi. 4.
Beulé, 256, 3.

As last, but left hand rests on shield ; to left of altar, olive, with snake and owl.

Æ Beulé, 256, 2.

11. ATHENE STANDING, ARMED.

Athene standing to left, her raised right resting on spear, shield behind her ; wears himation.

Æ Beulé, 390, 8. Imhoof (**AA** vii.)

Athene standing to right; holds in raised right hand spear, left rests on shield before her.

Æ Loebbecke (**AA** viii.)

Athene standing to right; holds in raised right hand spear, on left arm shield ; snake at her feet.

Æ Loebbecke (**AA** ix.)

12. ATHENE ARMED, RUNNING.

Athene running to right, looking back, right hand outstretched, in left shield and spear ; drapery flying from her shoulder ; before her, snake to right.

Æ Paris (**AA** x.)

Athene running to right, right hand outstretched, on left arm shield ; before her, snake to right.

Æ Loebbecke (**AA** xi.)

The former of these two types is closely like the above-described figure of Athene from a pediment (**Z** viii.-x.), the only noteworthy difference being in the position of the right arm, which in the pediment type is extended backward, in the present type is stretched to grasp the edge of Athene's shield. This latter type is remarkably like Athene (or Enyo) on the coins of the Lucanians and Bruttians of the third century.

Athene moving to left, spear transversely in right hand, on left arm shield ; before her, snake to left.

Æ Loebbecke (**AA** xii.) Rhousopoulos.

Athene moving to left, right hand advanced, in left shield and spear ; before her snake, behind her owl.

Æ Loebbecke (**AA** xiii.)

13. ATHENE FIGHTING.

Athene fighting to right ; in raised right hand thunderbolt, on left arm shield.

Æ B. M. (**AA** xiv.) &c. Before her snake, horse's head or other symbol. Beulé, 386, 1-3.

Athene fighting to right ; in raised right hand spear, on left arm shield.

Æ B. M. (**AA** xv.)

Similar figure ; behind her, olive-tree entwined by snake ; before her, owl.

Æ B. M. (**AA** xvi.)
Beulé, 390, 13.

Similar figure, charging rapidly to right.

Æ B. M. (**AA** xvii.)

Athene charging to right ; in right hand spear outstretched, on left arm aegis.

Æ Loebbecke (**AA** xviii.) B. M. (**AA** xix.)
Beulé, 390, 1 : 346, 3.

At her feet snake, owl, or other symbol.

These types seem to represent successive stages in the development of the normal Athene Polias.

14. ATHENE HOLDING OLIVE-BRANCH.

Athene standing to left, holds in right olive-branch over coiled snake, on left arm shield.

Æ Beulé, 390, 4. Hunter, xi. 10.

This type closely resembles some of those ranged under
Athene running. Compare especially **AA** XIII.

15. ATHENE VOTING.

Athene facing; left hand on hip, in right, vote which she
drops into amphora; beside her, shield.

Æ Rhousopoulos.

This coin is very obscure in details; it may represent Athene
Areia, of the Areiopagus, cf. Paus. i. 28, 5.

16. ATHENE SEATED.

Athene seated to left on throne; Nike in right hand, spear in
left; shield behind seat.

Æ Loebbecke (**AA** xx.)   Imh. &c.
Beulé, 390, 1.

Athene seated to left on throne; patera in right hand, spear
in left; shield behind seat; before her olive-tree.

Æ B. M. (**AA** xxi.)   Loebbecke.

17. ATHENE IN CHARIOT.

Athene, holding spear advanced, in galloping biga to right.

Æ B. M. (**AA** xxii.)   Imh.   Rhousopoulos (small size.)
Beulé, 390, 14 and 15.

Similar figure in quadriga.

Æ B. M.   Loebbecke (**AA** xxiii.)

Athene, with spear in raised right, in galloping biga.

Æ B. M.

18.   ATHENE-NIKE.   Cf. Paus. I. 22, 4.   Temple of Nike
Apteros.

Athene or Nike winged facing, clad in chiton and helmeted,
holds in left hand a standard surmounted by an archaic
Palladium.

Ꞃ Copenhagen (**AA** xxiv.)
Rev. Num. 1858, p. 357 : Wieseler, *Denkm.* ii. 220.
(Reverse, A⊙, Owl.)

This is a remarkable and unique drachm, assigned by
M. Beulé in the *Revue* to the time of Conon.   It was perhaps
intended to circulate in Asia, and in fact was probably issued
from an Asiatic mint.   It cannot be said with certainty whether
the representation should be called Athene or Nike : the helmet
and the Palladium are in favour of the former attribution.   We
have no reason to think that it reproduces a statue; certainly
not that of Athene Nike on the Acropolis.

2. (*a*) Paus. I. 1, 3.   At Peiraeus.   Bronze statue of Zeus,
holding sceptre and Nike.

(b) I. 1, 3. At Peiraeus. Statues of Zeus and Demos by Leochares.

(c) I. 1, 4. At Phalerum. Temple of Zeus.

(d) I. 2, 5. In the gymnasium of Hermes. Statue of Zeus.

(e) I. 3, 2. Near the royal stoa. Zeus Eleutherius.

(f) I. 3, 5. In the senate-house. Xoanon of Zeus Bulaeus.

(g) I. 18, 6. In the Olympieium. Colossus of Zeus in ivory and gold, set up by Hadrian.

(h) I. 18, 7. In the Olympieium. Zeus in bronze.

(i) I. 18, 9. Temple of Zeus Panhellenius and Hera, founded by Hadrian.

(j) I. 24, 4. On the Acropolis. Statue of Zeus by Leochares.

(k) I. 24, 4. On the Acropolis. Zeus Polieus.

(l) I. 32, 2. On Hymettus. Zeus Hymettius.

(m) I. 32, 2. On Parnes. Bronze statue of Zeus Parnethius.

(n) I. 32, 2. On Anchesmus. Zeus Anchesmius.

ZEUS naked, thundering, left hand advanced; archaic treatment of hair and beard ; at his feet, eagle ; sometimes symbols in field.

Æ B. M. &c. Imh. (**BB** I.)
Beulé, 249, 281, 357, 368.

Zeus naked, standing, thunderbolt in right hand which hangs down, left hand advanced.

Æ Munich. B. M. Imh. (**BB** II.)

Zeus naked, standing, thunderbolt in right hand which hangs down, in left patera over altar entwined by snake.

Æ B. M. (**BB** III.)
Beulé, 396, 1.

Zeus seated, naked to waist, Nike in right hand, sceptre in left.

Æ B. M. (**BB** IV.)
Beulé, 396, 2.

Jahn has proposed the theory (*N. Memor. dell' Inst. A.* p. 24) that the more archaic Zeus (I.) on the coins is a copy of the archaic statue of Zeus Polieus (k), and the later Zeus of a similar type (III.) is a copy of the statue by Leochares which stood beside it (j). On this theory Overbeck (*K. M.* p. 54) remarks that Jahn's identification of the archaic statue of Zeus Polieus though not certain is probable ; and certainly its parallelism with the recognized type of Athene Polias (**AA** XIV.) is in favour of such identification. To Jahn's argument as to the statue by Leochares, Overbeck adds that the altar in front of the figure on the coin (III.) may stand for the altar which stood before Zeus Polieus, where was performed the annual ceremony of the Buphonia or Diipolia (Paus. I. 28, 11.)

The seated figure of Zeus (IV.) is very probably copied from the colossal statue set up by Hadrian in the Olympieium (*g*) which would naturally be a copy of the chryselephantine statue by Pheidias at Olympia.

3. (*a*) Paus. I. 1, 3. At Peiraeus. Temple of Aphrodite, founded by Conon, after his victory at Cnidus.

   (*b*) I. 1, 5. Promontory Colias. Statue of Aphrodite Colias and the Genetyllides.

   (*c*) I. 8, 4. In the temple of Ares. Two statues of Aphrodite.

   (*d*) I. 14, 7. Near the Cerameicus. Temple of Aphrodite Urania : statue by Pheidias of Parian marble.

   (*e*) I. 19, 2. In the gardens (κῆποι). Temple of Aphrodite, and herm of Aphrodite near, called Urania, eldest of the Moerae.

   (*f*) I. 22, 3. South of Acropolis. Statues of Aphrodite Pandemos ; new, but good.

   (*g*) I. 23, 2. On the Acropolis. Statue of Aphrodite by Calamis, dedicated by Callias.

   (*h*) I. 37, 7. In the pass to Eleusis. Temple of Aphrodite.

   (*i*) I. 20, 2. In Street of Tripods. Standing Eros and Dionysus by Thymilus.

Aphrodite does not seem to occur on coins of Athens. The figure described by Beulé (p. 225) as the Syrian Aphrodite is Isis; that figured as Aphrodite with the Genetyllides is the Delian Apollo.

Eros facing, with right hand crowns himself; in his left a palm.

Æ Imh.

Beulé, 222.

Riggauer, *Eros auf M.* p. 8.

4. (*a*) Paus. I. 1, 4. At Munychia. Temple of Artemis Munychia.

   (*b*) I. 19, 6. At Agrae. Temple of Artemis Agrotera : καὶ τὸ ἄγαλμα διὰ τοῦτο ἔχει τόξον, κ.τ.λ.

   (*c*) I. 23, 7. On the Acropolis : καὶ Ἀρτέμιδος ἱερόν ἐστι Βραυρωνίας, Πραξιτέλους μὲν τέχνη τὸ ἄγαλμα, τῇ

θεῷ δέ ἐστιν ἀπὸ Βραυρῶνος δήμου τὸ ὄνομα. καὶ τὸ
ἀρχαῖον ξόανόν ἐστιν ἐν Βραυρῶνι, Ἄρτεμις, ὡς
λέγουσιν, ἡ Ταυρική.

(d) I. 26, 4. On the Acropolis : Τῆς δὲ εἰκόνος πλησίον τῆς
Ὀλυμπιοδώρου χαλκοῦν Ἀρτέμιδος ἄγαλμα ἔστηκεν
ἐπίκλησιν Λευκοφρυηνῆς, ἀνέθεσαν δὲ οἱ παῖδες οἱ
Θεμιστοκλέους.

(e) I. 33, 1. At Brauron. Archaic xoanon of Artemis.

(f) I. 29, 2. By the Academy : περίβολός ἐστιν Ἀρτέμιδος
καὶ ξόανα Ἀρίστης καὶ Καλλίστης.

(g) I. 38, 6. At Eleusis. Temple of Artemis Propylaea.

Archaic ARTEMIS facing, clad in chiton with diplois, hair in
formal curls ; holds patera and bow ; beside her, stag
looking up.

Æ B. M. (BB v.) Paris (De Luynes) (BB vi.)
Beulé, p. 287.

If the archaic figure of Artemis at Brauron was a copy of
the ancient xoanon carried off by the Persians to Susa and
given by Seleucus (Paus. III. 16, 7) to the people of Seleucia in
Syria, on whose coins (N XI. XII.) we find copies of it, the
present representation does not reproduce the Brauronian
statue as Beulé supposed, being of another type. It is far
more probably an Artemis Leucophryne. The statue dedicated
by the sons of Themistocles would in all probability be modelled
more or less closely on the cultus-statue of that deity in her
temple at Magnesia in Ionia, where Themistocles was dynast.
This cultus-statue is often reproduced on late coins of Magnesia ;
the goddess was represented in nearly the same form at Magnesia as at Ephesus, with polus on head, the body in term-like
shape, pendent fillets hanging from the outstretched hands.
The figure on our coin does not fully conform to this description ;
the feet are articulate, and in the outstretched hands are patera
and bow ; nevertheless the scheme seems rather Asiatic than
European, and it seems not unlikely that the sons of Themistocles may have innovated in details on the fixed traditional
type.

Archaic Artemis facing, clad in long chiton, holds torch in
each hand.

Æ B. M. (BB vii.)
Beulé, 380.

Artemis (not archaic) or Demeter facing, clad in long chiton,

D 2

holds torch in each hand : beside her seated Dionysus,
q.v.

Æ B. M. (CC viii.)
Beulé, 202.

Artemis running to right, clad in long chiton, holds two torches
—quiver at shoulder.

Æ Loebbecke (**BB** viii.)   B. M.   (**BB** ix.)   Rhousopoulos (**BB** x.)
Æ Loebbecke (**BB** xi.)   Rhousopoulos.   (Figure to left.)

Artemis Agrotera in short chiton, running, spear in her raised
right hand, her left outstretched ; beside her, hound.

Æ B. M.   (**BB** xii.)
Beulé, 214.

Artemis clad in short chiton, running, torch in both hands.

Æ B. M.   Imh.   (**BB** xiii.)   Æ Imh.   (**BB** xv.)   Loebbecke.   (**BB** xiv.)
Beulé, 375.

Artemis clad in short chiton, running, a torch in each hand :
beside her Demeter standing, clad in long chiton, holding
a torch.

Æ B. M.   (**BB** xvi.)
Beulé, 325.

On Athenian coins, Artemis, when she bears one or two
torches, is not easily to be distinguished from Demeter. The
figure with short skirts is of course Artemis ; as to the figure in
long skirts we may hesitate : but on some coins, notably x, a
quiver is distinctly visible, which can of course belong only to
Artemis.   When Artemis appears in company with Demeter
(xvi.) Beulé (p. 325) calls her Propylaea, there being a temple
of Artemis Propylaea at the sanctuary of Eleusis.

5. (a) Paus. i. 1, 4.   At Phalerum.   Temple of Demeter.

  (b) i. 2, 4.   Within the Peiraean gate : καὶ πλησίον ναός
       ἐστι Δήμητρος, ἀγάλματα δὲ αὐτή τε καὶ ἡ παῖς καὶ
       δᾷδα ἔχων Ἴακχος· γέγραπται δὲ ἐπὶ τῷ τοίχῳ γράμ-
       μασιν Ἀττικοῖς ἔργα εἶναι Πραξιτέλους.

  (c) i. 14, 1.   ναοὶ δὲ ὑπὲρ τὴν κρήνην ὁ μὲν Δήμητρος
       πεποίηται καὶ Κόρης. ἐν δὲ τῷ Τριπτολέμου κείμενόν
       ἐστιν ἄγαλμα.

  (d) i. 22, 3.   At entrance to Acropolis.   Temple of Demeter
       Chloe.

  (e) i. 31, 1.   In the Halimusian deme.   Temple of Demeter
       Thesmophoros and Cora.

  (f) i. 31, 1.   In the Prospaltian deme.   Temple of Demeter
       and Cora.

DEMETER or Cora standing; holds two torches turned downwards.

Æ B. M. (**BB** xvii.)
Æ Munich. (**BB** xviii.)
Beulé, 198.

Demeter standing to left clad in chiton and over-dress; holds in right ears of corn, left rests on hip.

Æ Oxford. (**BB** xix.)
Beulé, 210.

Demeter facing, head bound with ears of corn, clad in chiton with diplois, over-dress over arms; holds in left long sceptre, with poppy at top (?); right hand extended.

Æ Paris. (**BB** xx.)
Beulé, 253, 1.

Demeter seated to left crowned with corn; holds in right two ears of corn, in left torch.

Æ B. M. (**BB** xxi.)
Beulé, 334.

Demeter seated to left on throne; holds in right hand two ears of corn, left rests on sceptre.

Æ B. M. Loebbecke. (**BB** xxii.)

Demeter seated in chariot of snakes; ears of corn in her hand.

Æ B. M.
Overbeck, *Demeter*, pl. ix. 2ᵃ and 2ᵇ. Imh. *M.Gr.* pl. c. 26.

Demeter as above; torch in left hand.

Æ B. M. Beulé, 289, 6; 322-23.

Demeter standing in chariot of snakes; holds ears of corn and cornucopiae.

Æ Æ.
Beulé, 289, 2 and 4; 291, 1.

Demeter as above, holds ear of corn and torch.

Æ Paris. Cf. Beulé, 289.
Æ Imh. (**BB** xxiii.)
Overbeck, *Demeter*, pl. viii. 38.

Demeter, holding torch, standing in chariot of snakes: before her Cora holding long torch, behind her Artemis (?) who also holds torch.

Æ Parma. (**BB** xxiv.) Rhousopoulos.
Beulé, 291, 2. Overbeck, *Demeter*, pl. viii. 39.

Triptolemus naked, standing in chariot of snakes.

Æ Beulé, p. 291, 3.

Triptolemus naked to waist seated in chariot of snakes; holds ears of corn.

Æ B. M. Loebbecke.

In the above list we have not attempted to distinguish types which represent Demeter from those which represent Cora. Nor is it possible to determine which of the types represent sculptural originals. Most of them are discussed by Overbeck (*K. M.* III 497); and we have not space for so long a discussion as would be necessary if we attempted to discriminate them properly.

6. (*a*) Paus. I. 2, 5. In the Gymnasium of Hermes. Dionysus Melpomenus.

(*b*) I. 14, 1. In the Odeium. A Dionysus θεας ἄξιος.

(*c*) I. 20, 2. In the Street of Tripods. Temple with statue by Thymilus.

(*d*) I. 20, 3. Near the Theatre : Τοῦ Διονύσου δέ ἐστι πρὸς τῷ θεάτρῳ τὸ ἀρχαιότατον ἱερόν. δύο δέ εἰσιν ἐντὸς τοῦ περιβόλου ναοὶ καὶ Διόνυσοι, ὅ τε Ἐλευθερεὺς καὶ ὃν Ἀλκαμένης ἐποίησεν ἐλέφαντος καὶ χρυσοῦ.

(*e*) I. 29, 2. At the Academia. Temple to which on set days was brought the statue of Dionysus Eleuthereus.

(*f*) I. 31, 6. At Acharnae. Dionysus Melpomenus and Dionysus Cissus.

Bearded DIONYSUS, arms and shoulders bare, seated on throne, holds wine-cup and sceptre ; hair hanging in long tresses, and crowned with ivy.

Æ Paris. (CC I.)
Æ Imh. (CC II.) B. M. (CC III.)
Beulé, 261, 1—3.

Similar figure ; before him incense-altar on table.

Æ Imh. Photiades. (CC IV.)
Beulé, 261, 4.

Head of bearded Dionysus, crowned with ivy, hair falling in long tresses.

Æ Loebbecke. (CC V.)
Beulé, 376, 1 and 3.

There can be little doubt that the figure reproduced on these coins is, as Beulé has suggested, the Dionysus of Alcamenes. His likeness to the Pheidian Zeus is conspicuous in regard to his general attitude and the fashion of his outer garment, which does not cover the upper part of his body, but is brought over the left shoulder. There does not seem to have been a chiton under it. He is well adapted for a great cultus-statue, and that he served as such is proved by the table and altar of the coin IV. The head on the coin last described seems to be an exact enlargement of the head of the seated figure. It is certainly of noble type, but we may be somewhat surprised to find Alcamenes perpetuating so archaic a fashion of doing the hair.

Bearded Dionysus standing, clad in long chiton ; hair in
archaic fashion ; holds wine-cup and thyrsus transversely,
the latter bound with fillet.

Æ B. M. (CC vi.)
Beulé, 376.

Young Dionysus standing, clad in short chiton, holds wine-cup
and rests on thyrsus.

Æ Bunbury. *Num. Chron.* 1881, pl. iv. 4.

Young Dionysus, standing in long chiton ; holds in right hand
mask, in left thyrsus.

Æ B. M. (CC. vii.)
Beulé, 373.

Dionysus seated, facing, clad in long chiton, two torches over
shoulders ; beside him Demeter or Artemis standing,
holding torch in each hand.

Æ B. M. (CC viii.)
Beulé, 202.

Of these figures the first (CC vi.) seems undoubtedly a copy
of an archaic statue, of about the time of Calamis. The figure
holding a mask may be copied from one of the statues of
Dionysus in the Theatre or its neighbourhood. The female
figure in company with Dionysus should be Demeter rather
than Artemis ; the artistic type, however, would do for either.

Paus. i. 21. THEATRE OF DIONYSUS.

The Theatre of Dionysus ; above, the wall of the Acropolis,
over which the Erechtheum, the Parthenon and the
Propylaea of the Acropolis.

Æ B. M. (CC x.) Photiades. (CC ix.) &c.
Beulé, 394 ; Donaldson, *Architectura Numismatica*, No. 2.

It seems probable that this Theatre was chosen as a type for
coins in consequence of the great improvements effected in it
about the time of Hadrian, notably the erection of an elevated
logeion. See *C.I.A.* iii. 239. Donaldson has called attention to
the openings or niches which appear on the coin at the top of
the cavea and at the foot of the Acropolis rock, and has cited in
connexion with them the words of Pausanias, i. 21, 3, who says
that at the top of the theatre is a cave in the rocks, wherein is
a tripod, and in it Apollo and Artemis slaying the children of
Niobe. In Michaelis' plan of the Acropolis a cave is indicated
at the same spot, which was formerly blocked by the choragic
monument of Thrasyllus (*Descr. Arcis Athenarum*, 1880.) On
the Brit. Mus. coin (x.) there is an appearance of a monument

over one of the caves, but this appearance is probably due to accident only.

7. (a) Paus. I. 2, 5.   In a sanctuary of Dionysus.   Apollo made and dedicated by Eubulides.

(b) I. 3, 4.   In or near the temple of Apollo Patrous.   Apollo Patrous, by Euphranor; Apollo, by Leochares; Apollo Alexicacus, by Calamis.

(c) I. 3, 5.   In the Senate-House.   An Apollo, by Peisias.

(d) I. 8, 4.   By the temple of Ares.   Ἀπόλλων ἀναδούμενος ταινίᾳ τὴν κόμην.

(e) I. 19, 1.   Near the Olympieium.   Statue of Apollo Pythius.

(f) I. 19, 1.   Near the same place.   Temple of Apollo Delphinius.

(g) I. 19, 3.   Lyceium.   Temple of Apollo Lyceius.

(h) I. 21, 3.   Cave in Acropolis-rock.   Apollo and Artemis slaying the Niobidae.

(i) I. 24, 8.   Near the Parthenon.   Statue in bronze of Apollo Parnopius, by Pheidias.

(k) I. 28, 4.   On the north-west of the Acropolis.   Sanctuary of Apollo in a cave.

(l) I. 31, 2.   At Prasiae.   Temple of Apollo; connected with Hyperboreans.

(m) I. 31, 6.   At Acharnae.   Worship of Apollo Aguieus.

(n) I. 37, 6.   The pass to Eleusis.   Temple and statue of Apollo.

Archaic APOLLO, naked, polos on head, holding in right hand the three Charites on a sort of frame, in his left, bow.
Ⓡ Copenhagen.
Æ Imh. (CC XI.)   Loebbecke. (CC XII.)
Beulé, 364.
Wieseler,-Denkmaeler, No. 126, &c.

Similar figure, griffin rearing against him on each side.
Ⓡ Paris. (CC XIII.)   B. M. (CC XIV.)
Beulé, 364.
Furtwängler, Arch. Zeit. 1882, p. 331.

This figure has long been recognized as a copy of the Delian statue of Apollo by Tectaeus and Angelion, which held the Charites in its hand.   Furtwängler l.c. was the first to identify the griffins.

Apollo standing, naked, right hand outstretched, in left, bow.
Ⓡ B. M. (CC XV.)
Beulé, 271, 1-2.

Similar figure, holds branch and bow.
Æ B. M. (Facing.) (**CC** xvi.)
   Lambros. (To right.) **CC** xvii.)
   Beulé, 271, 3.

Apollo standing, naked, his right hand on his head, in his
   left, bow.
Æ B. M. (**CC** xviii.) (Beside him tripod on stand.)
   Beulé, 285.
Æ Beulé, 285. (Behind him laurel.)

Apollo standing, naked, his right hand on his head, his left
   rests on lyre.
Æ B. M. (**CC** xix.) Rhousopoulos.
   Beulé, 285, 3.

Apollo to left, clad in long chiton, holds patera and lyre.
Æ B. M. (**CC** xx.) Loebbecke. (**CC** xxi.)
   Beulé, 388, 2.

The descriptions of Pausanias are not sufficiently exact to
enable us to identify with certainty any of these figures of
Apollo. But the early figure **CC** xv.-xvii. is connected by
Furtwängler (Roscher's *Lexicon*, p. 456) with the so-called
Omphalos Apollo of Athens and the Choiseul-Gouffier Apollo of
the British Museum. T. Schreiber (*Athen. Mittheil.* 1884,
p. 248) maintains that it is probably a copy of the statue in the
Daphnephoreion at Athens (Athenaeus, x. p. 424 *F*). That in
which the hand rests on the head (xviii. xix.) seems from the
description of a statue of Apollo Lyceius (above, *g*) in Lucian
(Anacharsis, 7) to be meant for a copy of the statue in the
Lyceium. The tripod and the laurel would very well represent
such a locality as the Lyceium.

8. (*a*) Paus. i. 8, 4. Near the temple of Ares. Statues of
    Theseus and Herakles.
  (*b*) i. 17, 2-6. Temple of Theseus. Paintings of battles with
    Centaurs and Amazons.
  (*c*) i. 24, 1. On Acropolis. Fight of Theseus and the
    Minotaur.
  (*d*) i. 27, 8. Story of people of Troezen that Aegeus hid
    sword and sandals under a rock for Theseus to lift.
    On Acropolis, group in bronze embodying the tale.
  (*e*) i. 27, 9. On Acropolis. Dedicated group of Theseus
    driving the bull of Marathon.
    Also 3, 1 and 15, 2.

THESEUS standing, naked, right arm outstretched, left resting
   on club.
Æ Beulé, 398, 1.

Theseus standing, right hand extended, club in left.

Æ Loebbecke. (**DD** i.)

Theseus naked, raising with both hands rock, beneath whicn
are sword and sandals.

Æ B. M. Loebbecke. Imh. (**DD** ii.) Rhousopoulos.
Beulé, 398, 2.
Wieseler in *Berichte k. Ges. d. Wiss.* Göttingen, 1886, p. 71.

Theseus, holding in right hand club, seizing with left prostrate
Minotaur.

Æ B. M. Imh. Rhousopoulos. (**DD** iii.)
Beulé, 398, 4.

Theseus, club in raised right, lion's skin on left arm, rushing
on sinking Minotaur.

Æ B. M. (**DD** iv.) Loebbecke.
Beulé, 398, 5.

Theseus as in last, without Minotaur.

Æ B. M. (**DD** v.) Loebbecke. Beulé, 398, 3.

Theseus holding Minotaur by the horn, and striking him
with club.

Æ B. M. (**DD** vi.) Soutzo.
Beulé, 398, 6.

Theseus (?) driving a bull before him (the Marathonian
bull ?).

Æ B. M. Loebbecke. (**DD** vii.) Rhousopoulos. Vienna. (**DD** viii.)
Beulé, 392, 1.

Head of Theseus, beardless, club on shoulder.

Æ B. M. &c.

It is remarkable that the only sculptural records of Theseus
mentioned by Pausanias are: his statue beside that of Herakles
(*a*); his fight with the Minotaur (*c*); his lifting the stone (*d*); and
his driving the bull of Marathon (*e*). The subjects of all these
four representations appear on coins, but no other deed of Theseus,
none of the exploits, for instance, which were depicted in the
metopes of the so-called temple of Theseus. This is an interesting
fact, and shows that many people at Athens were, like Pausanias,
more impressed by separate groups than by those which merely
formed part of the decoration of a temple. It is likely that ono
of the coins (**DD** i.) gives us the type of the statue of Theseus;
and the group of Theseus raising the stone, as it appears again
quite similarly treated on coins of Troezen (**M** xi.), is probably a
copy of the bronze group on the Acropolis. As to the other
types we cannot say whether they are original or copies; but
the tameness with which the bull walks before the hero seems
scarcely worthy of a sculptural group.

9.—Paus. I. 8, 2. Near the Tholos, Εἰρήνη φέρουσα Πλοῦτον παῖδα. (A work of Cephisodotus.)

EIRENE clad in long chiton with diplois, over-dress at her back, holds in right long sceptre, on left arm young Plutus, who extends his right hand, and holds in his left cornucopiae ; her head turned towards the child.

Æ B. M. (**DD** IX.) Munich. (**DD** X.), &c.
Beulé, 202. (Demeter and Dionysus.)
Friedrichs, *Arch. Zeit.* 1859, 1-14 (Gaea Curotrophos.)
Brunn, *Ueber die sog. Leucothea*, 1867 (Eirene and Plutus.)
Friedländer, *Zeit. f. Num.* v. pl. I. 5.
Köhler, *Athen. Mitth.* VI. 363-71.

The identification of the group here presented has been attempted by many archaeologists, with varying results, which are above slightly indicated. The view usually accepted is that of Brunn, who sees in it a copy of the Eirene and Plutus of Cephisodotus, of which he supposes a sculptural copy to exist at Munich. Wieseler (*D.A.K.* II. 99*b*) is disposed to find difficulties in this view. He remarks that the sceptre does not properly belong to Eirene [she does, however, hold it on late Roman coins], and further that the statue of Cephisodotus was in marble while the original of the Munich group was in bronze. He therefore prefers the attribution of Cora and the child Iacchus. Overbeck (*Gr. Plastik.* II. 8) remarks that on the coin Eirene holds the end of the cornucopiae : this, however, does not seem to be the case in the specimens we have examined.

10.—Paus. I. 8, 4. Near the temple of Ares. Statues of Herakles and Theseus.

 I. 19, 3. Cynosarges. A temple of Herakles.

 I. 24, 3. On the Acropolis. Herakles strangling serpents.

 I. 31, 6. At Acharnae. Herakles worshipped.

 I. 32, 4. At Marathon. Herakles worshipped.

HERAKLES standing, naked, right hand resting on side; left hand, wrapped in lion's skin, rests on club.

Æ Loebbecke. Rhousopoulos. (**DD** XI.)
Beulé 397, 1.
(Beulé 397, 3, is of Uxentum in Calabria.)
Köhler, *Athen. Mittheil.* VI. p. 365.

Herakles clad in long chiton; right hand rests on club, in left, cornucopiae. The coin thus described by Beulé (397, 2) is identical with the following :—

Herakles as a term, lion's skin over shoulders, right hand
rests on club, in left, cornucopiae.
Æ Munich. (DD xii.)   Cf. Hartwig, *Herakles m. d. Füllhorn*, p. 51.
The Herakles first described (xi.) is exactly in the attitude
of Glycon's statue.
Herakles naked, standing to left; right hand advanced, in left,
club, which rests on ground.
Æ Rhousopoulos.   (DD xiii.)
11.—Paus. i. 8, 5.   Οὐ πόρρω δὲ ἑστᾶσιν Ἁρμόδιος καὶ Ἀριστο-
γείτων οἱ κτείναντες Ἵππαρχον· .... τῶν δὲ ἀνδριάντων
οἱ μέν εἰσι Κριτίου τέχνη, τοὺς δὲ ἀρχαίους ἐποίησεν
Ἀντήνωρ. Ξέρξου δέ, ὡς εἷλεν Ἀθήνας ἐκλιπόντων
τὸ ἄστυ Ἀθηναίων, ἀπαγαγομένου καὶ τούτους ἅτε
λάφυρα, κατέπεμψεν ὕστερον Ἀθηναίοις Ἀντίοχος.

HARMODIUS and ARISTOGEITON charging : Aristogeiton bearded,
holding sheath in left hand, chlamys over left arm :
Harmodius beardless, naked, sword in raised right.
Æ B. M. (DD xiv.).   Paris. (DD xv.)
Beulé 335 ; Friedrich, *Arch. Zeit.* 1859, p. 64-71, pl. cxxvii.
Harmodius naked, facing, holds sword raised, and sheath.
Æ Athens.
Köhler in *Zeit. f. Num.* xii. 103.
Harmodius naked, charging to left, right hand raised with sword.
Æ Loebbecke. (DD xvi.)
Aristogeiton advancing to right, sword in right hand, chlamys
on left arm.
Æ Loebbecke. (DD xvii.)
Aristogeiton (?) advancing to right, holds sword and chlamys.
Æ Loebbecke. (DD xviii.)
This group from the statues of Critius and Nesiotes has so
often been discussed that it is unnecessary to say anything more
about it. See Overbeck, *Gr. Plastik*, i. p. 118, and Michaelis in
Journ. Hell. Stud. v. 146. The three coins of Mr. Loebbecke
(xvi.-xviii.) seem to be unpublished, and the two first of them
are decidedly interesting in point of style ; the powerful forms of
the heroes remind us of the Naples statues.
12.—Paus. i. 15, 1.   Ἰοῦσι δὲ πρὸς τὴν στοὰν ἣν Ποικίλην
ὀνομάζουσιν ἀπὸ τῶν γραφῶν, ἔστιν Ἑρμῆς χαλκοῦς
καλούμενος Ἀγοραῖος καὶ πύλη πλησίον.
i. 22, 8.   At entrance to Acropolis. Hermes Propylaeus.
i. 27, 1.   Κεῖται δὲ ἐν τῷ ναῷ τῆς Πολιάδος Ἑρμῆς ξύλου,
Κέκροπος εἶναι λεγόμενον ἀνάθημα, ὑπὸ κλάδων μυρ-
σίνης οὐ σύνοπτον.

I. 28, 6.　On the Acropolis.　A Hermes.

HERMES as terminal figure, caduceus in left hand.
Æ Paris.　(DD xix.)
　Beulé 152.

Archaic Hermes bearded standing to right, holds caduceus in left hand.
Æ (DD xx.)
　Beulé 348 (Beulé mistakes the caduceus for a wreath, and calls the figure the hero Stephanephoros.)

Hermes running, chlamys flying, holds purse and caduceus.
Æ Loebbecke.　(DD xxi.)　Rhousopoulos.
　Beulé 362, 1.

Hermes naked, standing, holds strigil and caduceus (?)
Æ Vienna.　(DD xxii.)　Loebbecke.　(DD xxiii.)
　Beulé 362.

The archaic figure of Hermes (xx.) may be a copy of the Hermes Agoraeus set up before the Persian wars.　See Hermes, XXI. pp. 493, 600.　The figure carrying a purse (xxi.) would seem to be a later Hermes Agoraeus.　The third figure (xxii. xxiii.) we cannot positively identify; the strigil is clear and this seems to indicate Hermes if we compare the Hermes Promachus at Tanagra (X xiii.); but the caduceus is not certain; in fact the object looks more like a club.　Perhaps the figure may be Theseus or Herakles.

13.—Paus. I. 18, 1.　Τὸ δὲ ἱερὸν τῶν Διοσκούρων ἐστὶν ἀρχαῖον· αὐτοί τε ἑστῶτες καὶ οἱ παῖδες καθήμενοί σφισιν ἐφ᾽ ἵππων.

I. 31, 1.　The Dioscuri worshipped at Cephalae.

The DIOSCURI, naked, their arms about one another, one holds patera, the other spear.
Æ (EE i.)
　Beulé, 339.

This type of the Dioscuri seems to be a copy of an archaic work; they embrace one another like Dermys and Citylus on the Boeotian monument.　Hegias an Athenian artist of early times made statues of the Dioscuri, which were afterwards carried to Rome.　See Pliny, N.H. xxxiv. 78.

14.—Paus. I. 20, 3.　Ἦν Ἀριστίων Ἀθηναῖος, ᾧ Μιθριδάτης πρεσβεύειν ἐς τὰς πόλεις τὰς Ἑλληνίδας ἐχρῆτο· οὗτος ἀνέπεισεν Ἀθηναίους Μιθριδάτην θέσθαι Ῥωμαίων ἐπίπροσθεν.

Coins of Athens of the late type bearing the name of Aristion,

and the name of Mithridates, as well as his badge, a
star between two crescents.

Æ B. M. &c.   Beulé, 237.   Æ Berlin, *Zeit. f. Num.* iv. 9.

15.—Paus. I. 21, 4.   Τοῦ δὲ ᾿Ασκληπιοῦ τὸ ἱερὸν ἔς τε τὰ ἀγάλματά ἐστιν, ὁπόσα τοῦ θεοῦ πεποίηται καὶ τῶν παίδων,
καὶ ἐς τὰς γραφὰς θέας ἄξιον.

I. 23, 4.   θεῶν ἀγάλματά ἐστιν ῾Υγιείας τε, ἣν ᾿Ασκληπιοῦ
παῖδα εἶναι λέγουσι, καὶ ᾿Αθηνᾶς ἐπίκλησιν καὶ ταύτης
῾Υγιείας.

ASKLEPIOS clad in himation; his right hand rests on serpent-
rod, his left on his side.

Æ B. M.   (**EE** ii.)   Æ Loebbecke (**EE** iii.)   Rhousopoulos (**EE** iv.)
Beulé, 331 and 401.

Similar figure, but left hand raised.

Æ Beulé, p. 331.

Hygieia; holds in left hand patera, snake rising over her
shoulder.

Æ B. M.   (**EE** v.)
Beulé, 259.

Hygieia; holds in left hand patera; behind her, stem of tree
whence snake rises over her shoulder; her right resting
on her side.

Æ Beulé, 259.

16.—Paus. I. 18, 9.   Hadrian builds a gymnasium at Athens.

Table surmounted by head of Athene wreath and owl; beneath
it sometimes amphora, or in field, palm.

Æ B. M &c.

Similar; side of table inscribed ΑΔΡΙΑΝΕΙΑ.

Æ Berlin.   Rhousopoulos.

Similar table; on it small figure of Pallas and owl; beneath,
amphora; to the left, palm.

Æ B. M.   Rhousopoulos.

The Berlin coin proves that this agonistic table has reference
to games established by Hadrian.

17.—Paus. I. 22, 8.   Charites by Socrates, at the entry to the
Citadel.

Three female figures clad in long chitons, moving hand in
hand; the foremost with outstretched hand.

Æ B. M. de Hirsch (**EE** vi.)
Beulé, 297.
Benndorf in *Arch. Z.* 1869, 61.
Blümner in *Arch. Z.* 1870, 83.

This coin does not unfortunately help us in the interpretation
of this much discussed group, which appears frequently on

Athenian reliefs. Whether the figures represented are three nymphs, three Charites, or the three daughters of Cecrops remains uncertain.

18.—Paus. I. 23. Ἐπὶ δὲ τοῦ νοτίου καλουμένου τείχους, ὃ τῆς ἀκροπόλεως ἐς τὸ θέατρόν ἐστι τετραμμένον, ἐπὶ τούτου Μεδούσης τῆς Γοργόνος ἐπίχρυσος ἀνάκειται κεφαλή, καὶ περὶ αὐτὴν αἰγὶς πεποίηται.

A Gorgon-head also on the aegis of Athene, &c.

Head of MEDUSA.

Æ Æ B. M. &c.
Beulé, 346.

19.—Paus. I. 28, 4. Pan venerated in grotto near Propylaea.

PAN seated in grotto on side of Acropolis-rock.

Æ. See Acropolis.

20.—Paus. I. 32, 4. Monument of Miltiades at Marathon, and a trophy of white marble.

MILTIADES armed, dragging a captive Persian to a trophy.

Æ B. M. Imh. (EE VII.) Photiades. (EE VIII.)

In the Theatre were statues of Miltiades and Themistocles; beside each, a Persian prisoner. (*Schol. Aristid.* III. p. 535, Dind.).

21.—Paus. I. 33, 2. Μαραθῶνος δὲ σταδίους μάλιστα ἑξήκοντα ἀπέχει Ῥαμνοῦς .... μικρὸν δὲ ἀπὸ θαλάσσης ἄνω Νεμέσεώς ἐστιν ἱερόν. ... Φειδίας τὸν λίθον εἰργάσατο ἄγαλμα μὲν εἶναι Νεμέσεως, τῇ κεφαλῇ δὲ ἔπεστι τῆς θεοῦ στέφανος ἐλάφους ἔχων καὶ Νίκης ἀγάλματα οὐ μεγάλα· ταῖς δὲ χερσὶν ἔχει, τῇ μὲν κλάδον μηλέας, τῇ δεξιᾷ δὲ φιάλην.

Coin of Cyprus: fourth century B.C. Goddess facing, clad in long chiton, holds branch and patera.

Æ B. M. Cypriote legend.
Six in *Num. Chron.* 1882, 89.

The identification of the figure on the coin with the Nemesis of Rhamnus, a work of Agoracritus, not of Pheidias, is advocated by M. Six, and has much in its favour. In the flourishing times of Athens coins of Cyprus and the neighbouring coast bear not unfrequently copies of the great statues of Athens.

22.—OTHER TYPES at Athens:

Isis standing to left, lotus on head, holds flower.

Æ B. M. (EE IX.)

Isis or Demeter facing, clad in long chiton and over-dress, holds

ears of corn and long torch or sceptre : on head, head-
dress of Isis.

Æ Paris. (**EE** x.)
Beulé, 248.

Tyche facing, holds sceptre and cornucopiae.

Æ B. M. (**EE** xi.)

Nike standing to left, winged, holds cornucopiae (?) and drops
lot into amphora.

Æ Vienna. (**EE** xii.)

Hero facing, naked, spear in raised right hand, left rests on
side.

Æ B. M. (**EE** xiii.)

Metellus laureate seated facing, holds in right spear or sceptre,
in left, sword across knees.

Æ de Hirsch (**EE** xiv.)

Similar figure, crowned by Nike who holds wreath and sceptre,

Æ B. M. (**EE** xv.)

Draped female figure seated to right on rock, rests left hand
on a column.

Æ Berlin. (**EE** xvi.)   Loebbecke. (**EE** xvii.)

Published by Beulé (p. 400) as a figure of Solon : Lange
(*Athen. Mittheil.* vi. p. 69) is much nearer the mark in suggesting
that it may be a Demeter; but even this attribution is uncertain.

ELEUSIS.

1.—Paus. i. 37, 2.   Temple of Demeter and Cora on the sacred
way.

i. 37, 6.   Another in the pass to Eleusis.

i. 38, 6.   Temple of Triptolemus at Eleusis.

i. 38, 7.   The Sanctuary of the two Goddesses.

DEMETER seated in chariot of snakes, veiled, holds in right
hand ears of corn.

Æ B. M. &c. (**EE** xix.)
Imhoof, *M. G.* pl. C, 28.

Triptolemus, standing in chariot of snakes, holds two ears of
corn in right hand.

Æ B. M. &c.
Imh. *M.G.* pl. C, 29.

Triptolemus seated in chariot of snakes, naked to waist : holds
in right hand two ears of corn.

Æ B. M. &c. (**EE** xx.)
Imh. *M.G.* pl. C, 27.
Overbeck, *Demeter*, pl. ix. 1 *a* and *b*.
Athen. Mittheil. iv. 250 and 262.

OROPUS.

1.—Paus. I. 34, 2. Καὶ 'Ωρωπίοις ναός τέ ἐστιν 'Αμφιαράου καὶ ἄγαλμα λευκοῦ λίθου.

AMPHIARAUS seated on throne, naked down to waist; his right hand extended, in his left, long sceptre; at his feet, snake.

Æ Gallienus.   B. M.   (EE XVIII.)
Head of Amphiaraus bearded and laur.

Æ Auton.   B. M.
Koehler in *Athen. Mittheil.* IV. 262.

On these coins Amphiaraus is represented exactly in the guise of Asclepius, as a god rather than as a hero, in accordance with Pausanias' statements.

SALAMIS.

1.—Paus. I. 36, 1.   'Εν Σαλαμῖνι δὲ . . . . τρόπαιον ἔστηκεν ἀπὸ τῆς νίκης ἣν Θεμιστοκλῆς ὁ Νεοκλέους αἴτιος ἐγένετο γενέσθαι τοῖς "Ελλησι . . . . ναυμαχούντων δὲ 'Αθηναίων πρὸς Μήδους δράκοντα ἐν ταῖς ναυσὶ λέγεται φανῆναι.

THEMISTOCLES in cuirass, helmeted, standing on galley, holds wreath and trophy; on ship, owl; before it, snake.

Æ B. M.   Photiades.   (EE XXI., XXII.)   Imh.   Loebbecke.
Beulé, 305.

Owl and snake sometimes absent.

OTHER TYPE:

Demeter standing to left, holds in right hand ears of corn, in left, torch.

Æ Caracalla.   Welzl de Wellenheim, *Catalogue*, No. 3965.   (It is however doubtful whether this coin be not misread.)
Köhler, *Athen. Mittheil.* IV. 262.

SUPPLEMENT.

Since previous parts of the Commentary were published, several new types, or better specimens of types already published have been discovered, in most cases owing to the friendly cooperation of the custodians of the national collections at Berlin and Paris and to Prof. Rhousopoulos. These we subjoin, preserving the same order of subjects as in the earlier paper and the same numbers of sections where possible. In cases in which the passages of Pausanias have been already cited at length we here content ourselves with a mere reference.

MEGARA.

8. APOLLO facing, clad in citharoedic costume; holds branch
    and lyre.

Æ Anton. Pius.   Paris.   (FF I.)

This is a variety of **A** IX., and apparently a copy more or less
free of a statue of Praxiteles.   In this specimen the attitude of
the god appears less stiff than in **A** IX., and the body rests more
on one leg than the other.   It is of course a great gain if we
can trace a citharoedic type of Apollo to Praxiteles.

ARTEMIS holding bow and drawing arrow from quiver; Apollo
    as above; Leto leaning on sceptre.

Æ Commodus.   Rhousopoulos.   (FF II.)

It is interesting to compare this type with **A** x.   The figure
of Apollo in it is more closely like the detached Apollo of **A** IX.,
and thus the probability that the group reproduces that of
Praxiteles is increased.   There is a correction to make in
the description above under Megara, § 8: Artemis holds a bow,
not as there stated, a plectrum.

9.—ATHENE standing erect, spear in raised right hand, shield
    on left arm.

Æ L. Verus.   Rhousopoulos.   (FF III.)

This is a better specimen than **A** XI.

PAGAE.

1 A.—ISIS standing in temple; holds sistrum and vase.

Æ Commodus.   Rhousopoulos.   (FF IV.)

Isis to right, and Asklepius, standing face to face.

Æ Sep. Severus.   Rhousopoulos.

2.—HÓRSEMAN galloping right or left, chlamys flying.

Æ Sept. Severus.   Rhousopoulos.
     Geta.   Rhousopoulos.

Possibly this figure may represent Aegialeus, son of Adrastus,
whose tomb was at Pagae, Paus. I. 44, 7; but more probably it
stands for the Emperor.

CORINTH.

3.—Athene Chalinitis taming PEGASUS.

Æ Anton. Pius.   Paris.

Athene here takes the place of the more usual Bellerophon.
Chimaera.

Æ Commodus.   Rhousopoulos.

6.—ISTHMUS holding patera and rudder, seated in circular
    temple with conical roof surmounted by dolphins: on
    either side of temple, tree.

Æ Domna.   Paris.   (FF v.)

This coin seems to represent a different sacellum of Isthmus from that already figured (**C** XXXVII.). The form of the temple, and the pose of the statue within it, are quite different in the two cases.

10.—POSEIDON naked, standing; right foot rests on a rock; trident in raised left hand; in right hand, which hangs down, aplustre (?); behind, tree.

Æ Caracalla. Rhousopoulos.
Cf. **D** LIII.

Poseidon seated on throne, holds dolphin and trident transversely.

Æ Domitian. Berlin.

A variety of **D** LIV.

Poseidon, holding dolphin and trident, in chariot drawn by four horses.

Æ Plautilla. B. M.

11.—Quadrangular HARBOUR; at the top, temple, to which steps lead from the water, to left of it a shrine (?) to right a statue (?); at the two sides a range of colonnades: in the water, two Tritons, face to face.

Æ Caracalla. Rhousopoulos. (**FF** VI.)

As **D** LX. represents the harbour of Cenchreae, so the present coin seems to represent that of Lechaeum, which was a made harbour on the Corinthian gulf and the chief station of the Corinthian war-fleet. The temple in that case would be Poseidon's (Paus. II. 2, 3, ἔστι δὲ ἐν Λεχαίῳ μὲν Ποσειδῶνος ἱερὸν καὶ ἄγαλμα χαλκοῦν).

Poseidon standing naked, holds dolphin and trident; before him Aphrodite, holding shield, with her back to him; between them, Eros.

Æ Commodus. Berlin.

13.—APHRODITE, facing, draped, holds in right hand apple, in left hand the end of her dress.

Æ Auton. Rhousopoulos. (**FF** VII.)

Obverse, Head of Laïs or Aphrodite. A different type of Aphrodite from **D** LXX. The figure may however be Tyche, as there is an attribute which looks like a cornucopiae.

Aphrodite, holding mirror, in a biga drawn by Tritons.

Æ Nero. Munich. (**FF** VIII.)

Previously mentioned, but not figured.

19.—ZEUS seated to left on throne, holds Nike and long sceptre.

Æ Hadrian. Rhousopoulos. (**FF** IX.)
M. Aurelius. B. M.

Probably a representation of the Capitolian Zeus; the throne has no back, otherwise the type is closely like that embodied by Pheidias in the Olympian Zeus (**P** XXI.).

20.—PALLAS seated on throne; holds in right, Nike; in loft, spear; against which rests shield.

Æ Sept. Severus.   Rhousopoulos.   (**FF** x.)

Possibly Roma rather than Pallas.

Pallas standing, on basis : her right hand is extended, in her left spear.

Æ M. Aurelius.   Loebbecke.
Plautilla.   Rhousopoulos (**FF** xi.)

The basis shows that we have here a copy of a statue : that it is of Pallas is not quite certain, the head not being clear on either specimen.

23.—HERAKLES facing, head turned to left; holds in right hand club which rests on a cippus, on left arm lion's skin.

Æ Anton. Pius.   Berlin (**FF** xii.)

A different type of Herakles from **F** CIII., CIV.; but like them probably a copy of one of the numerous statues of Herakles which the city must have contained.

Herakles naked standing to left; right hand raised, in left, which is partly raised, club and lion's skin ; before him, Aphrodite holding shield.

Æ Commodus.   Berlin (**FF** xiii.)   Cf. **F** civ.

24.—PEIRENE personified as a nymph, naked to waist, seated on throne; holds on her lap water-pot; behind, snake to left.

Æ Caracalla.   Berlin.

Cf. **F** cvii., but in the present case Peirene is seated on a throne, a fact confirming the view that the coin-type is a copy of a figure by the spring.

25.—Paus. II. 2, 8.   Καὶ ᾿Απόλλων ἐπίκλησιν Κλάριος χαλκοῦς ἐστι.   Cf. II. 3, 2.

APOLLO naked, standing, holds in right plectrum, in left lyre which rests on tripod ; snake twined round tripod.

Æ Sept. Sev.   Berlin (**FF** xiv.)

This figure of Apollo is connected by tripod snake and lyre with the oracular functions of the god, and therefore probably stands for Apollo Clarius. The oracle of Apollo at Clarus was celebrated and said to have been founded by Manto, daughter of Teiresias.

28.—HERMES naked, seated on rock, ram (?) beside him ; the whole group on a basis, in front of which is a basin for water.

Æ Commodus.   Paris (**FF** xv.)

This adds another to the representations on coins of Corinthian fountains : the figure of Hermes seems to be a copy of that in the sacellum, **F** CXI. ; the figure of the ram, however, is not to be clearly made out in the present coin.

33.—APHRODITE, naked, but holding shield ; kneeling at the feet of the Emperor.

Æ Sept. Severus.   Berlin.

Aphrodite, naked to waist, turned to right, supporting with both hands shield which rests on pillar : the whole in tetrastyle temple on rock.

Æ Hadrian.   Rhousopoulos (**FF** xvi.)

This is a curious variety of **G** CXXI.—CXXVI., inasmuch as Aphrodite is turning in the wrong direction, and her shield rests on a pillar which stands in the place occupied on other coins by Eros.

34.—OTHER TYPES at Corinth.

Military female figure (Achaia ?) seated on rock, holds spear and sword, looks backward ; behind her, spears and shields.

Æ Plautilla.   B. M.

This specimen serves to correct our description of **G** CXL., in which we call the spears ears of corn.

Turreted female figure sacrificing left at altar ; holds in left hand rudder.

Æ Anton. Pius.   Paris.

This seems to be a form of Tyche.

Turreted female figure holding sceptre, standing beside trophy.

Æ Caracalla.   Berlin.

An embodiment of the city of Corinth.

The Emperor, standing, in a tetrastyle temple.

Æ Nero.   B. M.   Rhousopoulos, &c.

Male figure standing ; holds in right hand tessera ; over left arm chlamys.

Æ Domitian.   Rhousopoulos.

Perhaps an Athlete drawing lots for his turn in the Isthmian games.

Maenad clad in short chiton : holds in raised right hand torch
or knife (?), in left human head.

Æ Caracalla.   Rhousopoulos (**FF** xvii.)

Perseus facing, naked, holds in right hand head of Gorgon, in
left harpa.

Æ Auton.   Paris.

TENEA.

Cf. Paus. ii. 5, 3.

TYPES.

Dionysus (?) standing to left; holds in right hand kantharos,
in left thyrsus.

Æ Domna.   *Zeit. f. Num.* i. 320, pl. ix. 3.

Tyche standing.

Æ Sept. Severus.   B. M.   *Cat. Peloponnesus,* pl. ix. 23.

SICYON.

9. ASKLEPIOS seated on throne, sceptre in raised left hand,
right hand extended over the head of a snake.

Æ Geta.   Paris.

Cf. the statue at Epidaurus, **L** iii.—v.

OTHER TYPES at Sicyon.

14. Amazonian figure, clad in short chiton, on top of pillar; she
extends her right hand, and holds in left spear.

Æ Caracalla.   Paris (**FF** xviii.)

Either a statue of Artemis (cf. ii. 10, 2) or one of the numerous
memorials of notable persons which existed at Sicyon.

Isis to left; holds sistrum and vase.

Æ Geta.   Rhousopoulos.

Horse ridden by human head.

Æ Geta.   Rhousopoulos.

PHLIUS.

1.—Bearded male head crowned with reeds (ASOPUS ?).

Æ Auton.   B. M.   *Cat. Peloponnesus,* pl. vii. 6.

3.—ARTEMIS running to right, holds in left hand bow, with
right hand draws arrow from quiver : dog at her feet.

Æ Geta.   Berlin (**FF** xix.)

4a.—Paus. ii. 13, 7.   Οὐ πόρρω δέ ἐστιν ὁ καλούμενος
ὀμφαλός.

OMPHALOS represented as a circle in the midst of a wheel.

Æ Auton.   B. M.   *Cat. Peloponnesus,* pl. vii. 4.

5a.—Paus. ii. 13, 7.   Ἔστι δὲ καὶ ᾿Απόλλωνος, καὶ ἄλλο
Ἴσιδος.   τὸ μὲν δὴ ἄγαλμα τοῦ Διονύσου δῆλον πᾶσιν,
ὡσαύτως δὲ καὶ τὸ τοῦ ᾿Απόλλωνος.

APOLLO naked, standing to right; bow in advanced left hand.

Æ Geta. Rhousopoulos (**FF** xx.)

6.—APHRODITE (?) facing, right hand raised.

Æ J. Domna. Rhousopoulos.

It is impossible to determine whether this figure is of Aphrodite or some other goddess, owing to the bad preservation of the coin. It may be of Hebe.

CLEONAE.

OTHER TYPES :

Asklepios seated to left on throne, extends his right hand over head of coiled snake, in his left hand sceptre; dog lying behind him.

Æ Sept. Severus. Berlin.

A close copy of the Epidaurian statue by Thrasymedes : cf. **L** III.—V.

Artemis to right, holds in left hand bow, with right hand draws arrow from quiver; dog at her feet.

Æ Plautilla. Berlin.

Artemis facing, head turned to left, dog beside her; on either side a cypress.

Æ Sept. Severus. Brunswick (**FF** xxi.)

NEMEA. (Coins of Argos.)

2.—HYPSIPYLE running to left in alarm with arms spread towards erect serpent, which holds in its coils the body of Opheltes inverted.

Æ Hadrian. Berlin.

ARGOS.

8.—Perseus bearded (?) standing, chlamys over shoulders; holds in right hand harpa, in left Gorgoneion.

Æ Sept. Sev. Berlin (**FF** xxii.)

This type of Perseus is quite different from the conventional figure of **I** XVII., XVIII.

9.—APOLLO (Lycius ?) naked, facing, holds in right hand a branch ; rests left elbow on Ionic column.

Æ M. Aurelius. Rhousopoulos.
L. Verus. Rhousopoulos (**FF** xxiii.)

Above described, but not figured : possibly a reproduction of the work of the sculptor Attalus (Paus. II. 19, 3.)

16.—LETO, right hand raised to shoulder, the left extended over a small figure of Chloris, within a temple.

Æ Anton. Pius. Paris (**FF** xxiv.) Berlin.

These important coins complete the proof that the group of

these coins, as well as of **K** XXXVI.—VIII. is a copy of the work of Praxiteles.   On these specimens there is nothing in the left hand of Leto, her right hand is raised to her shoulder, whether to a quiver or to adjust her dress.   Chloris seems to be a somewhat stiffly-draped figure.

17.—DEMETER standing, clad in long chiton; holds in extended right hand poppy-head, in left ears of corn.

Æ L. Verus.   Berlin (**GG** I.)

Demeter, holding poppy-head and ears of corn, in a railed inclosure.

Æ Sept. Severus.   Paris.

The pose of this figure is not unlike that of Demeter on **K** XXXIX.   The inclosure in which she stands, probably the only occurrence of such a barrier on Greek coins, proves that the figure is a copy of a statue.   The coin is too ill-preserved to be reproduced.

18.—One of the DIOSCURI, naked, standing, holds spear and sword.

Æ Hadrian.   Rhousopoulos.
  Antinous.   Paris.

19.—Two figures of EILEITHUIA to left, each holding two torches, one raised, one lowered.

Æ Hadrian, Paris.

21.—ATHENE standing, holds in right hand patera, in raised right spear, against which leans shield.

Æ Hadrian.   Berlin (**GG** II.)

24.—ASKLEPIOS seated on throne, in the front of a temple with five Ionic columns at side.

Æ Anton. Pius.   Berlin (**GG** III.)

We have here further proof that the statue of Asklepios by Xenophilus and Strato is that reproduced on the coins.   The coin however on which the figure of Hygieia appears, **K** XLVIII, is not of Argos, but of Aegium : see **R** X.

29.—ARES standing, armed, clad in short chiton, holds patera and spear.

Æ J. Domna.   Rhousopoulos.

Compare **L** L.

30.—OTHER TYPES at Argos.

Goddess standing, clad in long chiton; holds patera and sceptre.

Æ Sept. Severus.   Rhousopoulos (**GG** IV.)

Goddess standing, clad in long chiton, holds pomegranate (?)

and sceptre; on either side of her, altar; behind her a
second figure clad in long chiton, who raises her right
hand and holds sceptre in left.

Æ J. Domna.   Rhousopoulos (GG v.)

Standing figure, apparently male, holding long sceptre in round
shrine on basis.

Æ Anton. Pius.   Paris (GG vi.)

Artemis running, discharging arrow.

Æ M. Aurelius.   Paris.

River-god reclining (Inachus ?).

Æ Ant. Pius.   Rhousopoulos.

EPIDAURUS.

2.—The ASKLEPIOS of Thrasymedes seated to left; before him,
snake.

Æ Anton. Pius.   Berlin (GG vii.)

Cf. **L** III.—v. The present coin is added because of its
remarkable execution and preservation. Even the head of
Asklepios is quite distinct; it is closely like that of Zeus on
fourth century coins.

3.—HYGIEIA standing in round temple.

Æ Anton. Pius.   Berlin (GG viii.)

In this coin as in **L** VI. the details of the figure are not clear,
nor even its identification certain. She stands to left, clad in
long chiton and over-dress; her right hand is extended, her left
hangs down.

6.—OTHER TYPES at Epidaurus.

Female figure facing, in chiton and over-dress; holds in raised
right long sceptre, in left a vessel (?).

Æ Anton. Pius.   Paris.   Berlin.

AEGINA.

3.—Nude figure of APOLLO, right, in the act of discharging an
arrow.

Æ Auton.   Munich (GG ix.)

This is a different type of Apollo from **L** II., but probably
like it a copy of a work of art of the early Aeginetan school.

7.—ISIS; holds sistrum and vase.

Æ Geta.   Rhousopoulos.

TROEZEN.

4.—APOLLO holding an arrow and leaning on a tripod, around
which is twined a serpent; he is draped from the waist
downwards.

Æ Sept. Severus.   Paris (GG x.)

5a.—Paus. II. 31, 10. Καὶ Ἑρμῆς ἐνταῦθά ἐστι Πολύγιος
καλούμενος ; close to the statue, an olive.

HERMES facing, right hand raised, in left hand chlamys and
caduceus ; at his feet, on either side, ram and lyre.

Æ Sept. Severus.   Paris (GG XI.)

Hermes advancing to right, drags goat by the horns, and holds
in left hand caduceus.

Æ Sept. Severus.   Paris (GG XII.)

7.—HIPPOLYTUS, standing, chlamys over shoulders, spear in
raised left.

Æ Commodus.   Rhousopoulos.
Sept. Severus.   Rhousopoulos.

HIPPOLYTUS, with spear and sword, before Phaedra (or her
nurse), who approaches him in an attitude of supplication.

Æ Sept. Severus.   Berlin (GG XIII.)

9.—ASKLEPIUS standing at altar, snake-entwined staff in his
left hand ; all in temple.

Æ Commodus.   Rhousopoulos (GG XIV.)

10.—FOUNTAIN, a pillar with lion sitting thereon, water flowing
into basin from his mouth.

Æ Sept. Severus.   Loebbecke (GG XV.)

A curious variant on the representation of the same subject
on M X., where the water flows from between the lion's feet, and
the basin is supported by a pillar, and not, as here, by legs.

12.—OTHER TYPES at Troezen.

Circular shrine, apparently surrounded by pillars : in the front
of it, closed doors.

Æ Commodus.   Berlin (GG XVI.)

HERMIONE.

1.—POSEIDON naked, standing to right, holds trident and
dolphin, left foot rests on rock.

Æ Caracalla.   Berlin (GG XVII.)

3.—The drapery of DIONYSUS on M I. is peculiar, consisting of
a skin or nebris reaching down to the knees : it may be that
this is the black goat's skin from which at Hermione Dionysus
took his name.

LERNA and NAUPLIA. Coins of Argos.

3.—POSEIDON naked, standing, left foot propped on a rock ;
holds trident and dolphin.

Æ Sept. Severus.   Rhousopoulos.

AMYMONE seated on rock, her right hand raised to her neck,

her left resting on hydria; before her Poseidon standing; holds trident in right, and carries chlamys over left arm.

Æ Ant. Pius.   Rhousopoulos (**GG** xviii.)

This description cannot be relied on, as the prongs of Poseidon's trident, and the hydria of Amymone, the two details which identify the scene, are obscure. There is an uncertain object (sea-snake?) above the left arm of Poseidon. Compare **L** liv.

Amymone seated on rock, hydria at her feet; right hand extended, left rests on rock.

Æ Paris (**GG** xix.)

Amymone standing, clad in long chiton; her right hand is raised to her neck, in her left she holds hydria.

Æ Antoninus Pius.   Rhousopoulos (**GG** xx.)

There is a curious likeness between this type and **L** li., the hydria on this coin appearing instead of the dolphin in the other. Probably in both cases the intention is to represent the nymph.

LACEDAEMON.

1.—ARTEMIS Astrateia facing, clad in short chiton with diplois; holds in right hand strung bow, in left spear and shield; beside her, stag.

Æ J. Domna.   Rhousopoulos (**GG** xxi.)

This interesting coin entirely confirms our attribution and description of **N** iii. as Artemis Astrateia.

GYTHEIUM.

1.—HERAKLES bearded in form of a term, clad in lion's skin, arm folded over breast.

Æ Sept. Severus.   Rhousopoulos.

Closely resembling **V** vi.

COLONIDES.

Niche or distyle TEMPLE, within which a female figure, indistinct.

Æ Geta.   Rhousopoulos (**GG** xxii.)

ASINE.

OTHER TYPES at Asine.

Perseus facing, naked, holds in right hand harpa, in left head of Medusa.

Æ J. Domna.   Rhousopoulos (**GG** xxiii.)

Coiled snake, on basis.

Æ Sept. Severus.   Berlin.
Plautilla.   Imh.

Apparently a reproduction of some votive work of art.
Terminal figure of Hermes, draped, right hand holds end of
nebris, in left caduceus.

Æ Sept. Severus. Berlin.

Draped female figure; holds what looks like a huge wreath or
shield.

Æ Sept. Severus. Berlin.

PYLOS.

1.—PALLAS standing to right, clad in long chiton; holds in
raised right spear, on left arm shield.

Æ Sept. Severus.   Rhousopoulos (**GG** XXIV.)

PATRAE.

Male figure standing on column in circular ENCLOSURE; he
seems to wear military dress, or short chiton; his left
hand is raised and rests on a spear or sceptre.

Æ J. Domna.   Rhousopoulos.

A variety of **R** I.; probably a figure of an Emperor, from a
market or gymnasium.

I.—INDEX OF ARTISTS.

(1, 2, 3, &c. refer to the sections under cities, 1*, 2*, 3*, &c. to the Supplement.)

II.—ORDER OF CITIES.

(With references to Plates).

III.—SUBJECTS REPRESENTED IN PLATES.

(Order of K. O. Müller).

SUBJECTS REPRESENTED IN NEW PLATES AND ILLUSTRATIONS

Museum, lxxix; relief from Brauron, lxxix.

Athena: bronze statue from Piraeus, lxxix, lxxxii.

Athena Parthenos: on gem by Aspasios, lxxx, 1; Varvakeion statuette, Pl. HH, 4; on Athenian theatre ticket, lxxx, 2.

Athens, Agora: relief of Demos and Demokratia, lxxx, 4; statuette of Apollo Lykios, Pl.HH, 2; Hephaisteion frieze: Pl. KK, 3.

Brauron: dedicatory relief to Artemis from, lxxix.

Deer hunt: in mosaic from Pella, Pl.KK, 8.

Demeter: in group by Damophon at Lycosura, Pl. 1; on coin, Pl. 1.

Demos and Demokratia: in relief on stele from Athenian Agora, lxxx, 4.

Despoina: in group by Damophon at Lycosura, Pl. 1; on coin, Pl. 1.

Harmodios: from a cast, Pl. KK, 1 on coin of Cyzicus, p. L.

Hephaisteion frieze: Theseus on west side, Pl.KK, 3.

Herakles Farnese: Pl. 2, on medal of Imperial period, Pl. 2.

Hermes Propylaios: copy from Piraeus, Pl. 4; on coin, Pl. 4.

Lion hunt: Theseus, from mosaic of lion hunt from Pella, Pl.KK, 4.

Lycosura: restoration by Dickins of statuary group by Damophon, Pl. 1; group on coin, Pl. 1; heads of Anytos and Artemis, Pl. 1.

Nemesis: on coin of Paphos, p. L.

Nike: bronze statuette from Spain, Pl.HH, 3.

Odeion of Pericles: on theatre ticket, lxxx, 3.

Pella: mosaics from, Pl. KK, 2, 4, 8.

Phryne: on coin of Thespiae, Pl. 3.

Piraeus: sculptures from lxxix, Pl. 4.

Theseus: on west frieze of Hephaisteion in Athenian Agora, Pl.KK, 3; in Pella mosaics, Pl.KK, 2, 4, 8; on Athenian coins, Pl.KK, 5, 6, 7.

Thespiae: The Aphrodite and Phryne group by Praxiteles on coin of, Pl. 3; copies of Aphrodite, Pl. 3.

Tyrannicides: On coin of Cyzicus, p. L; see also Harmodios.

In the four plates following, instances are given of identifications of ancient works of art by means of coins, identifications of coin representations through comparisons with actual statues, paintings and other forms of art, and the use of the descriptions by Pausanias in combination with the above to provide new knowledge of the lost original masterpieces of art of the ancient world.

The first plate illustrates a coin of Lycosura (upper right) with the archaelogical restoration of the sanctuary group by Damophon by G. Dickins (lower left). The head at the upper left is that of Artemis; the male head at lower right is Anytos; both are fragments of the original group found in excavations at the sanctuary of Despoina in Lycosura. These fragments were identified by means of the coin miniature and the literary description of the statues by Pausanias.

In the case of the Herakles Farnese (Plate 2), the numismatic representation orientates the search for the location of the lost original in the city of Athens and makes it possible to consider that the sculptor Glykon of Athens may have been a pupil of, or an imitator of the style of, Lysippos, rather than merely a commercial copyist as previously supposed. The medal (upper left) is one of the Imperial period showing a copy of the Herakles statue.

An inscription was used to provide a better understanding of a passage of Pausanias, restoring the correct epithet to Aphrodite Thespia, the patron goddess of the city, illustrated on the coins of Thespiae. At the upper left of Plate 3 is the "Aphrodite of Arles" which may be compared with the Thespian coin at its right. Below is a torso from a copy of the original Aphrodite of Thespia by Praxiteles, found in Athens.

From inscriptions, minor works of art and observations of stylistic developments we gain, step by step, an idea of the statuary art of the sculptor Alkamenes. Plate 4 illustrates the herm of Hermes Propylaios (upper left), the Ares Borghese (lower left) and a vase painting adaptation of the Aphrodite "in the Gardens," each of which can be recognized on the parallel coin representations (upper right). The numismatic representations have verified the identifications made through other media, and help to locate geographically the last originals.

Each of these typical cases is discussed in greater detail in the following pages in an effort to illustrate how important and useful is the study of coins and their representations to the archaeologist, numismatist and the art historian, especially when this study is combined with ancient literary texts such as that of Pausanias.

THE GROUP BY DAMOPHON AT LYCOSURA

Plate 1

Pausanias VIII. 37,3-6
The statues of the goddesses themselves, Despoina and Demeter, as well as the throne on which they are seated and the footstool beneath their feet were all sculpted from the same stone block . . . Both statues are about the size of the one of the Mother of the Gods in Athens, and they are works of Damophon. Demeter holds a torch in her right hand and rests her left on Despoina who holds a scepter and has the so-called 'cista' on her lap, being connected (with Demeter) from the right side of the cista. Beside the throne on this side (by Demeter) is erected a statue of Artemis clad in a deerskin and having a quiver on her shoulders, holding a torch in one hand and two snakes in the other. By her a dog of a hunting breed is lying down. On the other side (next to Despoina) is erected Anytos, represented as an armed warrior.

For the earlier bibliography and a brilliant discussion of the style of Damophon as it can be studied from the heads of Demeter, Despoina and Anytos discovered in the excavations of Kavvadias at Lycosura (1889-1896) see: Bieber, *The Sculpture of the Hellenistic Age*, Rev. ed. 1961, pp. 158-9.

From the discovery of the fragments found in the excavations, we now know that Pausanias was deceived, for they do not appear to be all from one block of stone as he indicated. The group could be reconstructed quite easily with the help of the coin from Lycosura, but unfortunately the minor fragments are in Lycosura and the major ones are in the National Museum of Athens, and to date, for reasons unknown, the staff of the museum has neglected this project which would be of so much help in the study of the revival of classicism in Hellenistic sculpture of the second and first centuries B.C. For a study of the reconstruction of the group see Dickins, G., *Hellenistic Sculpture*, Oxford 1920 and K. Kourouniotes in *Annual of the British School at Athens*, 13, 1906-7, pp. 384 ff. Figs. 24-25.

THE LYSIPPEAN "HERAKLES FARNESE"

Plate 2

The problem of the location of the original of the Lysippean "Herakles Farnese" is one of the most important ones for the study of the evolution of style in Hellenistic sculpture. This statue has been ascribed to Lysippos only on the grounds of stylistic criteria (see the almost complete list of known copies and theories in Johnson, F.P., *Lysippos*, 1927, pp. 197-203) and an inscription on the copy in the Palazzo Pitti which possibly may be forged. Thus it has become a major subject of archaelogical dispute on the basis of style.

The best example of the type is unanimously accepted to be the colossal statue in the National Museum of Naples which bears the signature of the sculptor Glykon of Athens. There are many who wish to discredit Glykon as the creator of the type for we have almost no knowledge of sculptors who were definitely pupils of Lysippos, and those names we have are not known by their works. For unknown reasons the possibly forged inscription *(Lysippou Ergon)* on the Pitti copy is considered by many to overshadow the signature of Glykon, simply because this artist is unknown from any other source. This fact and the archeological studies of the "dilettanti" type have resulted in the failure to come to any definite conclusions.

The suggestion of Professor Bieber that the original Herakles of this type stood in Athens *(Sculpture of the Hellenistic Age*, Rev. ed. 1961, p. 37), based on the fact that a similar figure appears on Athenian coins, is now supported by the discovery of a nearly intact small bronze copy found in the excavations of the Athenian Agora (*Guide*, 2nd ed. 1964, p. 181 : Shelf 46, S1241). This may be the opening of the road toward a solution. I see no reason for the omission of the Herakles of the Farnese type from the works of Athenian sculpture. Although Lysippos himself was the head of the school of Argos and Sicyon, why could not an Athenian sculptor of a later period imitate his style just as the Messenian Damophon followed the style of the Athenian Pheidias?

THE APHRODITE THESPIA AND PHRYNE GROUP BY PRAXITELES

Plate 3

Pausanias IX. 36,6

. . . *the city of Thespia is built at the foot of Mount Helicon. They say that Thespia who gave her name to the city was a daughter of the river-god Asopus . . . 36,7. On the acropolis of Thespiae is a bronze statue of Zeus Saotes (Saviour) . . . 36,8. . . . a statue of Dionysus and another of Tyche (Fortune) and in another place one of Hygieia (Health). As for the statues of Athena Ergane (Worker) and Ploutos (Wealth) standing beside her, they were made by ***. IX. 37,1. ***Eros (Love) is one of the gods highly honored of old by the Thespians . . . 37,5. The statue of Eros existing in my day was made by Menodoros the Athenian who imitated the statue by Praxiteles. Here are also Aphrodite and the portrait statue of Phryne, made by Praxiteles himself; both Phryne and the goddess are of stone. Elsewhere too is a sanctuary of Aphrodite Melainis (black) and a theatre and a marketplace worth seeing.*

In 1955 I came across an inscription (see *Platon* 7, 1955, pp. 342-5 ;*SEG* xv,324) on a bronze vase of the fifth century B. C. mentioning that it was "Sacred to Aphrodite Thespia." In searching through various sources for the location of this cult it occurred to me that the gap in the text of Pausanias between the end of IX. 36,8 and the beginning of IX. 37,1 which has been shown as containing the name of the sculptor of Athena Ergane and Ploutos, might well have been larger than previously supposed. If Aphrodite Thespia was the main cult of the city goddess in Thespiae, as we may assume from the epithet, then likely she was the one represented on the coins and not Aphrodite Melainis. We know from sanctuaries in other cities of Greece that Eros was always adored with Aphrodite and this fact was archaeologically confirmed in Thespiae by A. de Ridder (*BCH* 46, 1922, pp. 248 ff). Knowing the general reliability of Pausanias, we cannot imagine that he would have failed to visit the shrine of the main cult of Aphrodite in Thespia. I submit that he did, and that his writing on the subject is also missing from the manuscripts. This is a most likely description to fit into the gap just before the beginning of *IX. 37,1*. (See my restoration in *Platon* 12, 1960, pp. 52-54).

From the existent text we have hints that this was actually the subject of the missing portion. The marble group of Aphrodite and Phryne was *here* (where?) with the statue of Eros by Menodoros. We notice that the sanctuary of Aphrodite Melainis was *elsewhere,* thus distinguishing between the two cults of the goddess of love in the city of Thespiae.

Furtwaengler's suggestion that the Praxitelean Aphrodite at Thespiae was the original for the so-called "Aphrodite of Arles" in the Louvre seems likely (*Masterpieces* . . . , 2nd ed., Chicago 1964, pp. 319, 429). If we consider that the right arm and the left hand of the Arles copy are restored and that the head has been misplaced, it is easy to recognize the Aphrodite on the Thespian coin (Pl. X, xix) as a miniature of the same original. It was the idea of the restorer of the Arles copy that Aphrodite was holding a mirror in her left hand and the head has been placed to permit her to look into it. The identification becomes still stronger with the small draped female figure on the left side of the coin representation. Phryne, according to the text of Alkiphron, stood between the cult statues of Aphrodite and Eros *on the same plinth with Aphrodite* exactly as seen on the coin miniature.

THREE STATUES BY ALKAMENES IN ATHENS: HERMES, ARES AND APHRODITE "IN THE GARDENS"

Plate 4

An identification of coin DD, xix was impossible until 1903 when, in the excavations at Pergamon, a copy of the "Hermes Propylaios' by Alkamenes, so inscribed, was discovered. While the numismatic evidence of the Athenian coin had existed, together with the literary commentary on the existence of such a herm, it was impossible to link the two with the name of Alkamenes before this lucky find. (See Furtwaengler, A., *Masterpieces* . . . 2nd ed., Chicago 964, pp. 87,418).

In the case of the Ares Furtwaengler once again has been proved correct. He used stylistic comparisons to identify the Ares Borghese in the Louvre as a copy of the cult statue by Alkamenes in the temple of Ares in Athens. The numismatic representations seen on Plate DD, xxii-xxiii (cf. pp. liii-liv) might have been used earlier to verify his theory, but he did not consider them, apparently inasmuch as they had been identified as Hermes by Imhoof-Blumer and Gardner (p. 149).

The famous statue of Aphrodite "in the Gardens," long thought to be a standing one, was never associated with the correct coin representation due to its actual seated pose. Imhoof-Blumer and Gardner surmised that the seated statue represented on the Athenian coin was that of Demeter (BB, xxii, p. 141). Finally in 1953 E. Langlotz convincingly demonstrated that Aphrodite "in the Gardens" was a seated statue ("Aphrodite in den Garten," in *SB Heidelberg* 1953/4,2. Abh) ; thus we may conclude that this is now the correct identification for the miniature shown on the coin. Prior to my discovery of Langlotz's monograph I had proposed this identification, but lacked substantiating evidence, even as Imhoof-Blumer and Gardner had lacked support for their identification of the figure as Demeter (see p. lxiv).

Thus today we are better able to study the style of Alkamenes due to these verifications from numismatic representations and other industrial art than ever before.

SELECT BIBLIOGRAPHY

Following are a few of the many works on Greek and Roman coins and sculpture which are useful in the identification of sculpture from numismatic representations.

GENERAL WORKS

Head, Barclay V., *Historia Numorum*, 2nd ed., Oxford 1911.

Hill, G. F., *A Guide to the Principal Coins of the Greeks*, 1932. (Based on the work: *Coins of the Ancients* by Barclay V. Head). Rev. ed. by John Walker, British Museum. London 1959.

―――――――, *A Handbook of Greek and Roman Coins*, London 1899. First Amer. ed., Chicago 1964. Includes lengthy bibliography.

―――――――, *Historical Greek Coins*, London 1906.

―――――――, *Historical Roman Coins from the Earliest Times to the Reign of Augustus*, London 1909.

―――――――, *Select Greek Coins*, London 1927.

Seltman, C. T., *Greek Coins*, 1933. 2nd ed., 1955.

Vermeule, C. *Greek Numismatic Art, 400 B.C. — 300 A.D.*, Cambridge Mass. 1958.

STATUES ON COINS

Ashmole, B., "The Relation between Coins and Sculpture," in *Trans. Int'l Num. Congr.*, London 1936, pp. 17-22.

Babelon, Jean, *Le Portrait dans l'Antiquite d'apres les Monnaies*, Paris 1942.

Bieber, Margarete, *Alexander the Great in Greek and Roman Art*, Chicago 1964.

―――――――, *The Sculpture of the Hellenistic Age*, Rev. ed., N.Y. 1961.

Blanchet, A., "Representations de statues sur des stateres de Corinthe," in *Revue Numismatique*, 1907, pp. 317-323.

Frazer, J. G., *Pausanias's Description of Greece*. 6 vols. London 1898.

Gardner, P., *The Types of Greek Coins*, Cambridge 1883.

―――――――, "Copies of Statues on Coins," in *Corolla Numismatica*, London 1906, pp. 104-114.

Imhoof-Blumer, F., *Portraet koepfe auf antiken Muenzen hellenischer und hellenisierter Voelker*, 1885.

Imhoof-Blumer, F. and Gardner, P., "A Numismatic Commentary on Pausanias," in *Journal of Hellenic Studies* 6, 1885, pp. 50-101; 7, 1886, pp. 57-113; 8, 1887, pp. 6-63.

Lacroix, L., "Copies de statues sur les monnaies des Seleucides," in *Bull. de Corresp. Hellenique*, 73, 1949, pp. 158-176.

——————, *Les Reproductions de statues sur les monnaies grecques. La Statuaire archaique et classique,* Liege 1949. The basic reference work on the subject.

Lehman, Phyllis Williams, *A Numismatic Approach to the Sculpture of South Italy and Sicily in the Classical Period,* New York 1943.

——————, *Statues on Coins of Southern Italy and Sicily in the Classical Period,* New York 1946.

Levi, A. C., *Barbarians on Roman Imperial Coins and Sculpture,* Amer. Num. Notes & Monogr. 123, N.Y. 1952.

Mirone, S., "Copies de statues sur les monnaies antiques de la Sicilie," in *Revue Numismatique,* 1920, pp. 1-45; 1922, pp. 1-23 (Supplement).

Newell, E. T., *Royal Greek Portrait Coins,* New York 1937.

Smith, H. Wade, "Sculptural Style on Ptolemaic Portrait Coins," in *Berytus* 10, 1952-53, pp. 21-45.

Thompson, Margaret, *The New Style Silver Coinage of Athens,* 2 vols. New York 1962.

Vermeule, Cornelius, *Bibliography of Applied Numismatics,* London 1956. Excellent reference for numerous articles and books on special subjects and particularly valuable for its sections on statues as represented on coins. Additional references have appeared in *Numismatic Circular,* Nov., Dec., 1956 and Jan., 1957. Cf. also *Num. Chron.,* 1955, pp. 260 ff.

ANCIENT SOURCES

Jones, H. Stuart, *Select Passages from Ancient Writers Illustrative of the History of Greek Sculpture,* 1895.

Overbeck, J.: *Die antike Schriftquellen zur Geschichte der bildenden Kunste bei den Griechen,* 1868. (Rep. 1959).

Jones' book is the only one with English translations, but Overbeck's is more complete for the reader of German and Ancient Greek.

1. Marble head of Artemis by Damophon from Lycosura. Athens, National Museum. 2. Coin of the Imperial period (enlarged, reverse) picturing the statuary group by Damophon in Lycosura at the Temple of Despoina. 3. Restoration of the group by Damophon drawn by Dickins based on the fragments of the original sculptures found in the excavations at Lycosura. Left to right: Artemis, Demeter, Despoina, Anytos. (Same order on coin representation, Figure 2) 4. Marble head of Anytos by Damophon from Lycosura. Athens, National Museum.

PLATE 1

Herakles Farnese. The 'copy' by Glykon the Athenian. Naples, National Museum. Inset: Medallion of Imperial period representing the Emperor Maximianus Herculeus as Herakles, patterned from the Herakles Farnese.

PLATE 2

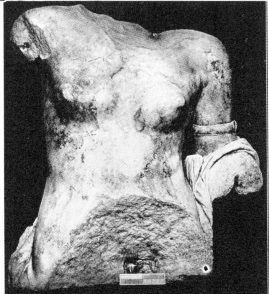

1. Aphrodite of Arles. Paris, Louvre Museum. A copy of the Praxitelean
   Aphrodite Thespia, according to A. Furtwaengler. The right arm and
   left hand are modern restorations; the head has been wrongly replaced.

2. Coin of the Imperial period from Thespiae. Reverse, depicting Praxitelean Aphrodite on the same base with Phryne.

3. Torso of early Hellenistic copy of the Praxitelean
   Aphrodite Thespia found in the excavations of the
   Theatre of Dionysus in Athens. Athens, Nat. Mus.

PLATE 3

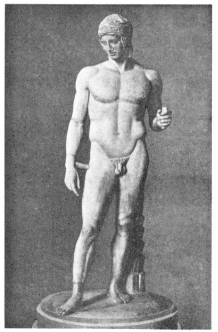

1a.

2a.

2b.

3a.

1. One of the two copies of Hermes Propylaios by Alkamenes found with treasure of bronzes in Piraeus in 1959. Piraeus, National Museum. 1a. Coin of Athens with representation of Hermes Propylaios by Alkamenes to the left of the owl. 2. Ares Borghese, identified by Furtwaengler as a copy of the statue by Alkamenes. Paris, Louvre Museum. 2a & b. Reverse of 2 coins of Athens illustrating statue of Ares by Alkamenes. 3. Echo of Aphrodite "in the Gardens" by Alkamenes on a red-figured vase painting showing Aphrodite playing with cupids. 3a. Reverse of coin of Athens illustrating the statue of Aphrodite "in the Gardens" by Alkamenes.

PLATE 4

A. MEGARA. PAGAE. AEGOSTHENA.

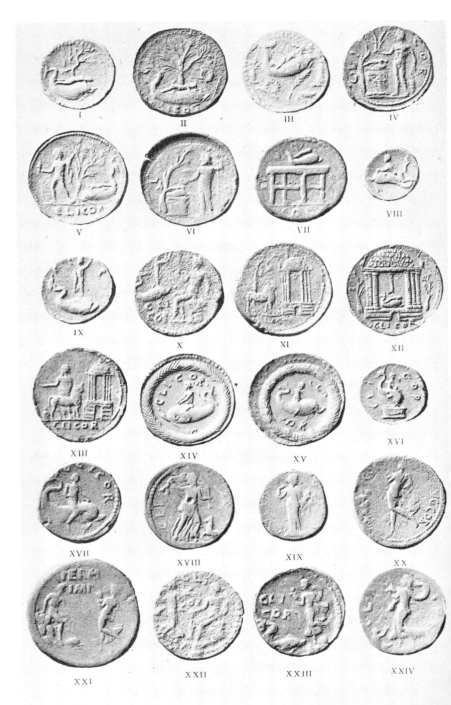

B. CORINTH I

XXV XXVI XXVII XXVIII
XXIX XXX XXXI XXXII
XXXIII XXXIV XXXV XXXVI
XXXVII XXXVIII XXXIX XL
XLI XLII XLIII XLIV
XLV XLVI XLVII XLVIII

C. CORINTH II.

D. CORINTH III.

LXXIII LXXIV LXXV LXXVI

LXXVII LXXVIII LXXIX LXXX

LXXXI LXXXII LXXXIII LXXXIV

LXXXV LXXXVI LXXXVII LXXXVIII

LXXXIX XC XCI XCII

XCIII XCIV XCV XCVI

E. CORINTH IV.

XCVII   XCVIII   XCIX   C

CI   CII   CIII   CIV

CV   CVI   CVII   CVIII

CIX   CX   CXI   CXII

CXIII   CXIV   CXV   CXVI

CXVII   CXVIII   CXIX   CXX

F. CORINTH V.

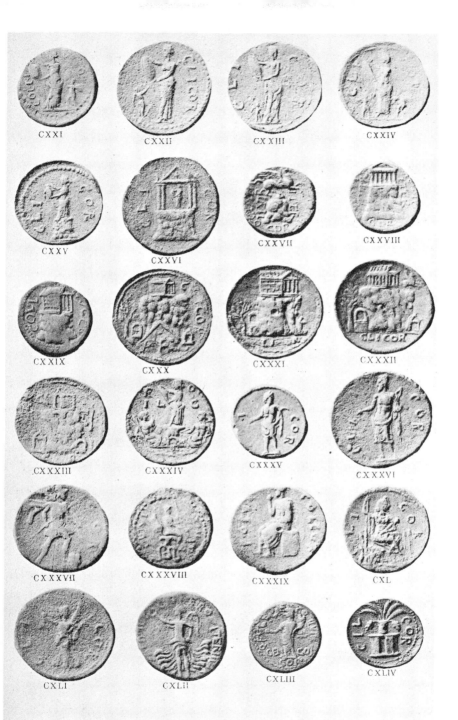

CXXI CXXII CXXIII CXXIV

CXXV CXXVI CXXVII CXXVIII

CXXIX CXXX CXXXI CXXXII

CXXXIII CXXXIV CXXXV CXXXVI

CXXXVII CXXXVIII CXXXIX CXL

CXLI CXLII CXLIII CXLIV

G. CORINTH VI.

H. SICYON. PHLIUS. CLEONAE.

I. ARGOS I.

XXV   XXVI   XXVII   XXVIII

XXIX   XXX   XXXI   XXXII

XXXIII   XXXIV   XXXV   XXXVI

XXXVII   XXXVIII   XXXIX   XL

XLI   XLII   XLIII   XLIV

XLV   XLVI   XLVII   XLVIII

K. ARGOS II.

XLiX   L   LI   LII

LIII   LIV   LV   LVI

I   II   III   IV

V   VI   VII   VIII

I   II   III   IV

V   VI   VII   VIII

L. ARGOS. EPIDAURUS. AEGINA.

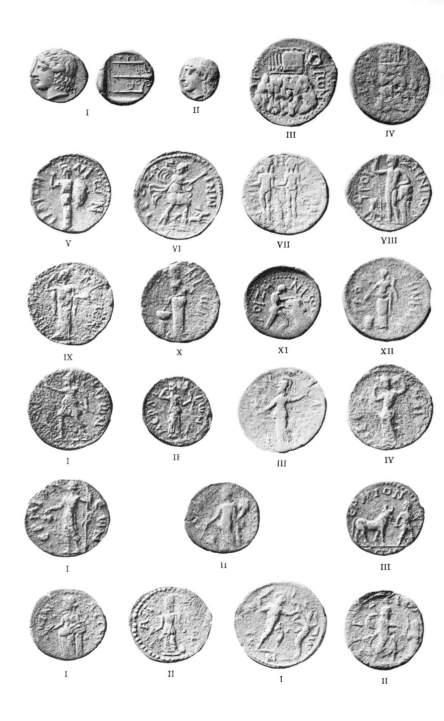

M. TROEZEN. METHANA. HERMIONE.
ASINE. LERNA.

N. LACEDAEMON. GYTHEIUM.

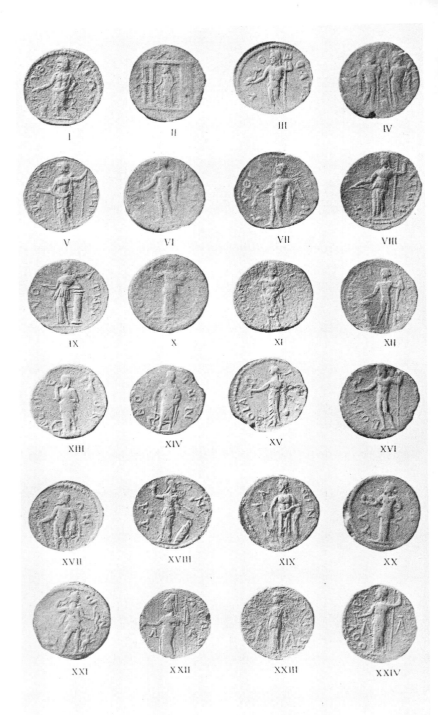

I   II   III   IV

V   VI   VII   VIII

IX   X   XI   XII

XIII   XIV   XV   XVI

XVII   XVIII   XIX   XX

XXI   XXII   XXIII   XXIV

O. GYTHEIUM. ASOPUS. BOEAE.
LAS. THURIA.

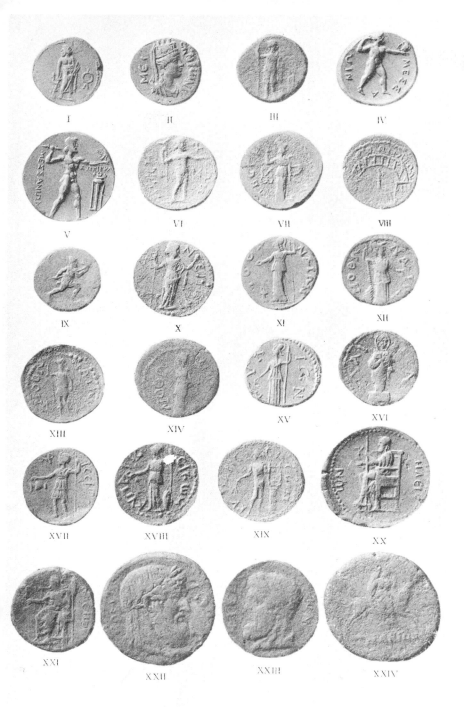

P. MESSENE, COLONE, MOTHONE, PYLUS,
CYPARISSIA, ELIS.

I   II   III   IV

V   VI   VII   VIII

IX   X   XI   XII

XIII   XIV   XV   XVI

XVII   XVIII   XIX   XX

XXI   XXII   XXIII   XXIV

Q: PATRAE.

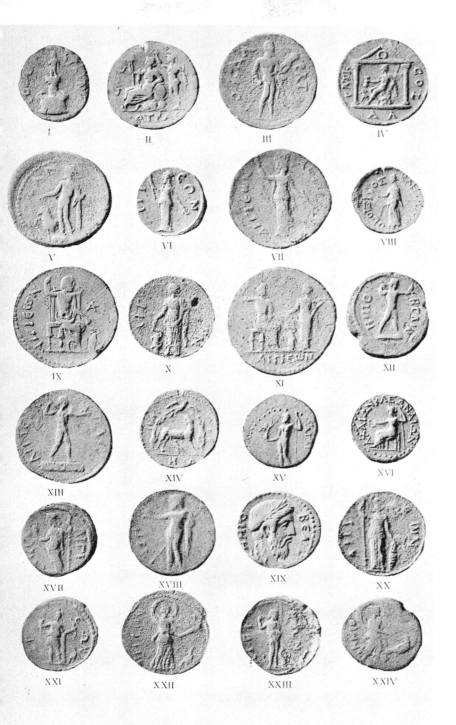

R. PATRAE. AEGIUM.

S. BURA. AEGIRA. PELLENE.
MANTINEIA. ORCHOMENUS.

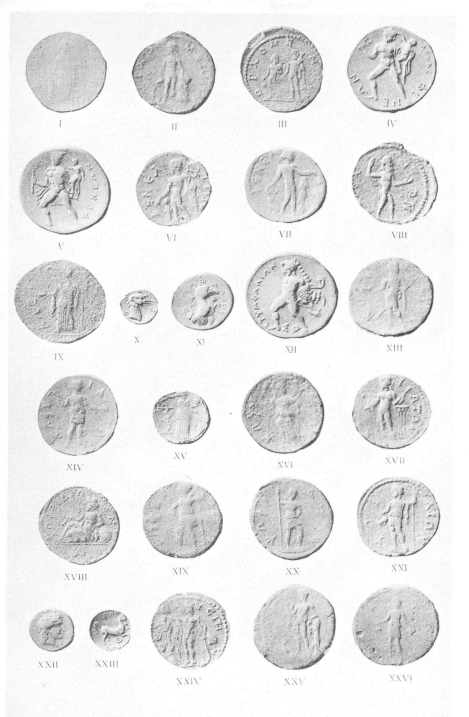

I II III IV
V VI VII VIII
IX X XI XII XIII
XIV XV XVI XVII
XVIII XIX XX XXI
XXII XXIII XXIV XXV XXVI

T. ORCHOMENUS. PHENEUS. STYMPHALUS.
CAPHYAE. PSOPHIS. THELPUSA. HERAEA.

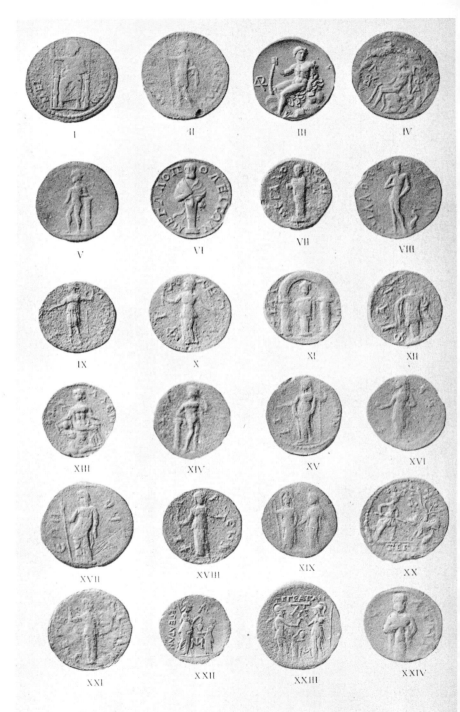

I   II   III   IV

V   VI   VII   VIII

IX   X   XI   XII

XIII   XIV   XV   XVI

XVII   XVIII   XIX   XX

XXI   XXII   XXIII   XXIV

V. MEGALOPOLIS. PHIGALIA. TEGEA.

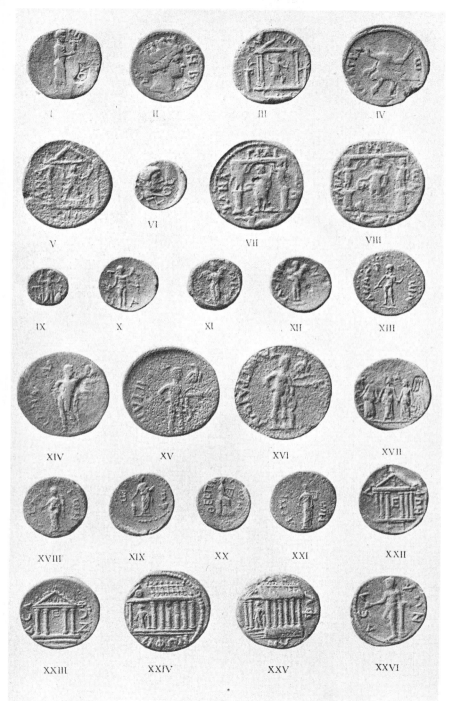

I   II   III   IV

V   VI   VII   VIII

IX   X   XI   XII   XIII

XIV   XV   XVI   XVII

XVIII   XIX   XX   XXI   XXII

XXIII   XXIV   XXV   XXVI

X. THEBES. TANAGRA. THESPIAE. DELPHI.

Y. DELPHI. ELATEIA. ANTICYRA. ATHENS.

I   II   III   IV

V   VI   VII   VIII

IX   X   XI   XII

XIII   XIV   XV

XVI   XVII   XVIII   XIX

XX   XXI   XXII   XXIII

Z. ATHENS. II.

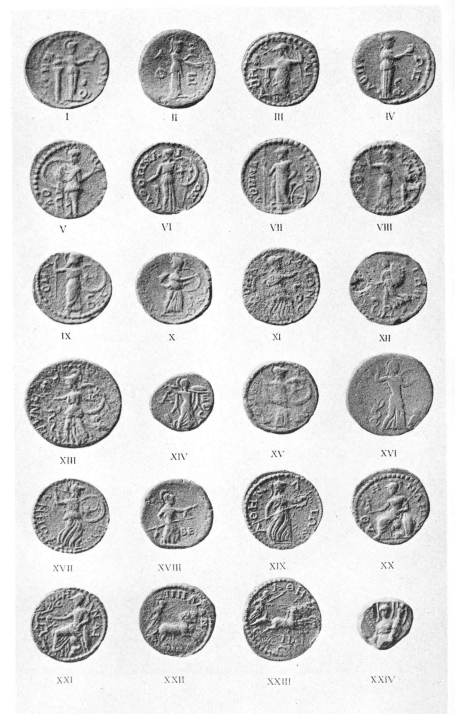

I   II   III   IV

V   VI   VII   VIII

IX   X   XI   XII

XIII   XIV   XV   XVI

XVII   XVIII   XIX   XX

XXI   XXII   XXIII   XXIV

A.A. ATHENS. III.

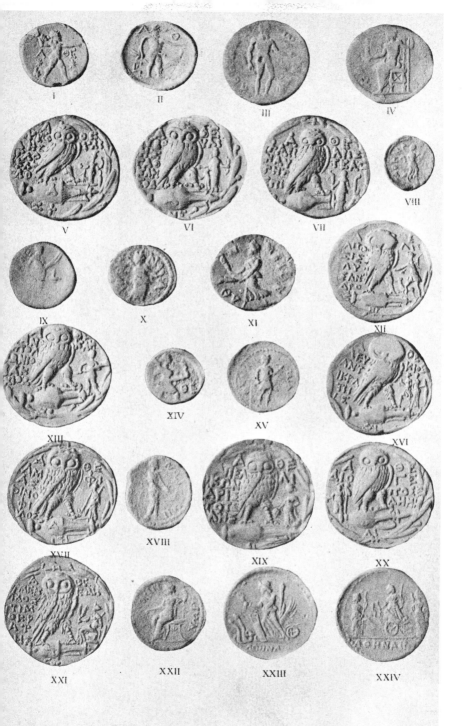

I
II
III
IV
V
VI
VII
VIII
IX
X
XI
XII
XIII
XIV
XV
XVI
XVII
XVIII
XIX
XX
XXI
XXII
XXIII
XXIV

B.B. ATHENS. IV.

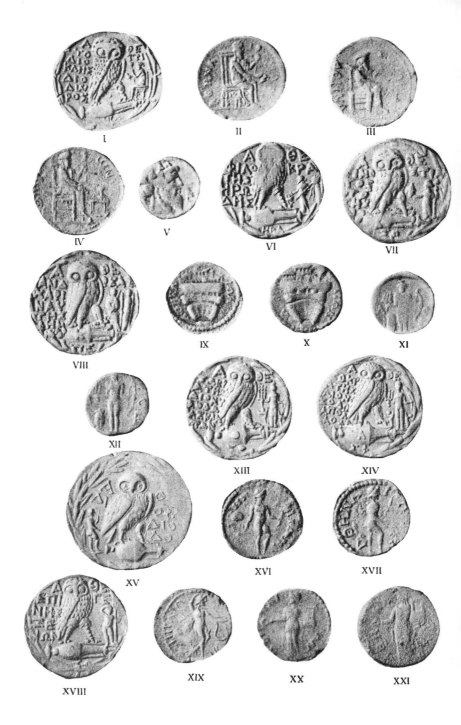

C.C ATHENS. V.

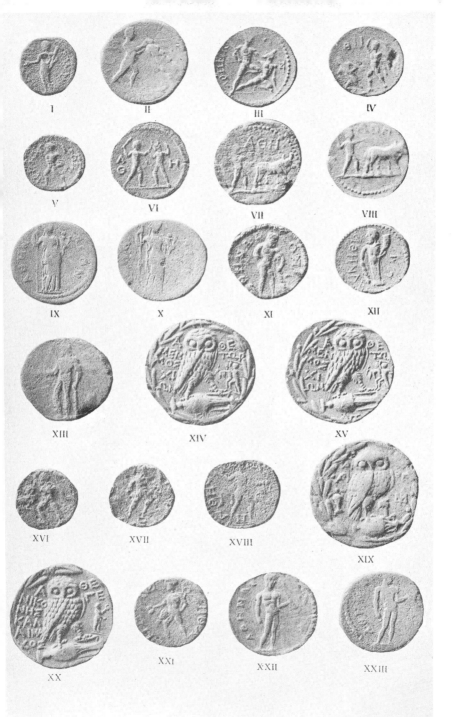

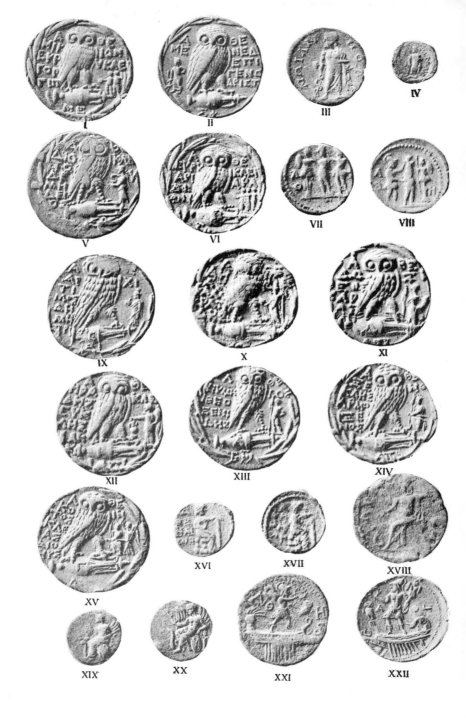

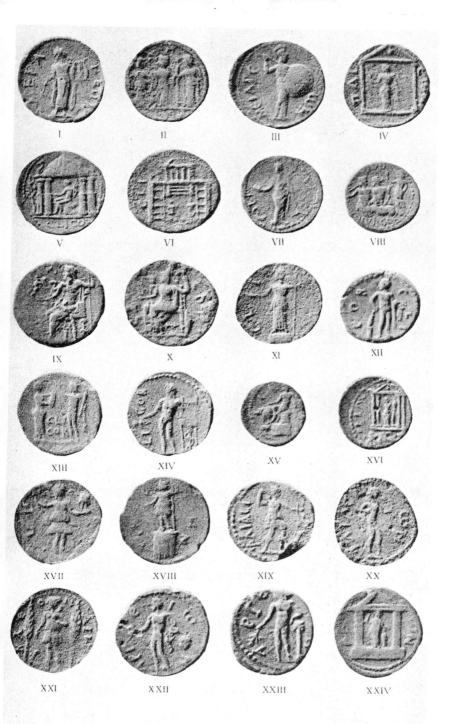

I II III IV

V VI VII VIII

IX X XI XII

XIII XIV XV XVI

XVII XVIII XIX XX

XXI XXII XXIII XXIV

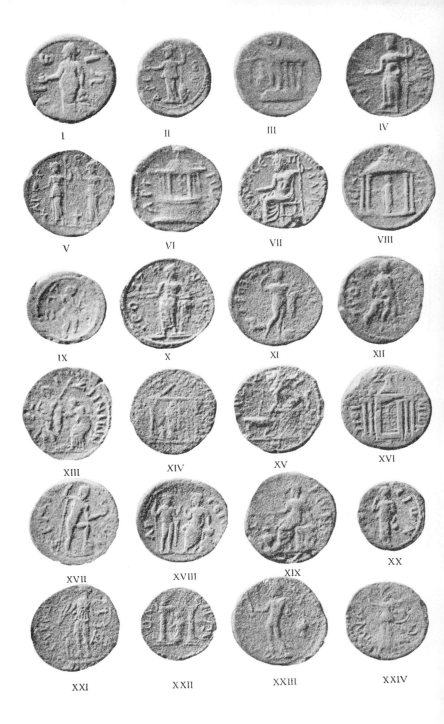

I   II   III   IV

V   VI   VII   VIII

IX   X   XI   XII

XIII   XIV   XV   XVI

XVII   XVIII   XIX   XX

XXI   XXII   XXIII   XXIV

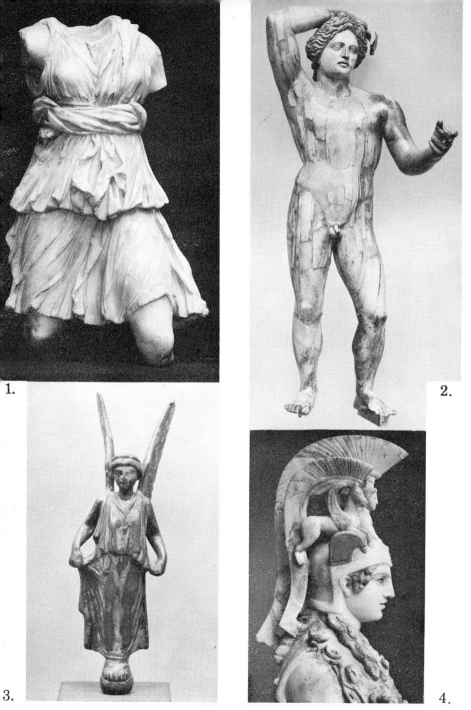

1. Artemis Agrotera. 2. Ivory statuette Apollo Lykios. 3. Nike. 4. Athena Parthenos stte.

H H. ADDENDA

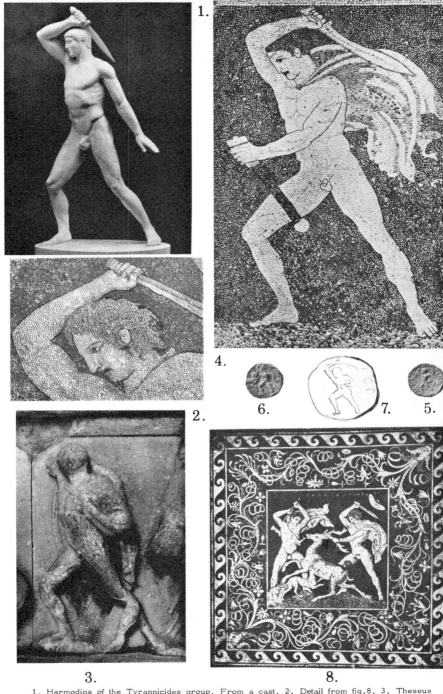

1. Harmodios of the Tyrannicides group. From a cast. 2. Detail from fig. 8. 3. Theseus from west frieze of the Hephaisteion. 4. Detail from lion hunt mosaic found ar excavations at Pella. 5,6,7. Theseus on Athenian Coins. 8. Deer hunt from mosaic discovered at Pella (cf. detail, fig. 2).

K K. ADDENDA

ANCIENT COINS ILLUSTRATING LOST MASTERPIECES OF GREEK ART

F. Imhoof-Blumer and Percy Gardner

EDITED BY AL. N. OIKONOMIDES

Must one travel abroad to search for lost treasures of ancient Greek art? No! You may hunt them in museums and books anywhere, for here is a guide illustrating hundreds of magnificent statues which once existed, but which have not yet been discovered.

While much is known of classical sculpture from copies by Greek and Roman artists, there are many statues, temples and sanctuaries of which no trace has yet been found. Somewhere they may still exist, perhaps buried beneath the earth or lying at the bottom of the sea, or often hidden, forgotten, in a museum basement storage room.

The cities and states of ancient Greece chose their most precious treasures of art and architecture to embellish their coins, and today these miniature numismatic representations, together with literary descriptions, provide us with our only knowledge of these masterpieces of antiquity. The work of an archaeologist is not only excavating, but knowing where to do so, what to look for, and perhaps most difficult, to correctly identify his discoveries. Often these identifications are pure guesswork or logical deduction. But by using numismatic evidence, together with literary descriptions, much can be definitely determined in the area of art treasures.

(continued on back flap)

Using the finest coins from all of the museums and collections of Europe, F. W. Imhoof-Blumer and Percy Gardner, both outstanding numismatists and archaeologists, compared the works of art shown on coins with the descriptions of Pausanias, a traveller in Greece during the second century A.D. They then compiled their *Numismatic Commentary to Pausanias* which is here revised and enlarged with translations of the original Greek texts, additional plates, and a completely new section concerning the coins of Athens.

Through the comparison of the art treasures depicted on these coins and the detailed descriptions of Pausanias, archaeologists, professional or amateur, numismatists and art historians identify copies of originals already found, or if very lucky, the originals themselves. The recognition, from a coin picture, of a distinctive pose or artistic style may lead to the identification, of a relic of the past or may revise an earlier opinion expressed without the valuable evidence from these coins.